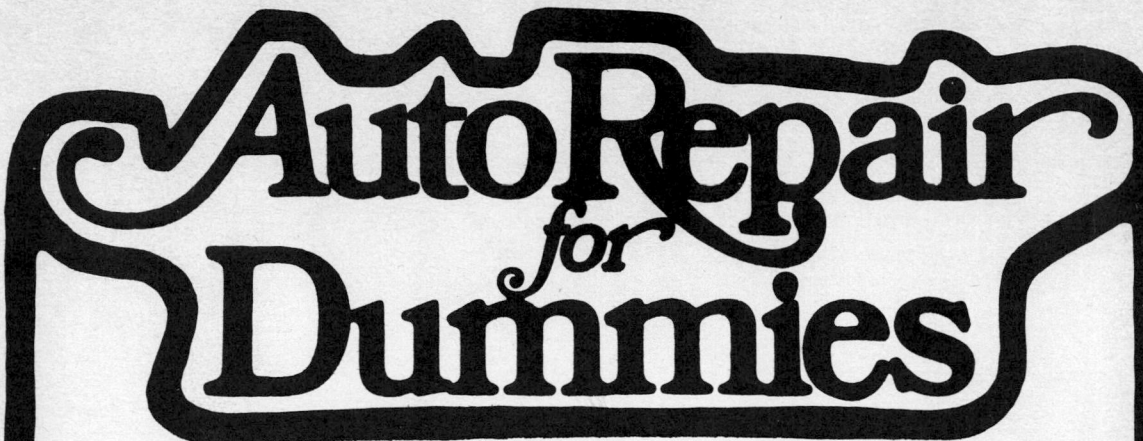

Deanna Sclar

Don Donesley
Technical Advisor

D0503404

McGraw-Hill Book Company
New York
St. Louis
San Francisco
Düsseldorf
London
Mexico
Sydney
Toronto

23456789 KPKP 79876

Library of Congress Cataloging in Publication Data
Sclar, Deanna.
   Auto repairs for dummies.
   Includes index.
   1.   Automobiles—Maintenance and repair.   I.   Title.
TL152.S42   629.28'8   75-45103
ISBN 0-07-055870-1
ISBN 0-07-055871-x (pbk.)

Quote on page viii is reprinted with permission of
William Morrow & Company from *Zen and the Art of
Motorcycle Maintenance*, copyright © 1974 by
Robert M. Pirsig.

What's So Special About

It Is *Not* Written for Confirmed "Do-It-Yourselfers"...

It *is* for You if

☐ You have never held a wrench;

☐ You are positive that, in your case, manual labor can lead only to disaster;

☐ You haven't the vaguest idea of how a car works;

☐ You cannot identify anything you see under the hood of your car;

☐ You have failed shop or arts and crafts;

☐ You believe that if you do something wrong, your car can blow up.

To Enjoy This Book It Would Help If:

☐ You do not believe that working on your car can possibly be *fun* but are willing to give it a try for any reason whatsoever;

☐ You are sincerely tired of being ripped off because of your own ignorance.

Why Should That Be Enjoyable?

Because you will be more delighted than anyone else to find:

☐ Cars run on principles that are as easy to understand as common sense;

☐ Most of the devices on your car will not hurt you unless you really go out of your way to hurt yourself;

☐ Not only can you get a fair deal, but you can save a tremendous amount of money, extend the life of your car, save on fuel, do your bit for the environment, and have a hell of a good time working on your car!

☐ The fun comes because it's so easy and you expected to hate it or be bored or befuddled.

Here's How *Auto Repair for Dummies* Accomplishes These Miracles

☐ By starting from scratch (it even shows you what a screwdriver looks like);

☐ By providing step-by-step illustrated instructions for even the simplest task;

☐ By telling you exactly what you'll need and how to know if you've been given the wrong thing;

☐ By covering each system thoroughly in simple terms *before* you get to work on it. It's easier to work on something that you understand.

It Tells You the Truth About	☐ What makes your car go (and how and why as well);
	☐ The easy work involved in keeping your car well tuned and running right;
	☐ A program of "preventive medicine" to avoid trouble, that takes about an hour or two a month;
	☐ How to tell what's wrong, when trouble strikes;
	☐ Whether or not you can handle a problem yourself (If it's easy, you'll be able to fix it yourself. If it's too difficult, you'll know enough to get it fixed at a fair price);
	☐ How to buy a used car that can perform as well as a new one.
There Are Fringe Benefits Too!	☐ Your car will run better and live longer;
	☐ Mechanics will respect you;
	☐ You'll have more money to spend on other things;
	☐ You will no longer be a dummy.
These Features Will Make Life Even Easier:	☐ A detailed Index and a Practical Glossary of Automotive Terms where you can look up a part, a problem, or a specific job and find a description of the terms or the work involved, along with the pages to consult for further details;
	☐ Bold type in the text for every term that is defined in the Glossary, so that you can refresh your memory if you've forgotten what a term means;
	☐ A Maintenance Record so that you can keep track of what you've done and when you did it
	☐ A Specifications Record, where you can keep all the information you need to buy the right parts for your car;
	☐ A Tool Checklist so that you can tell what you need, what you already have, and what you'd like for Christmas;
	☐ Almost 300 illustrations that show you how things look, where they are, and what to do with them;
	☐ A checklist that tells you if a used car is worth buying.
You Have to Supply a Few Things Too!	☐ You have to buy the book;
	☐ You have to take the time to read it through, just once;
	☐ You have to try to do one small, easy job yourself (and you can pick the job).

And That's What's So Special About This Book!

It is probably the only auto repair manual designed for people who think they *can't* do it themselves, feel they wouldn't like it anyway, but are willing to give it a try. How do I know it will work for these reluctant readers? Because it is written by a genuine, certified, ex-dummy who has found that despite total ignorance and a complete lack of manual dexterity, working on a car is enjoyable, rewarding, and easy. And, believe me, if I can do it, so can you!

DEANNA SCLAR

Acknowledgments

This book owes a great deal to a number of people who have gratuitously supplied the encouragement, expertise, and special materials to make it as accurate, comprehensive, and low-priced as possible. I am deeply grateful to them for their help and their friendship, and I'd like to thank them here:

Don Donesley, automotive guru, technical advisor, and good buddy. Thanks for having the genius to be able to reveal the "hidden mysteries" of auto mechanics in such simple terms that you not only made this dummy a confirmed grease monkey but prompted her to try to let the rest of the world in on the fun. Thanks, too, for the time, effort, and good advice you put into checking every page of the manuscript.

Jon Greene, dear friend, thank you for bribing me with the loan of an extra set of tools, dragging me down to that first auto class, and continuing to provide helpful suggestions until the book was finished.

Terry Miller (APAA), Tim Sullivan (Motor Racing Network), Rick Johnson (Union Carbide), and Jack Trotter (Guaranteed Auto Parts)—the "godfathers" of this book. Thank you all for taking such an interest in an unseen work and its unknown author. All of you provided a continuing supply of good advice, bright ideas, valuable leads, and unhesitating friendship for someone you'd never met. It has meant more to me than I can adequately express here, and I hope the good Karma flows back your way!

The Members of the Automotive Parts and Accessories Association (APAA) who, in answer to a letter from Terry, provided more than 250 free illustrations. Thanks for making the book easier to use, and for helping to keep the cover price low!

The Thursday Evening Auto Class at University High School, a truly communal group who share their ideas, tools, and good right arms; serve as guinea pigs for one another; change master cylinders in dark parking lots with only a flashlight and a wrench; and get it all together over beer and pizza afterward. The enthusiasm is contagious. Thanks for being your beautiful selves!

A special thank-you to my editor, Kathy Matthews, for her friendship, enthusiasm, encouragement, and unfailing capacity for hard work!

And, finally, thanks to *Tweety Bird*, faithful Mustang, who survived all the experiments and mistakes and grew up to be a fine car and a worthy steed!

Contents

Each machine has its own, unique personality which probably could be defined as the intuitive sum total of everything you know and feel about it. This personality constantly changes, usually for the worse, but sometimes surprisingly for the better. . . . The new ones start out as good-looking strangers and, depending on how they are treated, degenerate rapidly into bad-acting grouches or even cripples, or else turn into healthy, good natured, long-lasting friends.

Robert M. Pirsig
Zen and the Art of Motorcycle Maintenance

How I Became Intimately Involved with My Automobile, and Why You'll Want to Do It, Too

For many of us, getting a driver's license is an event that runs second only to getting a diploma or a marriage license. We study, practice, and take the test in a state of high anticipation, marred only by the fear of failing and being "grounded" forever.

Most of us succeed in passing and hop happily into our cars, headed for the freedom of the open road. Unfortunately, most of us don't know the first thing about the machine we've been licensed to drive—and this can turn a ticket to freedom into a ticket to trouble.

I'm not necessarily talking about physical danger. Our state motor vehicles bureaus have made fairly sure that we know how to drive defensively and can handle a car under poor driving conditions. What I am referring to is the kind of trouble that comes from being dependent upon other people for the care and repair of our automobiles.

If you are like most people who don't know anything about cars, you probably tend to drive around until something goes wrong, and then incur the expense of replacing worn and burnt-out parts—or the entire engine, for that matter—when low-cost, regular maintenance could have kept your wheels turning for a long time.

Even if your mechanics are honest, they are not going to notify you, as your dentist does, when it's time for a checkup. And charitable souls that they may be, they are not going to put their time and labor into your car without charging you for them. Since they have had to order, stock, and lay out cash for parts and supplies, they are going to want to make a profit on these too. Many of us have found that it simply isn't worth the extra money to get other people to do the things we can do for ourselves. And some of us are getting tired of having other people assume, just because we are teen-agers or women, that we aren't capable of handling repairs ourselves.

As a woman who has just gotten involved with her car, I'm here to tell you that we don't have to stand for this kind of thing! Getting involved with your car is easy and enjoyable and can save you a heck of a lot of money.

Whether you are trying to cut expenses, are tired of being patronized, or have just fallen in love with your first car, this book will tell you how your car works, what it needs in the way of tender loving care, and how to keep from getting ripped off if you have to entrust repairs to someone else. By handling the simple maintenance and tune-ups yourself, by being able to diagnose trouble and perform the less complex repairs yourself, you will earn the respect of your family, your mechanic, and your car—and, most of all, you'll feel pretty good about it! I know, because I've been there. . . .

Before I moved to California I was an ordinary urban cliff-dweller. Oh, I had a nodding acquaintance with cars; ours was locked up in a garage,

to be summoned forth by my husband for excursions to "the country." But aside from these occasions, I tended to think of transportation in terms of subways, buses, and taxis.

All the maintenance on our automobile was done by the garage that housed it. Every few months the garageman would comment, "Seems a little rough, could use a tune-up," and my husband would agree and give him the go-ahead. My sole contribution to our automotive life was choosing the color whenever we bought a new car (the only reason I had that much responsibility was that my husband is color blind), and since we rarely managed to put more than a few thousand miles on our car each year, these occasions were few and far between.

I had gotten a driver's license a few years back so I could go to the supermarket during our summers in the country or drive down to the lake for a swim, but driving in the city seemed to be a cross between foolishness and suicide, and I rarely, if ever, did it.

How did such a scared rabbit get to be an "authority" on automotive repairs, and where did she get the nerve to write about it? Funny you should ask. . . .

When we moved to California, I must confess, my enthusiasm for a life in the sun was considerably dampened by the knowledge that this would also include a life on the freeway. For the first few months my husband dutifully packed me into the family car and drove me to work, a distance of around 20 miles. Then he would turn around and drive home again. Each evening he would pick me up at work and take me home. Now, my husband is a very nice guy. And the drive took him through some very pretty scenery. But he had a business of his own to deal with, and the extra 80 miles and hour and a half a day did nothing to improve his temperament. And I was beginning to feel my oats. It began with a solo marketing excursion, and then that marvelous feeling of freedom that comes with sliding behind the wheel began to take hold, and before I knew it, I was looking for a car of my own.

Since the family budget had been considerably strained by the move West, the best I could do was a six-year-old Mustang with more than 70,000 miles on it. A friend of mine, who had grown up in Los Angeles—and was therefore a qualified expert on cars—checked the car out and pronounced it drivable. He said it might need "a little work." We took it to a reliable mechanic, who checked it over, tuned it up, and told me that it was a "classic." "They don't make them that way any-more," he explained. "Any time you want to get rid of it, just let me know. I can always use another car."

Thus reassured, I drove the car to the motor vehicle bureau for regis-tration. I parked the car, turned off the ignition, locked it, and found that, sitting there in the middle of the parking lot, the car was singing!

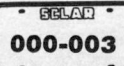

A bit puzzled, I rechecked the ignition and the radio, but everything was truly shut off. And still the car sang. By the time I returned, all was quiet. But that night, when I took the family out to dinner, old Tweety Bird began to sing again. Several weeks of filling and refilling the radiator, changing the coolant, putting gunk in the radiator to block any leaks, and so on managed to reduce the singing somewhat. But when I found out, $40 later, that all she needed was a new $2 radiator cap, I was made abruptly aware of two things:

First, Tweety was mine, and my responsibility. If she didn't work, I wasn't going to be able to either. And second, it was going to be impossible to enter this symbiotic relationship properly if I didn't know anything about her, because the garage bills were going to send both of us down the drain. The idea of putting myself into a piece of machinery and driving it at least 80 miles a day, at high speeds (this was pre-energy crisis), without the faintest idea of how it worked or what to do if it fell apart on the freeway, had become unthinkable.

So, after conning a friend of mine who happened to have two sets of car tools into taking an auto shop class with me at a local adult education center, I entered into what will probably turn out to be the closest relationship anyone has ever had with an inanimate object.

Of course the term "inanimate" is not really accurate. When you realize that a car exhibits most of the symptoms of life—it is self-propelled, reacts to outside stimuli, consumes fuel and discharges wastes, and even manages to sing a little tune now and then—it is really hard not to respond to it as though it were another living thing. (How far you go along with this idea is your own business. It is not a prerequisite for getting into auto repair, but it helps.)

The first thing I discovered was that cars are pretty simple things to deal with. Instead of a bewildering array of weird metal objects and miles of hoses, which threatened to blow up if I turned a screw in the wrong direction, I soon found that a car is just a series of simple Rube Goldberg mechanisms linked together. Since each repair, problem, or tune-up involves only a few, isolated gadgets, Tweety soon stopped being a mystery and began to be fun to hang around with.

Before long, just knowing what made the car go was not satisfying enough. After hanging around the auto shop watching other amateurs work on their cars, I began to itch to get into my own. The first steps were a bit awkward; I kept expecting the darn thing to blow up or break down if I made a mistake. Then I made the same discovery I'd made about my first child—the best way to handle a car (or a baby) is to take a firm grip on things and do the job without mincing around. Both the car and the baby seem to equate a little rough handling with assurance on your part. The results make for more security all around. From there, it was only a short step to forgetting about simply being able to communicate knowledgeably with a mechanic: I wanted to be the mechanic *myself* whenever possible.

One other note for my fellow females. No matter how liberated you've become, or how committed you still are to life as a "pussycat," you cannot fail to enjoy the heady pleasure that comes with being able to stride up to a garage mechanic and tell him you've recently rebuilt your carburetor! We'll get into all the money that moves like rebuilding your carburetor will save you, but just between us, knowing as much—or more—about cars than do the men you live with, or meet, is much richer stuff!

When I began to frequent auto-parts places, to get the things I needed for my work on Tweety, they used to go into the back and call out the other guys to see "the lady mechanic." Now we all stand around, peering under the hood, exchanging ideas, and I am "one of the boys." It beats getting whistled at, and it sure beats getting ripped off! To cap my pleasure, my husband, who had never gotten involved with auto repairs, recently respectfully requested that I teach him how to tune his car. Oh, bliss!

As a matter of fact, I've met a great many men who are intelligent, well educated, and know a great deal about law, business, literature, medicine, and other nonautomotive subjects but know absolutely nothing about cars. For some reason, most of them are ashamed of their ignorance and live as "closet dummies" who nod and smile wisely at the incomprehensible mutterings of their mechanics and shell out money for repairs neither fully understood nor always needed. For nonmechanical males this book can be "instant macho." You can finally learn what you need to know without having to admit you didn't, and you'll probably find that you enjoy being "one of the boys" as much as I do.

To my amazement, not only did learning about the inner secrets of my car turn out to be fascinating, but working on it myself soon became a great deal of fun. There is something about doing physical work and seeing the tangible results as soon as you drive away that is very, very rewarding. Another rewarding thing is seeing the difference between what it would have cost to have the work done professionally and the little bit of expense involved in buying the stuff yourself and doing your own **tune-ups** and repairs.

On the next page is a comparison chart that my instructor drew on our very first night in class. It impressed me tremendously, and I think you will have the same reaction.

Spark plugs from top manufacturers can be purchased for as little as 49 cents each, on sale. The full price can go as high as $1.35 each, but it is

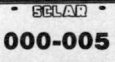

Comparison of Tune-up Parts and Labor Costs

Item	Do-It-Yourself	Have It Done for You
Parts:		
Spark Plugs (8)	$ 4.80 – $ 6.00	$10.80 – $ 14.00
Air Filter	1.50 – 4.00	7.50 – 8.50
Fuel Filter	2.00 – 3.50	3.00 – 7.50
Tune-up Kit	3.00 – 5.00	4.50 – 8.00
(points, rotor, condenser)		
PCV Valve (if necessary)	.99 – 2.50	2.50 – 4.00
Total Parts:	$12.29 – 21.00	$28.30 – 42.00
Labor:	0	$25.00 – 75.00
Total Parts and Labor:	$12.29 – $21.00	$53.30 – $117.00

Comparison of Oil-change Parts and Labor Costs

Item	Do-It-Yourself	Have It Done for You
Parts:		
Oil Filter	$ 1.50 – $ 3.00	$ 3.00 – $ 5.50
Oil (5 quarts)	2.50 – 3.50	5.00 – 7.00
Total Parts:	$ 4.00 – 6.50	$ 8.00 – 12.50
Labor:	0	$ 3.50 – 7.50
Total Parts and Labor:	$ 4.00 – $ 6.50	$11.50 – $ 20.00

Comparison of Radiator-flush and Coolant-change Parts and Labor

Item	Do-It-Yourself	Have It Done for You
Parts:		
Coolant	$ 3.50 – $ 5.00	$ 6.00 – $ 9.00
Thermostat (if necessary)	2.50 – 4.00	4.00 – 8.00
Total Parts:	$ 6.00 – 9.00	$10.00 – 17.00
Labor:	0	$10.00 – 14.00
Total Parts and Labor:	$ 6.00 – $ 9.00	$20.00 – $ 31.00

For a total of 2 to 5 hours of your time, you can save up to $160 in a single day, with your car properly tuned and maintained, because you *know* it's all been done—and done properly!

silly to pay this when you can get them more cheaply by keeping your eyes open. If you need additional items, like a new **distributor cap**, you will pay a garage nearly $5 for a cap that you can buy for $2.30. And if you know what you are doing, you may not need a new cap at all. There are tubes of gunk that seal minor cracks in distributor caps.

When you consider that any car should have a tune-up every 10,000 to 15,000 miles, you can get an idea of what you can save by doing it on your own. The work involved will take no more than a couple of hours (it can be done in less time once you know what you're doing), and it involves no heavy physical labor and nothing more than dirty hands.

Other simple jobs are comparable. I recently succumbed to laziness and allowed a local service station to change my **oil** and **coolant** for me. When the bill came to $30, I could only feel that I richly deserved it. When you consider that the coolant could have been purchased for around $5, and the engine flushed and refilled by merely turning the knob of a $2.50 attachment and attaching a garden hose, and that the oil would have cost about $3 retail and changing it involved removing a plug, allowing the **crankcase** to drain, replacing the plug, and pouring in the oil, you can see that I was paying a great deal for the convenience of having someone else do it.

I'm not saying I was charged unfairly—the prices seemed quite standard for my neighborhood—but the mechanics did neglect to change my **oil filter**—and now I'm going to have to wait until I need another oil change to do it. Since the filter is pretty old, that new oil change will come up long before it would have if I'd done the job properly myself.

If you are still with me and are now eager to get started (or at least are willing to read on while reserving judgment), then let me tell you a bit about what this book will cover and what it will not.

First, we'll talk about tools. Although you may not have a friend with a spare set, tools needn't be a major investment. You can borrow some of the more specialized ones, and there is really no need to go for the finest unless you are planning to start a business. There are, however, some tools that everyone should own, and we'll get into these in terms of what to buy, how to judge quality, and what they are for.

After a brief discussion of the basic principles and parts that make your car go—just so you'll know what you are dealing with—we'll get down to basics. We'll talk about each of the major systems in turn: the **electrical system**, the **fuel system**, the **cooling system**, **brakes**, **steering** and **suspension**, **lubrication**, and **transmission**. We'll discuss each system in everyday terms, with no jargon and no unnecessary technical details but with lots of simple illustrations. And we'll go into the tune-up and maintenance of each system with detailed instructions that leave nothing (I promise!) to the imagination.

There will be simple drawings that show *how* something works, with no attempt to show what it actually looks like, just the clearest possible picture of *what is actually going on*—and photographs that show *where* to find the part in your car and *what it really looks like*. I've tried to make the illustrations easier to follow than those instructions that tell you how to put together the toy you bought your kid for Christmas.

There will be chapters on how to lubricate your car and change your oil and oil filter, how to inspect your brakes (although we won't get into many repairs here; it really is too dangerous if you should goof), how to

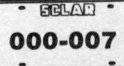

diagnose trouble by looking at your spark plugs and **tires**, how to tune your **ignition** and **carburetor**, how to buy tires and how to change a flat, how to flush out your **radiator** and change your coolant, how to diagnose transmission trouble and communicate it to your mechanic in terms that will assure that the work will be done properly (with a minimum of fuss and unnecessary labor and parts, and at a fair price), how to save fuel and cut down on air pollution, how to buy a good used car, and a host of other useful items.

If it is safe, and fun, to do the work yourself, I'll tell you how to do it. If it is just too hairy to deal with yourself, I'll tell you how to diagnose what's wrong, know what's needed, and make sure you get what you pay for.

There will be pre-trip safety instructions that should keep the "bugs" out of the car, even if they get into your picnic lunch, and tips on what to do if, despite your tender loving care, your car drops dead on the freeway. I'll provide a glossary, in case you forget what a **differential** is and don't want to search for the chapter that introduced you to it; a large index, in addition to the glossary, where you can look for a part, or a problem, when you return to this book for instructions for a specific area, and a **maintenance chart** that will remind you to get busy if you've let things go too long.

I suggest you read the book right through the first time. But after that initial excursion, just tuck the book into your trunk compartment, or under the front seat, so you can have it handy when it's time to tune up or make an adjustment or tell what the heck has gone wrong. I'd suggest you do your preliminary reading within walking distance of your car (you might want to curl up on the front seat) so you can open the hood and see for yourself that it's all in there just as I said. Then try an ignition tune-up for starters and, thus reassured, get into the rest of the stuff. I hope you'll find it as exhilarating as I did, and your car will love you for it!

2

The Way to
Your Car's Heart Is
Through Your Toolbox

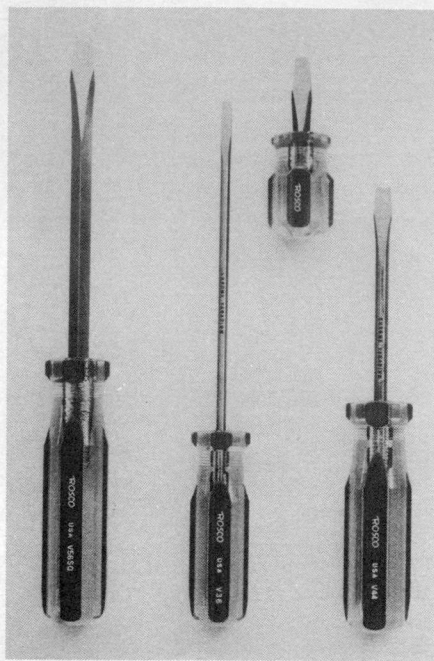

Standard Screwdrivers
Rosco Tools Inc.

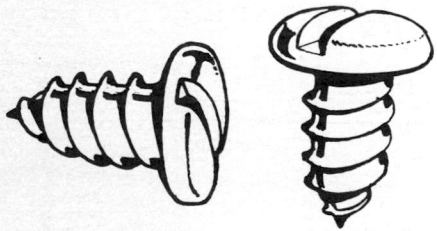

Standard Screws
Jack Herlihy

Whether you are trying to cook up a decent meal, paint a picture, run an office, or work on your car, you are only going to be as good as your tools will allow you to be. Just as you can't slice things super thin with a bent, rusty, dull knife—and you can't type a professional-looking letter on a broken-down type-writer—so it is impossible to do any kind of job on your engine if you lack the means to loosen or remove parts, clean or gap them, reinstall them, adjust them, and test the results.

Now, before you run off to return this book because you aren't prepared to spend a lot of money on tools that will probably never get used again after you've ruined your engine or cut off your thumb, let me tell you that all you really need are a few basic imple-ments and that they are not very expensive (we'll deal with the engine and your thumb later). In fact, you probably already own most of them. Prices vary wide-ly, but if you do your shopping in a major auto-parts chain store and stick to well-known brands, you will get good value at a fair price. Be sure to watch the paper for sales; most chains have them regularly, and you can save a lot of money. Also, if you buy each kind of tool in sets of different sizes, rather than buying at random, you will save there too. Look for high-grade steel, with no rough edges. Pick out friendly-looking salespeople and ask them what kind they buy. Most of them are auto enthusiasts who will be delighted that you are planning to do your own work (and be a future customer), and they will be glad to point out the best buys.

Screwdrivers First of all, you are going to need a couple of screw-drivers, so get out the toolbox and see what you al-ready have in stock.

There are two basic types of screwdrivers, and you will need a few of each type (not just for your car but for almost anything that has to be done around the house). The most common ones are called *standard screwdrivers* (or slot screwdrivers), and the others are called *Phillips screwdrivers*. They have different heads made to fit Phillips screws. You cannot use a standard screwdriver on a Phillips screw, or vice versa. Since your car is fitted with both types of screws, in a variety of sizes, it is necessary to have several of both kinds. Using a screwdriver of the wrong type or size will result in damage to the screw, the screwdriver, or yourself. Always use a screwdriver with a tip that is the same width as the head of the screw you are working on. The shafts will vary in length too, and this is useful, because a longer shaft will provide greater leverage for hard-to-remove screws, while a shorter shaft will get into tight places more easily. You can get all the screwdrivers you need for a couple of dollars. Look for sales of plastic-handled screwdrivers, in sets of varying sizes.

By the way, if you find yourself confronted with a screw that is difficult to start unscrewing, try giving it a slight twist in the *opposite* direction (clockwise), as though you were trying to tighten it. Then loosen it (counterclockwise). If this doesn't work, rap the screw on the head with a hammer, which should loosen it a bit. This works for bolts too. If strong-arm tactics aren't getting you anywhere, you can try squirting the troublemaker with a can of penetrating oil.

Keep your temper with difficult screws; otherwise you'll risk stripping the threads and turn a fairly simple job of replacing what you've loosened into a hair puller.

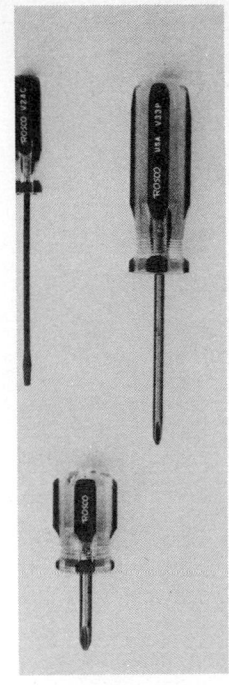

Phillips Screwdrivers
Rosco Tools Inc.

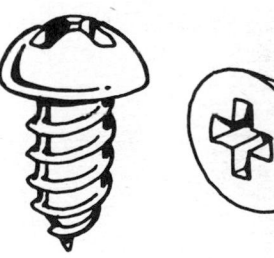

Phillips Screws
Jack Herlihy

Screwholders are perfectly marvelous for hanging on to screws that have to fit into tiny places. Instead of hanging on to the screw with the fingers of one hand while you wield the screwdriver with the other, you simply fit the screw into the screwholder and use the screwholder instead of a screwdriver. Some screw–holders have a magnet to hold the screw; others have a little gizmo that grabs the screw when you twist the screwholder. Both are lovely.

Screwholders

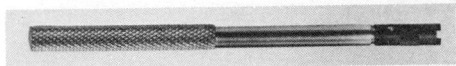

Screwholder
Pendleton Tool Industries, a subsidiary of
Ingersoll-Rand Company

Wrenches

Open-End Wrench
Husky Hand Tools

Box-End Wrench
Husky Hand Tools

These are probably the most basic tools for auto repair. You will need a couple of different kinds, in different sizes. Most wrenches are available in both standard measurements and in metric measurements, and you must know which system of measurement your engine is based on. As a rule, most foreign cars are based on the metric system, while domestic engines use standard fractions of an inch. However, in anticipation of the adoption of the metric system in the near future, at least one American auto manufacturer has switched to the metric system on one of its newer models, so it is best to check your owner's manual to be sure which type of engine you have.

There are several basic types of wrenches, some for very specialized purposes, but the following are the kinds you will need for most jobs. Again, look for sets made by well-known toolmakers and try to buy them on sale.

Combination Wrenches
Pendleton Tool Industries, a subsidiary of
Ingersoll-Rand Company

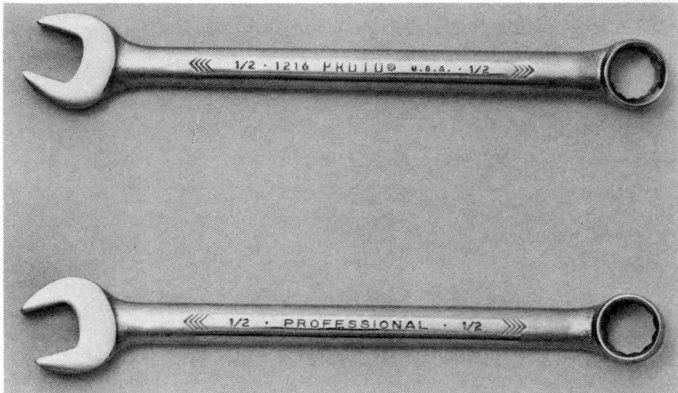

Combination Wrenches

There are *open-end wrenches* and *box-end wrenches*, but the very best kind to get are *combination wrenches*, with an open end and a closed end on each wrench. These wrenches come in sets of several sizes, and each wrench is made to fit a nut of a specific size, whichever end you use. You can get a good set of combination wrenches for from $5 to $8.

Some combination wrenches are sort of S-shaped. These are good for hard-to-reach spots and are called *offset wrenches.* You might want to add a couple to your tool kit. The most useful offset wrench is the *distributor wrench.* You use it to adjust your *timing.* Be sure to get one to fit the **distributor hold-down clamp** on your car. If you're not sure what a distributor hold-down clamp is or where to find it, see the Glossary or Chapter 5.

Offset Wrenches

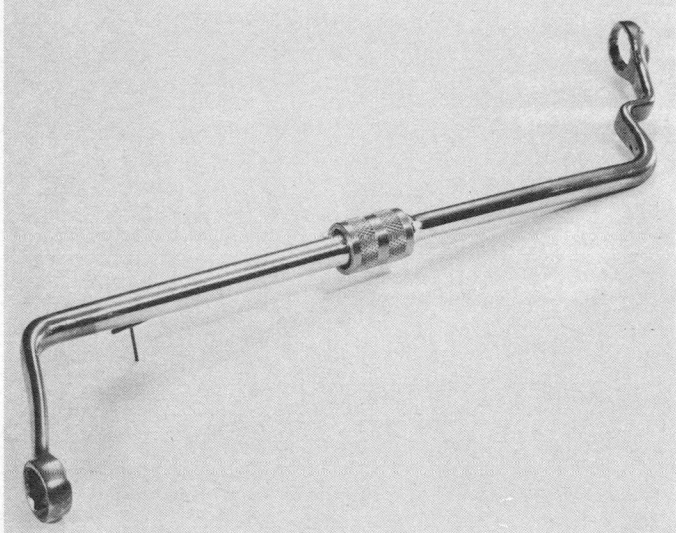

Offset Distributor Wrench
K-D Manufacturing Co.

Ignition wrenches are simply sets of combination wrenches in very small sizes for ignition work. They cost very little. I found a boxed set with a wire gauge and a feeler gauge (more about these in a minute) and a tiny screwdriver and file thrown in, all for $1.98.

Ignition Wrenches

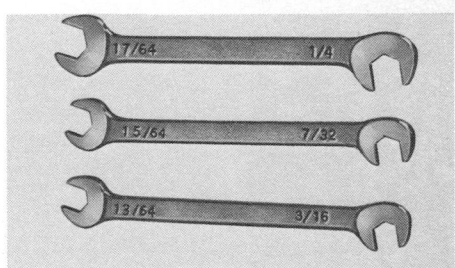

How to Use a Wrench

To use the open end of a wrench most effectively, place it around the nut you want to remove and move the wrench to the right so that the screw moves in a counterclockwise direction to loosen the nut. If the nut sticks, try a squirt of penetrating oil or give it a bang on the head with a hammer. Place your free hand over the wrench and the nut to give yourself some control and to stop the wrench from flying off the nut. When you move the wrench as far as it will go, the nut will have been loosened 15 degrees. (That's why the slot is at an angle.) By simply turning the wrench over so that the other surface of the same end is around the nut you can move the nut another 15 degrees without having to place the wrench at a different angle.

How to Hold a Wrench
Pendleton Tool Industries, a subsidiary of
Ingersoll-Rand Company

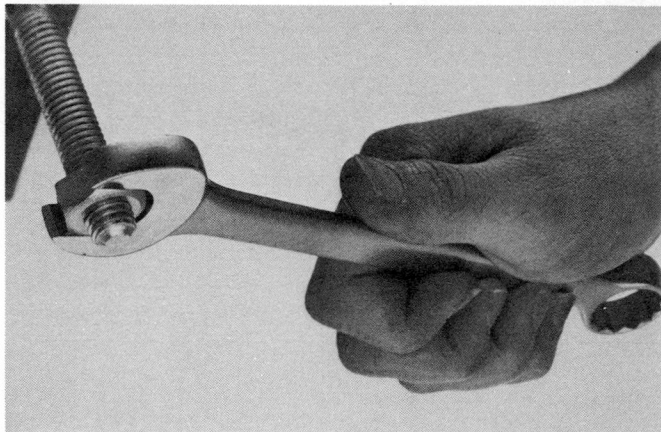

Always use the proper-size wrench. If you use one that is too big, it will slip and round off the edges of the nut. This will make the nut harder to tighten later on. It will also round off the inside edges of the wrench, with the same results.

A good set of **socket wrenches** will really make the difference between enjoying your work or killing yourself over it. These come in sets for around $20, less if you catch a sale. Your set of socket wrenches should contain the following basic items:

1 A variety of ¹/₄-inch or ³/₈-inch drive heads or *sockets*. The ¹/₂-, ⁹/₁₆-, and ³/₄-inch sockets are the ones you'll use the most, unless you need a metric set. The word "drive" refers to the size of the square hole in each socket where it attaches to the **ratchet handle**. It is easy to remember that the smaller the drive, the smaller the job you use it for. Quarter-inch drive is for tiny areas, ³/₈-inch is standard; other drives up to 2 inches are for really big jobs. You won't need these. You can use adapters to convert sockets of one drive to fit handles of another drive.

2 A **spark plug socket**. This is the large socket with a soft lining to hold the spark plug securely without damaging its soft jacket when you are removing and inserting it, or when you drop it on the floor by mistake.

3 At least one **ratchet handle**, to which you can fit any of the sockets. Most sets have one handle with at least one adapter. You might want to add additional adapters to extend the handle to different sizes and to adapt it to different drives. A *flex-head* handle or adapter is also very useful. It enables you to hold the ratchet handle at any angle when working in tight places—and engines are full of tight places!

The way to tell a good socket-wrench set is to look at the number of teeth in the ratchet handle. Most have 20 to 30 teeth. The really good ones have up to 60 teeth. The more teeth the handle has, the better it will fit into tight places. This is because you have to move the handle only a few degrees to turn the nut as much as a cheaper handle would in many degrees. In other words, a ratchet handle with 24 teeth must be moved 15 degrees to reach its limit. A handle with 60 teeth has to be moved only 6 degrees to turn a nut as far.

Socket Wrenches

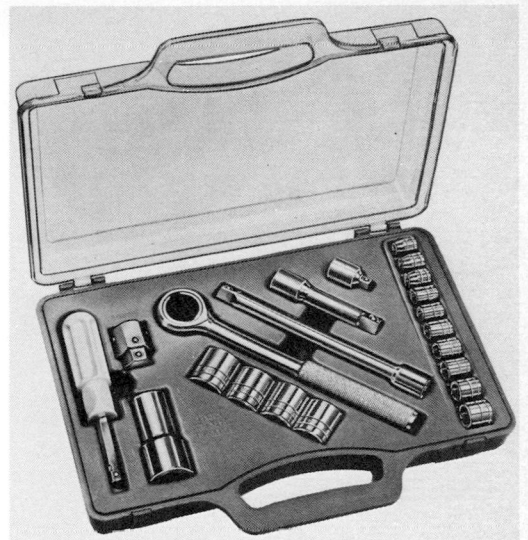

Socket Wrench Set
Oxwall Tool Company

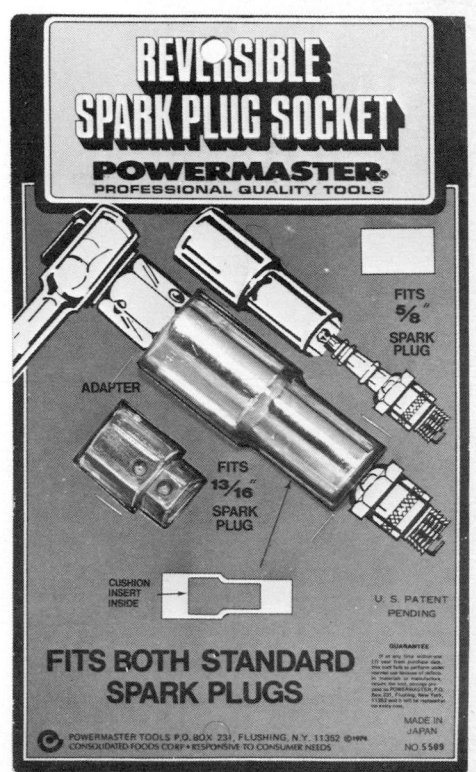

Spark Plug Socket
Oxwall Tool Company

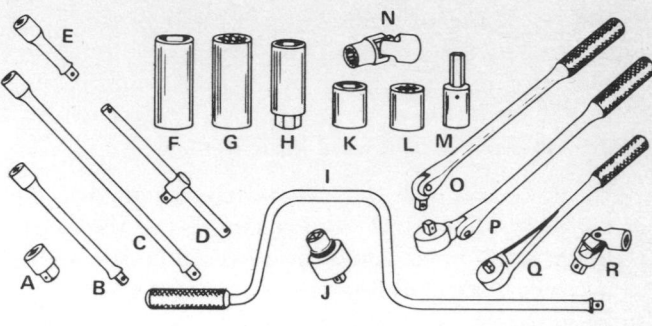

A	–Adapter	**K**	–Regular 6–point socket
B, C, E	–Extension bars	**L**	–Regular 12–point socket
D	–Sliding T handle	**M**	–Hollow screw socket bit
F	–Deep 6–point socket	**N**	–Universal 12–point socket
G	–Deep 12–point socket	**O**	–Flex handle
H	–Spark plug socket	**P**	–Flex head ratchet
I	–Speeder handle	**Q**	–Reversible ratchet
J	–Ratchet adapter	**R**	–Universal joint

Ratchet Handles, Extenders, and Adapters
Hand Tools Institute, New York

Torque Wrenches

A **torque wrench** is designed to tighten a nut, bolt, or screw to an exact degree. This is extremely handy because until one becomes familiar with a job, there is always the danger of undertightening or overtightening things. If you are replacing a spark plug and you do not tighten it enough, it will work loose and fail to deliver a spark. If you overtighten it you can strip the threads or crack the plug. Similarly, parts that have **gaskets** can leak if the bolts that hold them are not tightened enough. But if you overtighten the same bolts, the gasket will be crushed and it will leak anyway. Most really good torque wrenches are expensive, but you can get a cheap one for $10 to $12 which will serve your purposes. If you'd rather not spend the money until you are sure you are really going to like working on your car, it might be a good idea to borrow one, just to get the feel of how tight a nut, bolt, etc., should be. Or you can just forget the whole thing. I've never used a torque wrench; my set of socket wrenches has accomplished everything quite well, but I might just have been lucky. I'll probably borrow a torque wrench soon, and if I really like it, maybe I'll invest in one someday. Anyway, if you are planning to buy one, keep these things in mind:

1 Get a wrench with a slim profile, because torque wrenches are bulky anyway and will often not fit in tight places.

2 Get the kind that has an audible click when you reach the proper degree of tightness. The dial kind sometimes cannot be seen if you are working in a dark place or "by feel" in a remote corner of your engine. There is a torque wrench with a dial that lights up when you have tightened the bolt to the proper degree, but these are expensive. A click should do—if you don't sing while you work.

3 Torque wrenches should be gripped well down the shaft (not up close to the dial) and should be operated smoothly.

4 It is best to tighten a series of bolts out of sequence, to distribute the pressure evenly, instead of in strict clockwise or counterclockwise order.

5 When tightening a series of bolts, tighten them all just until they are snug. Then go back and tighten them all a bit more. Then go back and tighten them all the way to the torque specifications. This will ensure that the entire part you are tightening is under even pressure. It will prevent leaky gaskets and increase the life of the bolt and the part. This is good advice (so is 4) to follow when using any kind of wrench to tighten anything.

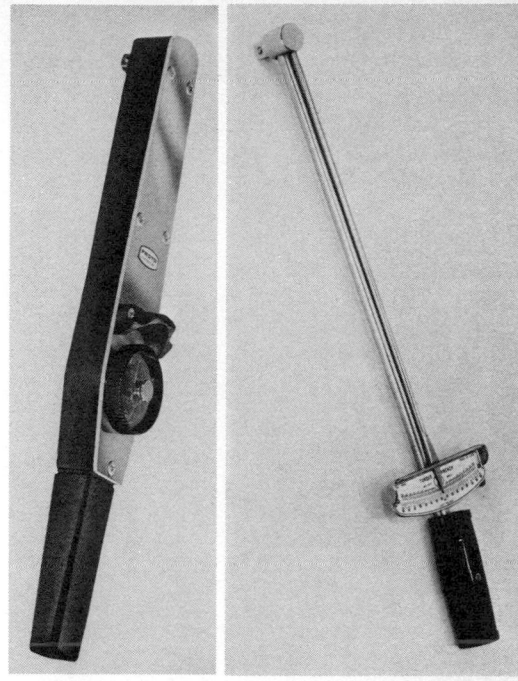

(*left*) Dial Torque Wrench (*right*) Deflecting Beam Torque Wrench
Pendleton Tool Industries, a subsidiary of Ingersoll-Rand Company

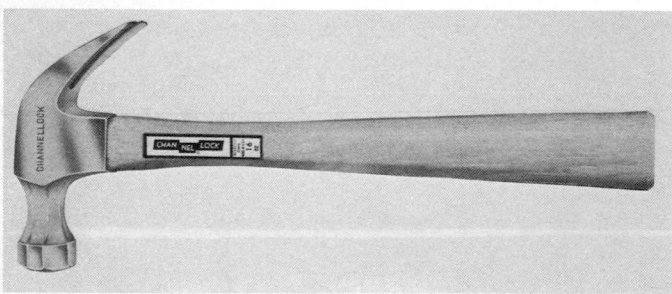

Carpenter's Hammer
Channellock, Inc.

You may associate these with carpentry, but they are useful in automotive work as well. A *carpenter's hammer* (*or claw hammer*) is not really designed for auto repair.

Hammers

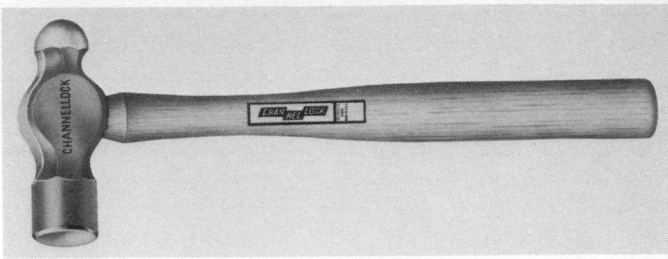

Ball-peen Hammer
Channellock, Inc.

You should have a *ball-peen* hammer. If all you have is a carpenter's hammer and you don't want to buy another one, you can probably make do with it. Just be sure that the hammer you use does not have a loose head. If the shaft is not securely sunk into the head, it can fly off and damage your car, yourself, or an innocent bystander. Claw hammers can also be dangerous because a hard, solid impact can cause the claws to break off, with dismal results.

Pliers Rummage through the family toolbox for these. Almost everyone has *needle-nosed* and *slip-joint* pliers, and these will be useful. If you are prepared to buy pliers, however, the very best kind to get are *combination slip-joint pliers*. These general-purpose tools can be adjusted to several widths by a sliding pin. They also usually have a wire-cutting slot built into them as well. If you are the only person on your block who doesn't possess these, by all means rush out and buy them before dark. Again, they needn't be expensive. A good pair should cost less than $5. Just be sure they work easily, are made of forged hardened steel and seem to be well finished.

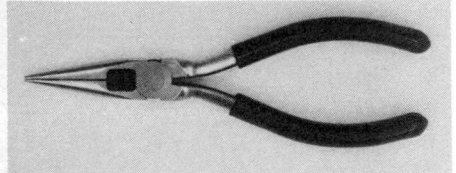

Needle-nosed Pliers
Rosco Tools Inc.

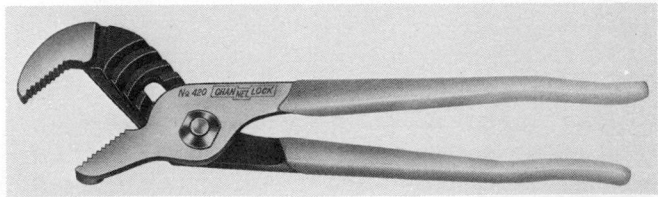

Combination Slip-Joint Pliers
Channellock, Inc.

A few notes on the use of pliers. If you are working on electrical wiring and want to be sure you won't get shocked, slip a length of rubber hose over each handle, leaving the hose in one piece. This will not only insulate the pliers; it will allow them to spring open quickly. Never use combination pliers on nuts and bolts—they will round off the corners and make them harder to replace. Besides, that's what you have all your lovely wrenches for.

Tool Kits

If, as you read this chapter, you are made painfully aware that you are going to have to go out and buy practically everything, you might want to look into pre-packaged tool kits. Nearly every major supplier carries a tool kit with everything you need already in it. These usually sell for around $50 (much less on sale), and if you are totally tool-poor, one of these may prove to be the best buy. Be sure you are getting good quality, however. It's better to have a couple of tools that work well than a large assortment of junk. And while we're on the subject, empty toolboxes are inexpensive and worth buying. They keep tools clean and in good shape and, most important, all in one place. Look for one that will fit easily into the trunk of your car. Although your tools will be useful around the house, it's very nice to have them handy if you get stuck away from home.

Gauges

The next two items are specialized tools that are used for "gapping" spark plugs, points, and valves. They are very inexpensive—some stores give them away as premiums. I will usually discuss specialized tools in the chapters that call for them, but I wanted to mention them now so you can pick them up while you're at an auto supply store buying other stuff.

Wire Feeler Gauges

Wire **feeler gauges** are used for gapping spark plugs. "Gapping" simply means sliding the proper gauge wire between the spark plug electrodes to be sure the surfaces are the proper distance apart, ensuring that

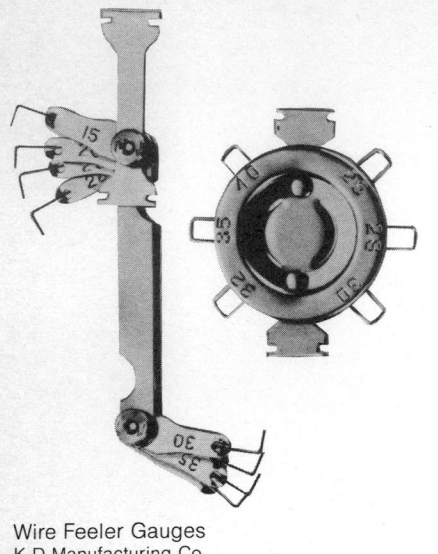

Wire Feeler Gauges
K-D Manufacturing Co.

Flat Feeler Gauge
K-D Manufacturing Co.

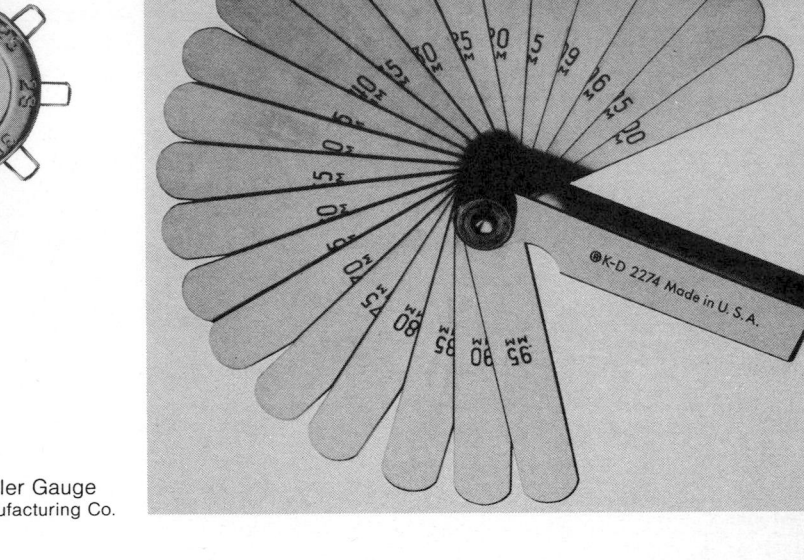

the spark can jump across the gap with the proper intensity. Wire feeler gauges usually cost around 59 cents, but sometimes they are included with sets of other tools.

Flat Feeler Gauges

Flat **feeler gauges** are used for adjusting valves and points, relatively simple jobs that are impossible to do properly without a feeler gauge. I found them for $1.19 at a local automotive supply store. Again, look for them as part of a set of other tools—or as freebies—first.

Compression Gauges

Compression gauges are used to check the pressure that builds up in each cylinder as your engine runs. They also reveal damage to piston rings and valves. If your car is new, this is probably not going to be a problem for some time, but if it is older, or second-hand, this easy-to-use gauge is a good investment. It

Compression Gauges
DIXCO
Karcheck Products

will help you spot trouble and save you money. I've found them for as low as $3.69. The screw-in kind is easiest to use, but these usually cost a bit more.

Whether you plan to work on your car in your home garage, in your driveway, at the curb near your house, or in a local auto shop, you will find that the lighting will be inadequate once you get under the hood—or under the car if you are that adventurous. A **work light** will provide all the illumination you need, with the capability of shining the maximum amount of light right on the work area and not in your eyes. If you will not be working near an electrical outlet, you might need an extension cord, but these, and the work light, are not expensive items at all.
Be sure your light has a protective cage around at least half of the bulb and that the cord is long enough and properly insulated. Look for the Underwriter's tag to be sure you are getting quality. Recently, a work light was recalled from the market because right under the bulb, there was a flexible handle with an

Work Lights

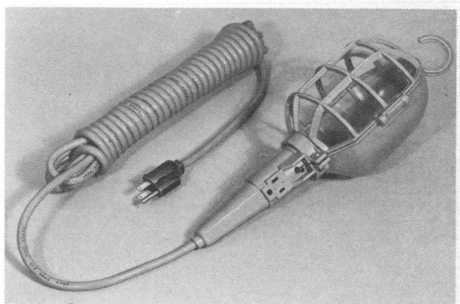

Work Light
Guaranteed Parts Company

open socket under that. You could plug additional accessories into this socket, but the convenience was considerably lessened because if you had nothing plugged into the socket, you ran the risk of "plugging yourself in" by gripping the work light on the socket area.

Most work-light cages have a hook at the top so that the light can be hung inside the hood of your car or on a nearby part. Just be certain you are not hooking the light to anything that carries electricity itself.

You can get a good work light, with a 25-foot cord, for under $5. Lights with 10-foot cords are only $3 or so, but a good extension cord will make up the difference in price if you need one.

You will find that a work light is useful for a variety of home repairs and for outside work at night, but if you are going to be working far from an outlet, there is also a work light that gets its power from your car's battery for around $4.50.

Scissor Jack

Jacks Most new cars come with a **jack** to be used when changing tires. If you have a secondhand car, or if your jack has been lying around neglected, you may need to buy one. There are several types of jacks available; just be sure the jack you buy is suited to your car's bumper design. Check your jack periodically and lubricate it. Never use a jack without the base plate, and never jack your car up unless the wheels are properly blocked. We'll get into this in detail in Chapter 9.

One last word, be sure your jack is in your trunk at all times. It is very depressing to know how to change a flat only to find that your jack is in your garage and your car is on the road.

Tripod Jack

Hydraulic Jack

Three Types of Jacks

Jack Stands **Jack stands** are quite inexpensive and very important if you are going to work under your car. Get two of them and look for instructions in Chapter 9 before you use them.

SCLAR
000-022

Jack Stands
Foxcraft/Philmont, a Division of Gulf & Western Mfg.
Co.

A **timing light** is a specialized piece of equipment that is used to check ignition **timing**. You can find out what timing is and how a timing light is used by checking the Glossary, and full details are given in Chapter 5. It is standard equipment at every garage, and if you don't want to undertake the expense right away, borrow one from someone else in your neighborhood who works on his or her car. If you live in an isolated spot, or in an old folks' home, you might drive down to your local garage—after you've done your tune-up—and ask them to check your timing. They will promptly haul out their timing light, shine it at your engine, and give you an answer. The only trouble with this is, if your timing is off, they will not understand why they can't fix it for you. And if you tell them you are going to fix it yourself, you'd better plan to go to another garage for a timing check when you're through. Then, when you've exhausted all the garages in the neighborhood, you'll have to go out and buy a timing light anyway.

Timing lights range in price from less than $10 to close to $40. There are two types—neon and xenon. The neon lights are cheaper but, because they operate off the spark plug circuit and use minimal voltage, the light they produce is not bright enough to see clearly

Timing Lights

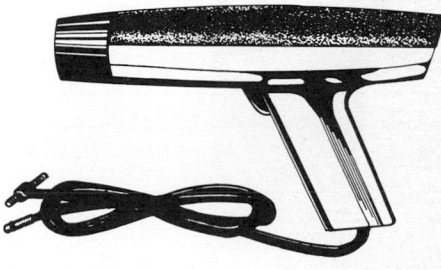

Timing Light
DIXCO

SCLAR
000-023

unless you work in almost total darkness. These can be obtained for $6.98 to $11.98. I would suggest you get the xenon light if you possibly can. They usually are available for under $20—if you scout around. I found one for $13.98, which is an incredible buy, since comparable timing lights can go as high as $35. Be sure that the cord is long enough and that the clamps are properly insulated so that you can grab them easily without getting shocked. The light should go on and off with a "strobe" effect when the clamps are properly affixed. When you shine the light at the timing marks on the moving **crankshaft pulley** of your engine, this strobe effect will make the marks appear to stand still, so you can see if you have tuned your car properly. We'll go into the proper way to use this gadget, and what "timing" really means, in Chapter 5.

Dwell Meters

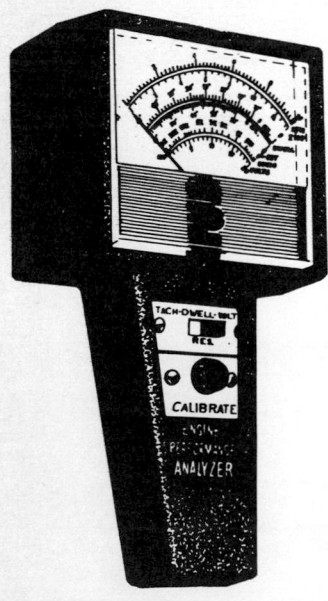

Tach-Dwell Meter
DIXCO

Although you can buy a gadget that is simply a **dwell meter**, try to find one called a *dwell/tachometer* or *tach/dwell meter.* This simply means that the gadget not only has a dwell meter for measuring your point gap but that it has a **tachometer** built in as well. The tachometer will measure the revolutions per minute (rpm) of your engine, and it is extremely valuable for adjusting your carburetor so that your car will idle properly. Look for a tach/dwell meter that has both high and low ranges on the tachometer—it will give you a more precise reading. Although you can get along without one, a tach/dwell meter (we'll just call it a "dwell meter" for short for the rest of the book) will provide a fast way to know whether you have set your **dwell** and idle properly. If you don't know what "dwell" and "idle" mean, relax. Basically they just mean that your car is running at a pace that ensures maximum mileage per gallon with optimum performance and minimum wear and tear. All shall be revealed to you in time; just have patience, fear not, and buy a dwell meter if you have the funds. If you don't, try to borrow a friend's until you are sure you are going to be working on your car regularly. I use the one at my auto shop class, but I am planning to ask Santa Claus for one this year, and if he fails me, I'll buy myself one for my birthday. If funds, friends, and

Santa all fail you, don't let the lack of a dwell meter keep you from tuning your car, however. The chapter on ignition tune-ups will tell you how to do the job with feeler gauges. A dwell meter would simply be more accurate and would help in adjusting your carburetor, but it can wait. You can buy a good dwell meter for around $25, and there are build-it-yourself kits available, if you swing that way. I've recently found a locally made dwell meter for $12.98, and another with a tachometer built in for $14.98, and the dealer swears they work beautifully.

Fire Extinguishers

A **fire extinguisher** is not really a tool, but it is a *must* for your car. Get the 2³/4-pound dry chemical type. Engine fires do not necessarily mean that the car is ruined—if you can put them out quickly. Sometimes gasoline can leak out of your carburetor and be ignited by a stray spark from your spark plugs or from a cigarette butt thrown from a car window. The resulting fire looks awful, but it is really burning on the outside of your engine. If you put it out quickly, you may have little or no damage. Cigarette butts can also land on your back seat, and fires can be caused by ruptured **fuel lines**, flooded carburetors, and faulty wiring as well, so an inexpensive fire extinguisher may not only save you money; it may also save your life. If the flames are anywhere near the **fuel tank**, however, forget the heroics; just run for it and throw yourself to the ground if you think it might explode. Because your fuel tank is located right under your trunk compartment, keep your extinguisher under the front seat of your car, or in the glove compartment if it fits.

Funnels

Funnels are used for filling your radiator, adding oil, and adding **transmission fluid** to your car. Steal a large one from the kitchen, or buy one at an auto supply or hardware store. Either metal or plastic is fine, and you should be able to find one for under a dollar.

Other Things You'll Want to Carry in Your Car

You probably have most of this stuff already, but here's a chance to check:

Rags Rags should be clean and lint-free. Get rid of gasoline-soaked rags—they're highly combustible. Never keep them in closed places, but you know that already, right? Don't use an oily rag on anything that isn't oily already. Because your car contains a variety of substances that must be kept away from other substances (engine oil, transmission fluid, and grease eat rubber hoses, for instance), it is best to throw out—or wash—dirty rags, and go for a clean one each time you start a job. Keep a clean rag in your glove compartment; you'll need it (if for nothing else) to defog your windshield.

Spare Parts When you replace your spark plugs and your **points**, save the old ones if they are not too worn. Carry them in your trunk compartment toolbox for a quick replacement if something goes wrong with those in your engine. The same goes for old, not-too-cruddy **air filters**, **fuel filters**, **rotors**, **fan belts**, and other minor gizmos. A couple of extra nuts, bolts, and screws will also help, in case you lose those you have or strip them accidentally. And hang on to extra pieces of hose, wire, etc., for makeshift repairs.

Spare Tires Just a reminder to check your spare tire often. It is humiliating to go through the work of changing a tire only to find that your spare is flat, too. If your spare is worn beyond belief, most garages will sell you a not-too-hideous patched tire at a low price.

Lug Wrenches A **lug wrench** is sometimes provided, along with the jack, on new cars. It is used to remove the wheel or lug nuts when you change your tires. But if you are going out to buy a lug wrench, get the *cross-shaft* kind. It will provide you with more leverage.

Jumper Cables One of the most common malfunctions of a car is the loss of power to start it, either from an old or faulty battery or because you've left the headlights on by mistake. Once in this situation, you can either wait for the AAA or a nearby garage to come and bail you out,

(*left*) Single-Shaft Lug Wrench (*right*) Cross-Shaft Lug Wrench
Alexandra Soto

or you can stop a passing car, whip out your **jumper cables**, attach them in seconds, and "jump a start" from the Good Samaritan's car to your own. Most people are willing to lend their cars to this sort of operation, because they lose nothing but a few minutes of their time. Full instructions for the proper way to "jump a start" can be found in Chapter 14. You can buy a set of jumper cables for as little as $1.79 to $4.50—less than you'd have to pay a garage if you got stuck with a dead battery and no cables. Good cables can cost as much as $20. The difference is in the way they are wired. Good cables have more strands of better-conducting wire which let more "juice" flow between the cars, with less loss of voltage. Sometimes the success or failure of an attempt to jump a start depends on the quality of the jumper cables and their grips. If you get a cheap set, there is an easy way to make them work better. Go under the plastic sheath that covers the place where the cables meet the grips and squeeze the connection tight with a pair of pliers. This will improve the connection, and the cheap set of cables will work beautifully—at least for the first few times.

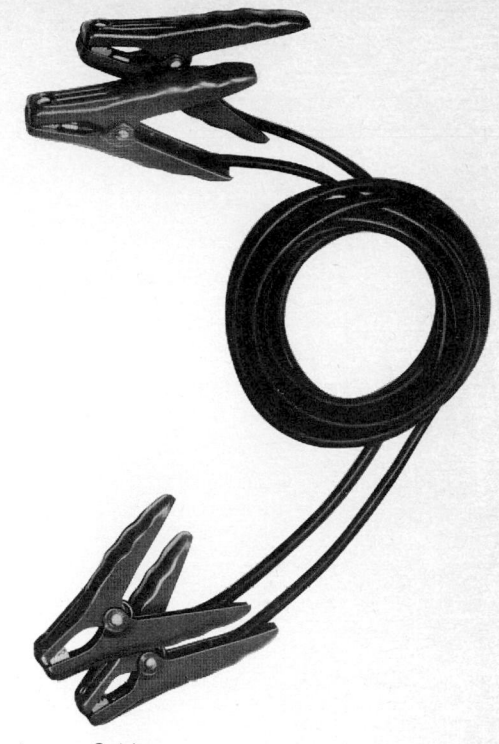

Jumper Cables
Guaranteed Parts Company

Snow and Ice Equipment

If you live in an area that is cold in winter, try to carry a bag of *sand*, or *tire chains*, in case you find yourself dealing with icy conditions. A small shovel might be useful for digging out, and a scraper will help to clear your windshield if you've been parked in the snow and it has iced over.

Flares and Flashlights

A flashlight is always a good addition to your glove compartment. It will help your kids to locate dropped toys on the floor of the car, enable you to see under the hood if your car breaks down, and serve as an emergency light for oncoming traffic if you have to stop on the highway for repairs. You can use flares, but they can be dangerous, and many states have rules regarding their use on the highways. A flashlight with a red blinker is safer, more versatile, and just as good. Of course you will be sure to put in fresh batteries now and then, or carry a couple of extras.

First-Aid Kit   It is a good idea for both workshop and car to keep on hand a couple of Band-Aids, something soothing for burns, and a good antiseptic.

Hand Cleaner   Most of these hand cleaners are basically grease solvents. They range from heavy-duty stuff that removes the skin along with the grease; through nice, soothing, good-smelling creams that leave you feeling reborn; to pre-cleaners that you put on your hands *before* you start working, in order to be sure that the grease will slide off easily afterward. I found a creamy hand cleaner at Sears which was cheap (a whole can for 89 cents), good-smelling, and effective. It can also be rubbed into work clothes to remove grease and oil stains before you launder them.

Spare Tools   If you can't carry your toolbox all the time, try to leave a couple of screwdrivers, some standard-size combination wrenches, and a can of penetrating oil in your trunk compartment. Remember, it is not necessary to buy everything at once in order to get started on your car; use the beg, borrow, and steal-from-the-family-toolbox method if you must. The important thing is to get to work!

Here is a handy checklist to help you keep track of what you have, what you need, and what you think you can do without. You can tear it out and take it to the store if you like.

TOOL CHECKLIST
(Starred tools are optional, but definitely worth buying!)

Tool	Have	Don't Have	Need Sizes:
Standard Screwdrivers			
Phillips Screwdrivers			
*Screwholder			
Combination Wrenches			
Ignition Wrenches			
*Distributor Wrench			
Socket Wrench Set			
*Flex-head Extension			
*Extra Handles & Adapters			
*Torque Wrench			
Ball-peen Hammer			
Needle-nosed Pliers			
Combination Slip-joint Pliers			
Wire Feeler Gauge			
Flat Feeler Gauge			
*Compression Gauge			
*Work Light			
Jack			
*Jack Stands			
*Timing Light			
*Dwell Meter/Tachometer			
*Fire Extinguisher			
Funnel			
Rags			
*Spare Parts			
Spare Tire			
Lug Wrench			
*Jumper Cables			
Flashlight			
First Aid Kit			
Hand Cleaner			

What Makes It Go?
The Inner Secrets
of Your Car Revealed

Anthropologists tell us that one of the major events that marked the transition of early man from "wise monkey" to a more civilized critter was the ability to get something else to do his work for him. Along with such major technological breakthroughs as the club and spear, the control of fire, and the invention of the loincloth was the eventual use of round logs, later called "wheels," to move things and people. Carts of various types, with wheels that allowed them to move easily, were pushed or pulled by men and animals for centuries. Eventually, some early science-fiction freak decided to invent a machine that could move itself, and the first engine appeared.

Today, most of us possess vehicles that can move themselves. True, we still have to tell our cars when to go and when to stop, and we have to steer them in the proper direction and keep them in good running order, but basically a car is simply a set of wheels and an engine to turn them.

The **internal combustion engine**, which forms the "heart" of your car, is a lightweight, fairly efficient, and relatively uncomplicated piece of machinery. It works on a mixture of gasoline and air to produce enough power to turn a shaft that turns the wheels. The basic gizmos on your car are simply the things that bring the fuel and air together in the proper quantities, ignite them, and channel the resulting power to the wheels. All the rest of the stuff is there to make this happen with ease and efficiency, to provide you with some control over what's going on, and to give you a place to sit and store your groceries. Power attachments provide comfort, at the price of additional cost and potential repairs. You pay your money and you take your choice.

O.K. Let's get down to specifics. First, let's take a look at your engine and the way it works.

Now remember, every car manufacturer has made sure to do something a little bit differently from the competition so that he can get patents and say that his cars are the best. Therefore, if any part of your car is not exactly where it is in the pictures in this book, don't panic. Just look for something that looks like it, in the same general area. Believe me, it will be in there someplace or your car would not go.

Your **owner's manual** should have a diagram that was probably gibberish to you until you bought this book. Now you can return to it and locate the parts of your car, if you can't find them on the car itself. If you are still up the wall, or if you didn't get an owner's manual, ask a friend who has the same make car, or ask your friendly garage mechanic, to point out these "missing" parts. I'm willing to bet, however, that if you read this chapter carefully, with an eye on your engine, you will be able to locate almost all the parts yourself.

By the way, if you don't have an owner's manual, ask your local distributor or car dealer to get one for you, or to tell you where you can get one. There are also **service manuals** available for every car, and it is a good idea to get one of these too. Again, ask the local distributor or dealer of your make car, or write to the company that made your car, with the words "Service Manuals" written on the envelope. The manufacturer will send you one for a couple of dollars. On the last pages of most owner's manuals there is information about obtaining service manuals. If all else fails, try your local library for one of the service manuals published by Chilton or Motor's which deals with your make and model. At first look, these seem very complicated; the schematic drawings are especially scary. But if you get to the point where you want to rebuild your carburetor, these drawings will show you where every little screw and washer fits, so you won't end up with a couple of "extra" parts at the end of the job. There's no need to rush out and get a service manual immediately, however. Most of the things we're going to cover right now can be learned without one.

And now back to our story . . .

First, I am going to run through the five basic systems very quickly, to give you a general idea of what goes on and how the parts and systems connect. Then we'll take it again, chapter by chapter and piece by piece, in greater detail. When we're done, you'll know about as much as I do concerning what makes your car go. Don't worry about what model you own; every car with an internal combustion engine works on the same principles in the same way.

The Electrical System

Although we tend to think of cars as being basically powered by gasoline, there are many parts of the car that function on electricity. These include the radio, headlights, clock, etc. Of course, you could get along without these devices if you had to, but did you know that it takes electricity to get your car to *start*? This is accomplished by an **ignition system**, which works in conjunction with your car's electrical system. It provides the power that allows your starter to make your engine turn over. And once your engine turns over, it can begin to run on gasoline, just as you expected it to. Here's how it works:

All the electrical current for your car is supplied by the **battery**, which is constantly being recharged with electricity by the **generator** or the **alternator**. Unless your car is quite old, it probably has an alternator, which generates alternating current (AC) and then converts it to direct current (DC) so that it can run the various devices on the car. Older cars have generators, which generate DC directly. If you aren't sure which one you have, alternators are short, round, and silver-colored; generators are cylindrical, long, and black.

Once your car has started running, the ignition system continues to provide electric current to the spark plugs so that they can provide the spark that causes

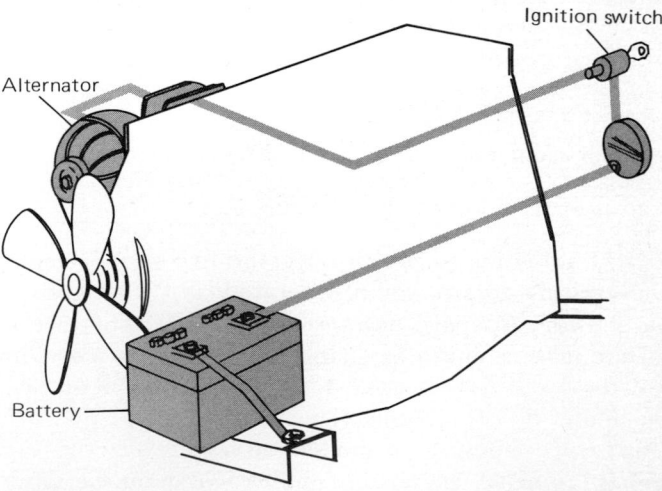

The Charging System
Automotive Information Council (AIC)

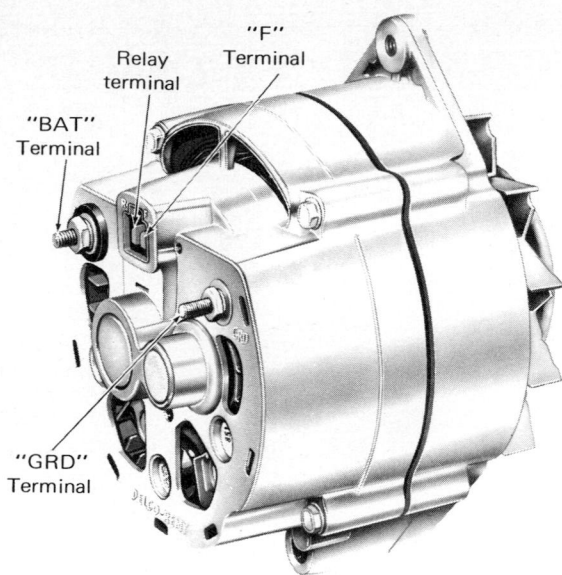

Alternator
Delco-Remy Division, General Motors Corp.

the fuel to burn. To do this, the current passes from the alternator (or generator) to the **coil**, where it is amplified. From the coil, it goes to the **distributor**, which directs the current to the proper **spark plug** at the proper time. This is a bit more complicated than it seems, and so I have devoted the next chapter to explaining the ignition system in detail. But now, back

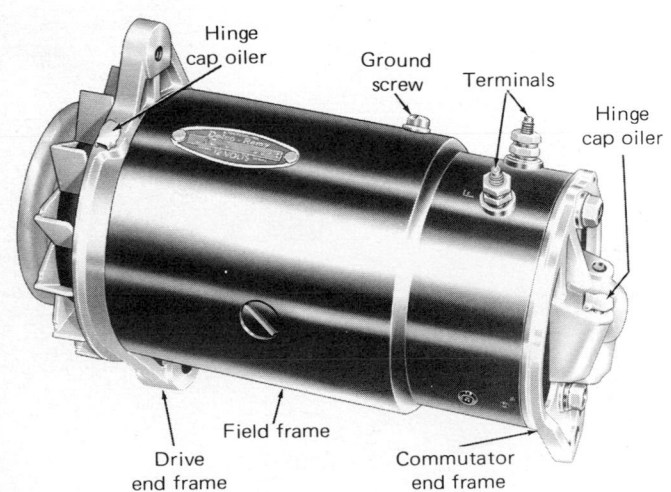

Generator
Delco-Remy Division, General Motors Corp.

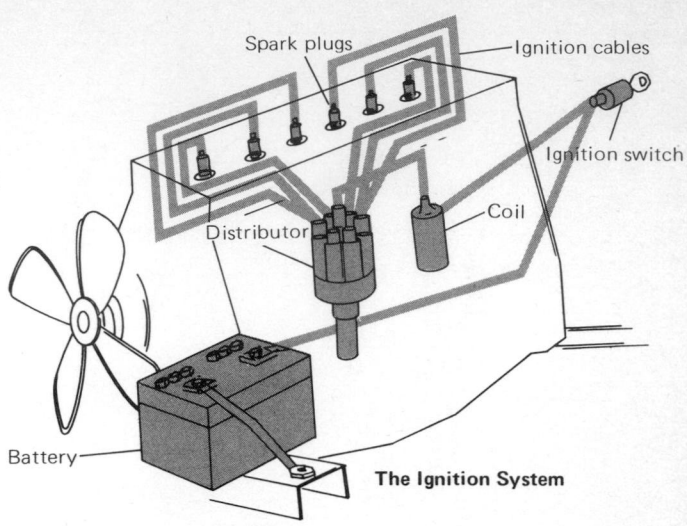

The Ignition System

The Ignition System
Automotive Information Council (AIC)

to a quick outline of exactly what happens when you turn on your car.

1 When you turn the key in your car's **ignition switch** to "Start," you close a circuit that allows the current to pass from your battery to your **starter**, via the **starter solenoid switch**.

2 Your starter makes your engine **turn over** (that's the growling sound you hear before the engine

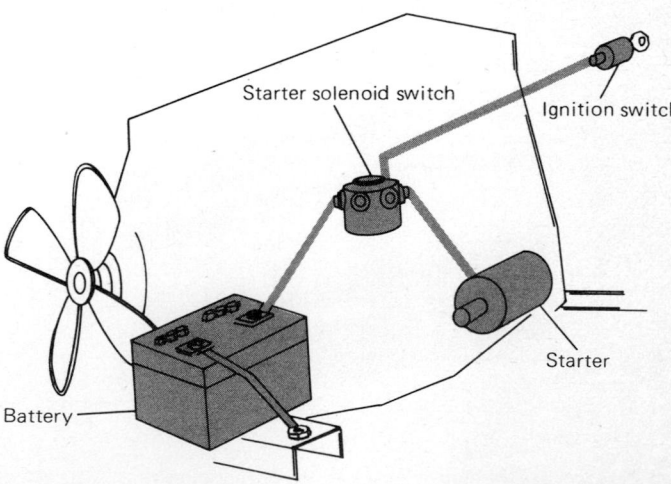

The Starting System
Automotive Information Council (AIC)

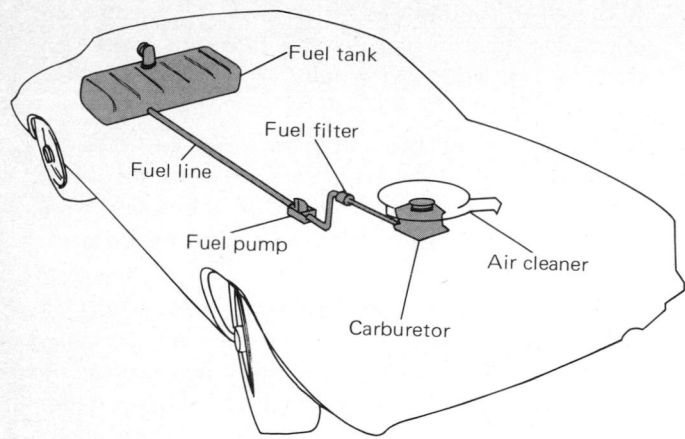

The Fuel System

The Fuel System
Automotive Information Council (AIC)

starts running smoothly). Once the engine is running, the following things happen:

3 Fuel (gasoline) flows from the **fuel tank** at the rear of the car, through the **fuel lines**, to the **fuel pump**, under the hood.

4 The fuel pump pumps the gasoline through a **fuel filter** into your **carburetor**.

5 The carburetor mixes each pound of fuel with 15 pounds of air to form a vaporized mixture, like a mist. Since fuel is much heavier than air, this mixture works out to something like one part of fuel to 9,000 parts of air, by volume. In other words, your car engine really runs on air, with a little fuel to help it!

6 This **fuel/air mixture** passes into the **cylinders** in your engine. Cylinders are hollow pipes with one open end and one closed end.

7 Inside each cylinder is a **piston**. These pistons fit the insides of the cylinders very closely and move up and down.

8 The piston moves *up*, trapping the fuel/air mixture in the upper part of the cylinder and *compressing* it, or squeezing it, into a very small space.

9 A spark from your **spark plug** *ignites* the fuel/air mixture, causing an explosion.

10 The explosion forces the piston back *down* again, with more *power* than it went up with.

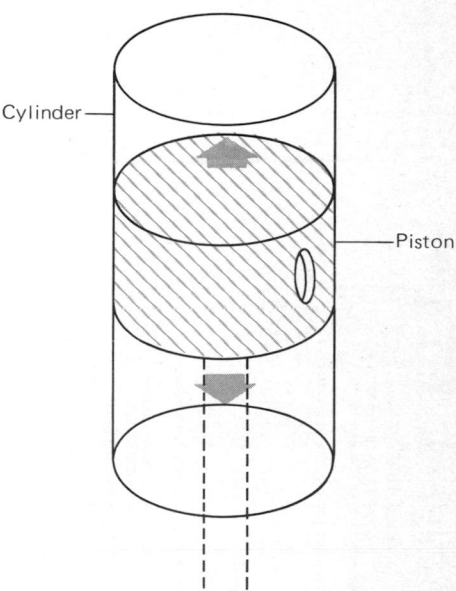

Cylinder and Piston
Alexandra Soto

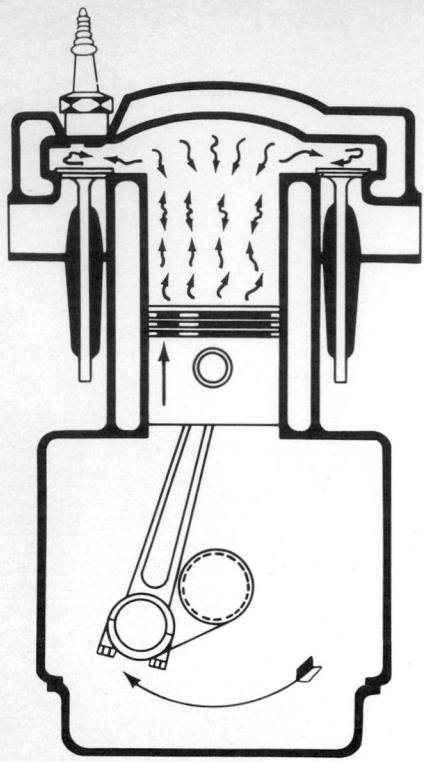

The Drive Train

11 Attached to the bottom of the piston is a **connecting rod**, which, in turn, is attached to a **crankshaft**, which leads, eventually, to the rear wheels of your car.

12 As the piston and the connecting rod go up and down, they cause the crankshaft to turn, in pretty much the same way as when your knee goes up and down while your foot goes round and round with the pedals of your bicycle.

13 At the other end of the crankshaft, somewhere under the front seat, is a box of gear wheels called the **transmission**. If your car has a **manual** (or standard) **transmission**, you will also find your **clutch** located here, between the crankshaft and the transmission. The clutch tells the transmission which gear you want. In a car with an **automatic transmission**, this is done automatically.

14 When you shift into "Drive," or "First," depending on whether you have an automatic or a standard transmission, a set of gears causes the rest of the crankshaft (which is called the **driveshaft** after it leaves the transmission) to turn at a particular speed.

15 The driveshaft runs to the rear of the car and ends in another set of gears called the **differential**. The differential converts the power of the rotating driveshaft into power to turn the **axle** that connects the rear wheels of your car.

16 Since, on most cars, the axle is set at right angles to the driveshaft, you can see that the differential is really changing the *direction* of the power, so your rear wheels can turn.

17 Your rear wheels turn and push your car forward (or backward) and off you go.

Still with me? If you are confused, go back through the preceding text slowly, looking again at the accompanying illustrations or try to explain it all to someone else. You'll be surprised at how much you know, once you're confronted by someone who knows less.

Now, let's fill in some necessary details.

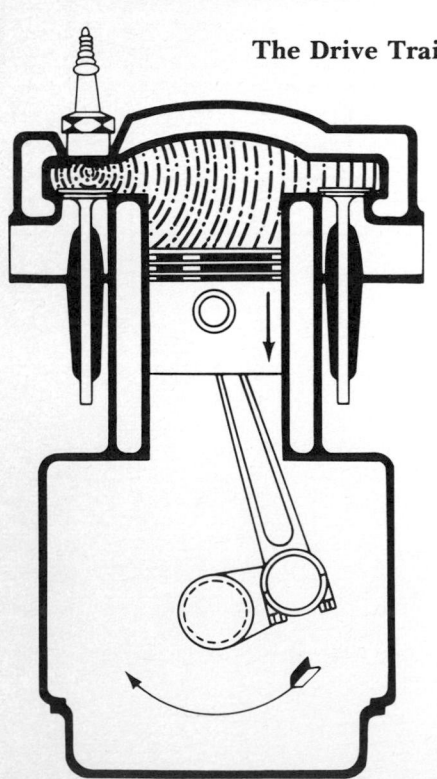

(*top*) Compression Stroke (*bottom*) Power Stroke
Echlin Manufacturing Company

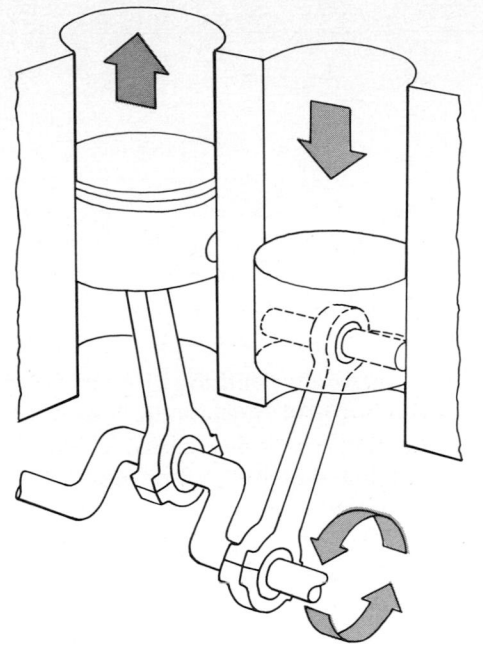

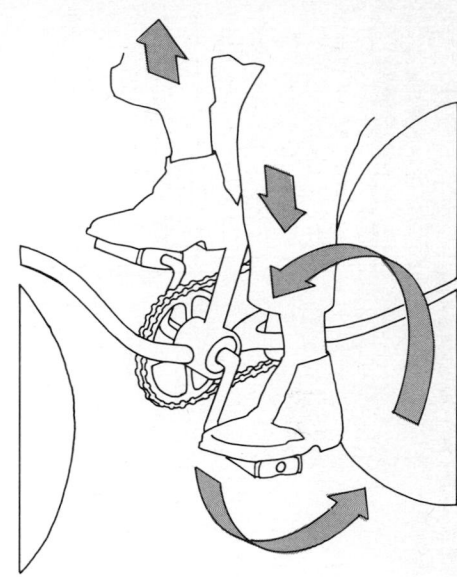

When you ride a bicycle, your knees move up and down to turn the pedals 'round and 'round—just as the pistons and connecting rods move up and down to turn the crankshaft in circles.
Jack Herlihy

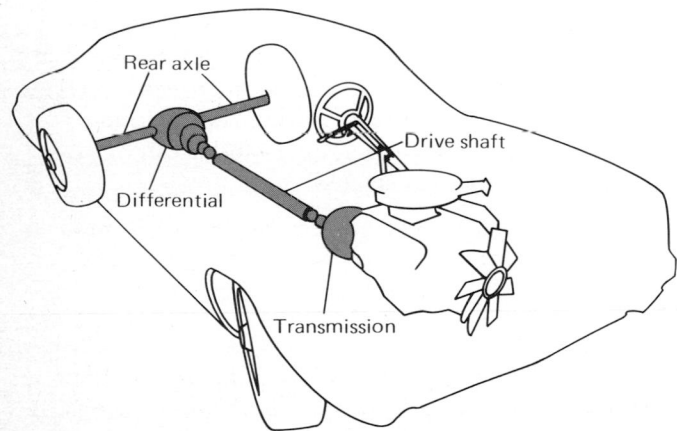

Rear axle

Drive shaft

Differential

Transmission

The Drive Train
Automotive Information Council (AIC)

The **exhaust gases** from the burnt fuel/air mixture that was ignited in the cylinders pass through **exhaust pipes** to the **tail pipe** at the rear of the car. On the

The Exhaust System

The Exhaust System
Automotive Information Council (AIC)

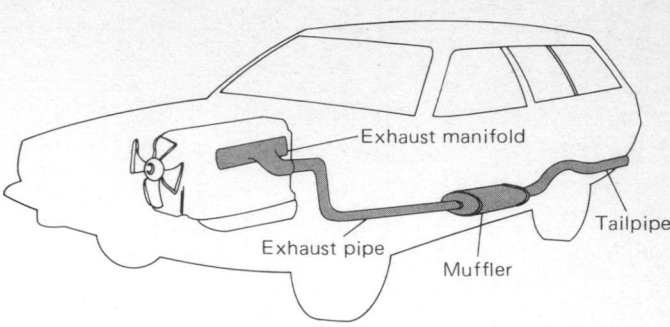

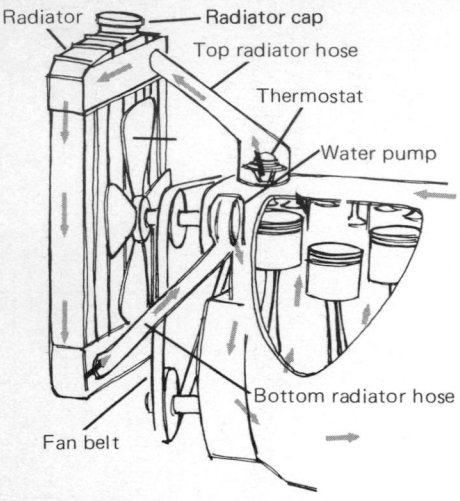

Radiator — Radiator cap
Top radiator hose
Thermostat
Water pump
Bottom radiator hose
Fan belt

The Cooling System
Automotive Information Council (AIC)

way, antismog pollution-control devices remove some of the harmful substances. A **muffler** controls the noise of the escaping gases, which contain carbon monoxide, which is poisonous.

The Cooling System

Since the temperature at which the combustion of the fuel and air takes place is around 4,500 degrees Fahrenheit, the temperature must be quickly lowered below the boiling point of fluid or your engine would break down rapidly. To do this, water and coolant circulate from your **radiator** through pipes called **water jackets** in your engine to keep your engine cool. A **water pump** keeps the water circulating, and a **fan** helps to get the cooling process started.

The Lubrication System

The Engine

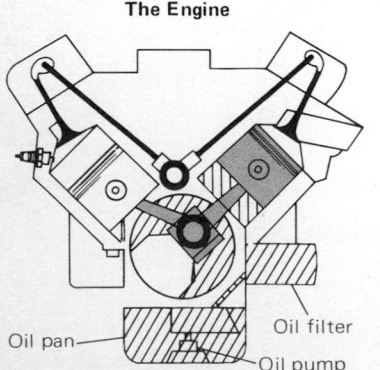

Oil pan
Oil filter
Oil pump

The Lubrication System
Automotive Information Council (AIC)

Oil circulates through your engine to keep its moving parts (pistons, connecting rods, crankshaft, etc.) lubricated to move freely and to reduce the friction that causes your engine to heat up. An **oil pump** keeps the oil circulating, and an **oil filter** keeps it clean.

And, while we're at it we might as well go into what makes your car *stop*. . . .

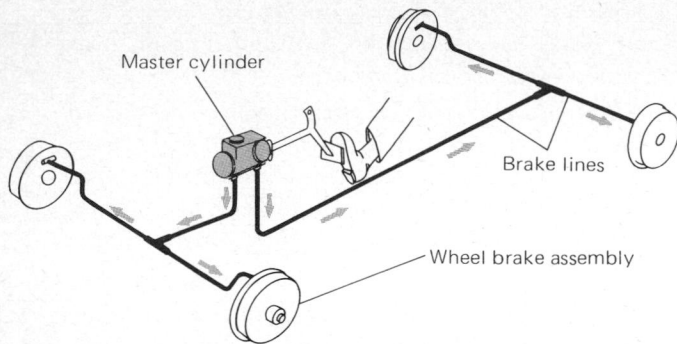

The Braking System
Automotive Information Council (AIC)

1. To stop your car, you step on the **brake pedal.**
2. The brake pedal pushes against another piston in a cylinder located under the hood of your car. This is called the **master cylinder**, and it is filled with a liquid called **brake fluid**.
3. When the piston in the master cylinder is pushed by your brake pedal, it forces the brake fluid out of the master cylinder into tubes called **brake lines**, which run to each wheel of your car.
4. Each wheel has a round, hollow, metal **brake drum** with another, smaller, **wheel cylinder** inside it.
5. The brake fluid goes into the brake cylinders and pushes against little **pistons** located at each end of each wheel cylinder.
6. These little pistons push against the **brake shoes**, which are curved, movable plates with friction-rough surfaces.

The Brake System

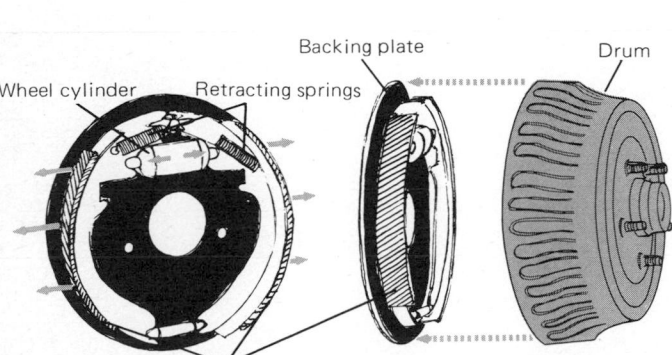

Drum Brake
Automotive Information Council (AIC)

7. The brake shoes push against the inside walls of the brake drum, and the resulting **friction** stops your wheels from turning.

8. When you take your foot *off* the brake pedal, the whole thing is reversed. Springs pull the brake shoes back; the pistons push back into the cylinders, squeezing the brake fluid back up the brake lines to the master cylinder. Now your wheels can turn freely again.

That's all there is to it! Of course, if you have **disc brakes** on your car, there is a slight difference, which we will get into in the chapter on brakes, but essentially, the same principles apply.

Now, let's go into each of the foregoing systems in more detail. As you learn how each part works, in view of what it does for your car, you'll get a better idea of how to keep it working well and what to do if it breaks down. By looking at your car as a series of simple systems, each with a specific job to do, you will soon cease to see it as a dismaying collection of gears, hoses, and gizmos and be able to deal with it easily and effectively.

The Electrical System:
Your Car's
"Spark of Life"

The **electrical system** provides your car with that vital spark that makes it start and keeps it running. Here are some of the services it performs:

1. It provides the initial power to get your engine started, through the **starting system**.
2. It fires the **spark plugs** so that they can cause the fuel and air to "combust" and drive your engine, through the **ignition system**.
3. It generates electrical power for the various systems in your car which depend on electric current, through the **charging system**.
4. It stores excess current for future needs, in the **battery**.
5. It runs a mixed bag of electrical gadgets like your car's horn, headlights, and so on, through various **circuits**.

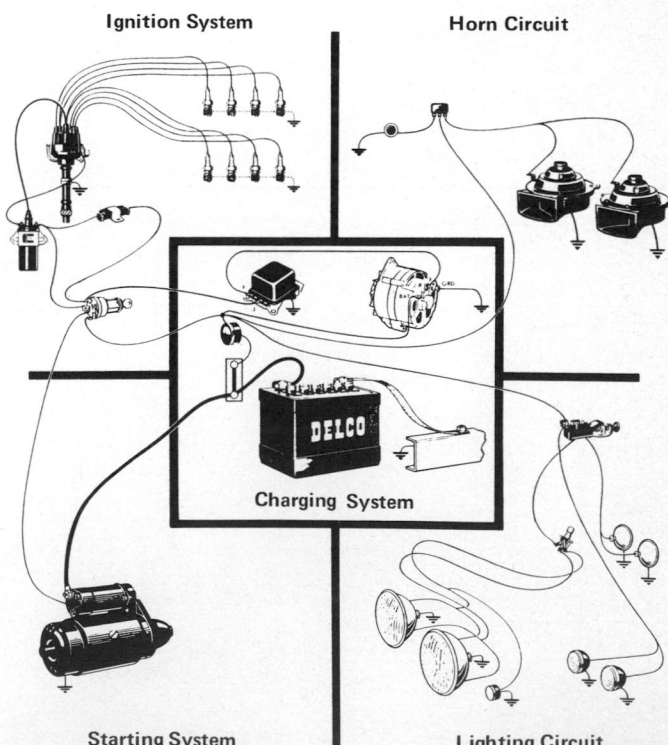

Ignition System **Horn Circuit**

Charging System

Starting System **Lighting Circuit**

The Electrical System
Delco-Remy Division, General Motors Corp.

In order to deal with the electrical system in simple terms, let's break it down into its basic functional systems and deal with each in turn.

The Starting System

This is the portion of the electrical system which gets your car started. When you turn your key in the **ignition switch** to "Start," it closes a circuit that lets electrical current flow from your car's **battery** to its **starter**. On the way, the current passes through a little device called the **starter solenoid**, which becomes important only if it malfunctions. Basically, all the solenoid does is pass the current along; you don't adjust or replace it unless it breaks down. So don't bother with it now; just know where it is and what it's called so you can impress your garage mechanic if it dies.

After I took my first class on the electrical system, I went out one morning and found that my car wouldn't start. I remembered that my instructor had said that if you hear a clicking noise (that's your solenoid) but your engine won't start running, it is probably simply a loose wire somewhere between the ignition switch and the starter. So I opened the hood (it was only the second time I'd gotten that far) and peeked in. Sure enough, there was a cluster of wires on the **firewall** in front of my steering wheel. (The firewall is the divider between the interior of your car and the under-the-hood area. It runs from the windshield down.) I could see where the wires ran to the battery, along the frame of the car, but after that I got lost. I ended up calling the AAA. When they arrived, I proudly informed them that I knew what was wrong. "It's just a loose wire between my battery and my starter," I announced. "Then why didn't you fix it yourself?" the mechanic asked. "Because I don't know which gadget is the starter!" He was nice enough to keep from laughing, and I felt better when it did turn out to be a loose wire on the starter. The mechanic also pointed out the starter and showed me where the wires ran that connected to it.

Anyway, why don't you stop here for a moment and try to trace the wiring from that cluster of wires on the firewall which lead from your ignition switch to

Voltage Regulator
ACCEL, Division of Echlin Manufacturing Co.

Under-the-Hood View of the Starting System
Richard Freshman

the battery, and from the battery to your starter solenoid and starter. Then you can be a hero if your car clicks but won't start running some morning. If you hit a couple of other things along the way (like a square box called a **voltage regulator**), just ignore them. Like the solenoid, you don't have to fuss with them unless they fail, and if they fail they have to be replaced. Actually, there are several things to look for if your car won't start, and they are all covered in Chapter 14. (By the time you get there, this will seem like kid stuff!)

How to Open the Hood of Your Car

It occurs to me that there may be some of you who aren't sure how to get under the hood of your car. Here's how:

1. Try to remember where the thing is that the service station attendant grabs when he opens the hood to check your oil and water. Does he ask you to pull a lever inside the car? Or does he go to the front grill?
2. Look around, and through, the grill to find a handle, lever, arm, or button, or feel under the grill and behind the bumper for a handle or lever. Then, pull, press, push front to back and side to

side on the thing you find. The hood should open a little, but it may be stopped by a safety catch that prevents it from coming open, and obscuring your vision, while you are driving.

3. Raise the hood with one hand, and feel along the underside for a metal lever which, when pressed one way or the other, releases the catch. Then raise the hood the rest of the way.

4. If it stays up, fine. If not, look for a safety rod attached to the underside of the hood. This should come down and fit into a slot. Other rods lift up from the frame and fit into a slot under the hood.

5. The easiest thing to do is to forget steps 1–4 and ask the person in the service station to show you how to open the hood, the next time you go in for gas.

Now, let's take a look at each part of the **starting system** (sometimes called the *cranking circuit*) and see what it does:

The **battery** is the box that sits under the hood. It is filled with acid and distilled water, and it has a set of metal plates inside it. The liquid should cover the tops of the plates. On top of the box, there are a couple of holes that you can peek into to see if there is enough water inside the battery. If there isn't, you can add distilled water through these holes. There are also two large metal terminals attached to the top of the box. One is a **positive terminal**, the other a **negative terminal**. You can tell which is which because the positive terminal is usually larger and may have a + or the word "Positive" on or near it.

The Battery

Most American cars are *negative ground*, which means that the wire from the positive terminal leads to the solenoid. The wire from the negative terminal is attached to the frame of the car to **ground** it. Other cars, especially foreign cars, are *positive ground* (or positive *earth*, as they call it in England), and this simply means that the reverse is true.

The battery stores electric current and passes it along to the parts of your car that need electric current to

000-047

The Electrical System

1 Container
2 Cover
3 Positive plates
4 Negative plates
5 Separators
6 Cell
7 Cell connectors
8 Terminal post
9 Vent caps

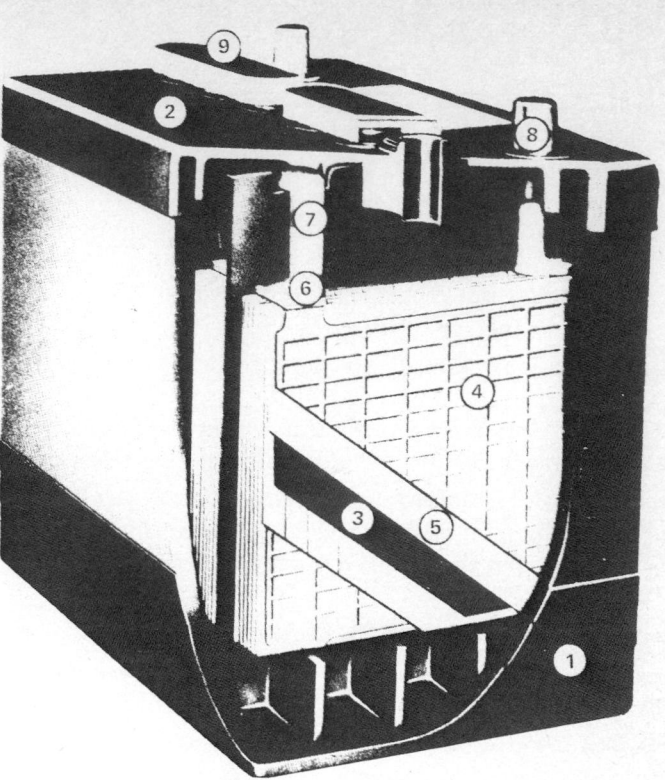

Anatomy of a Battery
Automotive Parts & Accessories Association (APAA)

Starter with Starter Solenoid
Delco-Remy Division, General Motors Corp.

function. We'll get into the right way to keep it functioning properly in the next chapter. Right now, let's continue to explore the starting system.

The Starter After the battery sends the current to the starter solenoid (which we've dealt with above), the current goes to the **starter**. If you've located the starter, perhaps you'd like to know what's inside it. Basically, it is a motor that makes your engine **turn over**. It has a shaft attached to a gear called a **starter drive**, which sits near a gear, called a *ring gear*, on the end of your **crankshaft flywheel**. When you turn your key in the ignition switch to "Start," the starter drive slides down the shaft and engages the ring gear. The motor starts the starter drive spinning, and it in turn starts the ring gear spinning. This makes the crankshaft turn, and your engine starts running because the turning crankshaft makes the **pistons** go up and down.

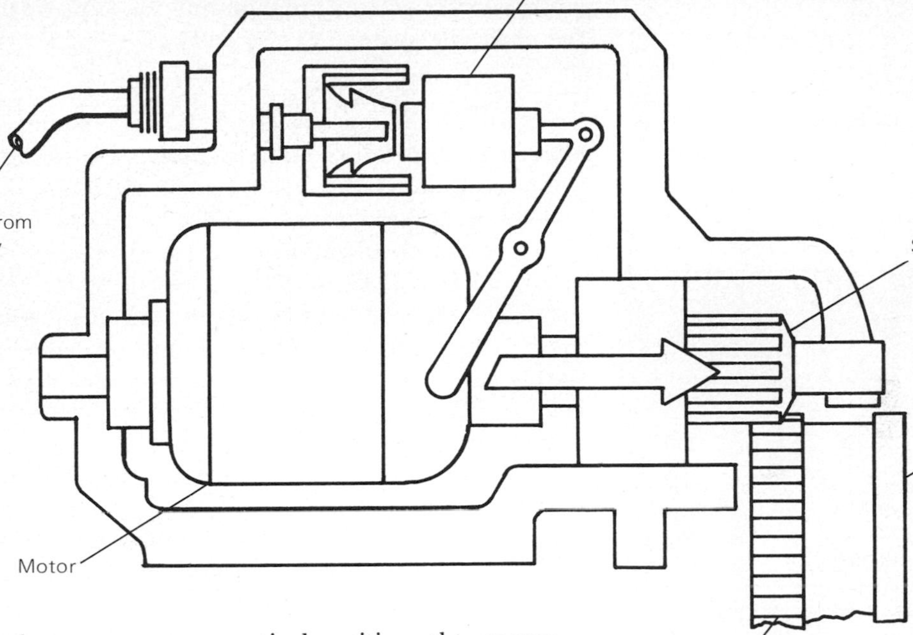

Starter
solenoid

Current from
battery

Starter
drive

Crankshaft
flywheel

Motor

Ring
gear

Anatomy of a Starter
Jack Herlihy

As your key returns to a vertical position, the starter drive and the ring gear disengage and your engine continues running on the fuel and air that are now being pumped into its **cylinders**. If you keep the key in the "Start" position after the engine starts running, the starter drive and the ring gear will continue to try to spin while they are still meshed together. The result is a horrible sound like metal grinding against metal—and that's exactly what's happening. If it happens too often, you will strip the teeth off the starter drive (or the ring gear), and have to get a new one. So be sure to let go of the ignition key as soon as your engine catches. When you release the key, it will automatically return to the "On" position and stay there until you shut the engine off.

O.K. Now your engine has started and is running at a nice steady rumble. This is because, as soon as the pistons in your cylinders started to go up and down, your car began to run on its usual diet of fuel and air.

The Charging System

And as your ignition switch went from "Start" to "On," the electric current stopped flowing from the battery to the starter but continued to flow through the **charging system**, as you will see.

The Alternator (or Generator)

The running engine drives a belt that enables your **alternator** to produce electric current for the rest of the trip. As we've discussed earlier, the basic difference between an alternator and a generator is that alternators appear on newer cars and produce alternating current (AC), which is then converted to the direct current needed to drive the various gadgets on the car. A generator is usually found on older cars. It simply generates direct current and passes it on. To keep things simple, let's just call the gadget an alternator, because no matter which you have on your car, it will do the same thing in the long run. There are pictures of an alternator and a generator in the last chapter, and since you won't have to take the thing apart, or adjust it, it really doesn't matter what we call it—as long as you know which one you have, where it is, and what it does. Try to find yours now.

Under-the-Hood View of Alternator
Richard Freshman

The first thing your alternator does is replace the electricity that was taken from the battery when you started the car. Then, every time your battery uses some of its "juice," the alternator replaces it. When the alternator is generating electric current, we say that it is charging. If you look at your dashboard, you will probably find a gauge with a "D" at one end and a "C" at the other. This shows you whether your alternator is charging or discharging. Other cars have a little light that lights up if the alternator is charging.

It is also the alternator that supplies your electrical system with current to run the car radio, headlights, etc., but let's go on to the ignition system.

The Ignition System

Since a basic tune-up involves inspecting, cleaning, replacing (if necessary), and adjusting the various gadgets that make up your ignition system, this chapter will help you to get to know what you'll be working on in the next chapter, which is about tuning your car.

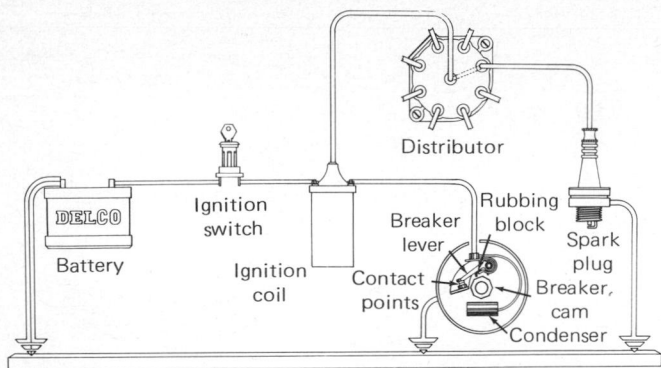

The Ignition System
Delco-Remy Division, General Motors Corp.

Meanwhile, back at the engine, the battery is busy sending the current it got from the alternator to the **coil**. The coil is a metal cylinder with three wires coming out of the top. One of the smaller wires goes to the battery via the ignition switch. The other small wire goes to the **points** and the **condenser**, which are inside the **distributor**. (Hang on, we'll clear all of this up in a minute!) There is also a big wire, which also goes to the distributor, entering through a hole in the center of the **distributor cap**. This sends current to the **spark plugs**.

The Coil

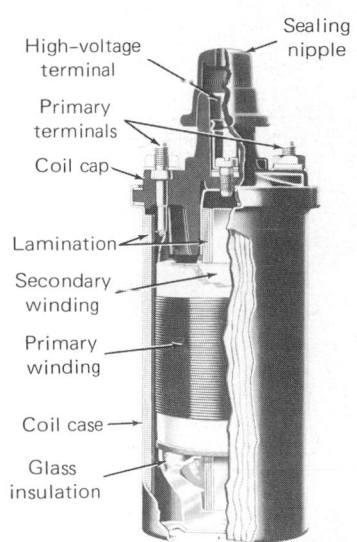

Anatomy of a Coil
Delco-Remy Division, General Motors Corp.

Under-the-Hood View of the Ignition System
Richard Freshman

000-051

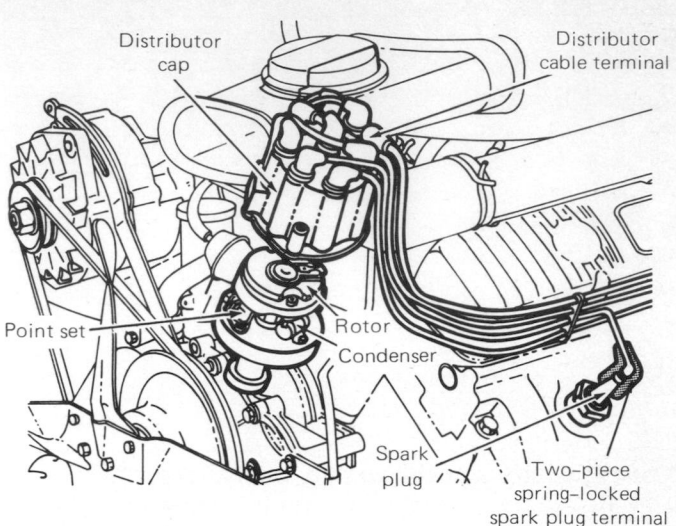

Traditional Ignition System
Guaranteed Parts Company

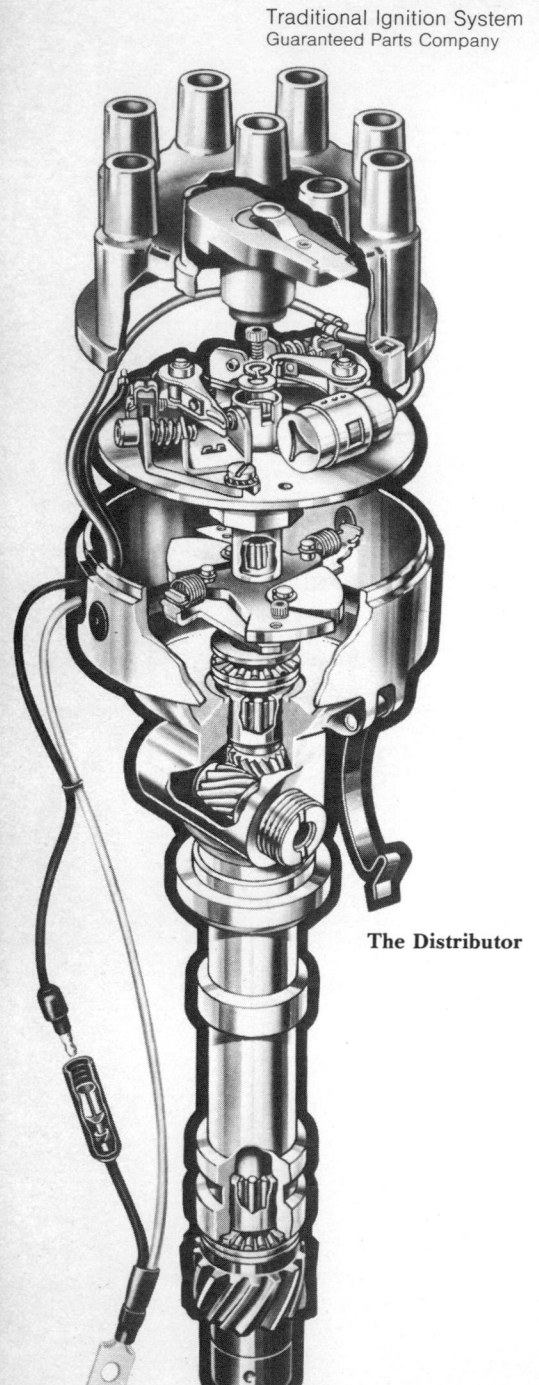

Anatomy of a Distributor
ACCEL, Division of Echlin Manufacturing Co.

The major job of the coil is to take a relatively small amount of electrical *voltage* from the battery and convert it into a big jolt of voltage and send it to the spark plugs via that large rubber-covered wire that comes out of the center of the top of the coil, travels a few inches, and enters the center of the distributor cap. In order to understand how it does this, we have to know a bit about the distributor. You will get to know your distributor quite well, because that is where a good part of your tune-up work takes place.

The Distributor

Your **distributor** is on either the side or the top of your engine, or up near the firewall. The coil is usually right near it. Since both are pretty distinctive-looking, they should not be hard to spot. Each of the wires that come out of the top of the distributor cap and give it its quaint, octopuslike appearance goes to a spark plug. (Except for the one that goes into the center of the cap from the coil, remember?) If you have a 4-cylinder engine, your engine will have four spark plugs and your distributor will have four wires leading from the cap to the spark plugs, plus the one to the coil. If you have an 8-cylinder engine, you will have eight wires going to the spark plugs, and your distributor cap will look like an authentic octopus. Have you found all of this on your car?

Now let's take a look inside the distributor. Most distributor caps are held in place by clips or screws on either side. Clips can be removed easily with the point of a screwdriver. If you want to take yours off right away, you will find instructions for removing the cap in Chapter 5. If you're not ready for this, you can probably get all you need to know from the illustrations in this chapter. If, when you look inside your distributor cap, you do not find the parts in our diagrams, you probably have an electronic ignition system (if your car is a 1973 model or a more recent one, you probably do) and can consider yourself pretty lucky. The proud owners of cars with an **electronic ignition system** do not have to deal with points, condensers, or their replacement or adjustment. All you have to do is change your spark plugs now and then. Meanwhile, for those of us in the traditional-system majority, let's get on with it.

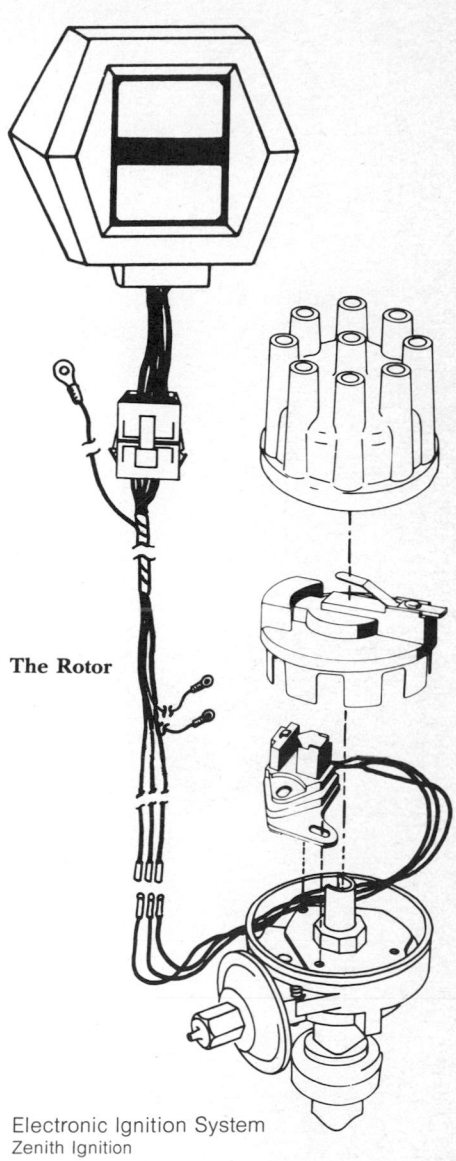

The Rotor

In the traditional ignition system inside the distributor cap, sitting on top of the **distributor shaft** is a piece of plastic called a **rotor**. This is designed to lift off and

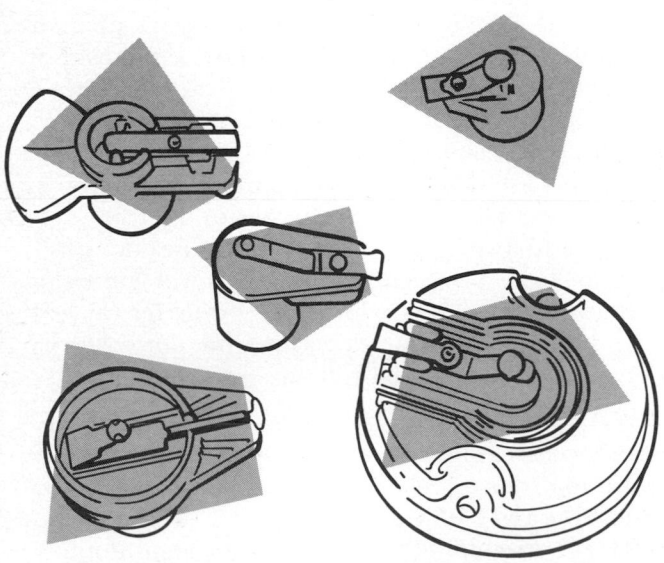

Electronic Ignition System
Zenith Ignition

Rotors
Delco-Remy Division, General Motors Corp.

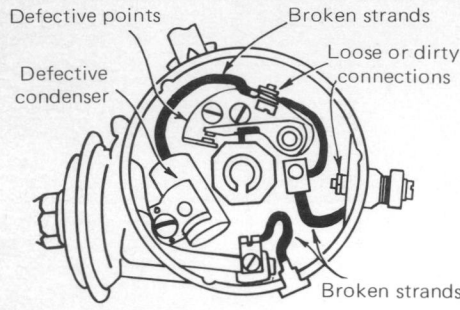

Typical Distributor Defects
A Close-up of the Major Parts Inside the Distributor
DIXCO

go back on in one position only (which means you have one less difficult decision to make). The tip of the rotor is made of metal, and it conducts the current that comes in from the coil through the center of the distributor cap to each of the wires that lead to the spark plugs. The way it does this is by turning with the distributor shaft. As the rotor turns, it points to each of the terminals at the base of the wires. When it is pointing at the terminal of the wire leading to your #1 spark plug, it will direct the current to that spark plug at precisely the time when the fuel/air mixture is in #1 cylinder, waiting to be exploded.

Attached to the **breaker plate** on the floor of the distributor you can see the **points** and the **condenser**. If you are looking at your own distributor, lift the rotor off to see them easily.

The Points

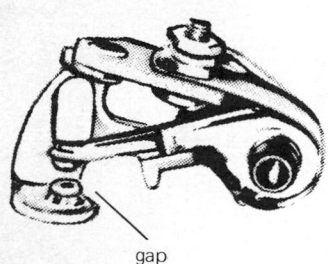

Points
Automotive Parts & Accessories Association (APAA)

The **points** (short for "breaker points") are two pieces of metal joined at one end so that they can touch and then draw apart. The space where they almost meet when they are open is called a **gap**. One point is stationary, and one can move. The way they do this is simple. If you look at that same distributor shaft that the rotor was sitting on, you will see, down at the base, a roundish wheel with bumps on it. The wheel is a **cam** wheel. The bumps, one for each spark plug, are **cam lobes**. The cam wheel is attached to the base of the shaft and moves with it. As it turns, each cam lobe comes against the movable point and pushes the points *open*. When the wheel turns past the cam lobe, the points are *closed* again by a spring. Each time the points open, electric current passes to the rotor, which directs it to a spark plug wire. This causes the spark plug to "fire," producing a spark that will ignite the fuel/air mixture in its cylinder. A 4-cylinder car will have four cam lobes on this wheel, one for each cylinder. A 6-cylinder model will have six lobes, and so on.

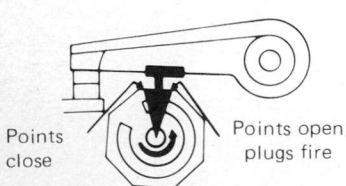

Normal Point Gap
DIXCO

The gap between the points must be set at a precise width in order to ensure that each spark plug "fires" at just the right time and intensity. If the gap is too wide, the spark plugs will fire before the piston has reached the top of its path. This can cause **pre-**

ignition and engine damage. If the gap is too narrow, the spark plug will fire after the piston has compressed the fuel/air mixture and has started back down. The loss of compression will result in poor combustion, loss of power, greater fuel consumption and more pollution. If the points cannot close enough to allow the current to pass properly, your car will stop completely. If they cannot get far enough apart to break the circuit, the current will arc across continuously and the points will burn out quickly.

This whole problem is referred to as having your points out of adjustment, which leads to poor ignition and faulty **timing**. That's why, when you tune up your car, one of the first things you do is check with a **feeler gauge** to see whether your points are correctly "gapped." Of course, if your points are badly worn or corroded, you replace them and carefully gap the new points you've installed.

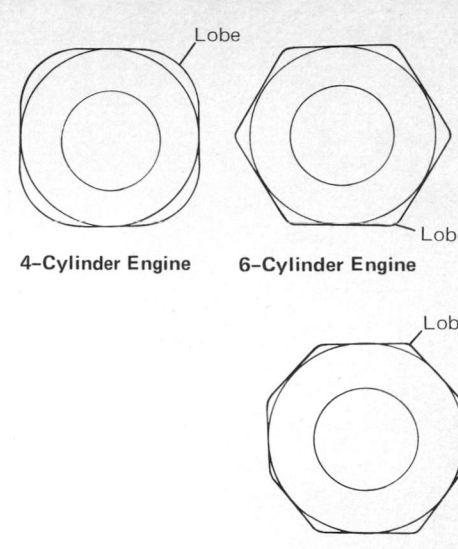

Cam Wheels for 4-, 6-, and 8-Cylinder Cars
Alexandra Soto

The Condenser

The small metal cylinder near the points on the floor of the distributor is called a **condenser**. The purpose of the condenser is to prevent the electricity from arcing across the gap when the points are open, since this would cause the points to burn. The condenser also is necessary for generating high voltage for the spark plugs. Just how it does this is not really important for our purposes, but if you can't stand not knowing, wait until you really understand how cars work and then get a more comprehensive book that will give you all the technical details.

Anyway, since condensers don't break down (they either work or they don't), just replace yours whenever you change your points and rotor (they all come together in a tune-up kit), and make sure that it is tightly in place and connected properly. Otherwise, ignore it. Just remember that one of those two little wires from the coil connects to the condenser to help it do its mysterious job, and the other little wire runs to the battery to bring in the voltage that makes the whole thing worthwhile.

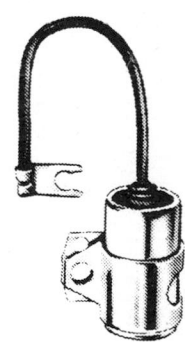

Condenser
Automotive Parts & Accessories Association (APAA)

Each one of the cylinders in your car has a **spark plug** that conducts the spark that will fire the fuel/air mixture in the cylinder to provide the power that will

Spark Plugs

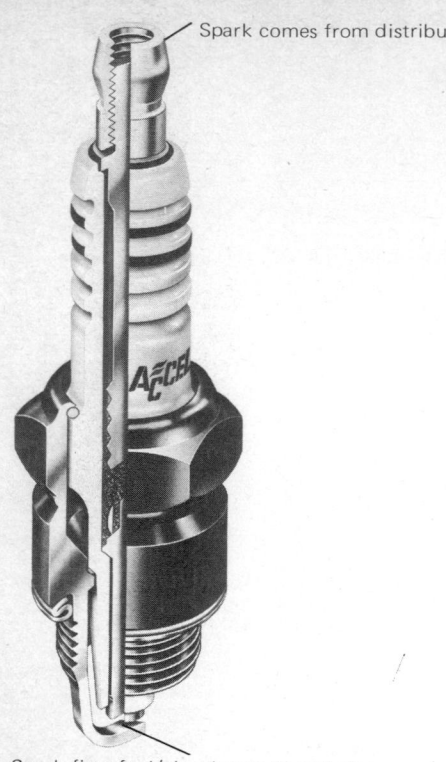

Spark comes from distributor

Spark fires fuel/air mixture in cylinder

Spark Plug
ACCEL, Division of Echlin Manufacturing Co.

turn the wheels. If your car is properly tuned, that spark will arrive at the precise moment when the fuel/air mixture is fully compressed by the piston, and the result will be that the fuel and air will burn as intensely and completely as possible. To achieve this, the spark plug has to deliver as strong a spark as possible. The strength of the spark is determined by the distance (or **gap**) between the **electrodes** at the tip of the plug. In the next chapter, you will learn how to gap your plugs properly. Right now, look at the illustration to see what a spark plug looks like. The side of the plug in the picture has been cut away to show you the metal shaft that runs from the top of the plug to the bottom. Since the wire from the distributor leads to the top of the plug, and since the bottom of the plug (where the hooklike electrode is) emerges into the cylinder, you can see how the electric current reaches the fuel/air mixture.

Another Way of Looking at The Electrical System

Is your head spinning? Don't worry, try looking at it this way: all that the electrical system does (all that matters for our purposes) is generate, store, and regulate the flow of electricity needed to start the car, fire the fuel/air mixture that drives the engine, and run the other electrical devices in the car. If you look at each part in terms of its position in this chain, the confusion will clear up. Let's trace the voltage once again:

Battery: *Stores* electricity to crank the motor and fire the spark plugs. Starts the starter.

Starter: Has a small motor that *starts* the crankshaft turning so the pistons can go up and down, the spark plugs can fire, and the engine can start running.

Alternator: *Generates* alternating current, *converts* it to direct current, and sends it to the battery. The equivalent on most older cars is called a *generator*. It serves the same function.

Coil: Takes a small amount of voltage (12 volts) from the alternator and *amplifies* it into the large amount of voltage (20,000 volts) needed to fire the spark plugs.

SCLAR
000-056

Distributor: Gets the voltage from the coil and *distributes* it to each spark plug in turn. Contains the points, rotor, and condenser.

Points: *Trigger* the flow of electricity so that it arrives at the spark plugs at the right point in time and at the right intensity.

Rotor: *Rotates* toward each spark plug terminal so that each plug fires in the correct order.

Condenser: An electrical *"sponge"* that keeps the points from burning up.

Spark Plugs: *Deliver* the spark to the fuel/air mixture in the cylinders at the point of greatest compression. The spark makes the mixture explode. The resulting power drives the engine and thus the car.

Try to look at the preceding in terms of the relationship between each part. You might trace the wires that carry the current from each part of your car to the next.

If you think you have it all digested, let's take a look at the rest of the electrical system, especially the gadgets that may someday need your attention.

As I've mentioned on several occasions, the alternator also supplies the electrical current for the car radio, head and taillights, etc., via electrical wiring under the dashboard. Most of this wiring is hard to reach, and since it doesn't go out of whack very often, we won't get into wiring problems here. But you should know about the fuse box that is usually located under or near the dashboard. Your owner's manual can help you find it, or you can crawl under the dashboard and trace the wires from your radio until you reach the fuse box.

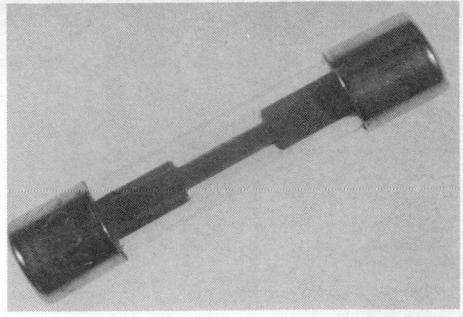

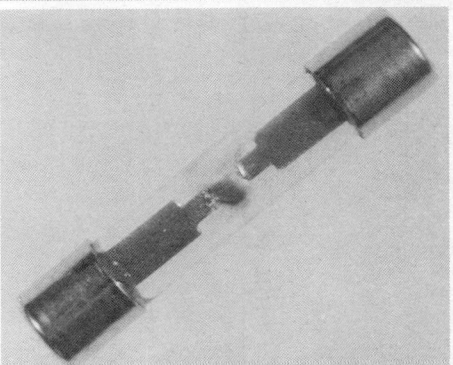

(*top*) A Good Fuse (*middle*) A Burnt-out Fuse (*bottom*) Fuse Box Located Under Dashboard
Bussman Manufacturing Division, McGraw-Edison Company

The Fuse Box

A fuse box is easy to recognize and replacing burnt-out fuses is a fairly simple matter. If your radio, clock, map light, or other electrical dashboard appliances stop, the chances are that a fuse has blown. It is much cheaper to change a fuse (even if you chicken out and have the garage mechanic do it) than to pay for a new clock or for repairs that you don't need. So take a flashlight, get down there, and find your fuse box, and look for a fuse that is black inside or no longer has its filaments intact. (Burnt-out fuses look like burnt-out bulbs.) Then take a bobby pin, bend it, and use it to pull the bad fuse out. Now press a new fuse into place. When you've replaced all the burnt-out fuses, try your radio or clock again. If it still doesn't work, then worry about having it repaired or replaced.

Directional Signal Flasher Lights

Here's something interesting. Did you know that the directional signal flashers on your dashboard have been designed to provide clues to malfunctions elsewhere on your car? If one of your directional flashers should stop flashing, or should stop making that ticking noise when it flashes, this does not mean that the light is out of order. It means that your car manufacturer has cleverly utilized these lights to tell you that a light on the outside of your car is not working.

Using the left-turn signal flasher as an example, if you find that the left flasher on your dashboard simply stays on, without blinking or without making a noise, get out of the car and check to see if your left directional signal lights are on in the front and the rear of your car. If only one is out, simply replace the bulb. Once the bulb has been replaced, your dashboard flasher should work normally again.

If there is no light on your dashboard when you move your directional signal lever, then the bulb in your dashboard flasher is out.

If your left *rear* directional signal light goes on but does not blink, and your left *front* directional signal light does not go on at all, but both your *right* directional signals lights are working perfectly, then your left front directional signal bulb is bad. Once it is fixed, the left *rear* light will start to blink again.

If *all* your directional signal lights go on but they don't blink, then your flasher unit is bad. This unit usually plugs directly into the fuse box, so look for trouble there first.

Once you replace the bulb or fuse that is defective, the dashboard flashers will go back to normal. Isn't that lovely? Be sure to replace burnt-out bulbs at once.

They cost practically nothing. Most service stations will replace them for the cost of the bulb, which is usually less than a dollar. Headlights are more expensive because they have to be replaced as a unit (see below).

It doesn't hurt to wash the outside of your headlights and taillights occasionally; they will provide better visibility at night. If you still have trouble seeing at night (and you've been getting enough Vitamin A), check to be sure your headlight beams are shining straight ahead and not shining wallcycd at thc sidc of thc road or in the eyes of other drivers. Check your headlights on both high and low beams. If one of your headlights won't work on low but does work on high, you will have to replace the bulb. Ask for a **sealed beam unit**. If it won't work on either high or low, you probably have a bad connection in the wiring.

Here's how to replace a sealed beam unit:

Before you can remove the bulb, you have to be careful to turn the correct screws to loosen the plate that holds the unit in place. (I'm going to refer to the sealed beam unit as the headlight bulb from now on.) There are six screws on the plate; three of them loosen the plate, and the other three adjust the angle of the bulb. If you turn the wrong screws, your headlights will go out of focus. Also, when you put in a new bulb, you have to put it back into its locking slots with the unit number at the *top*.

If you manage to goof up your adjusting screws, or if you find that your car is walleyed, or if you just aren't sure whether or not your headlights are properly adjusted, most service stations that do motor vehicle bureau inspections have the equipment to adjust your lights. Be sure to get a certificate saying that the lights have been adjusted and meet the proper standards. This certificate is usually part of the price. A cheap way to check it out is to look for a Highway Patrol station near your house. They usually have the facilities to check them for you. Or they can tell you where their current highway check points are. Of course if they find that your headlights aren't in focus (or find anything wrong with your car's emissions, etc.), you

Headlights

Headlight Removed to Show Adjustment Screws
Richard Freshman

Headlight Installation Screws
Richard Freshman

will have to get the trouble fixed within two weeks or face a fine. If you can fix it yourself, go back to the checkpoint for an O.K.; otherwise you will have to pay some service station that does motor vehicle bureau inspections for a certificate, whether they do the work or not.

Windshield Wipers Windshield wipers generally run in conjunction with the electrical system, too. The main things to check here are the blades (which can easily be replaced; most simply slide in and out, with maybe a button or a clip to hold them in place) and the fluid level in your windshield washer reservoir. More about this in the under-the-hood check section in Chapter 5.

Other Gadgets If you have trouble with your car's radio, defroster, heater, air conditioner, and so on, get professional help. Later on, if you have turned into a confirmed do-it-yourselfer, there are books that deal with these.

Have you got it all now? Then you are ready to stop living vicariously and get down to the nitty-gritty (which can always be removed with cleaning solvent).

How to Tune Your Ignition System and Do a Monthly Under-the-Hood Check-Up

There are several good reasons for tuning your **ignition system** yourself. First, as we mentioned in Chapter 1, it is a heck of a lot cheaper. And since it's cheaper, you can do it more often and cut down on expensive wear and tear on other parts of your car. Second, a well-tuned car is a gas saver. And gas savers, because they burn less fuel, add less pollution to the air. They also take less money out of your pocket to buy fuel. Third, since I've been hanging around with people who are tuning their cars themselves for the first time, I've found more and more evidence that if you don't do it yourself, it won't always be done properly.

It is hard to write a book like this without being called on the carpet for knocking professional garage mechanics. I have tried very hard not to do this, partially because most of them don't deserve it. They work hard, and most of them know their business. But they are human. So if some repair is very difficult and time-consuming—and if the customer would not understand an extra $24 charge because the car happens to have an air conditioner that makes one spark plug impossible to reach without disconnecting or moving the air conditioner (which takes at least $24 worth of time and labor)—and if the car seems to be running well with that one teensy-weensy plug left unchanged, then you just might find that you have a just-tuned car with seven brand-new spark plugs and one funky old one that's been in there since the car left the factory. I know this because it happened to me, and it happened on my husband's car, as well! One spark plug that is old and fouled can ruin the car's performance and increase fuel consumption. The car is like a piano that's been tuned, with one sour note left in.

By doing it yourself you can judge whether your plugs and points only need to be cleaned and gapped, or whether you should replace them. And you can replace them yourself for a fraction of what it would cost to have it done for you. Most of the parts involved in an auto tune-up are very easy to replace.

Of course, if you've bought this book, you've probably already decided that you want to tune your car yourself, so let's get started.

Tune-ups should be done every 10,000 miles or every six months, whichever is sooner. A fairly new car will run for 15,000 miles on a set of spark plugs; an older car with more than 50,000 miles should have its spark plugs changed every 10,000 miles. If you do a lot of stop-and-go driving, or pull heavy loads (like a camper or a boat), then you may need to tune your car more often.

How Often Should You Tune Your Car?

There are only a couple of parts that you will need for your basic tune-up, but in order to buy them properly, you should know something about car **specifications**.

Buying Parts for Your Car

1 Your owner's manual should give you specifications for everything you'll need for a basic tune-up.

2 If you don't have an owner's manual, or if yours lacks the necessary data, you can go to the auto supply store and use a general "tune-up specification guide." These are either in pamphlet form or printed on large sheets that are displayed near the parts section of the store. If you can't find a "spec sheet" at the store, ask a salesperson to show one to you. *Don't* ask what part you should buy, as you have a very good chance of getting the wrong one. First look up the specifications yourself; then ask for the part by number.

Where to Locate the Specifications for Parts for Your Car

Here is the proper way to read one of these specification sheets in order to obtain the proper parts for your car:

How to Read a Spec Sheet

1 Know the following things about your car:
   a The *manufacturer's name (General Motors, Ford, etc.).*
   b The *make* of the car (Pontiac, Mercury, etc.).
   c The *model* of the car (Catalina, Monterey, etc.).
   d The *year* the car was made (1968, 1974).
   e The *number of* **cylinders** in the car (4, 6, V-8, etc.).

1967

Make and Model	Dist. Rotation	Dwell	Contact Gap	Spark Plug Gap	Firing Order	Ign. Timing B.T.C. @RPM
CHRYSLER (Neg. Grd.) (INCLUDES IMPERIAL)						
383 Cu. In. V8 Eng. (2 bbl.)	CC	30	.016	.035	3A	12°@550
•383 Cu. In. V8 Eng. (2 bbl.)	CC	30	.016	.035	3A	5°@600[52]
383 Cu. In. V8 Eng. (4 bbl.)	CC	30	.016	.035	3A	12°@500
•383 Cu. In. V8 Eng. (4 bbl.)	CC	30	.016	.035	3A	5°@500[52]
440 Cu. In. V8 Eng.	CC	30	.016	.035	3A	12°@650
•440 Cu. In. V8 Eng.	CC	30	.016	.035	3A	5°@650[52]
DODGE (Neg. Grd.) (INCLUDES CHARGER, CORONET, DART)						
170 Cu. In. 6 Cyl. Eng.	C	42	.020	.035	5	5°@550
•170 Cu. In. 6 Cyl. Eng.	C	42	.020	.035	5	5°ATDC@650
225 Cu. In. 6 Cyl. Eng.	C	42	.020	.035	5	5°@550
•225 Cu. In. 6 Cyl. Eng.	C	42	.020	.035	5	TDC@650
273 Cu. In. V8 Eng. (2 bbl.)	C	30	.016	.035	3A	5°@500[56]
•273 Cu. In. V8 Eng. (2 bbl.)	C	30	.016	.035	3A	5°ATDC@650
LINCOLN (Neg. Grd.)						
462 Cu. In. V8 Eng.	CC	30	.017	.034	8C	10°@475
•462 Cu. In. V8 Eng.	CC	30	.017	.034	8C	10°@500
FORD (Neg. Grd.) (INCLUDES BRONCO, FAIRLANE, FALCON, MUSTANG, THUNDERBIRD)						
170 Cu. In. 6 Cyl. Eng.	C	40	.025	.035	5	6°@550[6]
•170 Cu. In. 6 Cyl. Eng.	C	40	.025	.035	5	5°@550
200 Cu. In. 6 Cyl. Eng.	C	40	.025	.035	5	6°@525[56]
•200 Cu. In. 6 Cyl. Eng.	C	40	.025	.035	5	4°@500[52]
240 Cu. In. 6 Cyl. Eng.	C	40	.025	.035	5	6°@550[6]
•240 Cu. In. 6 Cyl. Eng.	C	40	.025	.035	5	5°@550
289 Cu. In. V8 Eng. (2 bbl.)	CC	29	.017	.035	8C	6°@475
•289 Cu. In. V8 Eng. (2 bbl.)	CC	29	.017	.035	8C	TDC@550
289 Cu. In. V8 Eng. (4 bbl.)	CC	29	.017	.035	8C	6°@525
•289 Cu. In. V8 Eng. (4 bbl.)	CC	29	.017	.035	8C	TDC@550
OLDSMOBILE (Neg. Grd.) (INCLUDES F85, TORONADO)						
250 Cu. In. 6 Cyl. Eng.	C	32	.019	.035	5	4°@500
•250 Cu. In. 6 Cyl. Eng.	C	32	.019	.035	5	4°@500
330 Cu. In. V8 Eng.	CC	30	.016	.030	3A	8°@850
•330 Cu. In. V8 Eng.	CC	30	.016	.030	3A	7°@850

f Whether the car has **automatic** or **manual (standard) transmission**.

g The engine **displacement**—how much room there is in each cylinder when the piston is at its lowest point. A 300-cu.-in. 6-cylinder engine has a displacement of 50 cu. in. in each cylinder. The bigger the cylinder, the more fuel and air it will hold.

h The kind of **carburetor** it has. This is generally referred to by the number of **barrels**, or chambers for mixing fuel and air (2 bbl., 4 bbl., etc.). This is where the terms "single-barrel carburetor," "**dual carbs**," and so on, come from.

i Does the car have *air conditioning*? It is necessary to take this into account when buying certain parts but not usually spark plugs or distributor tune-up kits.

j The **horsepower** rating of the car. This is not
essential, but it's nice to know.

All this information should be in your owner's manual, and most of it is also printed on metal tags or
patches located inside your hood. These can be found
in front of the radiator, inside the fenders, on the
inside of the hood, anywhere the auto manufacturer
thought you'd find them. I know of one car that has
its patch inside the lid of the glove compartment.
Look around, you'll find it. These ID tags also give a
lot of other information about where the car was
made, what kind of paint it has, and so on, but you
needn't worry about these. I have included a Specifications Record sheet at the end of this book to provide a place to keep all this information handy. It also
has room for you to list the numbers and specifications of the things you should be replacing at regular
intervals. Once this sheet contains the necessary data
for each of your cars, you will be able to take it to the
auto parts store with you and keep it handy when you
are working on your car. If you don't want to take the
book along, and you have reservations about tearing
out pages, you might want to have it photocopied
before you fill it out, so you will have copies for future
cars. There is also a Maintenance Record sheet to help
you to keep track of what you've checked and what
you've changed during your tune-ups and monthly
checks. While you're at it, make copies of this one, too,
so you'll have one for each car and each new year.

2 Look up your car, by make and model, under the
proper year on the specifications record. For
Tweety, I look under 1967, then under Ford, then
under Mustang, then under "200 cu. in. 6 Cyl. Eng.
(1 bbl.)"—which means she has an engine displacement of 200 cu. in., a 6-cylinder engine, and a
single-barrel carburetor.

3 Take along a pencil and your Specifications Record
from the end of this book and mark down the
information in the columns under the following
headings:
a **Dwell**. (The number refers to the place on the
dwell meter that the needle should point to if
your points are correctly gapped. It is given in
degrees.)

b **Contact gap** (the proper **gap** for your **points**).

c **Spark plug gap** (exactly that).

d **Firing order** (to help you locate your #1 plug, which you will need to know in order to check your **timing**).

e **Ignition Timing**. The number given in degrees refers to the proper **timing mark** on your **crankshaft pulley** (I'll help you find it), and the number after "@" indicates at how many **rpm** to check your timing on your dwell meter/tachometer. (Don't get excited; it's not as complicated as it sounds.)

f Now, jot down the proper parts number given for spark plugs and for the distributor **tune-up kit** for your car.

5 Buy them. Most professional mechanics get a discount at auto parts stores. You might try to see if you can get one by telling them that you are going to install them yourself. It can't hurt to try. If not, you are still ahead of the game, especially if you shop at one of the discount auto shops—Sears, Pep Boys, Montgomery Ward, etc. You can use either the house brand or a very well-known brand like Champion or AC. Avoid little-known brands; they may not be made to the proper tolerances, and, with automotive parts, a fraction of an inch makes the difference between moving and standing still.

What You Will Need to Tune-Up Your Car

1 A new set of spark plugs. Buy one for each cylinder in your engine. Never change just a few plugs; it's all or nothing for even engine performance. If you are feeling especially wealthy, buy an extra plug in case you get home and find that one of them is defective, or in case you accidentally ruin one by dropping and cracking it, or by cross-threading it when you install it. If you don't use it, keep it in your trunk compartment tool kit for emergencies. Spark plugs don't get stale.

2 A tune-up kit. This will contain a new **rotor, condenser**, set of points, little capsule of **cam** lubricant, and any other things that the manufacturer thought you might like to have. Pick your kit out by part number; then read the package carefully to make

sure it says that it is for *your* make, model, year, and engine. This kind of double checking always pays off. If you don't see your car listed on the package, ask the salesman to clear up the situation.

3 Your tools. **Screwdrivers**, **screwholder**, **wrenches**, **feeler gauges**, a work light (or a flashlight, at least), a **socket-wrench** and a **ratchet handle** with a **spark plug socket**. If possible, a **dwell meter** and a **timing light** (in case you can't get these, however, I'll show you how to set your dwell and timing without them).

4 An old blanket, mattress pad, or a shiny new vinyl car protector to place over the fender where you'll be working, so you won't scratch it. The vinyl car protectors often come with handy pockets to keep tools and little parts in while you are working. You can make one yourself by pinning up the bottom edge of your folded blanket or pad—or you can forget about it completely if you don't mind rummaging in your tool kit a lot. Just don't place tools, screws, and little parts where they can fall into the engine. It can be difficult and time-consuming to get them out of the unreachable places they invariably head for once they are in a state of free fall. *Never* attempt to drive your car with something lost in the works. Even the smallest screw can find its way into something that will react violently to the intruder, ruining itself, and you, if you are on the freeway when it happens. Just hunt around patiently until you find whatever it is you've dropped. If you are lucky, it will drop through onto the ground, so check there first and rock your car a little, by leaning on the fender, to encourage the missing item to drop down.

While we're on the subject, check under the car *before* you start working. That way you will know that any bolts, screws, or unidentifiable objects that are there after you are done have *not* come from your car. Not knowing can be disquieting, to say the least.

5 Work clothes that you won't mind getting irrevocably stained with grease, oil, and other stuff.

6 Hand cleaner.

Safety Rules Before we go any further, I'd like to give you a few safety rules for working on your car:

1 Tie back long hair. If it accidentally gets into a moving fan or belt you can literally be scalped.

2 Never work on your car unless the **parking brake** is on, the car is in either "Park" or "Neutral"; and the engine is shut off. If you have to run the engine to adjust something, turn it on and off yourself to avoid the risk that a friendly helper may misunderstand and turn the engine on while your hands are in the way.

3 Never jack a car up unless the wheels are properly blocked. I'll go into this when we talk about changing tires. You won't need the jack for your tune-up.

4 Use insulated tools for electrical work.

5 Before using a wrench or ratchet on a part that is "stuck," be sure that, if it suddenly comes loose, your hand won't hit anything. To avoid this, *pull* on wrenches whenever possible, rather than *push* them.

6 Be sure the parts of the engine you are working on are nice and cold, so you won't get burned. If you are doing a job that calls for a warm engine, be very careful.

7 Don't smoke when you are working on your car—for obvious reasons!

So much for the scary stuff. It's all a matter of common sense, really. And remember, it is almost impossible to make a car "blow up" unless you drop a match into the gas tank. If you do something incorrectly, the worst thing that will probably happen is that the car won't start until you get it right. The first time I tuned my car I was sure that if I made the smallest mistake the car would explode when I started it. This seems to be a common delusion. It just isn't so. All you'll get is silence (which can be just as disconcerting, but not lethal, after all). And now, to work.

Changing Your Spark Plugs Before you can change your spark plugs, you have to find them. Look for a row of black-covered thick wires (or thin cables) that enter your engine in neat rows—

on both sides if you have a V-6 or V-8 engine, and on only the driver's side if you have a straight 4- or 6-cylinder engine (these are also called **in-line engines**). Since these spark-plug cables run from the **distributor** to the spark plugs, you can also trace a cable from your distributor to find your plugs for sure.

Cylinder Sequence

In all U.S.–made straight 4- and 6-cylinder cars, the cylinder nearest the radiator (nearest the front of the car) is #1. Then they run in sequence toward the **firewall**—#2, #3, #4, and so on. Some foreign-built cars have this reversed, with #1 at the rear, near the firewall. If you have a foreign car and no owner's manual, ask your local dealer where your #1 cylinder is. Your #1 plug is the spark plug in your #1 cylinder.

V-8 engines are not as easy. Most Ford V-8s have the #1 cylinder in the front on the passenger side of the car. Then, #2, #3, and #4 follow it toward the rear firewall. Number 5 is up front on the driver's side, with #6, #7, and #8 in sequence going toward the rear. On most other V-type engines, the #1 cylinder is up front on the driver's side, with #3, #5, and #7 proceeding rearward. Then, #2 is up front on the passenger side, with #4, #6, and #8 following. This goes for V-6s as well as V-8s: the three odd-numbered plugs are on one side and the three even-numbered plugs are on the other side, with the lowest-numbered plugs usually up near the radiator. Page 70 shows some examples of the **cylinder sequence** in U.S. engines.

Firing Order

Now, do not confuse cylinder sequence with **firing order**. Although your engine may have its cylinders in simple numerical sequence, if the cylinders were fired in that order the engine would rock violently as first the cylinders on one side (or toward the front) fired in rapid succession, and then the other cylinders did likewise. To avoid this, the firing order is carefully arranged to distribute the shock of **combustion** evenly throughout the engine. The cylinders fire in very swift

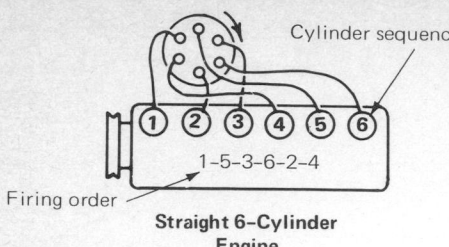

Cylinder sequence

1-5-3-6-2-4

Firing order

**Straight 6-Cylinder
Engine**

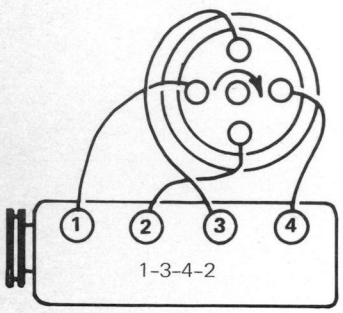

1-3-4-2

**Straight 4-Cylinder
Engine**

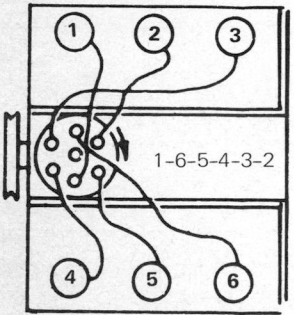

1-6-5-4-3-2

V-6 Engine

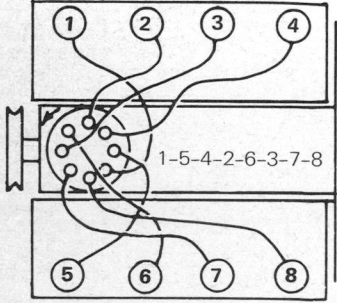

1-5-4-2-6-3-7-8

Ford V-8 Engine

sequence, and the result is a fairly stable engine. A typical firing order for a Ford V-8 engine (with cylinders #1 to #4 on one side and cylinders #5 to #8 on the other) would be #1, #5, #4, #2, #6, #3,#7, #8. The firing order has been printed inside each of the engines illustrated above. Trace the path of combustion back and forth throughout each of these engines so you can see how the shock of combustion is distributed to avoid rocking the engine. Remember, the whole thing happens very rapidly.

If you've digested all this, let's get back to work:

In order to keep the proper **firing order,** each spark-plug cable must go from the proper terminal on your **distributor cap** to the proper spark plug, so before you remove anything, you should label each cable with its proper number in the **cylinder sequence**.

1 To label your cables, place a piece of masking tape, or a clothespin with the tape on it, on the spark-plug cable near the **boot** that covers the tip of each spark plug. Put the proper number on each one. If you are really ambitious, label the boot where the cable enters the distributor cap terminal, as well. Then you will never be unsure about hooking things up properly. Of course, if you make it a habit to remove the cable from only one plug at a time, and to put it back before you remove another, you won't ever get into trouble—unless another cable comes off accidentally.

2 Gently grasp the #1 spark-plug cable by the boot, where it connects to the spark plug. Never yank on the cable itself (you can damage the wiring); just grasp the boot and twist it and pull it straight out so you can pull it off the plug. The shiny thing sticking out of the engine **cylinder block** is the *terminal* of the #1 spark plug.

3 Take a nice soft rag (old sweatshirts or flannel pajamas are lovely) and clean around the area where the spark plug enters the block. This will keep loose junk from falling down the hole into the cylinder when the plug is removed.

4 Find your **spark plug socket** (the big one with the rubber lining) and shove it down over the spark

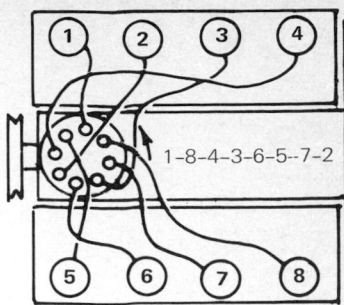
1-8-4-3-6-5--7-2

Many Other V-8 Engines

plug. Exert some pressure to be sure it's all the way down. Like everything else in auto repair, don't be afraid to use some strength. Just do it in an even, controlled manner. If you bang or jerk things, you can damage them, but you will never get anywhere if you tippy-toe around.

5 Pick up your **ratchet handle** and stick the square end into the square hole in the spark-plug socket. If you can work more comfortably by adding a couple of extensions between the handle and the socket, so that you can move the handle freely from side to side without hitting anything, go ahead. You add them in the same way you added the socket to the handle.

The little knob on the back of the ratchet handle is used to make the ratchet turn the socket either clockwise or counterclockwise. You want to loosen the spark plug, so you want the handle to turn counterclockwise. You can tell which way the handle will turn the plug by listening to the clicks that the handle makes when you move it in one direction. If it clicks when you move it to the right, it will turn the socket counterclockwise when you move it, silently, to the left. If the clicks are audible on the leftward swing, it will move the socket clockwise on the rightward swing. Every screw, nut, bolt, etc., that you encounter should loosen counterclockwise and tighten clockwise. If your ratchet is clicking in the wrong direction, just move that little knob and it will reverse direction.

Now, you may have some difficulty in loosening the spark plugs for the first time. This is because the mechanic who installed it may have used a "gorilla," which tightens things much tighter than you can. To get the proper leverage, place your free hand over the head of the wrench, grasping the head firmly, and pull the handle as hard as you can, hitting it gently with the palm of your hand to get it going. If you can't budge it, don't feel like a weakling. I thought it was because I was female, at first; but the biggest man in my class had problems starting my plugs. We recently had a discussion about it, and the general opinion was that strength depended less on the size or sex of the person and more on the way in which an

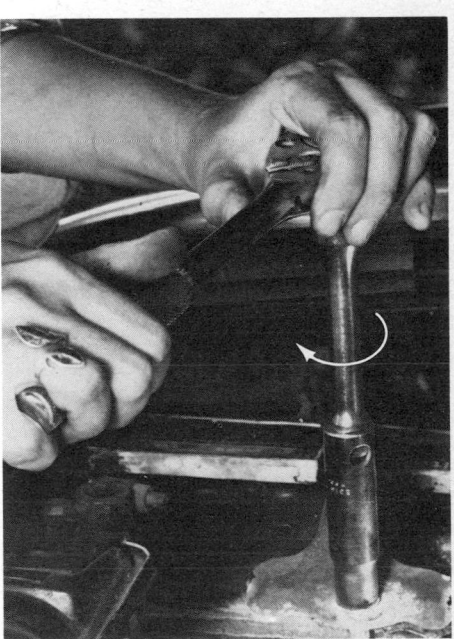

How to Use a Socket Wrench
Richard Freshman

individual had been taught to focus his or her strength in the hands or the tool with which one was working. I now approach hard-to-move objects with a wrench and the conviction that I can move it by pouring all my strength down my arms into my hands. You know, it works! Also, the longer the tool, the more leverage it will give you.

You'll feel better to know that after you've installed your new plugs by hand, it will be a lot easier to get them loose the next time. Also, grease, **sludge**, or

FIG. 5-4
WHAT YOUR OLD SPARK PLUGS TELL YOU
ABOUT YOUR CAR

CONDITION		CLUES	PROBABLE CAUSES
Normal plugs		Brown or grayish-tan deposit on side electrode.	Everything's fine. Just clean and regap the plug.
Carbon-fouled plugs		Black, dry, fluffy soot on insulator tip and electrodes.	Overly rich fuel/air mixture; malfunctioning choke; dirty air filter; or just too much driving at low speeds, or standing and idling for a long time. Switch to "hotter" plugs.
Oil-fouled plugs		Wet, black, oily deposits on insulator tip and electrodes.	Oil may be leaking into cylinders past worn pistons or poorly adjusted or worn valves. Clean and regap these, or replace them, but find out where the leak is coming from.
Lead-fouled plugs		Red, white, brown, or yellow deposits called scavenger deposits.	Highly leaded gas or other additives in gas or oil. Disregard, unless extensive. Clean and regap plugs.
		Shiny yellow glaze.	Same as above, but you'll have to throw these away.
Burnt plugs		Blisters on insulator tip, melted electrodes, burnt stuff.	Engine overheating; gap too wide, wrong or loose plugs; overly lean fuel/air mixture; incorrect timing. Replace plugs.
Worn plugs		Severely eroded or worn electrodes.	Plugs have been in there too long. Replace them.

other junk may have caused the plugs to stick in place, especially if it's been a long time between tunings. So persevere. I've never met a plug that didn't give up and come out, eventually.

6 Got it loose? Good! After you get the plug started, you can disconnect the ratchet handle, leaving the socket on the plug, and turn it the last few bits yourself so you'll know when it is free. Now take it out and remove the spark plug from the socket.

Take a look at your plug. The deposits you find on it will provide valuable "clues" to what your engine is doing. Here are a few clues to help you "read" your plugs and learn about your engine's past (and predict its future, in some cases):

1 Look at the end of your plug which was inside the cylinder. This is called the firing end. The hook at the top is the *side* **electrode**. The bump right under its tip is called the *center* **electrode**. The spark from the distributor comes up the center of the plug and jumps the **gap** between these two **electrodes**. And the gap has to be a particular distance across.

2 Take your *wire* **feeler gauge** and locate the proper wire (if your spark-plug gap specifications said .035, look for this number near one of the wires on the gauge). Now, slip the gauge wire between the two electrodes on your old plug. It probably has a lot of room to wiggle around in. This may be because your old plug has worn down its center electrode, causing a gap that is too large. If the gauge goes in and out with a lot of room on either side, the gap is too large. If the gauge will not fit between the center and side electrodes, the gap is too small. This means that the spark plug is not burning the **fuel/air mixture** efficiently.

3 Now, look at the little center electrode bump again. Is it nice and cylindrical, like the center electrodes on your new spark plugs? Or is it worn round, or worn down on one side? Chances are it's pretty worn. That's because it's old. Now that you are doing your tune-ups yourself, you'll probably check your plugs more often and replace them before they get too worn to operate efficiently. When the

Reading Your Spark Plugs

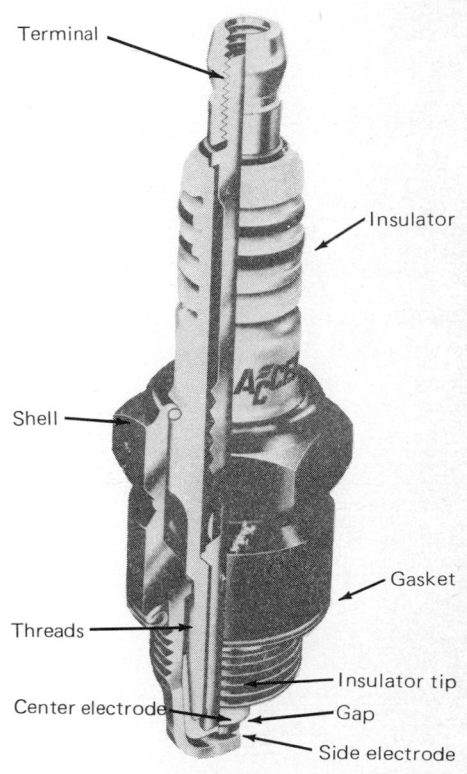

Terminal

Insulator

Shell

Gasket

Threads

Insulator tip

Center electrode

Gap

Side electrode

Anatomy of a Spark Plug
ACCEL, Division of Echlin Manufacturing Co.

center electrode wears down, the gap becomes too large.

If you should find that your plugs seem to indicate that there is something wrong with the way your engine is running, ask a professional mechanic for his opinion. If he says that it is a serious problem, requiring extensive or expensive work, get a second opinion at another station without telling that you went to the first station. This is a good policy to follow whenever major garage work is indicated. We tend to get a second opinion whenever a doctor tells us we need major surgery; why not give your car the same thorough attention? Sometimes a problem can be cured by going to a "hotter" or "cooler" burning plug. These can be identified by the plug number. The higher the number, the hotter the plug. Never go more than one step hotter or cooler at a time.

If you find that a few of your old plugs were not too worn, and in fairly good shape, clean them and regap them and keep them in your trunk compartment tool kit for emergencies. When tuning your car, either replace all the plugs or clean them all and use them all. Don't mix plugs in varying states of wear. Your engine will not operate efficiently. And please don't use a *flat* feeler gauge to gap old plugs.

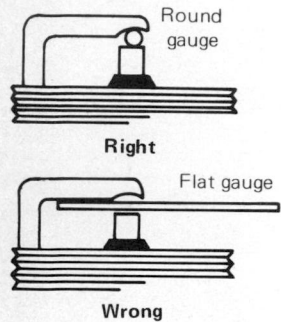

Right

Wrong

Why You Can't Use a Flat Feeler Gauge on Old Spark Plugs
DIXCO

Gapping Your Spark Plugs

1 Now, locate a place where you can keep the used plugs in cylinder order and put the #1 plug there. An egg carton works well.

2 Get out a shiny new spark plug and take a look at it. It should be clean and new-looking, with the tip of the side electrode centered over the center electrode. There should be no cracks or bubbles in the porcelain insulator, and the threads should be unbroken.

3 Take your wire feeler gauge, select the proper wire, and run it between the electrodes. If it doesn't go through, find the part of the feeler gauge that is used for bending electrodes, hook it under the side electrode, and tug very gently. Now run the gauge through the gap again.

4 Did it go through this time? Did it go in too easily, without touching the electrodes? Then you've got

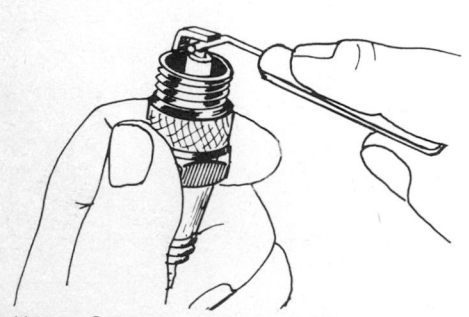

How to Gap a Plug with a Wire Gauge
Rogers and Greenberg

the gap too wide. Press the side electrode against a clean, marproof surface, *very gently*, until it is *slightly* bent down toward the center electrode. Now try the gauge again. Does it go through fairly easily, just catching the electrodes as it passes? Fine! (If the gap is now too small again, don't feel bad. Everyone I know goes through the "too large–too small–too large" bit a couple of times for each plug, especially the perfectionists.) The wire should just "hang" in the gap but go through with a little guidance.

Now you are ready to reinsert the plug in the engine.

How to Replace a Spark Plug

1 Clean the hole in the cylinder block with a clean cloth. Wipe *away* from the hole; don't shove any dirt into it.

2 Slip the spark-plug socket over the new plug, pressing the plug, terminal end first, into the socket as far as it will go, leaving the threads and electrodes exposed.

3 Place the plug in the socket back in the entrance of the hole and gently turn it clockwise, by hand, as far as it will go comfortably. This is called *seating the plug.* You have to do it by hand, or you run the risk of starting the plug crookedly and cross-threading it. Cross-threaded plugs are useless, unless you know someone who has a gadget that can rethread them.

4 Attach your ratchet handle to the socket (be sure that the knob is adjusted to make it turn the socket clockwise) and tighten the plug. Don't overtighten (you can crack the plug); just get it in nice and tight with no wiggle. It should stick a little when you try to loosen it, but you should be able to loosen it again without killing yourself. Tighten and loosen it once or twice to get the proper "feel" of the thing.

If you have a **torque wrench**, look in the manual for the proper setting and use it, once you have seated the plug by hand. Then try to loosen the plug by hand. This will give you the proper "feel" for how tight it should be. Most do-it-yourselfers tend to do plugs without torque wrenches because they are difficult to work with in the small space between the block and the other parts of the car.

5 Slip the cable **boot** over the exposed terminal of the new plug and press it firmly into place.

Well, you've just cleaned, gapped, and installed your first spark plug. Don't you feel terrific? Now you only have 3, or 5, or 7 more to do, depending on your engine. (It's at times like these that owners of 4-cylinder cars have the edge on those who drive those big, expensive 8-cylinder monsters.)

6 Taking each plug in order, and working only on *one plug at a time*, gap and replace each plug. Most of them should be easy to reach. If you find that one or more plugs is blocked by an air conditioner, a power-steering device, or some other part, try using various ratchet handle extensions to get around the problem. There are *universal* extensions that allow the ratchet handle to be held at odd angles; *T-bar* handles for better leverage; and *offset* handles for hard-to-reach places. (See the tool chapter for examples of these.) Almost every car has at least one plug that is a miserable thing to reach. If you have one, save it for last. Then you can work on it with the satisfaction of knowing that, when you get the darn thing finished, you will have finished the job. I bet that when you get it out you will find that it has never been replaced during all those professional tune-ups you've paid for. And you've paid even more because that one funky plug can cut your gas mileage (and add to air pollution). Your car will be really glad to get rid of it.

If you absolutely cannot reach the offending plug, you can always drive to your service station and humbly ask them to change just that one plug. They won't like it, but it *is* a last resort. If you get to that point, you'll probably be glad to pay to have it done. But do try very hard, first. If you can't get to the plug in the ordinary way, go under, over, around, or through gaps in the thing that's blocking it. Or get someone to help you move what's in the way (but be sure that you can get it back in place correctly). Use your imagination; it's the only hard part of the job. And you won't have to do it again for a long time. Of course, if you are lucky enough to own a car without air conditioning, power steering, power brakes, etc., chances are that all your plugs will be easy to get at. Think it over next time you are tempted to buy a car with all the "extras." Those "extras" tend to block the things you want to work on, and they often go wrong themselves. Some, like air conditioning if you live in a hot climate, are worth it. Others, like power brakes on a small car, are not.

Done? Great! Go and start your car to prove to yourself that everything still works. Then wash your hands with hand cleaner. You want to be nice and fresh for your distributor. If you have had a hard time with a hard-to-reach plug, you can put off the distributor part until tomorrow, but you should be able to do both, in a couple of hours, without getting fed up.

There are some differences between **distributors** on different make and model cars, but the basic steps are the same for all, except those new cars with **electronic ignition systems**. These, as I've mentioned before, do not need to have their points changed, so, if you have one, just forget this section and go on to the next. All testing and servicing of these systems should be left to trained professionals. They work on magnetic principles and are easily damaged if hooked up improperly. All you need to do is to change your spark plugs and check the wiring to be sure your cables and connec-

Servicing Your Distributor

Anatomy of a Distributor
DIXCO

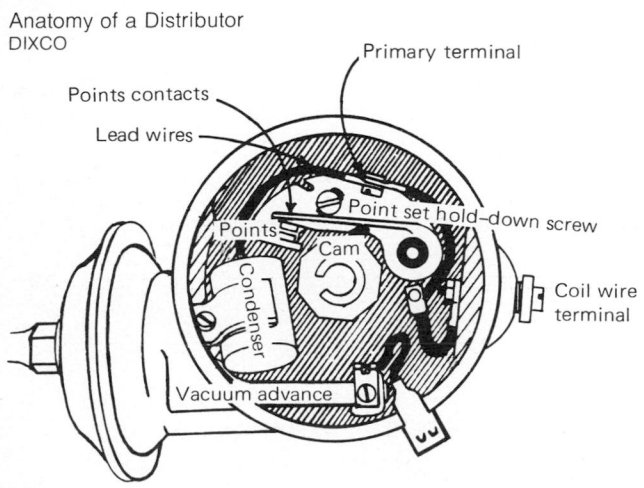

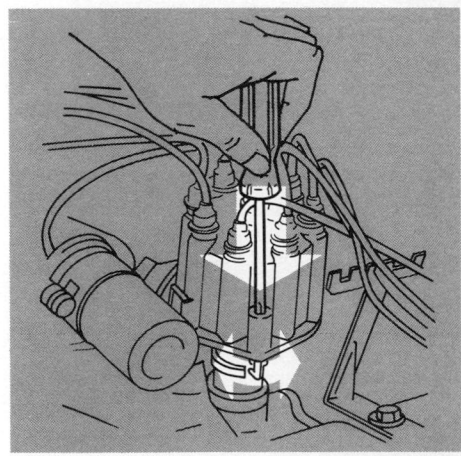

Removing a Distributor Cap with Screw Clamps
Delco-Remy Division, General Motors Corp.

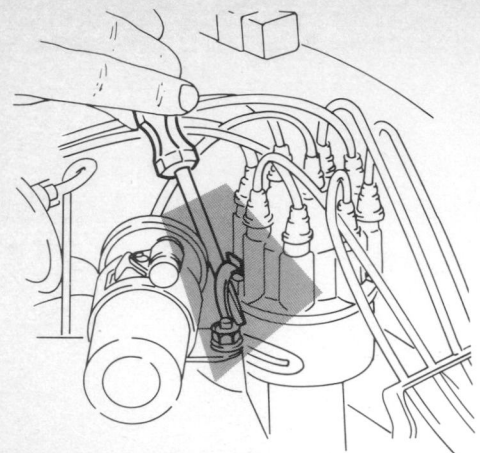

Removing a Distributor Cap with Clips
Delco-Remy Division, General Motors Corp.

Removing Your Distributor Cap

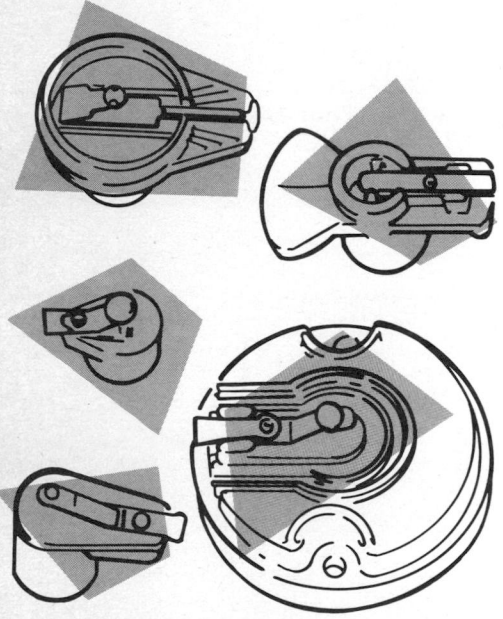

Various Types of Rotors
Delco-Remy Division, General Motors Corp.

Removing Your Rotor

tions have not become corroded or unstrung. How do you know if your car has an electronic ignition system? You don't have one if your car was made before 1973. If it is a 1973 model, or newer, check your owner's manual or ask your dealer.

For those of you who are still with me, the **tune-up kit** you have bought for this purpose contains everything you will need to do the job except for tools such as a screwdriver, a screwholder (optional, but nice), and a timing light and dwell meter (if you have them).

Let's begin:

1 Find your **distributor**. If you are still not sure about it, go back and reread the description of the distributor—where it is, what it does, and what it contains—in the previous chapter. I'll wait. . . .

2 Using a screwdriver with a nice long handle, remove the **distributor cap**. Most caps are held in place by either clips or screws. Which kind does your car have? The illustration on this page will show you how to remove both types.

3 Now that your distributor cap is free, remove it without removing any of the wires that are attached to the top of the cap. Place it to one side and take a look inside your distributor. Does the stuff in there look like the stuff in your kit? Look at the structure of the **rotor** and the **points**. They should be similar, although some parts may be made of plastic instead of metal. If they look different, you've got the wrong kit. Go back to the auto parts store and start over (Do Not Pass Go, etc.).

Sitting on top of everything in the distributor is the **rotor**. Rotors vary in size from small plastic gizmos that simply lift off the **distributor shaft**, to big round plastic plates that have two screws to remove. The illustration to the left shows different kinds of rotors.

1 Before you remove your rotor, move it on its shaft. Does it move easily? If not, you really need this tune-up badly!

2 Now remove the rotor from the shaft. The illustrations on this page will show you how to remove big and small rotors.

3 Take a close look at it. You can see the metal contacts that conduct current to the spark plug terminals. Are they corroded? Broken? Cracked? Then you really needed a new one! You'll put a new one in anyway, because you've paid for it and it will last longer than the one that's in there now. But don't put it in yet; you have other things to do. Just be sure to see how the old one fits onto the shaft so you can put the new one in properly, later on. All rotors will go on one way only. They either have a square-pin-in-square-hole/round-pin-in-round-hole arrangement, or they are notched or shaped so that they fit on the shaft in one direction only. Still, it is a good habit to take a long look at anything you are removing, because later on you will tend to forget how it went, and sometimes you have to make a choice. Don't be afraid to draw pictures if you aren't sure you'll remember how something fitted together.

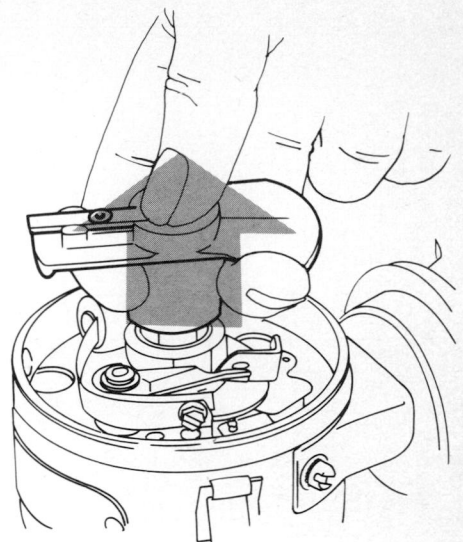

Removing a Small Rotor
Delco-Remy Division, General Motors Corp.

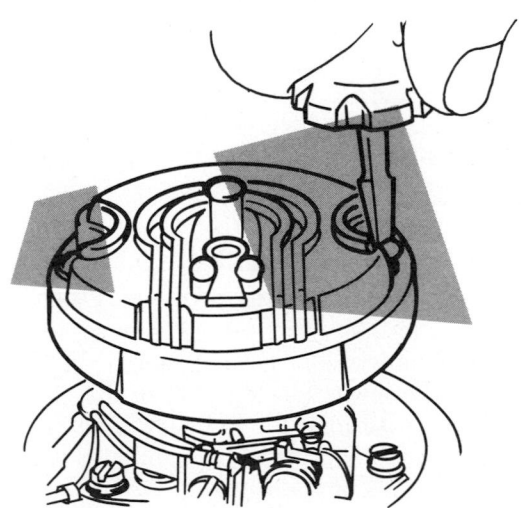

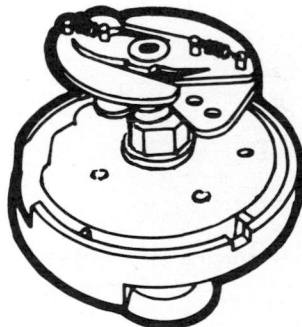

Centrifugal Advance
Guaranteed Parts Co.

Removing a Big Rotor
Delco-Remy Division, General Motors Corp.

This type of rotor is released by removing the screws.

Under the rotor are the points and condenser. Under the rotor on some General Motors cars, you will find something called the **centrifugal advance**. Its function is rather complicated, and it has nothing to do with our minor tune-up and hardly ever breaks. Just leave it where it is and forget it.

Static Shield On certain newer cars, you will find a two-piece **static shield**, which must be removed before you can change

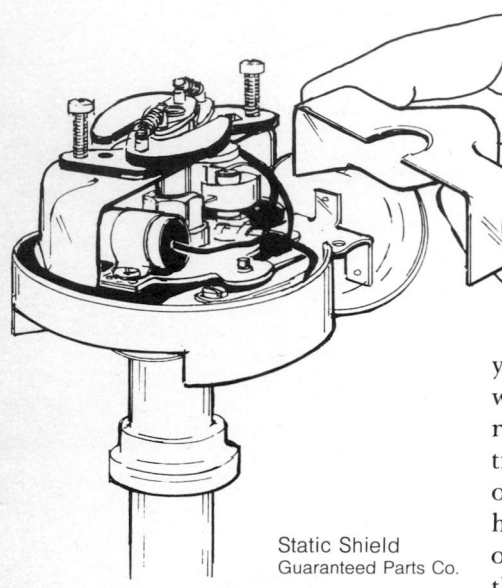

Static Shield
Guaranteed Parts Co.

your points and condenser. The figure below shows what this shield looks like. Its purpose is to prevent radio interference. Sometimes the working of the electrical system in your car will produce strange noises on the car radio. This gizmo prevents that. It isn't hard to remove, but when you are finished working on your distributor, be careful to put the shield back the way it was. If you cannot get it back properly, your car will run perfectly without it, so just put the pieces in a paper bag and drive to your friendly service station. They'll put it back for you (although you may have to take a little kidding).

How to Remove and Replace Your Condenser

1 You will notice that there are two little wires, one leading to the **points**, and one to the **condenser**, that join together—usually with some sort of little screw and washer arrangement. Take a good look at how these wires fit together in the gadget that holds them (it is called the **primary terminal**). The main purpose of the primary terminal is to keep the clips at the ends of the wires (or *leads*, as they are sometimes called) from touching the floor of the distributor, which is called the **breaker plate**. If they touch this, they will short out and the car will not start. Look again. Are the little clips at the ends of the wires touching each other? Or are they separated with something? Does the screw that holds them in

place touch them? Or is there something in between? If you don't think you can remember how they go, draw a picture of them. The figures on this page show how to disconnect several types of primary terminal arrangements.

2 Now disconnect the leads. Put the screws, or other parts that came off, down on a clean area, so you'll know where they are in case you need them later.

3 The **condenser** is that little cylinder in there. Push it through the ring that holds it, and put it down near the screws. Some condensers are attached to the clips that hold them, and you will have to remove them clip and all. Wipe around the breaker plate where the condenser was resting with a clean, lint-free rag. The figures on this page show a few of the most common set-ups.

4 Now take the new condenser and slide it in where the old one was. If there is a new clip in the tune-up kit but you were able to slide your old condenser out without removing the old clip, forget the new clip as long as the old one seems to be in good condition and does not wiggle around. Congratulations, you've just replaced your condenser.

Disconnecting the Lead Wires from the Primary Terminal of Various Popular Distributors
Delco-Remy Division, General Motors Corp.

(*above*) On some types of distributors, the leads must be loosened from the primary terminal as shown. Leads should be removed from the terminal after noting their relative positions.

(*below right*) On other types of distributors, the nut on the primary terminal must be loosened to release the contact spring and lead wires. Here again the lead arrangement must be noted. (*below left*) Still another type of distributor has its leads attached as shown. These must be removed by loosening the nut at the primary terminal.

ow) Here is another arrangement of the ary terminal. To release the contact point g and leads, a special tool must be to remove the primary terminal nut.

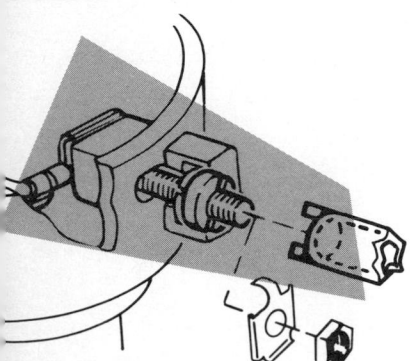

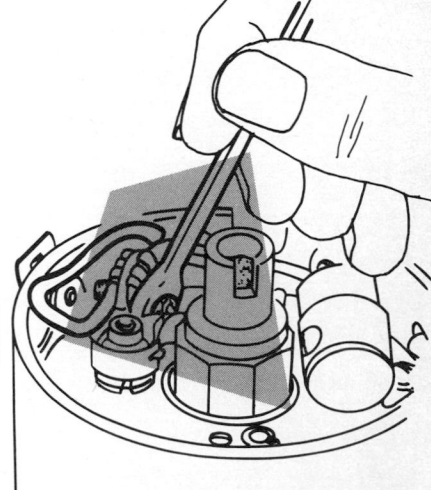

How to Remove Old Points

How to Remove the Condenser from Various Popular Distributors
Delco-Remy Division, General Motors Corp.

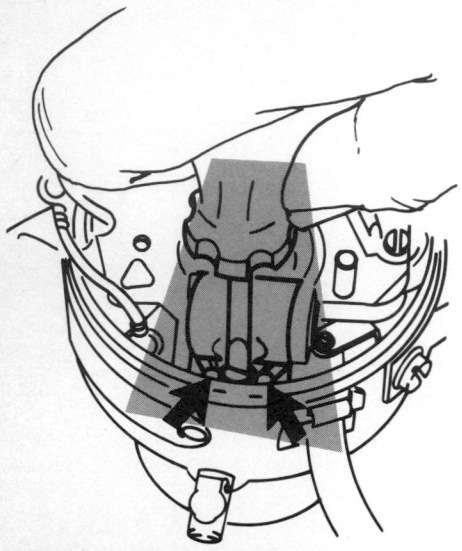

This type of condenser has one screw to remove and two locating bumps to help you position the new one correctly.

1 Take a look at the **points** in the tune-up kit. They may look a bit different from the ones in the illustration, but they work the same way. Some points are made in a single unit; others consist of two halves that fit together. Some Chrysler products have dual sets of points, but these are no more difficult to install or change. Some foreign cars have little springs that come out separately from the points. If you have points like these, be sure to hold your free hand over the distributor when you loosen the points or it will spring out and get lost. Some points have two screws that fit into slots in the points—these can be loosened, and the points will slide out. Others have a screw to hold the points down and another screw to adjust them. Which kind do you have?

2 Take your screwdriver and open the points up so you can see between them. Are the contacts rough where they meet? This is usually the result of normal wear and tear, and if they are badly burnt or pitted, they should be replaced. If the points are relatively new, excessive wear can be a sign that something is improperly adjusted or malfunction-

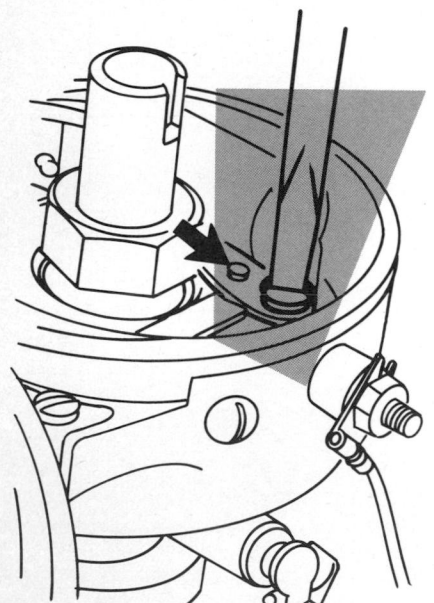

Other types of condensers have a locating hole in the mounting bracket.

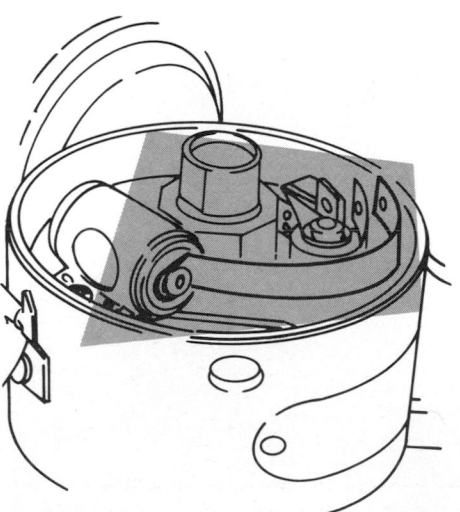

Some types of condensers are connected to the primary terminal by a copper strap that must be released before the condenser can be removed.

Actual point opening .025

.020
Feeler gauge

Why You Can't Get an Accurate Gap Reading on Old Points
Delco-Remy Division, General Motors Corp.

How to Remove Points
Delco-Remy Division, General Motors Corp.

Remove the screw(s) that hold the points in place. If you have slotted points, simply *loosen* the screw and slide the points out.

ing. Excessively worn points or burned points usually result from either poor adjustment when they were installed (this means that they were incorrectly gapped) or a bad condenser, or the accidental introduction of oil or cam lubricant between the point contacts. Because used points are impossible to read accurately with a feeler gauge, you will not be able to tell if this was a case of poor adjustment. But if your old points looked badly burned or worn, be sure to check your new points after about 1,000 miles of driving, and if these look bad too, ask your garage mechanic for an opinion.

3 Remove the old points by removing the screw or screws that held them in place. This is a good time to use your screwholder. Because it will hold onto the screw until you release it, it cuts down on the chances of dropping the screw into the works, and makes it easier to operate in the relatively tight

distributor area because you don't have to cram your fingers in to hold onto the screw. Some screw holders work on magnetic principles; others have a twist handle that grabs the screw. The magnetic ones are super for retrieving metal screws, nuts, and washers that you've dropped into relatively inaccessible places; the other kind may hang onto the screw more securely. Take your pick!

4 Put your old points aside. With the clean rag that you used to clean around under the condenser, wipe the rest of the floor of your distributor (the breaker plate).

How to Lubricate Your Distributor

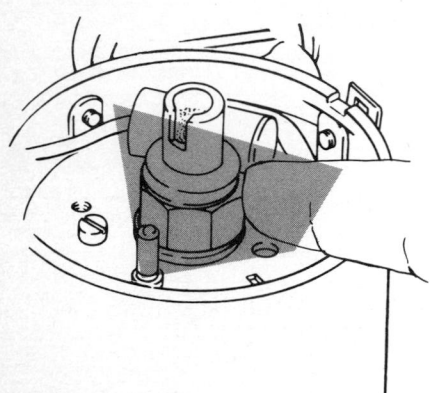

Applying Lubricant to the Cam Wheel
Delco-Remy Division, General Motors Corp.

The cam wheel should have a light coating of cam lubricant applied to its surface prior to point installation. The amount of grease applied should be kept to a minimum to prevent the grease from being thrown off at high speeds and/or at high temperatures.

1 Here is something that seems inconsequential but is really very important. In your tune-up kit there should be a little capsule of cam lubricant. If there isn't any, you can buy a tube of it very cheaply. Take a *little bit* of cam lubricant on your index finger and wipe it around the sides of the cam wheel. Use it very sparingly. You don't want lumps, just a nice greasy finish on the cam wheel *only*. If you don't lubricate this wheel, your points could burn out very quickly. If you use too much, the

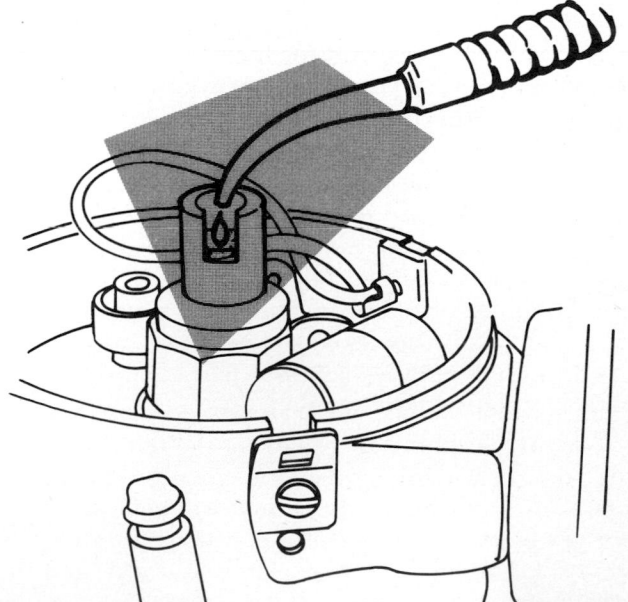

Lubricating the Distributor Shaft
Delco-Remy Division, General Motors Corp.

Place a few drops of light engine oil on the wick in the shaft under the rotor, if a wick is present. Do not over oil!

stuff will fly around inside the distributor when the wheel spins, and foul things up or cause your points to burn. Since your points open and close at around 12,000 times a minute when you drive a V-8 engine at 60 mph, you can see why the lubricant is necessary and why it might tend to fly around if you've been too generous. You want just enough to make your cam wheel lobes slide easily past the points.

2 Look at the top of the distributor shaft, where the rotor was sitting. If there's a wick inside it, place a few drops of light engine oil on the wick in the shaft. If you don't have the proper kind of oil, forget it this time and pick up some in time for the next tune-up.

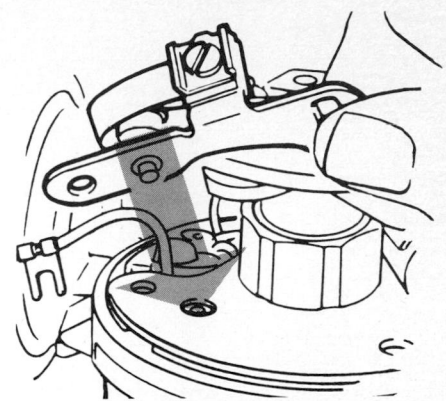

Installing New Points
Delco-Remy Division, General Motors Corp.

Some points have a knob that fits into a locating hole on the floor of the distributor.

How to Install New Points

1 Now pick up the new points. Gently rub the two contact tips together. They usually come from the factory with some kind of coating on them, and this coating can keep the spark from going across the gap. Gently rubbing them together will remove this coating. Don't use cloth, paper, or a file to remove this coating—the lint or tiny filings will foul the points. A little rub is all you need.

2 Install the new points where the old ones were. Sometimes it is easier to connect the lead wires that come from the points and the condenser before you replace the points in the distributor. In any case, just be sure that the clips on both wires *touch each other* but *do not touch any other metal.* They are designed to go back to back so they will fit snugly into the clip on the primary terminal. Check back on page 81 to see the different types of clips and the way to assemble yours. If you don't see it and you've neglected to make a drawing of the way yours were, use your imagination. If you get it wrong, your car won't start until you get it right. Nothing else will happen, so don't worry. Just fit the wire clips together and put them in the clip so that they are not touching anything metal (this includes the side of the clip, if it's made of metal, and the distributor base). As I said before, this can be done either before or after you've got the points in place, whichever is easier.

3 If you haven't already done so, install the new

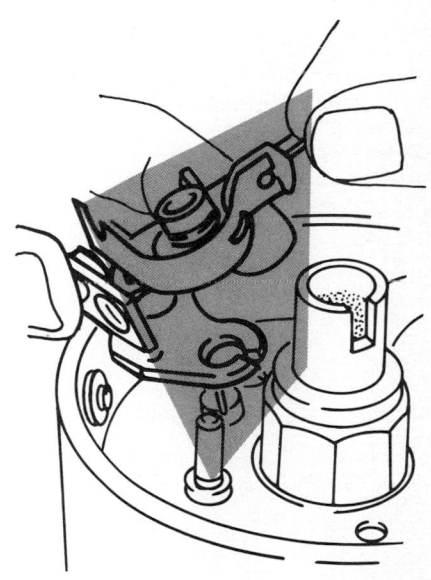

Other points fit over a locating post on the floor of the distributor.

points. Don't tighten down the screws that hold them in place until you have adjusted the gap.

How to Gap Your Points

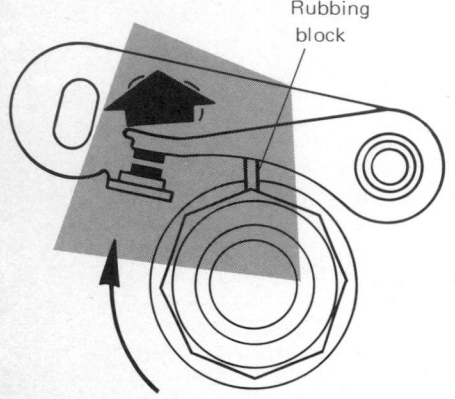

Rubbing block

How the Rubbing Block Causes the Points to Open
Delco-Remy Division, General Motors Corp.

The rubbing block is pushed upward by the highest point on the cam lobe, which causes the points to open to their widest gap.

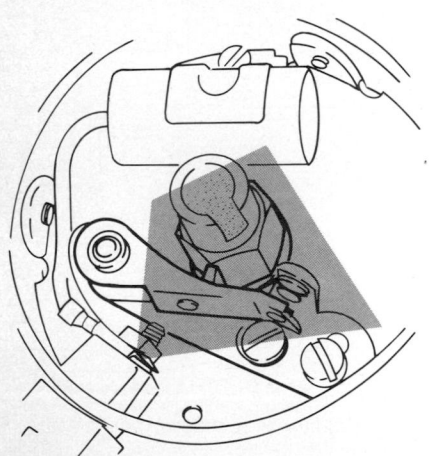

How to Bring Points to Their Widest Gap
Delco-Remy Division, General Motors Corp.

Crank the engine with the starting motor until the point rubbing block is on the peak of the cam lobe. This is the position of maximum point gap.

Now it's time to adjust your point gap (or gap your points).

1 Look at your specifications for the proper gap. Then take your flat feeler gauge and select the correct blade. Before you can adjust the point gap, the little **rubbing block** that protrudes from the side of the points nearest the cam wheel must rest on the highest point of one of the cam lobes. This forces the points open to their widest gap—and that is the gap that you are going to adjust.

2 If the rubbing block is not resting on the point of the cam lobe, bump your starter with the ignition key until the cam wheel turns to the correct position. If you can't seem to do this, run a chalk mark down the side of the distributor and on to the base, or whatever it is sitting on. This will help you later to get it back the way it was. Then turn to page 97 of this chapter where we deal with setting the timing, and see how to locate the **distributor hold-down clamp**. Loosen it and turn the distributor until the rubbing block is resting on the point of the cam lobe and the points are wide open.

3 Slide the blade of the feeler gauge between the points. Is the gap too small to let the blade in? If you left it like that, your car would be hard—or impossible—to start and your points would get burnt and pitted. Is the gap so wide that the gauge doesn't touch both surfaces as it goes in and out? This would result in a weak spark and poor engine performance at high speeds. So, if your gap is either too wide or too small, it needs adjusting.

4 There are three basic kinds of point-adjusting set-ups. Let's see which one your car has. Some cars have an *adjusting screw* (in addition to the screw or screws that hold the points in place). Other cars have an *adjusting slot*. Still others have a little *window* in the distributor cap which allows you to adjust the points without removing the distributor cap.

a Loosen the screw or screws that hold the points in place.

b Turn the off-center adjusting screw.

c Place the feeler gauge between the point contacts (these should still be at their widest gap; if they aren't, turn the distributor shaft until they are).

d Turn the adjusting screw until the gauge can slip in and out between the contacts, just touching them as it slides. There should be a minuscule grab as it goes through, but it should go through easily. If you aren't sure, try the next thicker and thinner gauges. Neither should work properly.

e When you've got the gap just right, tighten up the screws that hold your points in place (*not* the adjusting screw) and recheck with gauge.

f If you have moved the distributor, put it back where it was, with the chalk marks lined up.

a Loosen the locking screw or screws that hold the points in place.

b Making sure that the points are at their widest gap (if they aren't, move the distributor shaft until they are), insert the tip of your screwdriver into the adjusting slot and, by moving it one way or the other, open the gap so that the correct feeler gauge blade can slip in.

c Insert the correct feeler gauge blade and, using your screwdriver in the adjusting slot, adjust the contacts to allow the feeler gauge to slide in and out properly. It should just touch both contacts as it moves, but it should move easily, with just a little bit of grab as it goes by.

d Tighten screws that hold points in place and re-check with gauge. If you have moved the distributor, put it back the way it was, with the chalk marks lined up.

a Reassemble your distributor and put the distributor cap back on. (You'll find instructions for doing this on the next page or so.) Your points will probably *not* need adjusting—they come pre-

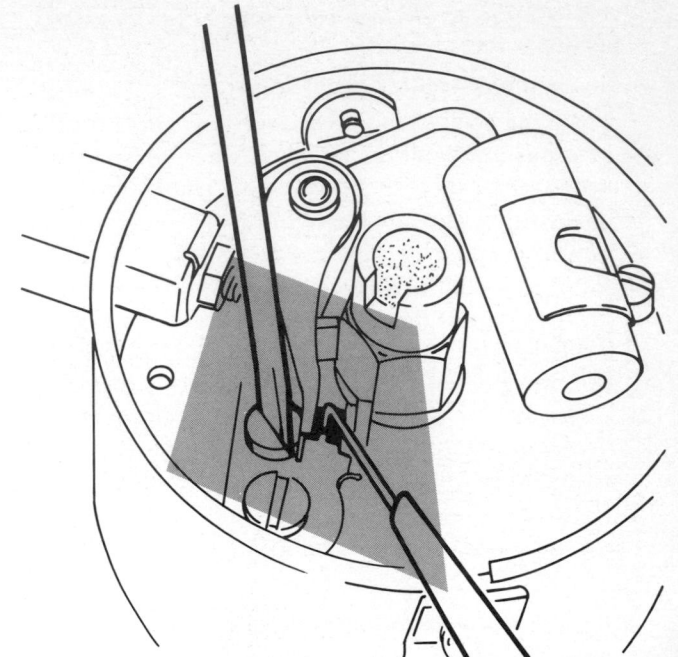

Adjusting Screw-Type Points
Delco-Remy Division, General Motors Corp.

Insert a *flat* feeler gauge between points and turn adjusting screw until points grasp gauge firmly but not so tightly as to obstruct its movement. (Do *not* use wire gauge shown in illustration.)

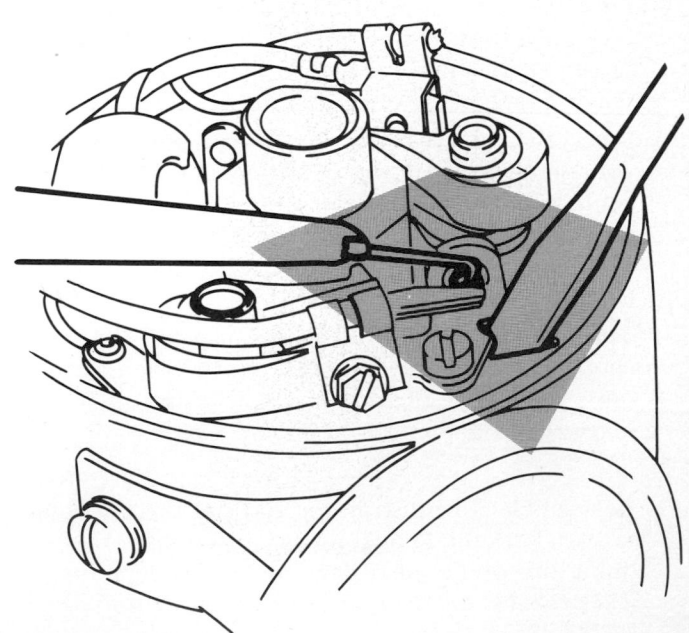

Adjusting Slot-Type Points
Delco-Remy Division, General Motors Corp.

Insert tip of screwdriver into adjusting slot and twist until points grab feeler gauge firmly but not enough to impede its movement. (Use *flat* gauge rather than wire gauge shown in illustration.)

set from the factory—but if you do need to adjust them, then follow the rest of these instructions. You will know if they need adjusting if your car won't start and if you've hooked the wires from the points and the condenser together so that they don't touch any other metal but each other.

b (Only if your points need adjusting) If the car won't start, use a wrench as in c below to turn the adjusting nut. If turning it one way won't get the car started, try turning it the other way. Start your car and leave the engine running with the emergency brake on and the car in either "Park" or "Neutral" gear.

c Use the little "hex" wrench in the tune-up kit, or your own, to turn the adjustment nut behind the sliding window in the distributor cap. Turn the nut clockwise until the engine starts to "miss." Then turn the screw *half a turn* counterclockwise, remove the wrench, and close the window.

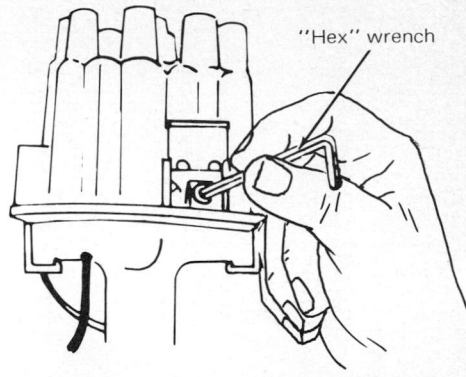

Adjusting Points with an External Adjustment Window
DIXCO

Insert "hex" wrench into adjustment nut. With engine idling, turn nut clockwise until engine "misses," then half a turn counterclockwise.

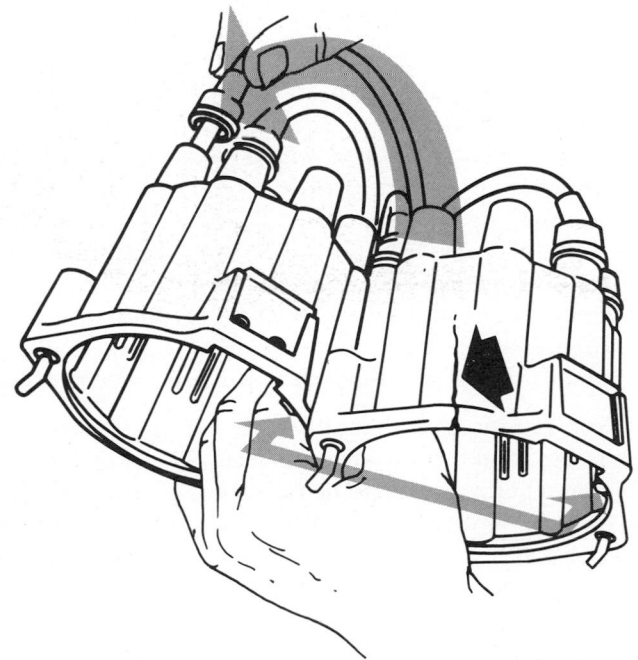

How to Replace a Defective Distributor Cap
Delco-Remy Division, General Motors Corp.

To replace a defective cap, place old and new caps side by side in same relative position, noting locating lugs or slots. Remove one lead at a time from the old cap, placing it in the same relative tower on the new cap. Lead must first be pushed to bottom of tower and then the rubber boot replaced securely.

How to Reassemble Your Distributor
Replacing the Rotor

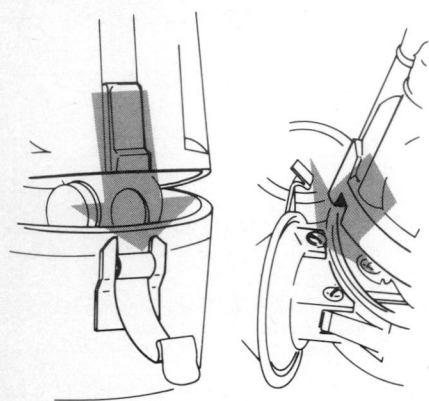

Some distributor caps have either a locating lug that fits into a slot in the cap spring hanger, or a groove or slot in the cap which fits over a boss on the distributor housing.

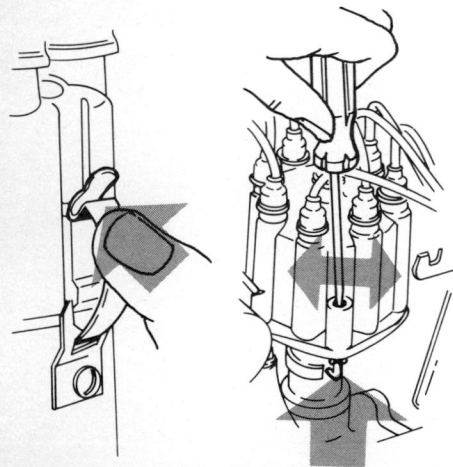

After replacing the cap, with the locators in place, fasten it to the housing by either (a) pressing on the center of the cap spring, forcing the spring over the mounting lugs on the cap, or (b) by pressing down on the screw and turning it until the clamp is under slot on the bottom of the housing.

How to Replace Your Distributor Cap
Delco-Remy Division, General Motors Corp.

1 You've got your points adjusted, the condenser in place, and the little lead wires screwed into the clip, right? Now install the rotor from the tune-up kit, making sure that you put it back the way it was. (Of course if you have one of those **static shields**, you want to put that back before the rotor.) All rotors will fit properly one way only.

2 Turn your rotor to see if it settles back in place easily. Can you turn it in more than one direction? If you can, you don't have it back in place properly.

3 Pick up the distributor cap (don't let any wires come off) and take a look inside it. Wipe the inside clean with a lint-free rag. Are there any cracks in the cap when you hold it up and shine a light through it? If there are, you can buy another cap very cheaply. (The wires snap in and out of the cap, and as long as you hold the two caps in the same direction and pull the wires off the old cap and insert them in the new cap *one at a time* in the *correct order*, you should have no trouble.)

4 Look at the inside of the cap where the wires enter it. Push gently on each wire where it enters its "tower," and make sure it is in tightly. Are the insides of the towers clean? Each little metal thing you see inside the cap is an electrode that transfers the electricity to the rotor, so you don't want them to be too fouled to conduct the electricity. If they look dirty, scrape them with a small screwdriver to remove the carbon. If they are very dirty, or burnt, you may need to replace your wires. At this point, you are probably better off having someone do this for you. Later, when you are more confident, you can do these things yourself and wonder why I suggested you have someone else do the job. But I don't want to hit you with too many things at once.

If you are satisfied that all is well, replace your distributor cap, making sure it is on securely and will not budge when you wiggle it. Be sure you've got all the clamps or screws back in place. Now start your engine to see if you've got everything right. If your car won't start (this is not unusual), go back and recheck the following:

a Is your car still in "Park" or "Neutral"? It won't start in any other gear.

b Is your distributor cap on correctly? If it is, take
it off.

c Are the lead wires from the condenser and the
points correctly replaced and tightened down? If
they are touching anything metal but each other,
the spark is grounding out instead of passing
through the points while they are closed.

d Are your points properly gapped? Check them
with the feeler gauge. Sometimes they move back
together when you tighten them down after adjusting them. Run a bit of very clean, lint-free
cloth between them—maybe something got in
there and is preventing the spark from going
across. Do they close completely? They must open
and close to work.

e Did you accidentally disconnect any other wires
while you were working?

One of these questions will solve your problem.

Now, put your distributor cap back again and start the
engine. It should start this time. Don't panic if you
have trouble—everyone does the first time. But you
ran the car after you changed the spark plugs, so if
there is a problem it has to be in the distributor,
right?

If you still can't get started, remove the new condenser and put the old one back in. Maybe the new one is
defective. This could also be true of the points or
rotor. I'm pretty sure you are not *going to resort to this
strategy* without being able to start your car, but if you
do, and nothing is still happening, the worst that can
happen is that your friendly garage mechanic will
come and get you out of the hole. So how bad can it
be?

Anyway, for the nine-hundred-ninety-nine out of a
thousand of us who have managed to start our cars,
now it is time to check the **dwell**, if you are lucky
enough to have a **dwell meter**. The difference between the cost of doing this tune-up yourself and
having it done for you is probably what a dwell meter
and maybe even a **timing light** would cost, so why not
get them?

Checking Your Distributor with a Dwell Meter

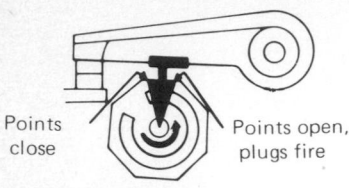

Points close — Points open, plugs fire

Normal Gap, Normal Dwell

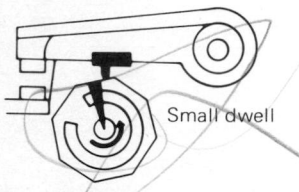

Small dwell

Wide Gap, Insufficient Dwell

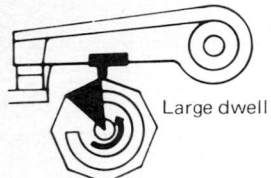

Large dwell

Small Gap, Excessive Dwell

"Cam angle" or "dwell" is the time the points are closed, measured in degrees of cam rotation. Point gap, therefore, has a definite bearing on the cam angle. Both cam angle and point gap should be checked when new points are installed.

What "Cam Angle" or "Dwell" Means
DIXCO

A **dwell meter** is a handy gadget for determining whether or not your points were properly gapped—a wise double-check, even for a professional—and whether your distributor is operating properly. It checks the distance that your distributor shaft rotates when your points are closed—which is the same as saying that it measures how long the points stay closed (or "dwell together"). This distance is called the *cam angle* and, like all angles, it is given in degrees.

1 Here's how to hook up two of the most popular types of dwell meter:

The kind with two clips:

a With the engine shut off, hook the RED clip to the clamp that holds the little wire on the side of the **coil** that leads to the distributor.

b Hook the BLACK clip to "**ground**." "Ground" can be anything that is made of metal, through which electricity can pass back to the battery. In this case, it can be any part of the metal frame of the car, but the best ground is an unpainted pipe or bolt bolted directly to the engine (but not too near the carburetor, please!).

The kind with three clips:

a Connect the RED clip to the positive terminal of the battery.

b Connect the BLACK clip to the negative terminal of the battery.

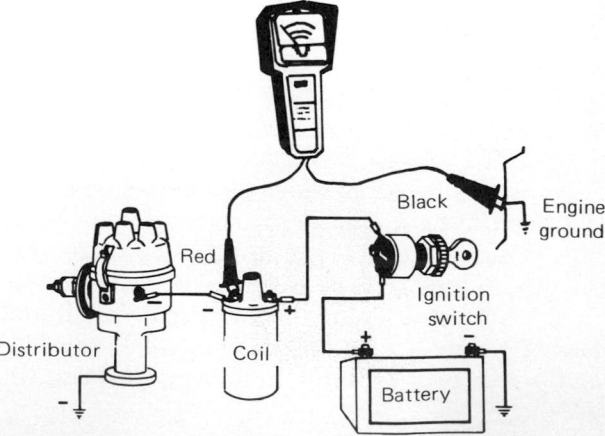

Black — Engine ground

Red

Ignition switch

Distributor   Coil   Battery

How to Hook Up a Dwell Meter with Two Clips
DIXCO

CONNECTIONS:

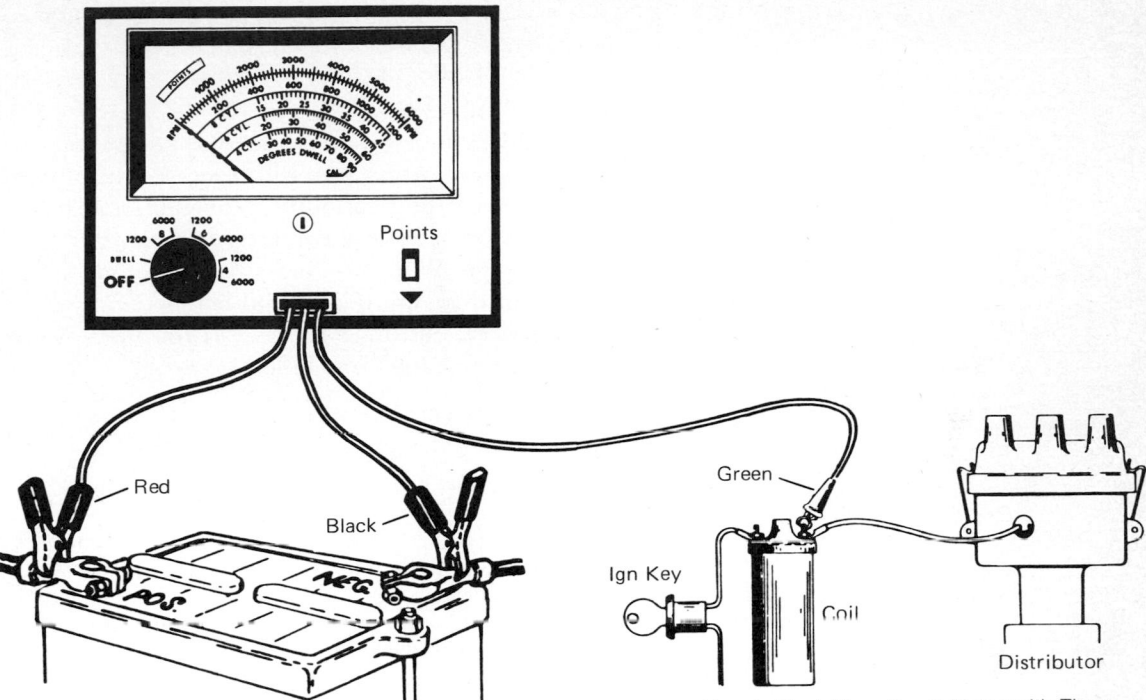

How to Hook Up a Dwell Meter with Three Clips
Actron Manufacturing Co.

c Connect the GREEN clip to the clamp that holds the little wire on the side of the coil which leads to the distributor.

If you have a Ford, see the figure to the right.

2 If your dwell meter has one, turn the *calibrated* knob to set it.

3 Turn the proper knob to the number of cylinders that your car has.

4 Start the engine and let it idle, with the emergency brake on, in "Park" or "Neutral" gear.

5 Look at the dwell meter, on the line that has the same number of cylinders as your car. Is the needle pointing to the correct figure listed under "Dwell" on your Specifications Record sheet? It can be + or − 2 degrees (if your spec sheet shows a dwell of 38 degrees, the dwell is fine if it is anywhere between 36 and 40 degrees). If it is further off than that, you will have to readjust your points.

6 a If you have a distributor with an external *adjusting window*, let the engine idle and keep the dwell

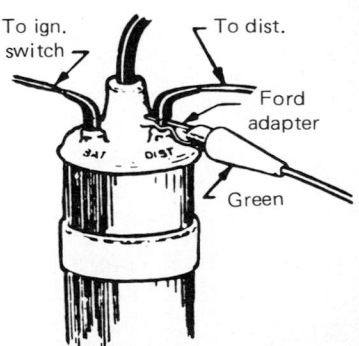

Using a Ford Adapter Clip
Actron Manufacturing Co.

Late model Ford cars have an insulated slip-on terminal on the wire lead from the distributor to the ignition coil. Lift this terminal and slide the Ford Adapter clip in place as shown, then push the terminal down. Attach the GREEN clip to the adapter clip as shown.
Do Not Allow the Ford Adapter Clip or the Green Clip to Touch Any Other Metallic Part of the Coil Case or the Engine.

meter in place. Then open the little window in the side of the distributor cap (it slides up) and turn the adjustment screw with the hex wrench until the needle on the dwell meter points to the correct number.

b If you have the kind of points that adjust with an *adjusting screw or slot,* you will have to shut off the engine, open the distributor cap again, and readjust your points to the correct gap with your feeler gauge. When you are sure you've got it right, put everything back and check the dwell again. Sorry, but that's life. . . . If the dwell is too low, the gap is too large, and *vice versa.*

Everything on target? Then it is time to check your **timing**. Did you get a timing light? I hope so. I've heard of a variety of ways to check your timing without one, but none of them has proved very accurate, and many turned out to be impossible. So, beg or borrow one if you can't buy one, or, as a last resort, ask your garage to check your timing.

7 If you have a *tach/dwell* meter (a dwell meter with a **tachometer** built in), then turn the knob to set it to the tachometer readings. Some tach/dwell meters have both Hi and Lo readings; if yours does, choose either line for right now. Start your engine and let the car idle. After it warms up a bit, check the tachometer to see at how many rpm the car is idling. Try to keep the tach/dwell hooked up while you check your timing, but if it is too difficult to clip both the tach/dwell and the timing light to the battery terminals, disconnect the tach/dwell and keep it handy.

How to Check Your Timing with a Timing Light

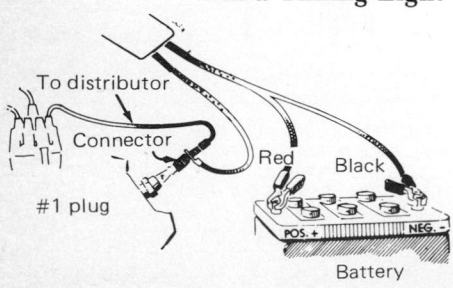

How to Hook Up a Timing Light
DIXCO

1 Read the instructions that came with the light. This is a good idea with any piece of new equipment. Then, hook up your **timing light** as they suggest. Most lights have three clips on them. Cheap neon timing lights have a clip and a plug that fits a wall outlet. These lights are generally too dim to read by in anything but total darkness, so try to avoid this kind when you go out to borrow or buy one. If you have no instructions, the ones in this book will work for most timing lights with three clips.

2 Be sure your engine is shut off.

3 Clamp the big RED clip to the **positive terminal** of your car battery.

4 The big BLACK clip goes on the **negative terminal** of the battery. Make sure the battery terminals are clean enough to allow current to pass through them. If they look *very* funky, scrape the clip around on them a little, or wash off the junk with a clean rag dipped in water and baking soda. Don't get the stuff from the terminal on your hands—it has acid in it. But if you do get it on your hands, just wash them off with water; it won't burn holes in you right away.

5 The third clip, with the thickest insulation, attaches to your #1 spark plug. Way back on page 70 there is an illustration that will tell you where the #1 plug is on your car—in case you've forgotten. You can either place the clip by removing the **boot** from the plug; putting the clip on the terminal end of the plug, where it is sticking out of the engine; and replacing the boot so that it fits snugly and allows the current to pass through from the cable to the plug. Or you can use a small metal spring or clip that will fit over the end of the plug, leaving a gap between the boot and the plug on which to clip the third clip from the timing light.

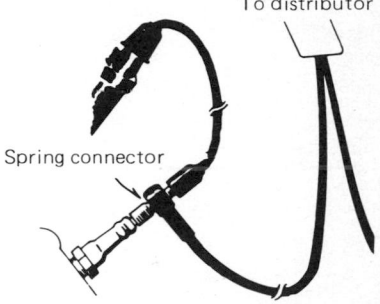

To distributor

Spring connector

Using a Spring Connector
DIXCO

If your #1 spark plug is hard to get at, you can attach the third clip to the distributor terminal tower where the cable from the #1 plug enters the distributor cap. Just trace the cable from the plug to the distributor, remove the boot from the distributor cap terminal, add a metal extension (usually supplied with the light), replace the boot, and clamp the clip to the extension.

6 Keeping your engine shut off, try to pull up on your fan belt with one hand to tighten it, and turn the fan with the other hand in order to rotate the wheel that has the fan belt hooked around it (the lower wheel). This wheel probably has your **timing marks** on it. It is called the **crankshaft pulley** (or the harmonic balance wheel). On some cars, the timing marks are located elsewhere, so if you cannot find yours on the crankshaft pulley, consult your owner's manual for their location, or call your dealer. If you cannot move the fan by hand,

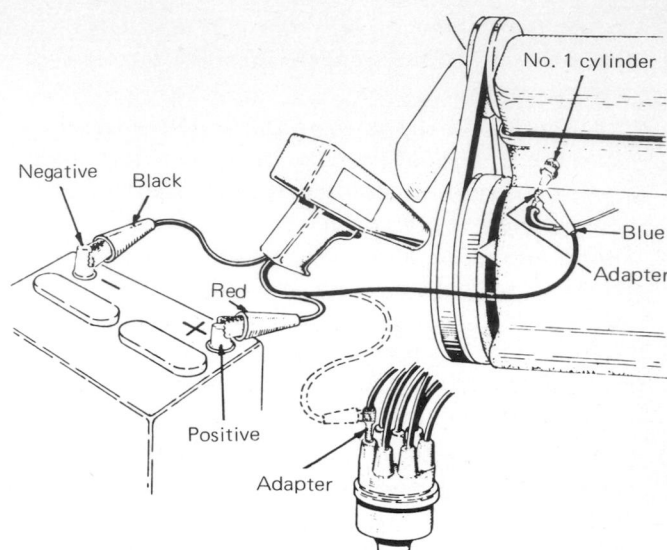

How to Attach the Third Clip to the #1 Spark
Plug or the #1 Distributor Terminal
Actron Manufacturing Co.

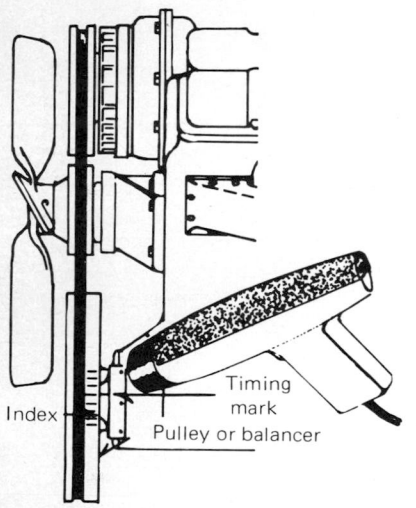

Timing Marks on the Crankshaft Pulley of a
Car
DIXCO

remove the big wire from the center of your distributor cap and lay it on something metal to
ground it. Then turn the key in the ignition to
"bump" the starter without starting the engine.
This will turn the pulley, and as it turns, a set of
lines should come into view. These are your timing
marks. A pointer attached to the engine block usually points to these marks. To set your timing, you
will have to get the pointer to point to the correct
timing mark while the engine is running.

7 Look at your spec sheet to see what your timing
degree should be. It will say something like "10°@
550," which means that you want to line the pointer up with the 10° timing mark when the engine is
idling at 550 rpm. It may say something about
"BTDC" or "ATDC." This simply means that your
timing marks will have a line labeled "0," with
marks above and below it, and these will be the
marks that come before and after the "0," which is
"top dead center" (**TDC**). Depending on the direction that the wheel rotates, the lines that come into
view before the "0" (or TDC mark) are "before top
dead center" (BTDC), and the ones that appear
after TDC are "after top dead center" (ATDC). In
case you are curious, "top dead center" is the point
at which the piston has reached its highest point in

the cylinder and compression is greatest. (How's that for cocktail party chatter?)

8 Have you found your timing marks? Do you know which mark you want to set your timing at? Then use a piece of chalk to make that mark stand out. You can also chalk the tip of the pointer to make it more visible.

9 Attached to the side of your distributor is a round gizmo called a **vacuum advance**. Disconnect the little rubber hose that comes from it, and put a piece of tape on the end of the hose—or stick a screw in it—to seal it off.

10 Start your engine, making sure that your emergency brake is on and that you are in "Park" or "Neutral", and let the car warm up.

11 If your dwell meter/tachometer is still hooked up, look at the rpm line to see if the car is idling at the proper speed. If it isn't, you will have to adjust your **idle**. You will find instructions for doing this in Chapter 7. It is a simple matter of turning one screw, so don't be dismayed. And just think, if your idle is off, you have been wasting fuel and your car hasn't been running properly.

12 Is your car idling properly now? Fine! Now aim the timing light at the timing marks and press the button on the light. The fact that the light is hooked to your #1-cylinder spark plug means that current will pass through the light every time your #1 plug "fires." This makes the light go on and off with a strobe effect. The timing marks should appear to be standing still, although the crankshaft pulley is actually turning rapidly. Is the pointer pointing to the correct mark? If it isn't, you must adjust your timing.

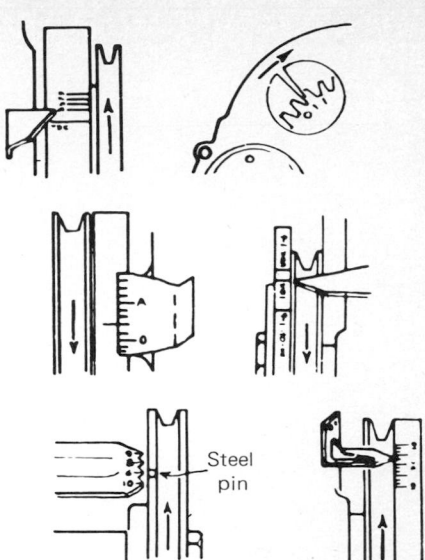

Timing Mark Locations on Various Popular Cars
DIXCO

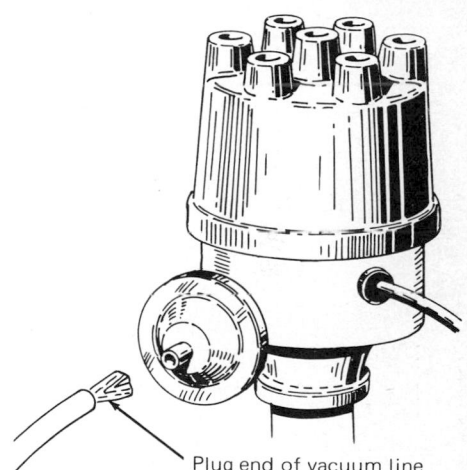

Plug end of vacuum line

The Vacuum Advance Shown Disconnected
Actron Manufacturing Co.

How to Adjust Your Timing

1 On the base of your distributor shaft, below the distributor, is a nut called the **distributor hold-down clamp**. Use a combination wrench to loosen this nut so the distributor can turn a bit on the shaft when you grasp the vacuum advance and move it back and forth. If you have trouble reaching the hold-down clamp, use your *distributor wrench*.

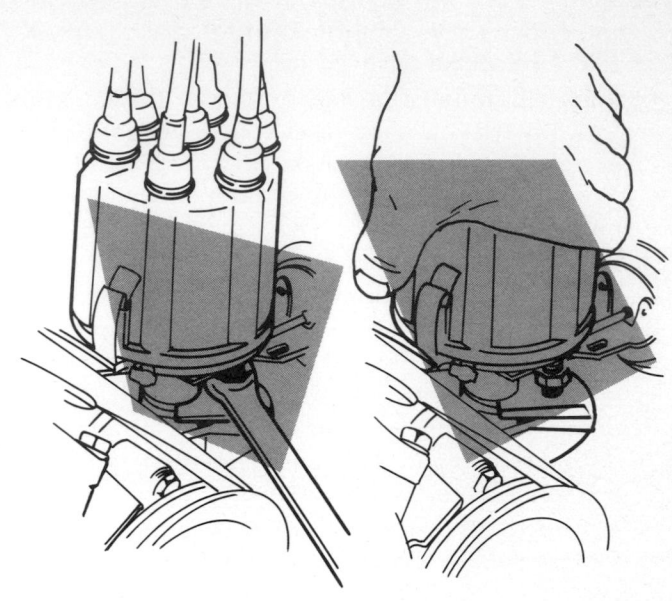

How to Adjust Your Timing
Delco-Remy Division, General Motors Corp.

To change the timing, the clamp holding the distributor to the engine block must first be slightly loosened. The entire distributor is then turned in the direction of rotation of the rotor to retard the timing. To advance the timing, turn the distributor in the direction opposite the rotating rotor. Tighten the hold-down clamp securely after adjustment is completed.

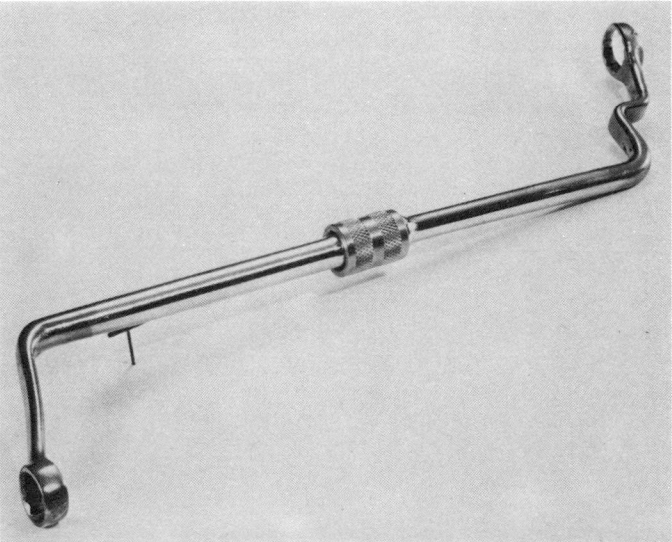

Offset Distributor Wrench
K-D Manufacturing Co.

2 Move the distributor *a little bit* on the shaft, then shine your timing light at the timing marks again. Is the pointer nearer the right mark? Is it farther away? Then you have moved the distributor in the wrong direction. Go back and move it the other way.

3 Now go back and check again with the timing light. Continue doing this until the pointer is pointing to

the correct timing mark. If your idle speed changes, adjust your idle to specifications and recheck your timing. Then tighten the distributor hold-down clamp again, making sure you don't move the distributor when you do it. Check again with the light. Are the timing marks dead on? Good! (You can be off a little bit without causing trouble, but be as accurate as you can without driving yourself crazy.) You now have your car timed perfectly, and this will lead to much better engine performance and fuel consumption. And cut down on air pollution.

4 Shut off your engine, and disconnect the timing light and the tach/dwell meter. Be sure to remove the metal extension if you've used onc on your #1 plug, and put the boot back on the plug.

Well, you've changed your spark plugs, serviced your distributor, and checked your dwell, idle, and timing. You have just completed a basic tune-up! If you've had a little trouble, would it have been worth $40 to $90 to avoid it? (As I write this book, the cost of tune-ups seems to be going up daily.) And you *know* that all the work has been done, and done properly. If you are still game, there are a couple of other things that you can do to be sure your engine is operating at peak efficiency. If you are pooped, you can check them tomorrow, or next weekend, without ruining anything. Then, make it a habit to set aside an hour or two on a specific day each month for your under-the-hood check.

Under-the-Hood Check

We all know people who are chronic "tire kickers." These are the people who habitually walk around their car, kicking the tires to make sure they aren't flat, before they get in and drive off. These are the same people who habitually open and close all the cabinet doors in the kitchen and turn the gas jets to make sure they are completely off, every time they go past the stove. We tend to laugh at them, and yet they are probably rarely caught with flat tires, open cabinets, or leaking gas. We can learn a little from these people and make a habit of checking the little things under the hood of our cars—maybe not *every* time we

go anywhere, but definitely once a month and before starting out on long trips. I've provided a Maintenance Record sheet at the back of this book to help you keep track of what you've checked and what you've replaced.

What should you check now? Well, you are probably already doing a lot of these things. Here they are:

Radiator Check

1 Open the cap on your radiator and check to see if the water in it is running low. You should be able to see the water a couple of inches below the cap. If the level is low, add water or coolant. Tap water is fine. Since you will be doing this *before* driving anywhere, you won't have to be careful about removing the cap. But if you should have to remove a radiator cap from a car that has been running, be sure to turn to Chapter 8 for instructions on how to remove radiator caps from hot engines!

If the water in your radiator looks pinkish, that's the coolant, or antifreeze. If the water looks rusty or has things floating around in it, you should flush your radiator and add new coolant. You can find details on how and how often to do this in Chapter 8.

2 While you are messing around with your radiator, feel the big hoses that go into the top and come out of the bottom of the radiator. If they are leaking, cracked, bulgy, or squishy, they should be replaced. It's easy to do this—see instructions in Chapter 8.

Fan Belt Check

Take a look at the belt that goes around the fan and the alternator (or generator) on your car. Is it cracked or frayed inside or outside? If it is, it should be replaced. Is the inside of the belt glazed and shiny? This means it should be replaced, too. Does the belt "give" more than half an inch when you press on it midway between the alternator and the fan? You might be able to adjust it if the belt is otherwise in good condition. If not, replace it.

Here's how to tighten your fan belt:

1 Loosen the nuts and bolts that secure the alternator bracket.

How to Replace Your Fan Belt
The Gates Rubber Company

1. Loosen the alternator (or generator) by loosening the pivot bolt.

2. Loosen the adjustment bolt.

3. Move the alternator toward the block by grasping the belt and pulling sharply upward. If the belt is broken or missing, use a hammer handle to move the alternator.

4. Remove the old belt by slipping it off the alternator pulleys and working it up and over the fan blades.
   NOTE: On some cars the fan is too close to the radiator to slip it into the crankshaft and alternator pulley grooves.
5. With a new belt, reverse the process. Work the new belt down and over the fan blades and slip it into the crankshaft and pulley grooves.

6. Pull the alternator by hand until the belt is snug. Then use a hammer handle to apply leverage until there is about $1/4$ to $1/2$ inch of "play" on the belt. Use that hammer handle carefully to avoid applying pressure to parts of the engine or alternator which could be damaged. Tighten the adjustment bolt.

7. Run the engine for about 15 minutes at varying speeds, and check the belt again for the proper amount of tension. After about 100 miles of driving, check the belt again. New belts will stretch. If it has more than $1/4$ to $1/2$ inch of play, readjust the tension.

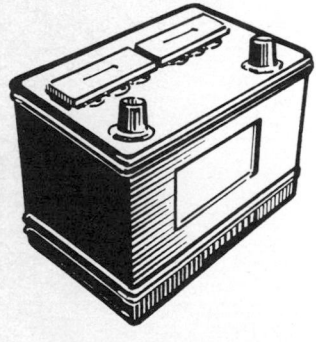

2 Pull the alternator back, away from the fan end of the belt, so that the belt is drawn tighter. Then tighten the nuts and bolts. Check again after about 100 miles of driving to see if it has loosened again.

If you want to do it yourself, go to the auto parts store with the year, make, and model of your car. Buy the fan belt you need. Then follow the instructions in the "How to Replace Your Fan Belt" illustration.

Keep the old belt in the trunk of your car for emergencies. If replacing it yourself does not seem worth the effort, you can have the fan belt adjusted or replaced at almost any service station.

Battery Check

Two Types of Battery Covers

1 Open those little caps, or remove the bars, on the top of your battery. Look inside. If you can see the tops of the plates inside the battery, add water. This should be distilled water, or water with a low mineral content.

Caution: Never open a battery with a lighted cigarette in your mouth. For that matter, don't smoke when working around your car. Batteries are filled with acid, which generates hydrogen gas, so you want to be careful when working around them.

2 The cruddy deposits that form in lovely colors on the top of your terminals are made by this acid. Brush it off with a wire *battery brush*, or remove it with some baking soda and water. Try to avoid getting the powdery stuff on your hands or clothes, but if you do, just wash it off with water *right away* and neither you nor your clothes will be damaged. If you coat the terminals with grease and stick two pennies near each terminal, you will prevent these deposits from forming.

3 Check to see that the wires leading to the terminals are not frayed. If they are, they should be replaced, or the battery may short circuit. A battery that is kept clean and filled with water should last a long

Battery Brush
K-D Manufacturing Co.

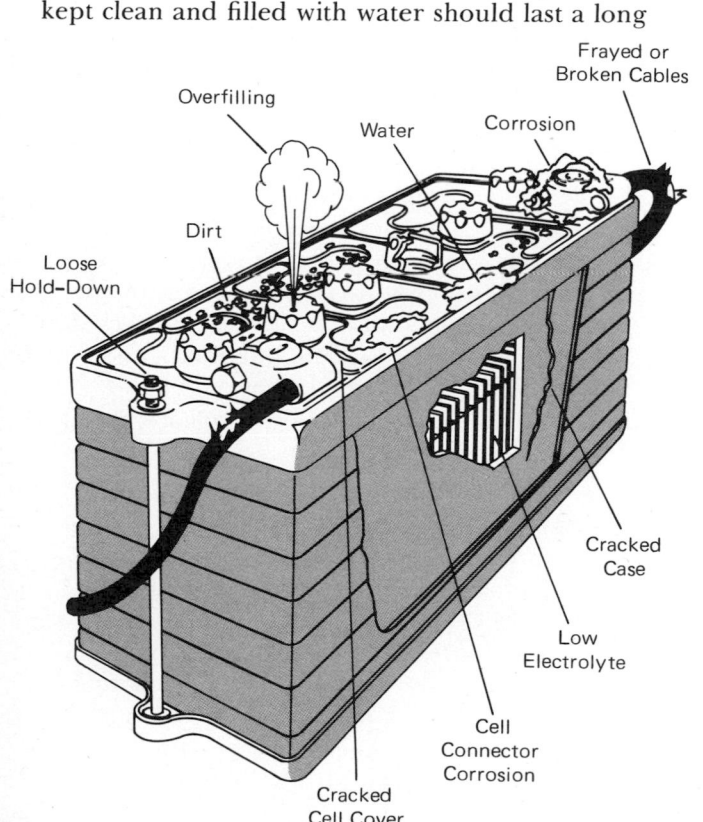

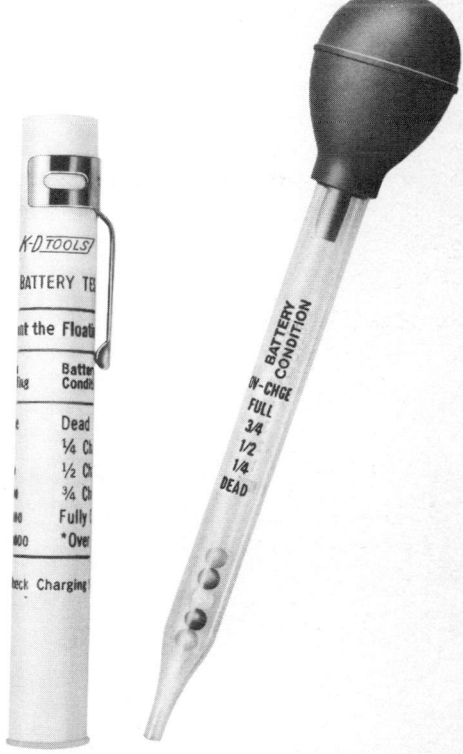

(*left*) Check Your Battery for These Problems
Automotive Parts & Accessories Association (APAA)
(*right*) Battery Tester
K-D Manufacturing Co.

time. By the way, if those caps or bars look beyond help, you can buy replacements cheaply at the auto supply store.

4 Check the rest of these trouble areas shown in the illustration on page 103.

5 If your battery has been acting up lately—if you are having trouble starting your car or your lights dim out—or if the battery is very old, buy a battery tester and check to see if the acid level is high enough. These testers cost less than $1, and you simply draw some of the battery fluid (**electrolyte**) into the tester and look at the floating balls inside it. A scale on the tester will tell you the condition of the battery fluid. If you get a very low reading, you can get the fluid changed at a service station. But if they tell you that the condition of the plates inside the battery is also deteriorating, you are probably going to have to buy a new one.

Hose Check Walk around the hood area, squeezing every hose you encounter. If you meet any that are leaking, bulgy, soft and squishy, or hard and brittle, turn to Chapter 8 for instructions on how to replace them. Replacing a hose is an easy job. It pays to replace hoses *before* they break; any saving of time or effort is not worth the aggravation of having your trip come to an abrupt stop on the freeway because of a broken hose. Most emergency trucks do not carry spare hoses (they'd have to carry too many different kinds, and they don't have the time to change them on the road), and you may end up paying an expensive tow charge for $2 worth of hose that could have been replaced ahead of time in about 10 minutes.

Oil Check Sticking out of the side of the engine block is a little **dipstick** with a ring on the end of it. That's the one the gas station attendant is always showing you and saying, "Looks like it needs oil. Shall I add some?" Now, look at it yourself. First, be sure that your engine is cold or has been shut off for a few minutes. Then, pull the little stick out and wipe it off on a clean rag. Now shove the stick back in again. If it gets stuck on the way in, turn it around. The pipe it fits into is

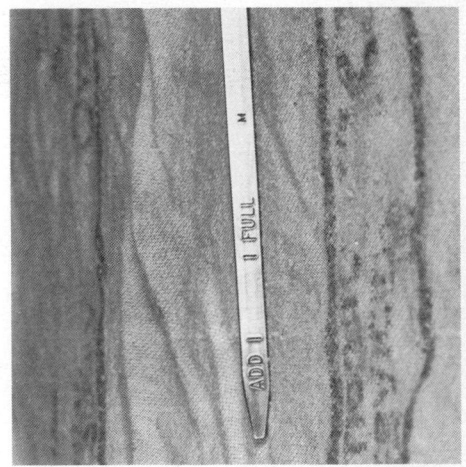

Where to Find the Oil Dipstick on Many
Popular Cars
Richard Freshman

curved, and the metal stick will bend naturally in the
direction of the curve if you put it back the way it
came out. Now pull it out again and look at the tip of
the stick. You will see a film of oil. Does the oil film
reach only to where it says "add oil" on the dipstick?

Or does it reach to where it says "full"? Is the film of
oil on the dipstick very black and gooky? Stick the tip
of your finger in it. Does it leave your fingertip dirty
when you wipe it off? Then you should probably have
your oil changed. Chapter 12 will tell you how to
change your oil yourself. It's easy and will save you a
lot of money.

Let's say that your oil looks clean enough but that it
only reaches to the "add oil" level on the dipstick. You
can get some oil next time you fill up at the gas
station, or you can buy a can at the auto supply store
and add it yourself. Chapter 12 will help you to determine the proper weight oil for your car, and provides
instructions for locating the place to add it.

An Oil Dipstick
Richard Freshman

Automatic Transmission Fluid Check

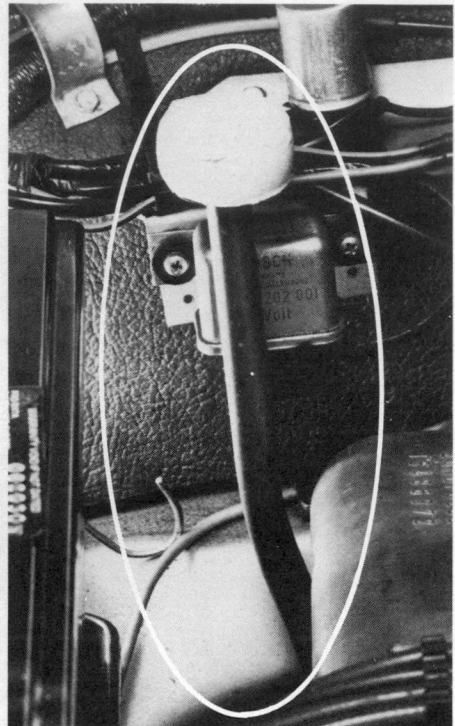

Where to Find the Transmission Dipstick on Many Popular Cars
Richard Freshman

Look toward the rear of the engine, and you will find another dipstick handle. This one is sticking out of your **transmission**, where the end of the crankshaft meets the gears and turns miraculously into a drive-shaft, remember? Let your engine run with the car in "Park." When it is warm, leave the engine running and pull out the dipstick. Wipe it with a clean, lint-free rag. Reinsert it and pull it out again. If the stick shows that you need more **transmission fluid**, buy it and put it in yourself, down the same hole the dipstick fits into.

If you have a Ford with an **automatic transmission**, you need Type F transmission fluid (if your owner's manual specifies Type A, use Type F anyway, it's better). If you have a General Motors car, or one from another popular manufacturer, you need Dexron transmission fluid. Check your owner's manual, or with your dealer, if you aren't sure; or have your service station put it in for you the first time and check to see which kind they use.

Of course, if you have a car with a manual (standard) transmission, disregard all of this. The grease level in **manual transmissions** must be checked with the car on a hoist, to enable the mechanic to easily reach a plug in the bottom of the transmission. It's best not to monkey around with this yourself. But the next time your car is in for repairs, or for lubrication, have them check the level for you.

If the transmission fluid on the dipstick looks or smells burnt or has particles in it, have the fluid drained and changed by a mechanic. It should be pinkish and almost clear.

Incidentally, if your car has been hesitating when you change gears, the first thing to check is the transmission fluid level before you let anyone start talking about "bands." If you are burning white smoke from under your car, you probably need transmission fluid badly, although it can also be a bad **vacuum modulator**. If the smoking has been going on for a long time, you may need a new transmission!

Brake Fluid Inspection

On the driver's side of your car, usually up near the firewall, is a little box or bottle with pipes, or a pipe,

coming from it. This is your **master cylinder**. It holds
the **brake fluid** that gets pushed down the lines to
each wheel of your car when you step on the brake
pedal. If there is insufficient brake fluid, your car
won't stop properly. So, let's check to be sure that
there's enough brake fluid in your master cylinder.
You can find instructions on how to open your master
cylinder and how to buy the proper brake fluid in
Chapter 10. Newer master cylinders have two chambers as a safety feature. This way, if one well of brake
fluid goes dry—owing to a leak in the brake lines, or
something like that—then the other chamber still has
enough fluid in it to stop the car. Is the brake fluid up
to within ½ inch or so of the cap? Then you are O.K.
If it isn't, get some brake fluid and add it. Be careful
not to get brake fluid on anything painted. It eats
paint. If there are spills, wipe them up and get rid of
the rag. Be sure not to get grease or oil into your
brake fluid (you can cause this by wiping your master
cylinder with a greasy or oily rag), because either will
ruin your hydraulic brake system. One more thing:
Don't open a can of brake fluid and leave it standing
around. If the air gets to it for as little as 15 minutes,
the fluid is ruined. (Air oxidization lowers its boiling
point.) So keep it tightly closed until you are ready to
use it, and if you have some left over, throw the stuff
away.

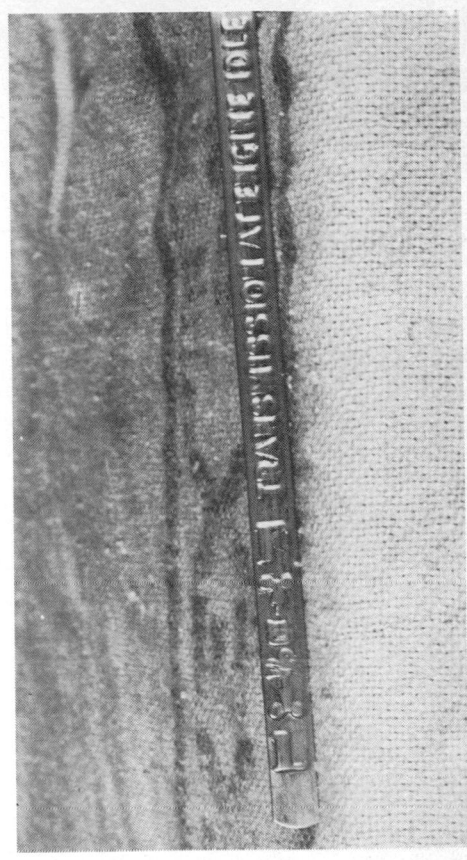

A Transmission Dipstick
Richard Freshman

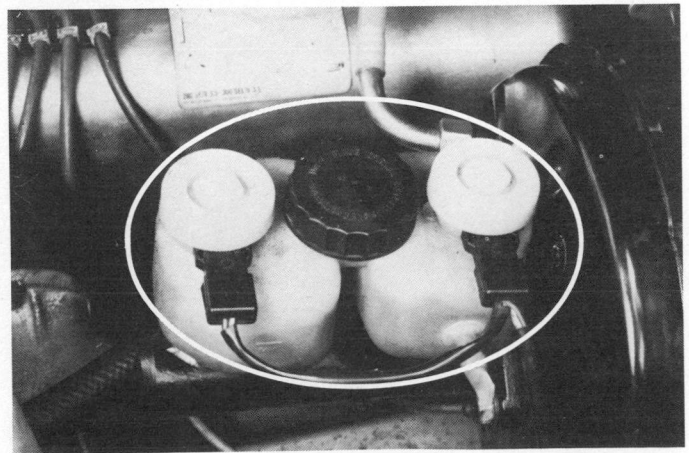

Where to Find the Master Cylinder on Many
Popular Cars
Richard Freshman

Power-Steering Fluid Check

Locate the **power-steering pump** in your car. Your owner's manual should tell you where it is. Unscrew the cap and check to see that the fluid is up to the fill mark on the dipstick, or near the top of the bottle. If it isn't, get some automatic transmission fluid and add it.

NOTE: If any of the water, oil, transmission, brake, or power-steering fluid levels are very low and it has been only a short time since that particular fluid was added to your car, it might be a wise idea to find out why you are losing fluid. Your garage attendant has a special device to locate leaks in your cooling system. It is a replacement radiator cap that has a short hose attachment that leads to a meter and a hand pump. If you ask him to pressure-test your radiator, he will put the cap on your radiator and use the pump to pump air into your cooling system. This increases the pressure in the cooling system to where it generally is when your engine has been running. (The meter tells him when the proper pressure is reached.) If you have a leak in your cooling system, the pressure will make the water squirt out of wherever the leak is.

Similar devices will give you the answers to other fluid-loss problems. It is usually simply a leaky hose, or a gasket that has come loose. Sometimes a loss of

Where to Find the Power Steering Pump on Many Popular Cars
Richard Freshman

transmission fluid, or radiator water, can be cured with a single dose of the proper **sealer**. It is wise to get professional advise about leaks, but be sure that they cover the simple, inexpensive answers (like changing a hose or adding sealer) before you let them sell you expensive parts (like water pumps) or major overhauls.

Windshield Washer Fluid Check

Under your hood there is a plastic bottle or bag that connects to the washers on your windshield wipers. Is it full of liquid? If not, you can fill it with any one of a variety of windshield washer solutions. Some are concentrated, and are mixed with water before adding, or you can use a home window cleaner. Don't use detergent, however. It can leave a residue that can plug up your lines, and it isn't easy to drive with suds all over your windshield!

If you live in an area that gets cold in the winter, you can buy a premixed washer solution that contains antifreeze. This comes in quart and gallon sizes and will keep your windshield clean while it prevents the liquid from freezing up in cold weather.

If your wipers have been making a mess of your windshield, buy new blades for them. These are generally inexpensive, and usually just slide or snap into place. Consult your owner's manual, if you can't figure it out by looking—or ask the person in the auto parts store to tell you how the blades are inserted.

Wiring Check

Feel the wires that you encounter under the hood. If they feel hard and inflexible, if there are bright metal wires showing through the insulation, or if the wires look corroded or very messy where they attach to various devices, they may need to be changed before they short out. Have a garage do the rewiring until you really get to be an expert.

Tire Pressure Check

And lastly, for those tire kickers among us, buy a *tire pressure gauge* ($1.50 or less), and check the pressure in each of your tires. Chapter 11 has full instructions on how to perform this easy task. Tires that are low wear down faster and make your car harder to steer. Tires that have too much pressure may blow out or steer erratically. So try to keep them within the manufacturer's specified range.

You're through for the day! You know that your car is in tune and that it has had everything it needs in terms of fuel, oil, water, and other exotic beverages. And you did it all yourself! Doesn't it feel good? There is nothing like working on your own car for instant rewards. Get in and drive it around. It feels smoother, right? The pickup is better. The car is happier, and you can hear the engine purring. Your car knows that *you* did it, and it has drawn you closer. Silly romanticizing? Well, either I have an extremely affectionate car or a wild imagination.

For more tangible evidence, I offer this: A few months ago I showed my husband (who used to run at the sight of anything mechanical) how to do everything in this chapter. After just changing his spark plugs and servicing his distributor, his mileage increased from 10 miles per gallon to 17.5 miles per gallon. He was so impressed that the next weekend he changed his radiator hoses and did his under-the-hood inspection (which involved fixing a windshield washer pump that had gotten stuck), and now he is a confirmed do-it-yourselfer. This was a relief to me, because I had visions of taking care of *two* cars, and that is *one* car too many for a "working girl"—unless she is a garage mechanic!

Now that you are hooked, let's get on to the Fuel System so that you can see what *really* makes that engine run and can learn to tune your carburetor.

The Fuel System:
The Heart and
Lungs of Your Car

Let's go back to our earlier discussion of how an **internal combustion engine** works. We zipped through it rather quickly, way back in Chapter 3, but now you are sufficiently sophisticated about cars to bear a couple of additional technical details. It is always easier to work on a machine that you understand, and if you are going to get involved with your **fuel system**, you should be able to relate to it in terms of what it does to make your engine operate efficiently.

Basically, the fuel system stores the fuel for the car; passes it along to the **carburetor**, which mixes it with air; and sends it on its way to the engine. Probably the most coherent way to get this stuff across to you is to take each step in the process separately, discuss its form and function, and let the total picture emerge from the relationship of its parts. With characteristic perversity, let's begin at the rear of the car and work our way forward. . . .

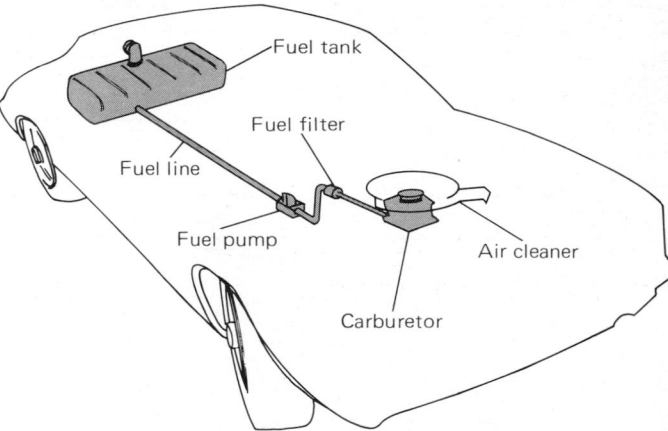

The Fuel System
Automotive Information Council (AIC)

The Fuel Tank   The **fuel tank** is a metal container located under the trunk compartment of most cars, although others have some fairly interesting other locations for it. Your owner's manual will tell you where yours is located, but since fuel tanks very rarely go wrong, you probably won't have to deal with it personally.

Inside the fuel tank is a little float that bobs up and down on the surface of the fuel. It sends messages to the fuel gauge on your dashboard so you can tell when it is necessary to buy more gasoline.

Since the rest of the space in the fuel tank, above the fuel level, is filled with air—and since air contains quite a bit of water vapor—on cool mornings the water in the air tends to condense on the sides of the fuel tank, and elsewhere. This water vapor can rust the insides of your fuel tank, it can mix with the fuel, and it can act in a variety of pesky ways to keep your car from operating efficiently. Of course, if you keep your fuel tank well filled, there will be less room for air and therefore less water vapor hanging around. This is an excellent reason for *not* driving around until your fuel gauge reads "Empty."

Another reason for making those extra trips to the gas station is that the rust that is formed by the water vapor in the air tends to sink to the bottom of the fuel tank. These sediments can do no harm as long as they are happily sloshing about in the bottom of the tank. But if you let the fuel level in the tank get too low, the fuel that gets fed to your engine could be like the last bit of coffee in the bottom of the pot—full of sediment that tends to stick in the throat. Some tanks have filters to prevent this, but they can get choked up if you consistently drive on an empty tank.

Why You Should Keep Your Fuel Tank Full

It might make those refueling trips more fun—and cheaper too—to turn them into another do-it-yourself adventure. Since the energy crisis, some gas stations have offered their customers the option of operating the pumps themselves and buying the gasoline at a lower price. This kind of consumer self-sufficiency has a lovely "rightness" about it. Everybody wins. The station attendants can devote their time to more financially-rewarding projects, and the customer gets a lower price.

Here's how to pump your own gas:

1 Look at the price window on the pump. If there is a price registered there, have the attendant clear the machine so that the price window reads "$0.00."
2 Move the little handle on the pump to the "ON" position.
3 Remove the cap from your fuel tank.
4 Take the pump nozzle off the pump and place it into the fuel tank opening.

How to "Fill 'Er Up" Yourself

5 There is a trigger on the pump nozzle. When you press it, gasoline flows out of the hose and into your fuel tank. There is usually a little latch near the trigger which will keep the trigger open so that you don't have to stand there holding it. Don't worry about overflows; these pumps automatically stop pumping gasoline when your tank is almost full.

6 When the gasoline stops flowing (you'll know because those numbers in the window of the pump will stop moving), remove the pump nozzle from your fuel tank. If you want to bring the price up to an even figure, you can add a small additional amount of gasoline by pressing the trigger on the pump nozzle and watching the figures on the pump. I don't do this, because I don't want to overfill my tank. My tank cap is old, and if the gasoline is right up to the top of the tank, it might leak out. Another reason for not "topping off" your tank is that if you fill up when the car is cold and then you park it in the sun, the gas will expand and run out through an overflow outlet, causing waste, pollution, and a fire hazard.

7 Return the pump nozzle to the pump. Find the attendant who will then write the bill for the amount shown on the pump. *Don't* clear the pump, or you will find yourself unable to prove how much gasoline you've taken, and that could lead to a very unhappy station-attendant/customer relationship!

While you are standing around waiting for the fuel tank to fill up, you can divert yourself in a variety of ways. You can get a couple of those treated towels and some water and wash your windshield. Or you could whip out your tire gauge and check your tires and maybe add some air. Most pump areas have water faucets, towels, and air hoses near them. Or you can kibitz with the attendant about cars and what you've been doing to yours. Most attendants are totally enchanted with customers, especially female customers, who do their own work. I haven't encountered any attendant whose first reaction was that I was going to deprive the station of its income. Most of them are delighted to have found a fellow car freak. Once you've made friends, they won't react too badly if you have to drop in occasionally to get a little help.

O.K., now your fuel tank is nice and full. What happens next?

The **fuel pump** under the hood of your car pumps the gasoline through the **fuel lines**, which run under your car from the fuel tank to the **carburetor**.

We aren't going to get into the inner secrets of the fuel pump, here. If your fuel pump goes wrong, I'd let a professional take care of it, for now. *But*, before you let anyone talk you into buying a new one, be sure the trouble really does reside in the fuel pump. Remember, any problem that seems to be the result of a faulty fuel supply could be caused by a variety of other things. There could be a block in the fuel lines, your fuel filter could be stuffed up, or the problem could be in your carburetor.

An easy way to see if fuel is getting pumped to the carburetor is simply to locate the hose that carries the fuel from the fuel pump to the carburetor, unhook it at the carburetor end, and stick the end of the hose in a clean can. Then have someone start the car while you see if fuel comes out of the hose. Be careful not to spill the gasoline—it can cause a fire. If fuel comes out of the hose, your fuel pump is doing its job and the trouble is farther up the line, in the carburetor, the fuel filter, etc. Be sure to shut the engine off before the fuel overflows the can.

If your fuel pump does need replacing, a rebuilt one is often as good as a new one, and a lot less expensive. So ask your garage to locate a rebuilt fuel pump for your car. Some manufacturers supply rebuild kits and you can take your pump apart with a screwdriver and rebuild it for a few dollars, if you are ambitious.

The Fuel Pump

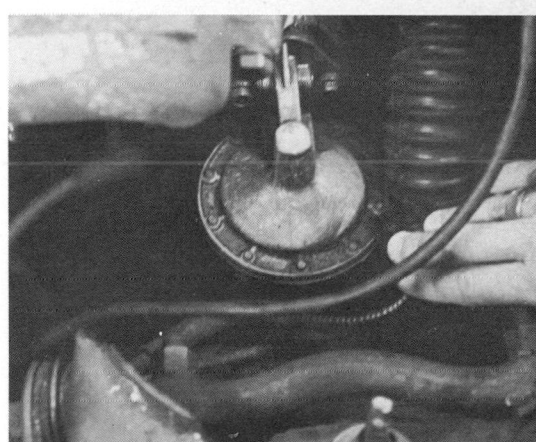

The Fuel Pump at Home
Richard Freshman

Between the fuel pump and the carburetor is a little metal cylinder called a **fuel filter**. It does exactly that. As the fuel passes along the hose, it goes through this thing, and a small screen inside it traps the dirt and rust that might have got into your fuel (especially if you've been riding around most of the time on a near-empty tank). It is wise to change this filter about once a year, and we'll get into how to do that in the next chapter.

The Fuel Filter

The Carburetor

The **carburetor** is probably the most easily located part under the hood of your car. It usually sits under a large, round, pot-shaped thing that dominates the view under your hood. This is called an **air cleaner**, and it is easily removed by turning the wing nut situated in the center of the lid and removing the nut and then the entire air cleaner. Smaller cars, especially foreign cars and sports cars, often have more than one carburetor, and these are topped with air cleaners that look like metal cans, neatly in a row.

The main job of the carburetor is to mix the proper proportions of air and fuel together and pass them along in the proper quantity to the engine. Along the way the carburetor performs a couple of other functions, and we'll get into these as we go along.

You may remember that the proper proportion of air to fuel is *one* part of fuel to 15 parts of air, by *weight.* Since air is considerably lighter than gasoline, if we were to view this in terms of the amount of space taken up by these parts, it would come out to one part of fuel to 9,000 parts of air, by *volume.* That's enough air to fill a room 10 feet square for every gallon of gasoline we burn!

The Carburetor is Under the Air Cleaner in Your Car.
Richard Freshman

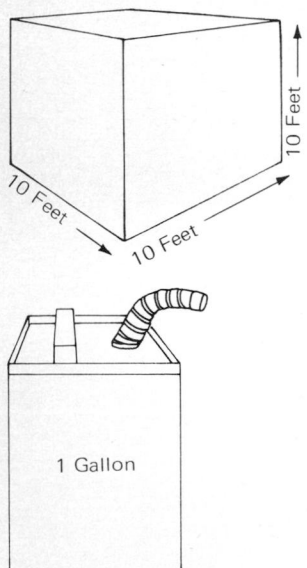

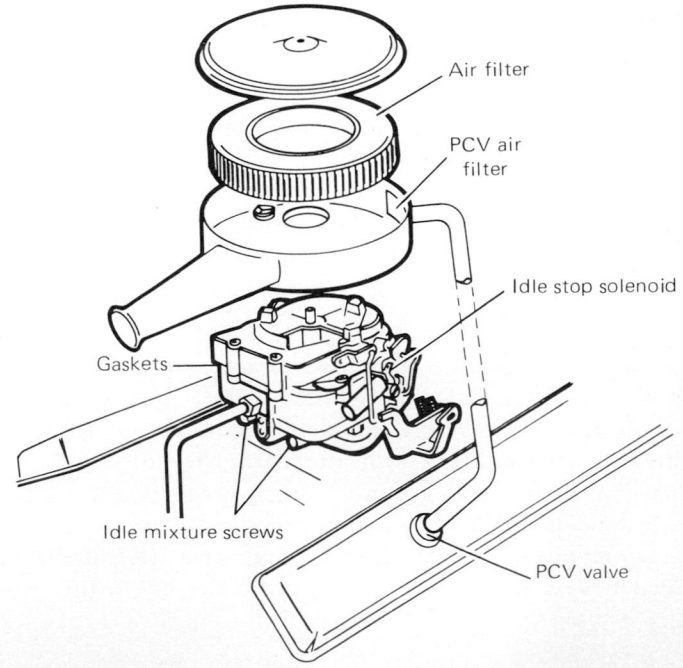

(*above*) For Every Gallon of Fuel, Your Car Consumes Enough Air to Fill a Room 10 Feet Square!
Alexandra Soto

(*right*) The Carburetor and the Air Cleaner
Guaranteed Parts Company

Luckily, the car does not have to store air; it simply draws in astonishing quantities of it through the **air cleaner**. The air passes through an **air filter** located inside the air cleaner and then goes down the throat, or barrel, of the carburetor.

Since dirt and dust particles are extracted from the air by the air filter, you will want to change it at least once a year, as well. We'll get into how you tell if the air filter needs replacement, and how to do it, in Chapter 7.

The air travels down the **carburetor barrel**, and on its way, it passes a small pipe that leads to a fuel reservoir called a **float bowl**, which holds a small supply of gasoline.

The Float Bowl

This small chamber on the carburetor is located next to the carburetor barrel. It contains a small amount of raw fuel to ensure a readily available fuel supply when you start or accelerate the car. This is more efficient than having to pump each new portion of gasoline all the way from the fuel tank at the rear of the car. The amount of fuel that stays in the float bowl is controlled by a little float (surprise!) that bobs up and down on the surface of the fuel in the chamber. The float bowl is kept filled by a hose that leads to it from the fuel pump.

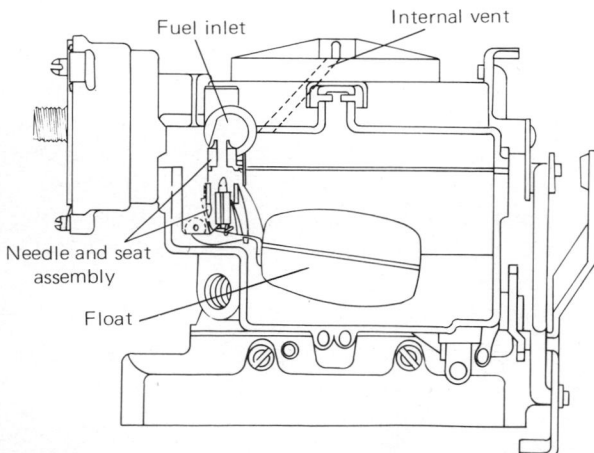

The Float Bowl
Echlin Manufacturing Company

If your car has too little fuel in its float bowl, it is going to hesitate or stall when you want that extra surge of power or when you try to start it in the morning. The float in the float bowl is adjustable, but adjusting it involves taking apart at least a portion of the carburetor. This isn't too hard, but putting the thing back together again can get hairy; so again, if you think your carburetor needs overhauling, let a professional do it. Of course, there are overhaul kits with instructions available, and if you are determined to do the job yourself, look for a good auto repair course and do it under the instructor's supervision.

The Fuel/Air Mixture

As the air passes the small opening at the end of the little pipe that leads to the float bowl, it picks up fuel, and the result is a mist, or a vaporized **fuel/air mixture.** The air and the fuel travel in this form to the cylinders, where combustion is going to occur.

How does the vaporizing process take place? The principle is the same as the one that operates "flit guns." If you look closely at one of these insecticide sprayers you will see that when you push the plunger, you are sending a jet of air past an opening in the top of the chamber where the liquid is stored. The air rushing past the opening creates a vacuum that draws the liquid out of the storage chamber and mixes it with the air. The carburetor works the same way.

The Venturi

Because the faster the air moves, the more liquid it will pick up, the carburetor has been very cleverly designed so that air will pick up speed as it passes through the barrel. Inside the barrel is a chamber called a **venturi**. This gets narrower as it nears the opening that leads to the float bowl. When the air gets to this narrow part of the venturi, it picks up speed, creating a vacuum just at the point where the opening occurs. This draws the fuel out of the float bowl and mixes it with the air. The resulting fuel/air vapor is carried to the cylinder.

In case you are wondering why all this is necessary, you must remember that liquid gasoline will not explode. Oh, it will burn all right, if you drop a match into it, but it will not explode. And it is the pressure caused by the rapid expansion of exploding gases that drives the engine. The only way to get gasoline to explode is to mix it with air. Gasoline/air vapor is explosive; plain old gasoline isn't. This, incidentally, is why so many accidents occur with near-empty gasoline cans. We tend to think that if a can of gasoline is almost empty, it is harmless. This is just when it is at its most dangerous! The "empty" can still contains a tiny bit of gasoline, and remember, we need only one part of gasoline to 9,000 parts of air to get a combustible mixture! So, if there is a lot of gasoline sloshing around in the can, there might be *too much* gasoline to explode. But if all there is is a bit of gasoline vapor, or fumes, it can mix with the air in the "empty" can, and any kind of spark can set off a really big explosion. Gasoline/air vapor is more explosive than TNT! Now you can see why we are not encouraged to store gasoline around the house or in the trunk of the car. If you have an old gasoline can around, throw it out! Fill it with water before you dispose of it so it doesn't do any damage to any innocent bystanders it may encounter. Some people keep gasoline to clean parts with. This is dangerous. Mechanic's Solvent, available at gas stations or auto supply stores, works better, and it has been treated with a flame retardant to keep it from burning too freely.

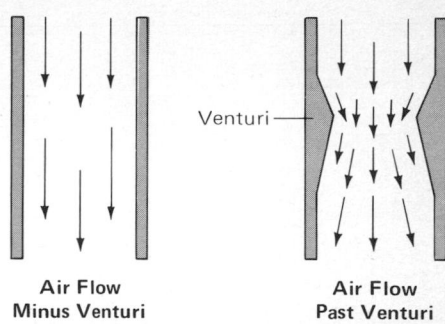

Venturi

| Air Flow Minus Venturi | Air Flow Past Venturi |

How Air Picks Up Speed in the Venturi
Echlin Manufacturing Company

Single-, Double-, and Four-Barrel Carburetors

To increase the amount of fuel/air mixture that is passed along to the engine, auto manufacturers have developed carburetors with more than one barrel. A double-barrel carburetor has two venturis, and a four-barrel carburetor has four venturis. These are generally found on large engines, like V-8s, where more fuel and air is needed fast to supply all those cylinders with stuff to feed on. In a four-barrel carburetor, two of the four barrels are reserved for extra power at high speeds or stress, and you can see why V-8 engines consume more fuel than most four- or six-cylinder engines do. Of course they put out more power, too. And if you like to drive a big, impressive car around—or if you want to drive up hills at high speeds—that's the kind of engine you need. Just don't confuse *power* with *efficiency*. A smaller engine will do just as good a job, if it is not hauling a lot of extra junk around.

You may ask, If that is all the carburetor does, what are all those other gizmos attached to it? Good question. Let's take them in order.

The Choke At the top of the carburetor, looking up at you after you've removed the air cleaner, is the **choke**. This consists of a little **butterfly valve** that can open and close, and a means of adjusting it.

When your car is cold, the butterfly valve will stay closed. This way, when you go out to start your car in the morning, the choke will help you get the car started and warmed up faster. Here's how it does this:

1 When you start your car and the engine is cold, the gasoline condenses on the cold metal parts. As much as ¹/₃ of it can settle out in this way, leaving only ²/₃ of the fuel/air mixture on its way to the engine. This is not enough for proper combustion, and your car won't start properly. The mixture must be enriched.

2 The choke limits the air supply by closing the butterfly valve at the top of the carburetor barrel(s) so there is a greater vacuum created in the venturi.

(*below right*) When You Look Down the Carburetor Barrel, You Can See the Choke Butterfly.
Richard Freshman

(*below left*) The Choke Butterfly Can Restrict the Amount of Air Entering the Venturi.
Echlin Manufacturing Company

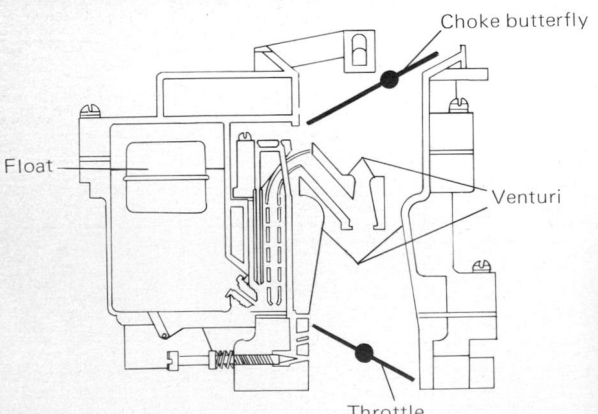

This causes more fuel to come out of the pipe that comes from the float bowl. This larger quantity of fuel mixes with the restricted amount of air, forming a richer mixture. Now, even though some of the fuel condenses on the walls of the pipes leading to the engine, there is still enough left for proper combustion.

3 When the engine warms up, the butterfly valve opens, letting more air into the barrel(s), and the fuel/air mixture returns to normal.

Remember, the choke limits the supply of air entering the venturi. It does not prevent all the air from coming in. The resulting fuel/air mixture is richer than the stuff you usually drive on, but it returns to normal when the car warms up enough to stop the fuel from condensing. Simple, isn't it?

Automatic Chokes

Cars used to have manual chokes, which you controlled by a knob on the dashboard. Today, most cars have an **automatic choke** that works by means of a spring that coils and uncoils in response to the amount of heat present. It is this spring that eventually causes the butterfly valve to open and close.

If you have an automatic choke (see illustrations on pages 146–147 in Chapter 7), chances are it is controlled by a thermostat located on the outside of the carburetor, either at the top of the barrel near the butterfly valve, or near the carburetor at the end of a long rod. The first type looks like a little round cap, and there are little arrows on it that say "Lean" and

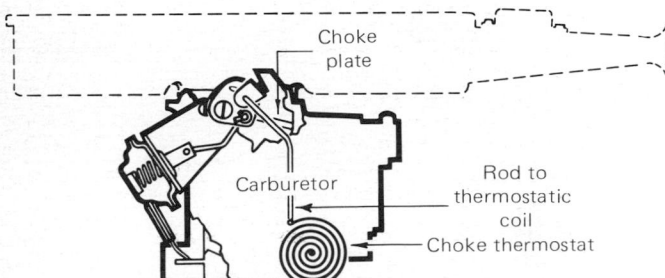

Choke plate

Carburetor

Rod to thermostatic coil

Choke thermostat

The Choke Thermostat Causes the Butterfly to Open and Close.
Guaranteed.Parts Company

"Rich." By turning this knob, you can adjust the proportion of air that is allowed into the carburetor barrel past the butterfly. The second type uses a rod
attached to the thermostat to make the butterfly open
and close. In the next chapter, we'll get into how, and
when, to adjust your automatic choke.

**How to Tell If Your Choke
Is Working**

If you want to see whether or not your choke is
working (and, if you have trouble getting started in
the morning, it may not be working properly), take
the air cleaner off some morning before you start your
car. Does the butterfly valve seem to be closed? If it
isn't, step on the gas pedal a couple of times before
you start the car and it should close. Now, run the car
for a few minutes. (You can run your car with the air
cleaner off, but never drive around like that. The
amount of dirt that gets into your engine will determine the life of your car. This dirt creates the kind of

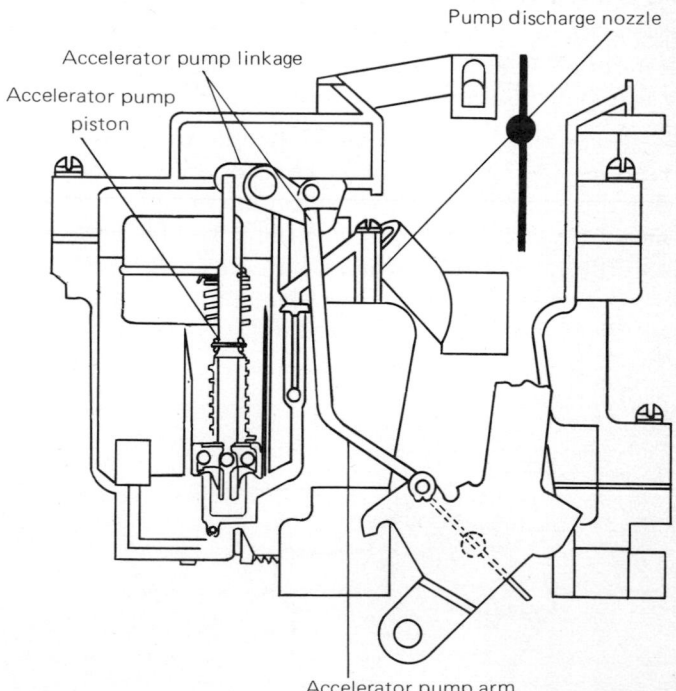

Accelerator Pump System
Echlin Manufacturing Company

wear that causes engines to break down.) By the time the car is warmed up, the butterfly should open so that you can see down the barrel of the carburetor. If you are driving a car with a manual choke, see if the butterfly valve opens and closes when you push the knob on the dashboard in and out, but don't let anyone accelerate the car while you are looking down the carburetor. It could backfire.

If the butterfly valve refuses to open or to close, it may simply be stuck because of poor lubrication or dirt. Try wiggling it with your finger. If that doesn't work, squirt a little carburetor cleaner or automatic choke cleaner on the moving parts. Then wipe them dry and put a drop of oil on them. If this doesn't work, the next chapter will tell you how to adjust your choke properly.

The Accelerator Pump

Have you ever stopped to wonder just what makes your car speed up when you step on the gas pedal? It's really a very simple device, so unsophisticated that you'd think the inventor would have been embarrassed to suggest such a "mickey mouse" gadget.

When you step on the gas pedal to accelerate, there is a rod that connects the pedal to a little lever located on the outside of the carburetor. This little lever pushes on a little piston inside the carburetor which squirts a little extra fuel into the venturi. That extra fuel creates a richer fuel/air mixture, which explodes with a bigger bang in your cylinders, and your car gets that extra push we call "acceleration."

If you have the air cleaner off your carburetor, look for the little lever on the side. (Not the big one, that's the throttle; and we'll get to that in just a minute.) If you push that little lever in, even if the engine is not running, you will see a little squirt of fuel inside the barrel of your carburetor. So, if your car has been hesitating when you step on the gas, it may be that your **accelerator pump** is not working properly. If no gasoline squirts into the carburetor when you push the lever, or if the lever won't move when you try to push it, then that's where the trouble is.

If your **accelerator pump** is not working properly, your carburetor will probably have to be rebuilt (which means taking it apart, cleaning it, and replacing various parts) or replaced. Again, if you need a new carburetor, you may be just as well off with a cheaper, rebuilt one. Ask the person who is going to do the work to try to get one for you.

The Throttle

And now for the bigger lever on the outside of your carburetor. This is the *throttle arm.* It too is attached to your gas pedal. It controls the **throttle**, a butterfly device, very much like the choke butterfly but located at the *bottom* of the carburetor barrel, where it joins the **intake manifold**. The intake manifold is a pipe that branches into as many smaller pipes as you have cylinders. It carries the fuel/air mixture to each cylinder.

The throttle controls the amount of fuel and air that comes into the carburetor. The more air, the higher the vacuum developed in the venturi. The greater the vacuum, the more fuel is drawn out of the float bowl and mixed with the air. The richer the fuel/air mixture, the faster the car will go. At high speeds, the throttle is wide open to allow a lot of air to come into the carburetor. At low speeds, the throttle closes, so less air can get in. If you get someone to sit at the wheel of your car, with the emergency brake on and the car in "Park" or "Neutral," and have them step on the gas pedal while you look at your carburetor, you will see that every time your friend revs up the engine, the throttle arm moves. Now, with no one stepping on the gas, and the car just idling by itself, press the throttle arm with your finger. The car will rev up just as though you were stepping on the gas pedal. What a very simple device! And yet it controls that most important flow of fuel and air which determines how effectively your car performs!

There are a couple of other gizmos on your carburetor that make your car run smoothly. I'll show you in the next chapter how to adjust them, but I thought I'd introduce you to them here:

(*top*) The Accelerator Pump Arm Is Located on the Outside of the Carburetor.
Richard Freshman

(*bottom*) The Throttle Arm Is Also Located on the Outside of the Carburetor.
Richard Freshman

The **idle speed screw** is a little screw located at the bottom of your carburetor, on the outside, but right near the throttle. It keeps the throttle from closing completely when your foot is off the gas pedal and the car is idling. (Idling is what the car is doing when it just sits there humming to itself without moving. Cars **idle** while they wait for stoplights to turn green.) It is important that you locate this screw on your carburetor, because it is easy to adjust and will do wonders for your engine performance and fuel consumption if it is set properly after you've tuned your ignition system. The next chapter is going to tell you how to do this, so get out your owner's manual and hope that it tells you where the idle speed screw is. If not, look at your carburetor and try to identify it. It is near the throttle on the outside of the carburetor. If you turn it clockwise, with a screwdriver, your car will idle faster; counterclockwise, and it will idle more slowly. Do not get it confused with the **idle mixture screw**, however (see page 126).

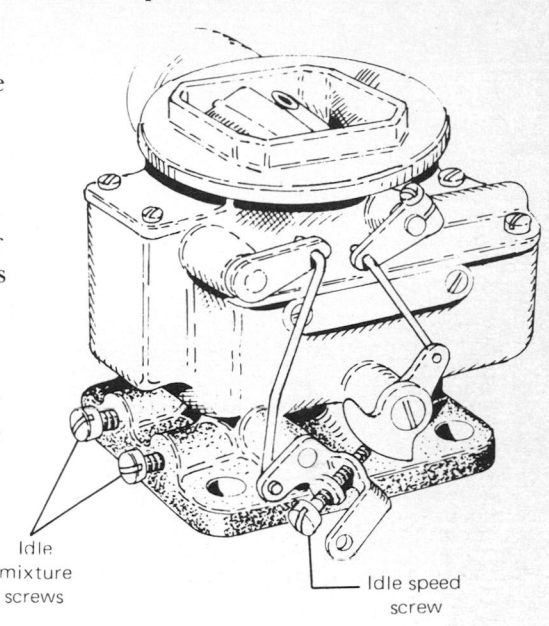

The Idle Speed Screw

Idle mixture screws

Idle speed screw

Some of the newer cars do not have only an idle speed screw and an idle mixture screw; they have an **idle stop solenoid** as well. This is really easy to spot. You can see one in the figure on page 144. Cars with engines with controlled exhaust emissions tend to idle at faster speeds. Often, if such an engine is shut off abruptly, the engine simply cannot stop fast enough and it keeps going, or dieseling. The idle stop solenoid prevents the car from continuing to idle after it has been shut off.

If you think you have an idle stop solenoid on your car, look for a little can-shaped device attached to the carburetor near the throttle. When it is time to tune your carburetor, read the instructions in the next chapter about adjusting the idle stop solenoid.

Some cars do *not* have an idle speed screw. They have an **idle air bleed screw** instead. The theory behind this one is that when the throttle is closed during idling, there should still be some air coming through

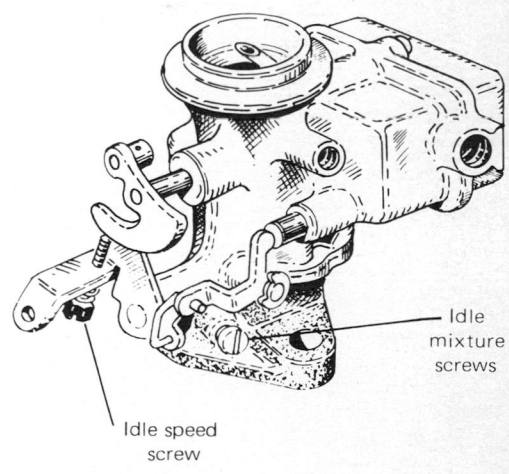

The Idle Stop Solenoid

Idle mixture screws

Idle speed screw

Idle Speed and Idle Mixture Screws on Two Popular Carburetors
Actron Manufacturing Company

The Idle Air Bleed Screw

to prevent the formation of carbon and gum deposits that tend to collect around the throttle area. The idle air bleed screw, or *idle air adjusting screw*, as it is sometimes called, simply determines how much extra air is allowed to come in when the throttle is closed. By turning this screw clockwise, you can decrease the amount of air that gets in and slow down your idle. By turning it counterclockwise, you get more air and more idle speed. Wait for the next chapter before fiddling with it. Air bleed screws are usually found on Lincolns, Caddies, and other big cars.

The Idle Mixture Screw

(We're almost through with the carburetor gadgets now; don't lose heart!)

The **idle mixture screw** looks like the idle speed screw, but it controls the *proportion* of air and fuel that get to your engine while your car is idling. By turning this screw, you can determine how rich the fuel/air mixture will be. If you adjust it properly, you can get maximum engine performance and still save fuel.

Carburetors with more than one barrel can have more than one idle mixture screw. The screw (or screws) can be found in a variety of locations, depending on your car. It can be identified by the fact that if you turn it counterclockwise, the end of the screw will come out of the carburetor. Locate your idle mixture screw(s) in your owner's manual, or ask your friendly garage attendant to identify it for you. We'll get into how to adjust it in the next chapter, with more pictures of all of these adjustment devices to help you locate yours.

I realize that all of this has been a bit complicated. Before we continue to follow that fuel/air mixture into the engine, it might be wise to check yourself to be sure that you have it all straight. Try to see if you can find the following parts on your carburetor, and then tell yourself what each one does. If you have problems, reread the chapter until you get it straight. It may seem like gibberish at first, but I promise you that it will all fall into place! My instructor used to make us promise not to think about what he'd told us until the next class. He'd say, "Forget everything I've said. It will just confuse you if you think about it. When you start to actually work on the car, it will become clear." And you know, it did!

O.K., find these:

Automatic Choke
Butterfly Valve
Float Bowl (just the outside will do)
Accelerator Pump Arm
Throttle Arm
Idle Speed Screw, or, if you don't have one:
Idle Air Bleed Screw
Idle Mixture Screw
Idle Stop Solenoid (you may not have one)

Do you know what these mean?

Venturi
Single-, Double-, Four-Barrel Carburetor
Throttle
Fuel/air Mixture (and what causes the fuel to vaporize)

You do? Then you are ready to get into your engine!

If you take a look at what we've covered in the past few chapters, you will see that you now know about the source, and control, of the three things you must have to drive an **internal combustion engine**. These three things are *air*, *fuel*, and *fire*. (Of course we're not dealing with actual fire here, but rather with a spark that ignites the air and fuel. One should really say "air, fuel, and *ignition*," but "air, fuel, and fire" has a more poetic ring to it—and it's easier to remember.)

Well, if you've got the air and fuel coming together, in the form of a vapor, from the carburetor; and you've got the spark plugs and the distributor timed to provide that all-important ignition spark; then all you need is a spot for that passionate meeting to take place. That rendezvous occurs in the cylinders of your engine, and it is truly a triumph of timing (as all successful rendezvous must be!).

The Engine Block—Where the Action Is

This is what happens:

The Intake Manifold

The fuel/air mixture travels past the throttle at the bottom of the carburetor to the **intake manifold**. (We've already described this cluster of iron pipes, remember?) There are actually *two* sets of manifold pipes. The other set is the **exhaust manifold**, which carries the carbon-monoxide and other vapor wastes away from the engine for disposal. The intake manifold pipes are generally found near the top of the engine, between the carburetor and the engine block. The exhaust manifold is either lower down on the same side of the engine, or on the other side of the cylinder heads.

Inside the engine there are a variety of fascinating objects. At the top are the **cylinder heads**, which contain the mechanisms that allow the valves to open and close to let the fuel/air mixture into the cylinders and allow the burnt gases to leave. You open the cylinder heads to adjust your **valves**.

Below the cylinder heads is the **engine block** itself. This contains the **cylinders**, which in turn contain the **pistons**.

At the bottom of the engine is the **crankcase**, which houses the **crankshaft** and the **oil pan**. Water circulates throughout the engine to keep it cool, and oil

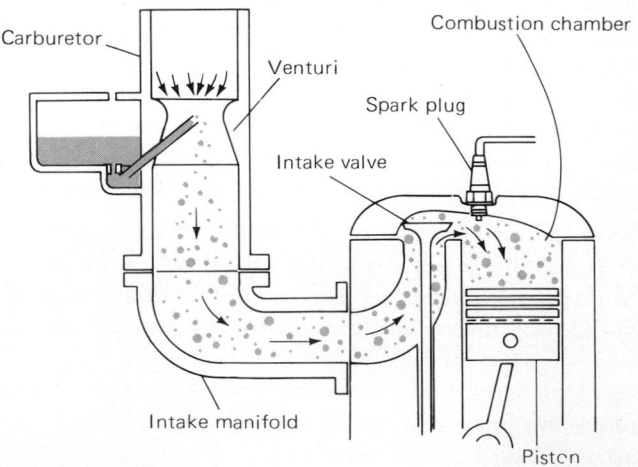

The Fuel/Air Mixture Travels from the Carburetor, Through the Intake Manifold, to the Combustion Chamber, Where Ignition Takes Place.
Echlin Manufacturing Company

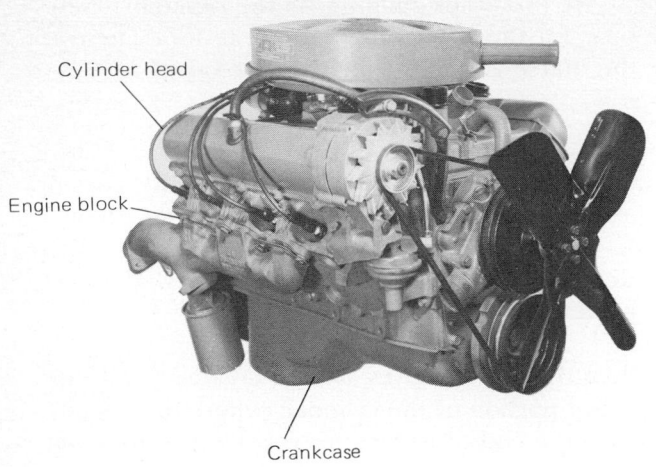

Cylinder head

Engine block

Crankcase

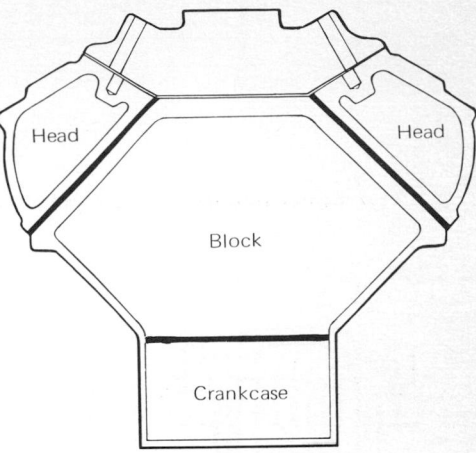

Head

Head

Block

Crankcase

Cylinder Head, Engine Block,
Crankcase—The Main Parts of the Internal
Combustion Engine
Automotive Marketing Division, Dana Corp.

circulates, as well, to keep the parts moving freely.

Let's look inside one of the cylinders and see what
goes on in there.

The Cylinders

A **cylinder** is an empty iron pipe. A **spark plug** is
inserted in the pipe, with its **electrodes** available for
action. Inside the pipe there is a metal **piston**, which
fits snugly against the walls of the cylinder, so nothing
can get past it. There are **piston rings** on the outside
of the piston that ensure that it fits snugly. Those
"ring jobs" that people have to pay for involve taking
the engine apart to replace the rings on the pistons.
This is a time- and labor-consuming job, so it usually
costs a good deal of money. If your car needs one you
generally have to "bite the bullet" and pay. But sometimes people pay for these jobs when they don't really
need them. Or people need ring jobs when simple
maintenance could have prevented the trouble. If you
know how your engine works, you are in a better
position either to prevent the trouble or to determine
if such costly work is really necessary. And that is what
this book is all about.

The piston rides up and down, inside the cylinder, on
a **connecting rod** that attaches to the **crankshaft**. (You
remember that from Chapter 3, right? If you don't,
take another look at that chapter; it will make this a
lot easier to grasp.)

There are two other openings in the cylinder besides the ones for the spark plug and the piston. These are for the **intake valve** and the **exhaust valve**.

The Four-Stroke Power Cycle

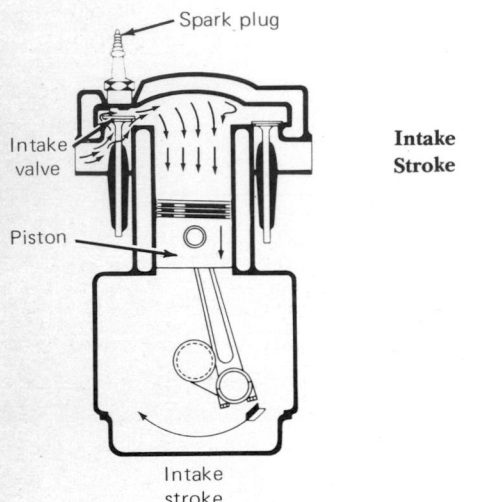

Spark plug

Intake valve

Piston

Intake stroke

Inside the cylinder, the piston (as we've said) goes up and down. Each movement it makes—either up or down—is called a **stroke**. It takes four strokes—down, up, down, and up—to complete the cycle that creates the power to drive the engine.

Intake Stroke

1 When the piston moves *down*, it creates a vacuum in the top portion of the cylinder (where the piston was at the end of its last upstroke). Air cannot get in from the bottom of the cylinder, because the rings on the piston have sealed it off.

2 The **intake valve**, conveniently located at the entrance of the **intake manifold** pipe to the cylinder, opens up and lets the fuel/air mixture into the cylinder. It rushes in to fill the vacuum left by the piston.

The Compression Stroke

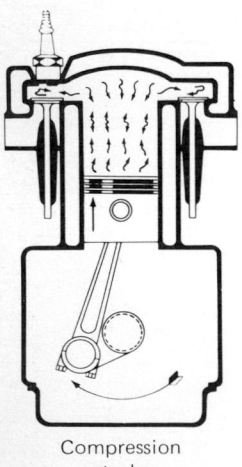

Compression stroke

1 The piston moves back *up*, compressing the fuel/air mixture into a tiny space between the top of the piston and the top of the cylinder. This space is called the **combustion chamber**. It also happens to be where the spark-plug electrode end enters the cylinder. The fuel/air mixture is compressed into about $1/10$ the space it occupied before the piston moved up, and this 10:1 **compression ratio** increases the pressure in the combustion chamber to about 200 psi (pounds per square inch). Normal air pressure is 15 psi. The reason this is necessary is that compression will make the explosion much more intense than it would have been if the fuel/air mixture had been allowed to spread out. So, when the compressed mixture is ignited, the pressure will increase another *four times*, creating a heck of a lot of power when it explodes!

2 At this point, the intake valve has closed, so the compressed mixture can't get out. Both the intake and exhaust valves have seals to ensure that nothing can get past them when they are closed.

1 The spark plug produces a spark across the gap between its electrodes, which ignites the compressed fuel/air mixture.

2 The burning fuel/air mixture explodes, creating intense pressure that forces the piston *down* again. The power that pushed the piston down is transmitted, via the **connecting rod**, to the **crankshaft**. It then travels, via the **drive train**, through the **clutch**, the **transmission**, the **driveshaft**, to the **differential**, and so on to the wheels. (Aren't you glad you reread Chapter 3?)

1 The piston moves *up* again, pushing the burned gases up with it.

2 The **exhaust valve** opens and lets the burned gases out into the **exhaust manifold**.

3 From there, they travel through the exhaust system (which, on newer cars, includes antipollution devices), through the **muffler** and out the **tail pipe** into the air.

Now you can see why your ignition tune-up is so important. If it is done properly, it will ensure that a full measure of electricity is transferred from the battery, amplified by the coil, and directed by the distributor to the proper spark plug at the proper time. If the spark was insufficient, or if it arrived before, or after, the fuel/air mixture was at full compression by the piston, the result would be less power and poorly burned fuel. Consequently, your car would produce more air pollution and use more gasoline—a dangerous, and costly, price to pay for laziness or ignorance.

The Power Stroke

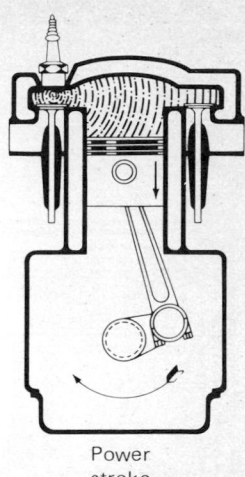

Power stroke

The Exhaust Stroke

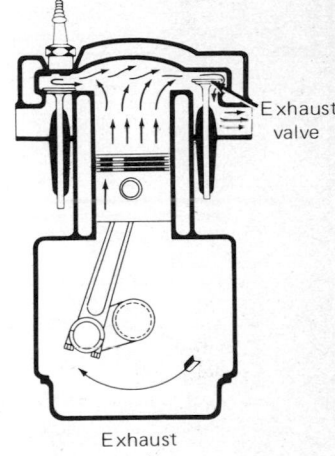

Exhaust valve

Exhaust stroke

The Four-Stroke Power Cycle
Echlin Manufacturing Company

If your car has a **fuel injection** system or a **diesel engine**, it will not have a carburetor. These systems are too difficult to repair yourself and it would be best to call in a professional if problems develop. However, just to give you an idea of how these systems differ from conventional fuel systems, let's stop for a moment and talk about them in general terms so that you can deal with your mechanic properly. Later, if you want all the details, you can refer to books or instruction manuals that deal with them specifically.

Cars without Carburetors

000-131

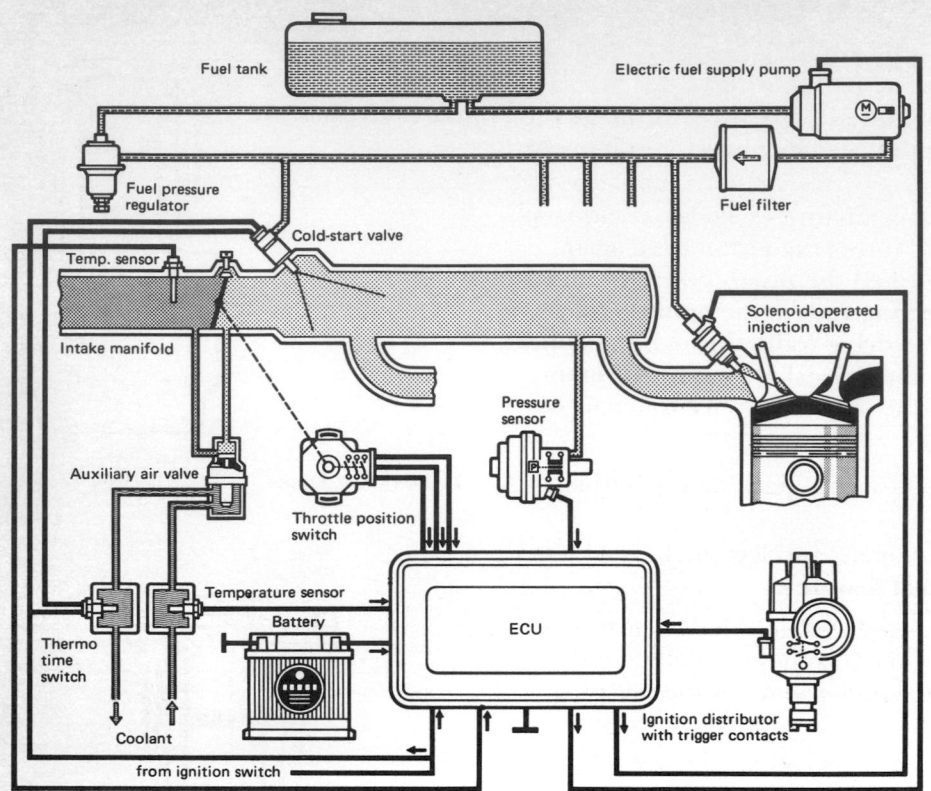

Fuel tank

Electric fuel supply pump

Fuel pressure regulator

Cold-start valve

Temp. sensor

Fuel filter

Intake manifold

Solenoid-operated injection valve

Auxiliary air valve

Pressure sensor

Throttle position switch

Temperature sensor

Battery

ECU

Ignition distributor with trigger contacts

Thermo time switch

Coolant

from ignition switch

Fuel Injection System
Robert Bosch Corporation

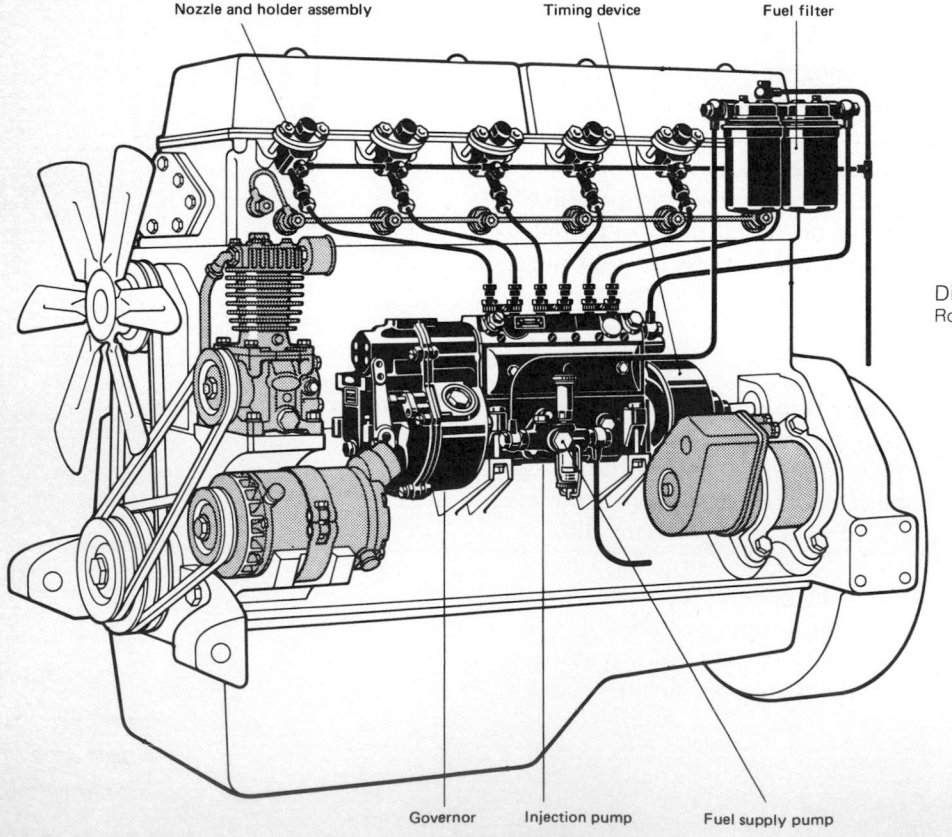

Nozzle and holder assembly

Timing device

Fuel filter

Diesel Engine
Robert Bosch Corporation

Governor

Injection pump

Fuel supply pump

Fuel injection eliminates the need for a carburetor by bringing the fuel and air together right in the **intake manifold**, just outside the **combustion chambers** of the engine. A constant supply of air is drawn through the **air cleaner** and past a **throttle** into the **intake manifold**. Here, tubes of equal length deliver an equal amount of air to each cylinder. This air is mixed with varying amounts of fuel from **fuel injector valves** located close to the combustion chambers. The valves respond to commands from an **electronic sensing device** (ECU) which receives data on intake manifold pressure, intake air temperature, the position of the throttle, and the temperature and speed of the engine. Impulses from the ECU determine the length of time that the valves stay open. The longer a valve is open, the more fuel it delivers to the combustion chamber. The richer the resulting **fuel/air mixture**, the more power it delivers. Fuel injection systems provide greater fuel economy, cleaner exhaust emissions, and more controllable power. Since the newest electronic sensing devices are computers that measure changes in speed and load much more accurately than carburetors can, you save fuel and contribute less unburnt fuel to the atmosphere. You will probably pay considerably more for these sensitive electronic systems and their repair, but I think that, as they are perfected, costs will be reduced because of mass production.

Diesel engines run on diesel fuel instead of gasoline. Instead of having carburetors, they have an injector which drops a finely calibrated spray of fuel into the compressed air in the **combustion chambers**. Here, the **compression ratio** is 16 to 20:1, rather than 8:1 as on ordinary cars. The intense heat created by this compression is enough to ignite the fuel without a spark from a spark plug. Diesel engines consume less-expensive fuel, give better mileage (in most cases), need no spark plugs, or ignition tune-ups, and have no carburetors to adjust. They are becoming more popular as diesel fuel is generally available now, and several manufacturers are considering or producing diesel cars in response to the current fuel and energy crisis. Cars with diesel engines are said to be noisier and relatively less powerful than conventional models,

but I have met several diesel owners who adore them and say that their cars are just as quiet and responsive as everybody else's.

Most American-made cars, and a good many foreign cars as well, have carburetors that work on the same principles. They may look a bit different, vary in size and the number of barrels, but they all do the same job and are adjusted in the same manner. So, unless your car has a diesel engine or a fuel injection system, just remove your air cleaner (or air cleaners), take a look at what you've got, and try to relate the information in this chapter to the carburetor(s) on your car. If you really have a rough time finding the adjustment devices on your carburetor, either ask a mechanic to point them out to you or get a service manual for your car (you can probably borrow one at the local public library or buy one at an auto parts store). The service manual will have a picture of your carburetor, with all the parts labeled. It might be wise to make a photocopy of the page and keep it in this book, for future reference. Some owner's manuals have this information, so check yours before you go shopping elsewhere.

In the next chapter, we'll discuss the proper way to keep your fuel system in tune. By adjusting the carburetor, you will enable your car to use a minimum amount of gasoline to produce the maximum amount of power. And the best thing about carburetor tune-ups is that they can cost *nothing*—if you do them yourself.

How to Keep Your Fuel System in Tune

When you have tuned your ignition system, it is nice to complete the job by tuning your carburetor and taking care of the other devices that provide the air and fuel for your engine. Unlike the basic ignition tune-up discussed in Chapter 5, the fuel system tune-up does not usually involve hard, or messy, work (unless you get into major overhauls). And if you've already acquired the tools you needed to tune your ignition system, you probably possess all the tools needed to complete this job, as well.

All the work is under-the-hood stuff, so you won't need to jack up your car. Most of the adjustments take place on, or near, the carburetor, so you won't have to undertake any acrobatics to reach the scene of the action. I'll take the adjustments in the order in which they should be made, if you need to make them. Various filters should be replaced on a regular basis, but if your car is running well—starting right up in the morning, idling without conking out at stoplights, and producing readings within the acceptable range on your tach/dwell meter—you needn't bother with most of the adjustments mentioned in this chapter. Just do what's necessary, and refer back to this book if trouble crops up later on. It will tell you what to look for, and how to fix it. In the meantime, let's get started with the basics.

How to Replace Your Air Filter

If you unscrew the wing nut on the lid of your **air cleaner** (or undo whatever device your car has instead), you will find a doughnut-shaped **air filter** inside. Some automobiles have permanent air filters, and these should be cleaned according to the instructions in your **owner's manual**. Today, however, most cars come with paper air filters that can be replaced for a few dollars.

To see whether your air filter needs replacement, just lift it out (it isn't fastened down) and hold it up to the light. Can you see the light streaming through it? If not, try dropping it *lightly*, bottom side down, on the ground. This should jar some dirt loose. Don't blow through it—you can foul it up that way. If it is still too dirty to see through after you've dropped it a few times, you need a new one.

It's a good idea to change these filters at least every year or every 20,000 miles, whichever comes first—unless yours gets very dirty before then. If you do most of your driving in a dusty or sandy area, you may need to replace your air filter every 5,000 miles, or less.

To replace your air filter, just go to your local auto supply store, tell them the make, model, and year of your car, buy a new one, take the old one out, and drop the new one in. Look for well-known, quality-brand filters; you can often get them quite cheaply at a discount store. Unknown brands sell for very little, but they are not always of good quality, and if your air filter lets a lot of junk get into your carburetor, you may find that a cheap filter is very costly in the long run. Be sure the filter you get matches your old filter in size and shape. That way you'll be sure you've been sold the proper filter for your car.

The Air Filter is Inside the Air Cleaner.
Richard Freshman

Take the rest of the air cleaner off your car—it will just lift off. Underneath is your carburetor, and inserted into the little hose or pipe that comes out of the carburetor and leads to the fuel pump—usually just an inch or two away from the carburetor—there often is a little metal or plastic cylinder called the **fuel filter**. On most cars, the fuel filter is held in place by metal clamps on either side of it, either in the fuel line or in the carburetor inlet fitting. These are called *in-line* filters. Some cars have the fuel filter inside the carburetor or the fuel pump, but it is no more difficult to get at these. They are called *integral* filters. If you haven't already found yours, find it. It is important to get in the habit of changing your fuel filter every 10,000 miles or six months, whichever is sooner. More often if you tend to ride around with an almost-empty fuel tank.

To replace your fuel filter, buy a new one at the auto supply store (on the basis of your car's make, model, and year—plus type of carburetor, in some cases).

How to Replace Your Fuel Filter

Filter

An In-Line Fuel Filter Near the Carburetor
Richard Freshman

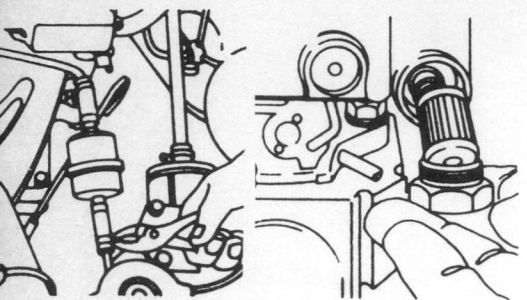

In-line Filter   **Integral Filter**

Replacing In-Line and Integral Fuel Filters
R&S Auto, Division of Roth-Schlenger

Again, go for well-known brands at discount prices. Buy new gear-type clamps, too, if yours look old, rusty, brittle, or are the wire-ring type illustrated on page 168. The total cost of this package should come to less than $3.

Back home, simply unfasten the clamps that hold the filter in place, slip the filter out, slip the new one in (there's usually an arrow on it to show you which way it goes, or look at the way the old one is pointing before you remove it), and replace the clamps. If you get the clamps on nice and tight (without cutting or shutting off circulation in the hose), there will be no leaks and no trouble.

How to Tune Your Carburetor

There are several things you can do to keep your carburetor in tune. You can adjust the **idle speed screw** to keep the car idling at the proper number of revolutions per minute (rpm); you can adjust the **idle mixture screw** so your car is idling on just the right amount of fuel necessary for good performance; you can readjust the **automatic choke** if your car is not starting properly in the morning; you can check and clean your **PCV valve** or, if necessary, replace it; and you can determine if more radical surgery is in order. I'll show you how to do all these things in the following pages.

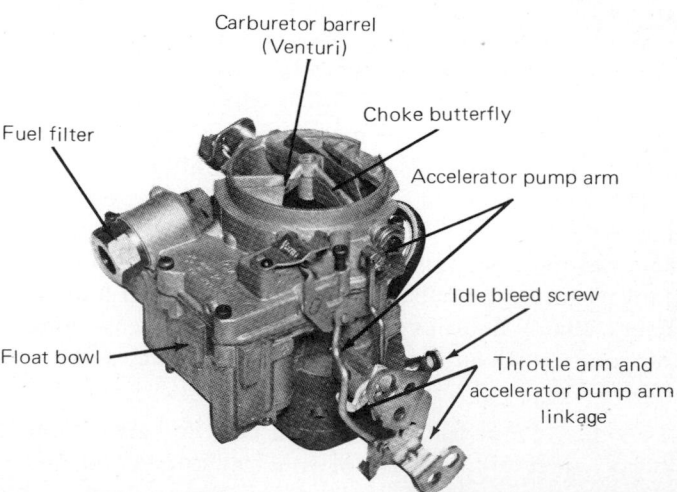

Carburetor barrel
(Venturi)

Choke butterfly

Fuel filter

Accelerator pump arm

Idle bleed screw

Float bowl

Throttle arm and accelerator pump arm linkage

Typical Carburetor
Echlin Manufacturing Co.

An Exploded Drawing from a Carburetor Kit

Ref. No.	Nomenclature
1	Clamp screw
2	Thermostatic cover clamp
3	Thermostatic spring cover
4	Thermostatic cover gasket
5	Choke baffle plate
6	Retainer clip
7	Washer
8	Fast idle link
9	Pin spring
10	Choke housing screw and washer
11	Choke housing assembly
12	Choke housing assembly
13	Air horn screw and washer
14	Air horn
15	Air horn gasket
16	Screw and lockwasher
17	Choke seal retainer
18	Choke rod seal washer
19	Choke rod seal
20	Float pin retainer
21	Float assembly
22	Float pin
23	Needle and seat assembly
24	Needle seat gasket
25	Pump discharge nozzle screw
26	Pump discharge nozzle screw gasket
27	Nozzle and venturi assembly
28	Venturi assembly gasket
29	Pump discharge ball
30	Main metering jet
31	Pin spring
32	Pump rod
33	Pump cover screw and washer
34	Pump cover assembly
35	Pump diaphragm return spring
36	Pump diaphragm assembly
37	Pump inlet ball retainer
38	Retainer gasket
39	Pump inlet ball
40	Economizer screw and washer
41	Economizer valve cover
42	Economizer valve cover gasket
43	Economizer valve assembly
44	Economizer valve gasket
45	Idle mixture screw
46	Idle mixture screw spring
47	Main body
48	Pump cavity filler
49	Pump diaphragm return spring
50	Elastomer inlet check valve (When used, replaces parts 37–39)
51	Idle limiter cap (Beginning 1968)*

*Do not remove unless new cap is available.

Late design replaces 20

Late design replaces 36

Accelerator pump design beginning late 1964

SCLAR
000-139

If your carburetor doesn't respond to any of these, and if it is still carrying on by causing your car to stall, accelerate improperly, burn enormous quantities of gasoline, etc., *and* if the inside of your carburetor looks foul and gunky, you might want to undertake a carburetor overhaul. This can be accomplished by means of an inexpensive kit (they range from $3.50 to nearly $8.00, depending on type of car and where you shop), but it is a difficult job, and I'd suggest that if you decide to undertake it, you ask a friend who has already overhauled a carburetor to help you. The basic problem is not one of *skill*, or of mechanical genius, but simply that the darn things have so many nuts, screws, washers, and gizmos that it can be very difficult to remember where everything goes when it's time to reassemble. The kits come with "exploded" drawings, but these can be confusing unless you've had some experience. If you have no mechanically inclined friends, you might want to find yourself an auto repair course at a local school and try the job under the supervision of an instructor. Right now, let's get back to the easy jobs!

How to Check Your PCV Valve

When your car is running, a certain amount of fuel and exhaust fumes find their way past the piston rings and into the crankcase. Originally, these fumes were simply dispelled into the air through a tube, because if they were left to accumulate, they would foul the oil in the crankcase. In the early sixties a new method, called *Positive Crankcase Ventilation* (PCV), was put into general use. This was much more efficient because, instead of allowing these fumes to pollute the air, it rerouted them back to the carburetor so that they could be reburned in the cylinders along with the rest of the fuel/air mixture. This was much more desirable. It increased fuel economy, since the engine could now run on the fuel in the exhaust fumes as well as on the regular fuel/air mixture.

Whenever you tune your car you should check your **PCV valve** to make sure it has not become clogged with sludge from the contaminants in the fumes. If it

PCV Valve
Automotive Marketing Division, Dana Corp.

ceases to function, the fuel/air mixture that has been adjusted to take these fumes into consideration will go out of balance and your car will not operate as efficiently. Most car manufacturers suggest that PCV valves be cleaned or replaced after about 12,000 miles of driving. Here's how to locate your PCV valve:

1 Look for the hose that leads from the bottom area of the carburetor to the top of the **cylinder head** or to the **oil filler hole.** (If your car has *both*, you want the one that does *not* lead to the oil filler hole.) Some PCV valves screw into the base of the carburetor; some push into a rubber grommet in the cylinder head valve cover, at the end of the hose that leads from there to the carburetor; and still others screw or push into the oil filler cap or tube. If you can't find yours, consult your **owner's manual** or dealer.

A PCV Valve Located on the Cylinder Head with the Hose That Leads to It Removed
Richard Freshman

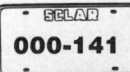

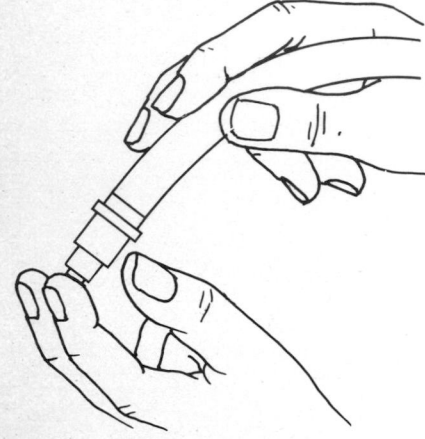

One Way to Check Your PCV Valve
R&S Auto, Division of Roth-Schlenger

2 With the engine idling, pinch the hose hard to shut off any air that may be going through it. Don't puncture the hose, however. If the PCV valve is operating, the idle speed should drop perceptibly. You'll be able to *hear* the change. If your car has been idling roughly, you might want to check the PCV valve before you make other adjustments.

3 You can also check your PCV valve by removing it from the cylinder head, with the hose still attached, and placing your finger over the open end of it. If it is working well, you will feel a strong suction.

4 Another way to check your PCV valve is to remove the oil filler cap from the cylinder head cover and place a stiff piece of paper over the opening. The paper should be sucked against the hole within seconds if your PCV valve is working properly.

5 If your PCV valve is not working, it must either be replaced or cleaned. A new one costs about $2. If you have the kind that comes apart, you can clean it instead. Just take it apart and immerse it in carburetor cleaner or PCV solvent, if you can get some cheaply. Lacquer thinner and fuel oil can also do the job. There should be no gummy deposits or discolorations on a clean valve.

6 While you have the valve off, check the hose by removing it and blowing through it. If the hose is dry, brittle, soft and spongy, or full of sludge or hard deposits, replace it. When everything is ship-shape once more, reassemble hose and valve and replace them.

How to Check Your Accelerator Pump

Check to see that, when someone steps on the gas pedal (with the emergency brake on and the car in "Neutral" or "Park"), the **accelerator pump** arm moves freely. If it catches, bend it a little to clear the obstruction. Some accelerator pumps have more than one hole where the arm hooks up, to allow you to adjust it. Adjusting for a shorter stroke will give you a leaner mixture of fuel and air; a longer stroke will give you a richer one. If your accelerator pump arm is moving when the gas pedal is stepped on, and if you are still having "getaway" problems, try adjusting the arm for a longer stroke. Did you look into your carburetor barrel to see if fuel is squirting in when the accelerator pump arm moves? We talked about this in the previous chapter.

1 You've already located your **idle speed screw** after reading the last chapter, right? Now, get out your tach/dwell meter (a plain tachometer will do as well, but a dwell meter without a tachometer is useless here) and hook it up according to the instructions that came with it. (If you have no instructions, refer back to Chapter 5.)

2 With the emergency brake on, and the car in "Neutral" or "Park," start your motor and let it run until the engine is hot and the choke butterfly is fully open.

3 When the engine is hot enough, turn the knob on the meter to "tach" and look on the rpm line of the tach/dwell meter to see at how many rpm your car is idling. Check this against your spec sheet or owner's manual to determine at how many rpm it should be idling.

4 If your car is not idling at the proper number of rpm, check your owner's manual to see whether idle speed should be adjusted with the air cleaner off or on the carburetor. Most cars are adjusted with the air cleaner off. If there is a hose that goes from the carburetor to the air cleaner, plug the hose after you take the air cleaner off.

5 With a screwdriver, turn the idle speed screw until the tach/dwell needle rests on the proper number of rpm. Turning the screw *inward* (clockwise) will *increase* idle speed; turning it *outward* (counterclockwise) will *decrease* it. And that is all there is to it.

How to Adjust Your Idle Speed Screw

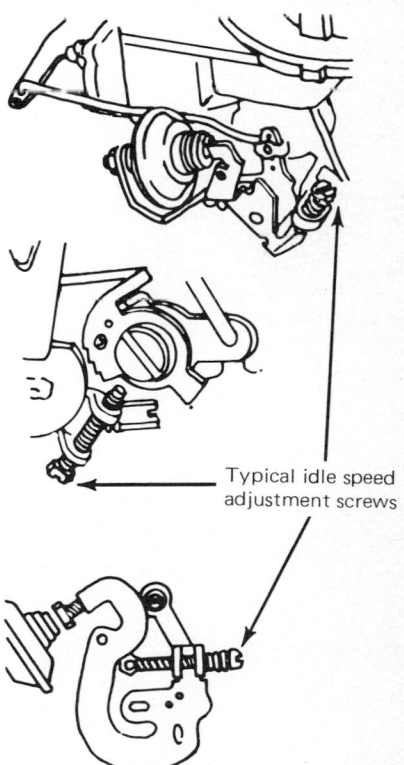

Typical idle speed adjustment screws

Typical Idle Speed Adjustment Screws
Karcheck Products, Otsego, Michigan

How to Adjust Your Idle Air Bleed Screw

If you have an **idle air bleed screw** instead of an idle speed screw, just do exactly the same thing to adjust it. However, in this case, turning the screw *clockwise* will *decrease* idle speed, and turning it *counter-clockwise* will *increase* idle speed. Otherwise, they are just the same in terms of adjustment.

How to Adjust Your Idle Stop Solenoid

If you have an **idle stop solenoid**, you will probably find a tag somewhere under the hood of your car that will give you special instructions on how to adjust it. If you can't find yours, and your owner's manual either is not helpful or is too difficult to follow, and you have hooked up your dwell/tach and found that your car is *not* idling at the proper speed, then do the following:

1 Adjust the nut on the end of the solenoid until your car is idling at the proper number of rpm (at least 700 rpm is usual).

2 Disconnect the little wire that runs from the end of the solenoid to whatever it leads to. Your idle speed will drop.

3 Then adjust your **idle speed screw**, following the instructions above.

Your manual will usually indicate that this last adjustment is at a lower number of rpm. This is called *shutdown idle speed*, and it is the reduced speed that allows your engine to stop running when you shut off the ignition.

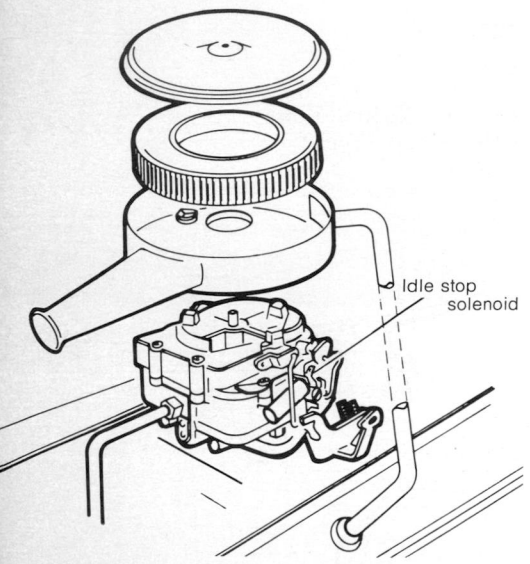

Idle stop solenoid

An Idle Stop Solenoid Is Sometimes Located on the Outside of the Carburetor
Guaranteed Parts Company

How to Adjust the Idle Mixture Screw(s)

1 With the engine still at idle speed, locate the **idle mixture screw** (or screws) on your carburetor. They can be almost anywhere, and two- and four-barrel carburetors can have two idle mixture screws. You can consult your owner's manual or service manual to locate yours. If yours is hard to reach, you may need a screwdriver with a flexible shaft, although, in some cases, you can turn them with your fingers. Some idle mixture screws have been provided with plastic caps called *limiters*, which do not allow you to adjust the screw, or which limit adjustments to

around a quarter of a turn. This was done as an air pollution control device to keep you from adjusting for a too-rich mixture that would result in an increase in the exhaust emissions that pollute the air. If your carburetor has these limiters, leave it alone (they were preset and sealed at the factory and are probably set properly) unless you are having problems that nothing else seems to cure.

2 If you feel that your mixture needs adjusting because your car is not idling smoothly now that you've corrected its idle speed, turn the idle mixture screw inward until the engine starts to falter. Then turn it back the other way, about half a turn. If the car is still idling roughly, continue to turn the screw outward until the engine sounds smooth. If you turn it too far outward, the engine will begin to falter again from too rich a mixture. The best position for most cars is when the tach/dwell meter returns to the highest idle speed after its initial drop when you turned the idle mixture screw inward. If your car has two screws, do them one at a time.

NOTE: Some cars are adjusted according to special instructions provided on a tag or decal under the hood. You can find these tags almost anywhere, usually on the cylinder head cover or on the air cleaner lid or up front on the frame. If you have one, follow the instructions on the tag instead of those given above.

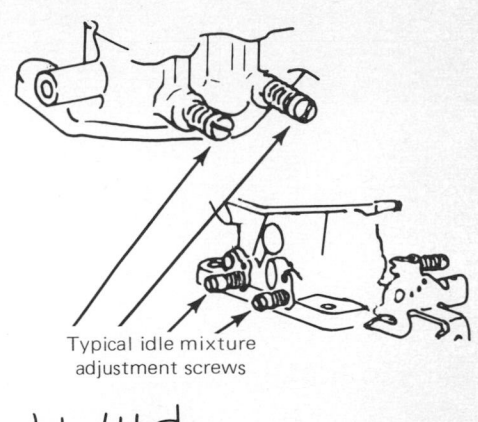

Typical idle mixture adjustment screws

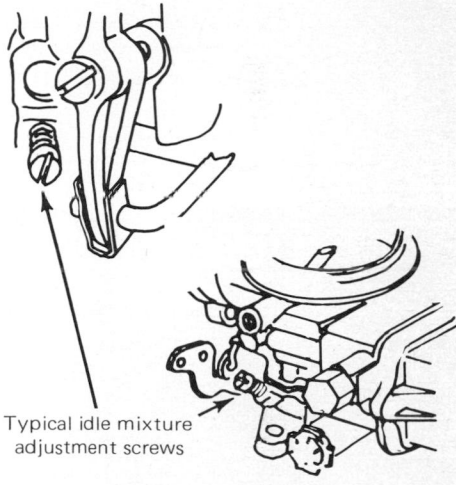

Typical idle mixture adjustment screws

Typical Idle Mixture Adjustment Screws
Karcheck Products, Otsego, Michigan

How to Adjust Your Automatic Choke

Many cars have a **thermostatic spring choke**, like the one we discussed in the previous chapter. If you have one of these on your carburetor, and if you have trouble starting your car in the morning, you might want to adjust this too.

1 Check the specifications for your automatic choke, and see if it is properly set (if the proper notch on the carburetor housing is opposite the indicator on the plastic cap). If it isn't, then you will have to adjust the thermostatic spring choke to the proper setting. If it *is* properly set and you are still having trouble getting the car started in the morning, first wait until the car is very cold (like the next morn-

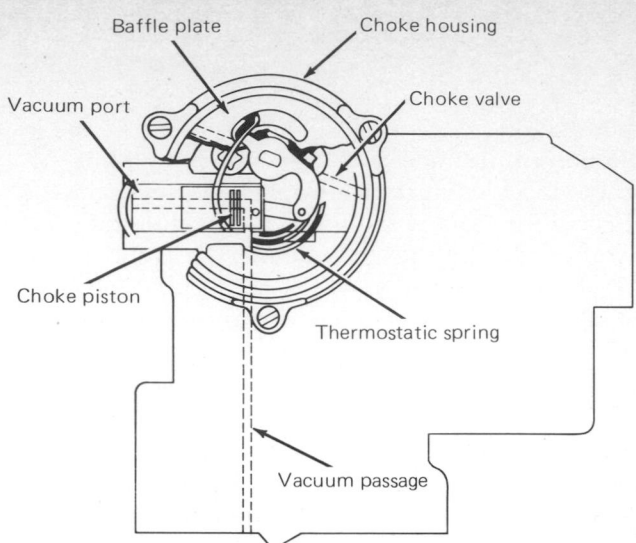

Baffle plate

Choke housing

Vacuum port

Choke valve

Choke piston

Thermostatic spring

Vacuum passage

Thermostatic Spring Choke
Echlin Manufacturing Company

The Three Screws to Loosen When Adjusting
a Thermostatic Spring Choke
Richard Freshman

ing), step on the gas pedal, and check to see if the **butterfly valve** is closed before you start the car. If it *isn't* closed, then it may need adjusting or cleaning, in case it is simply stuck. The butterfly valve should open again after the car has been running for a few minutes and is sufficiently warmed up. If the butterfly valve is closed and the car still won't start properly, you can try adjusting the thermostatic spring choke to a richer setting.

2 First loosen the three screws that keep the plastic cap in place.

3 Next, turn the cap until the notch lines up with the proper mark on the carburetor housing. You will notice that on the back of the cap, there are the words "Lean" and "Rich" with arrows to indicate direction. Your specifications may read "one notch Lean," in which case you would turn the cap until the indicator lined up with the first mark on the "Lean" side of the carburetor housing. If your car was already set at the specified mark, just turn the cap one notch to the richer side and see how that works the next morning. If it is still not starting properly, try one notch richer. Never adjust more than one notch at a time. These chokes are generally set on the lean side, so they often run better cold when set a notch richer. Don't forget to tighten down the three screws when you are finished.

If your automatic choke is the **thermostatic coil** type, it will have a rod leading from the top of the carbu-

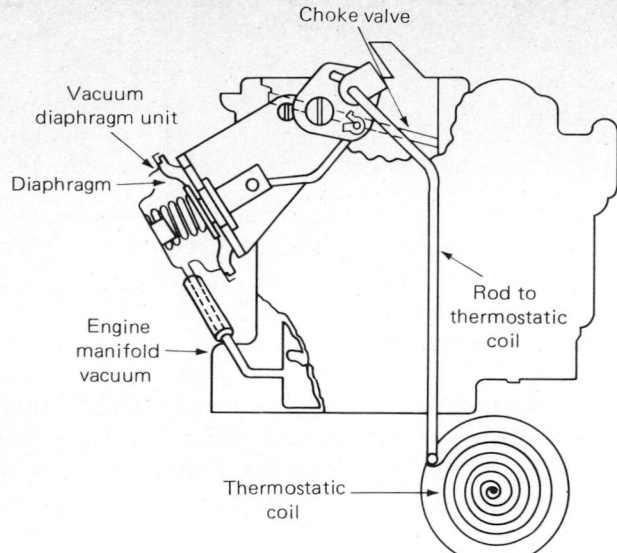

Thermostatic Coil Choke
Echlin Manufacturing Company

retor near the choke butterfly to a small box mounted not far away, usually on top of the exhaust manifold. Unless it's been tinkered with since the car came from the factory, an automatic choke of this type stays set properly until it breaks down. It is quite cheap to replace, and if you think your choke is not working properly—either because the butterfly won't close when the car is cold or won't open when it warms up, or because you can't get the car started properly in the morning—get a new one, for a couple of dollars. You can install it yourself if you want to.

There are other types of automatic chokes, but these should be adjusted by a professional. If you have one of these and your choke does not seem to be working properly, ask your garage mechanic to have a look at it. Be sure that all the above-mentioned gizmos are checked before you let them talk you into a new carburetor or any other major expense. If you are told that your carburetor needs replacement, get another opinion (without telling the second garage that you've been to the first one). You can probably get a **rebuilt** carburetor for your car at a much lower price than a new one would cost. Ask whoever is going to do the work to find a rebuilt one, if possible—they usually work just as well, and should be guaranteed for thirty days—or call the auto wreckers to locate a rebuilt carburetor and either bring it with you or install it yourself.

Installing a New or Rebuilt Carburetor

You can probably install another carburetor yourself, with the help of a knowledgeable friend or an auto shop instructor. It's easier than overhauling one!

1 Go down to the local auto parts store or auto wrecker. Ask them for a rebuilt carburetor for your car. Give them the make, model, year, how many cylinders the car has, how big the engine is, etc. If your carburetor still has a metal tag on it, bring the tag along; that will tell them what they need to know. Check out a couple of places by telephone, using the Yellow Pages. Prices can differ drastically from one place to another. Ask for a discount, since you are going to do the job yourself. (Who knows, you might get it!) Or ask if they will accept your old carburetor in exchange for a discount.

2 When you get the carburetor, there will be a **gasket** with it. The gasket goes between the carburetor and the thing it sits on. Compare the new gasket with the one under your carburetor. They have to be the same; if not, you have bought the wrong carburetor. Now, before you go any further, skip ahead to chapter 10 for instructions on How to Disassemble Anything (and Get it Back Together Again).

3 Remove the throttle arm and choke linkages (the things that attach the moving parts of your old carburetor to the other parts of your car, and all the pipes, hoses, and other things that connect your old carburetor to your car. (Leave the other ends attached to the car so you can hook them to your new carburetor.) Be sure to remember, or draw, the way they were attached.

4 Remove the carburetor nuts that fasten the base of your old carburetor to the top of your engine, and lift the old carburetor out of your car. If fuel spills out, wipe it up—and for heaven's sake! *don't smoke* while you do this job! There will be fuel in the float bowl of the old carburetor and in other parts of it, so handle it carefully and dispose of the old fuel before setting the old carburetor aside. Don't throw the old carburetor out—you may be able to sell it to a place that can rebuild it and sell it again.

5 Clean the gasket surfaces where the old gasket was. If the old gasket is stuck to the car, clean it off and be sure to keep the pieces of the old gasket from

falling down the manifold. Maybe stuff a clean, lint-free rag into the top of the hole while you are getting the junk off—just don't forget to remove it before you put the new gasket on!

6 Be sure the new gasket goes on the way the old one was. If you are afraid you'll forget, draw a picture before you take the old one off.

7 Never use anything to cement the new gasket in place. Just place it where it belongs. The weight of the carburetor will hold it in place.

8 Place the new carburetor on the gasket and replace the carburetor hold-down nuts. Don't get these, or any other bolts, too tight; you don't want to break them, or crush the gasket. Have an experienced friend check it over when you are through—or ask your auto mechanic to check it for you. It is impossible to *tell* someone how tight or loose to make a bolt—you have to *feel* it for yourself. And only experience can bring that sense of tightening something properly.

9 Assemble the linkages, pipes, hoses, etc., in the reverse order in which you took them off. If you still think you won't remember, write little numbers next to each thing you disconnect as you disconnect it. Again, remember to have someone with experience check your work when you are through, before you head for the freeway.

Float Level Adjustments

As we mentioned previously, if the float in your **float bowl** is set improperly, you may find that your car will hesitate or stall when it is accelerated, or it may be hard to start. Since the float level is pre-set, it will only be incorrect if someone has worked on it since the carburetor was installed. If you suspect that this is your problem, then have a professional overhaul your carburetor and reset the float level to the manufacturer's specifications. If he finds that the float level was correct, then chances are that the tiny passages in the carburetor have become plugged with dirt. An overhaul (dismantling and cleaning of the carburetor) will correct this. As I've said before, don't try this yourself unless you have at your elbow someone who has done it before.

What to Do When All Else Fails If you've made all the adjustments in this chapter and your car is still not idling properly; is not starting up in the morning without a hassle; or is hesitating or stalling at corners or when it is accelerated sharply, then you are going to need extra help. *But,* you don't want to seek help like a lamb being led to the slaughter. If you want to drive into the service station like someone who knows the score and is prepared to judge intelligently whether or not the proposed remedies are necessary or not, here's what you should do:

1 Take the car to your friendly garage mechanic and ask him (or her) to use an **oscilloscope** to test your ignition system, in case that is the culprit.

2 Then ask them to use their *exhaust gas analyzer* to test your exhaust to see if your car is running on a fuel/air mixture that is too lean or too rich. The easy way to spot this for yourself is to run your finger around the end of the inside of your tail pipe (when the car is cold, please) to see if there is a black, *sooty* deposit there. If there is, your fuel/air mixture is too rich. If there is a black, *greasy,* or *shiny* deposit, you are burning oil. A car that is running "too lean" runs poorly only when it is cold. A choke adjustment should help. In either case, you will need a professional for the necessary carburetor adjustments if the adjustments you've made to the idle mixture screw and the choke haven't helped.

After the garage has isolated the problem, remember to get a second opinion if the remedy seems costly or overly drastic. Also, remember to request a *rebuilt* carburetor, if you need a replacement.

You have just finished the most difficult jobs in this book! If you've gotten this far, what is to come should be a breeze. The next chapters will deal with the rest of the systems at work in your car. None of them are so complex, and none of them needs the kind of adjustments that your ignition and fuel systems did. So, if you've just finished your tune-up work, relax and enjoy yourself—you're practically a professional! And if you've "chickened out" so far, there are still a lot of things you can do to save money and keep your car running well.

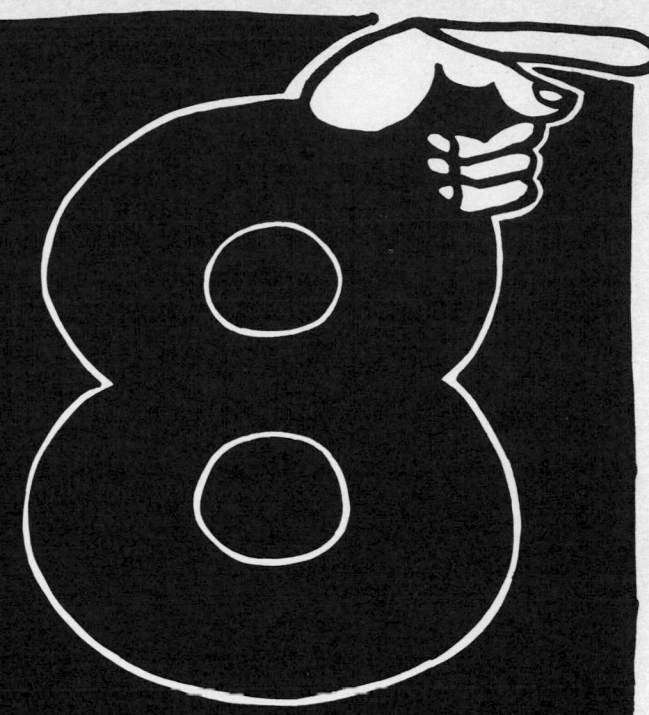

The Cooling System:
How to Keep
Your Car from
Getting Heartburn

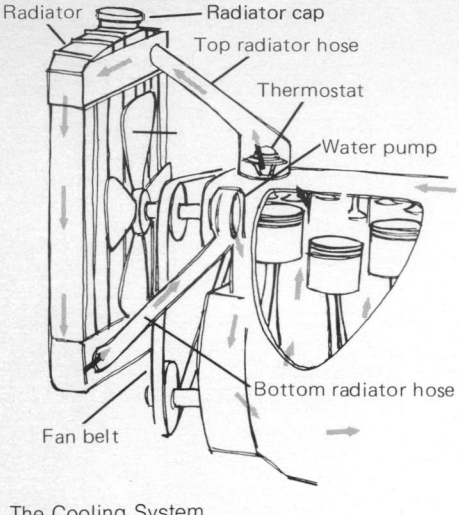

The Cooling System
Automotive Information Council (AIC)

With all that "air, fuel, and fire" stuff going on in its engine, your car needs something to help it keep a cool (cylinder) head! Since water is cheap, plentiful, and readily available, car manufacturers have found it to be the simplest answer to the problem. (Except for a few who found that air was even cheaper and more abundant. They designed the air-cooled engine. If you have a pre-1975 Volkswagen, you won't find a drop of water in it.)

Of course, nothing is as simple as it seems, and so the car manufacturers have added a couple of gimmicks to keep the water from boiling too easily. These include a **water pump** to keep the water moving; a **fan** and a **radiator** to cool it off; a **pressure cap** to retard boiling; a **thermostat** to help you warm the car up fast on chilly mornings; and **antifreeze/coolant** to raise the boiling point of the water, keep it from freezing in the winter, and keep it from rusting your engine. Put them all together, and you have the **cooling system** in your car. This system is highly efficient. It requires almost no work to keep it operating—only a watchful eye for leaks, and an occasional check or change of coolant, should do it.

Let's take a look at the way the system works; then we'll discuss the things that you can do to help your car keep its cool. If your car has been overheating lately, it may *not* be the fault of the cooling system, and we'll get into the other possibilities as well.

The Radiator

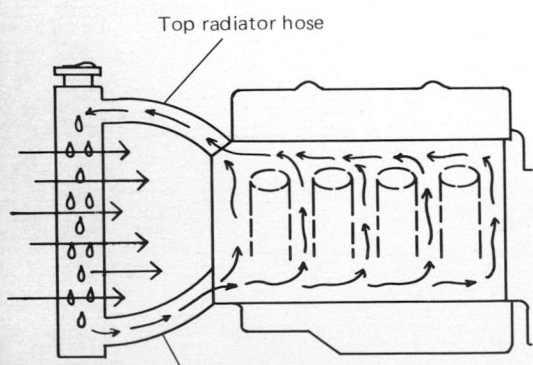

Water Circulates Between the Radiator and the Engine via the Radiator Hoses.
Jack Herlihy

When the fuel and air mixture is ignited in the cylinders, it burns at a temperature of 4,500 degrees Fahrenheit! It takes only *half* that heat to melt iron, and your 500-pound engine would be a useless lump of metal in about 20 minutes if you couldn't keep things cool. Naturally, the water that circulates around the cylinders in the engine block gets very hot, and so it is continually circulated back to the **radiator**, where it cools off before heading back to the scene of the action.

The radiator is designed to cool the water quickly by passing it over a larger cooling surface. The water enters the radiator through a *radiator hose* that is usually connected to the top of the radiator. As the water descends, it runs through channels in the radiator which are cooled by air rushing in through *cooling fins* between the channels. When the water has cooled, it leaves the radiator through another hose that is generally found at the bottom of the radiator.

It is easy to see how air rushing through the radiator can cool things off when we are driving merrily down the freeway—but what happens when the car is standing still or crawling its way through heavy traffic? To keep a fresh supply of air moving through the radiator fins, there is a **fan** located behind the radiator. It is positioned so it can draw air through the radiator.

When the car is running, a **fan belt** drives the fan, which keeps the car cool until it is moving fast enough for the inrushing air to do the job itself. Formerly, the fan continued to be driven at all speeds, but many newer cars (from 1966 on) have *fan clutches* that automatically limit the fan's movement at speeds over 25 mph. On these cars, the fan will continue to "coast" at high speeds because of the air rushing past it, but it will not be using any power (and that means less fuel consumption and air pollution from exhaust fumes).

The fan belt is also connected to the **water pump**. This pump draws the water from the radiator through the *bottom* radiator hose and sends it to the engine, where it circulates, through **water jackets** located around the cylinder combustion chambers, and other hot spots.

The Fan

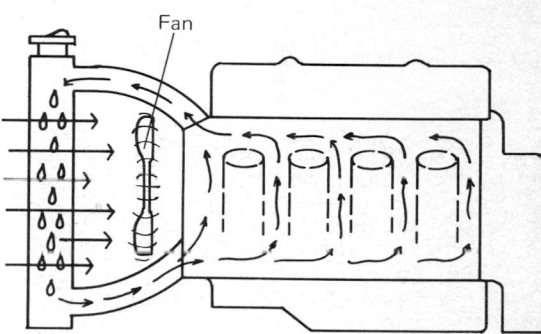

The Fan Draws Air Through the Radiator to Cool the Water Even When the Car Isn't Moving.
Jack Herlihy

The Water Pump

Water pump

(*left*) The Water Pump Forces the Water from the Radiator Through the Water Jackets in the Engine.
Jack Herlihy

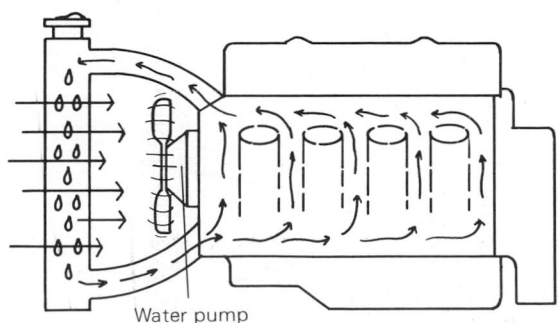

Water pump

Antifreeze/Coolant To keep the water in the cooling system from boiling or freezing, the water is mixed with **antifreeze/coolant**. This contains a chemical called "ethylene glycol," which can keep water from freezing at temperatures far below the 32 degrees F. usually required to freeze water at normal pressures and can retard boiling so that the resulting mixture of water and antifreeze/coolant will not boil and turn to steam until it reaches a much higher temperature than the 212 degrees F. normally required.

Most antifreeze/coolant (after this, let's just call it "coolant," for short) contains about 95 percent ethylene glycol, plus rust, corrosion, and foaming inhibitors. This means that coolant does more than just keep the water in the system in a liquid state. It helps to prevent the formation of rust on the metal surfaces of the engine and the radiator, lubricates the water pump, and keeps the liquid from foaming as it circulates through the system. Since the early 1960s, car

Antifreeze (Coolant) Raises the Boiling Point and Lowers the Freezing Point of the Water in Your Cooling System.

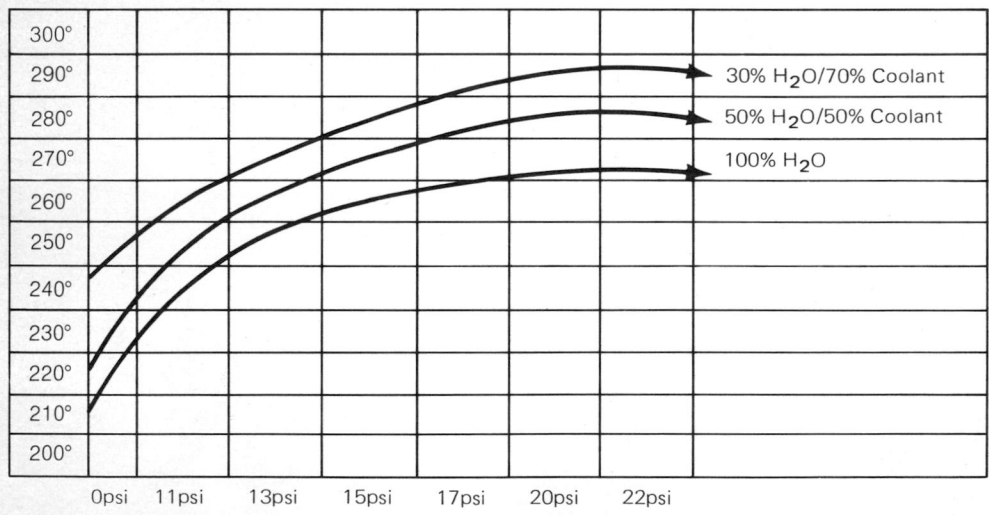

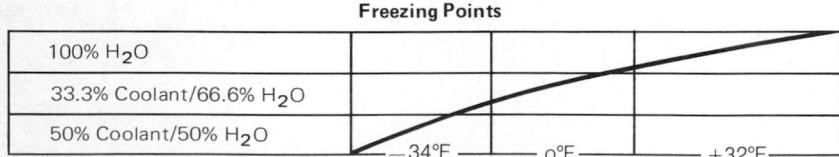

manufacturers have designed the cooling systems of most cars for a 50–50 mixture of ethylene glycol and water—and that is generally considered the proper proportion of coolant and water for the cooling system of your car.

If your car's cooling system is operating properly, you should not have to keep adding water to it. The more water you have to add, the more you dilute the coolant in your system. Since the generally recommended proportion of coolant and water is 50–50 (although you can use a higher proportion of coolant if you need it), sooner or later you are going to tip that balance in favor of water if you keep adding it without adding coolant. Even if your car is not losing water, you should flush the system and replace the coolant at least once a year. We'll get into how to do this as soon as we finish with the technical stuff.

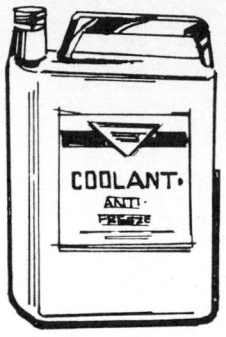

Anti–freeze/Coolant

To further retard the boiling point of the liquid in the cooling system, the entire system is placed under pressure. This pressure generally runs between 7 and 16 pounds per square inch (psi). As the pressure goes up, the boiling point rises as well. This combination of pressure + coolant results in the ability of the liquid in your cooling system to resist boiling at temperatures that can rise as high as 250° F., or more, in some new cars.

The illustration on the opposite page gives you an idea of the ways in which coolant and pressure affect the boiling and freezing points of the water in the system.

To keep the lid on the pressure in the system, and to provide a place to conveniently add water and coolant, each car radiator has a removable **radiator pressure cap** on its **radiator fill hole**. These are relatively inexpensive, but if you have a cap that is not working properly, or if you have the wrong type of cap, you will be amazed at the amount of trouble it can cause. A modern cooling system that has been designed to operate normally at temperatures over 212 degrees F. and that is filled with water and in perfect condition, will continually boil over if the radiator cap is no good.

The Radiator Pressure Cap

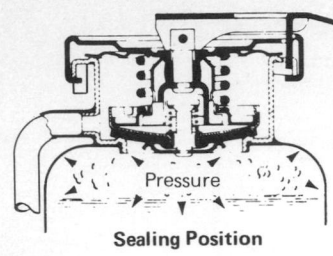

Sealing Position

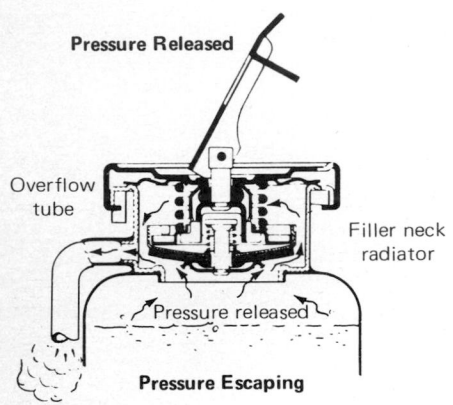

How a Safety Pressure Cap Works
Stant Manufacturing Company, Inc.

If the gasket (rubber ring) inside the cap is not working, the pressure in the system will escape, allowing the water to boil at a lower temperature. As the water boils, it will escape through the overflow pipe in the form of steam. The car will overheat, and the resulting inconvenience and possible danger to your engine—and yourself—are just not worth the risk.

Most cars come equipped with a simple radiator pressure cap that resembles the lid of a jar. You just screw the cap on and off the **radiator fill hole**. If you have this kind of cap on your radiator, *get rid of it*, whether or not you are losing water!

What you want is a **safety radiator pressure cap** because it will help to keep you from getting burned if it becomes necessary to remove the cap before the car is cool.

Most safety caps have a little lever on them. Whenever you want to remove the cap, you lift the lever *first*. This allows the pressure to escape (it sounds like the "poof" you hear when you open a fresh can of coffee) *before* you unscrew the cap.

Since the stuff in the radiator has been restrained from boiling by the pressure in the system, if you just whip off the radiator cap the pressure in the system will go down suddenly and the liquid in the system will boil instantly. The result can be a terribly hot spray of liquid and/or steam which can scald you badly. So, whether or not you already have a safety cap on your radiator, it is important that you know how to remove the cap safely.

How to Remove a Radiator Cap and Add Water or Coolant to Your Radiator

1 First of all, *never* remove the cap from a radiator when the engine is hot. If your car overheats on the freeway, get to the side of the road and shut off the engine. Then just sit there for 15 or 20 minutes until things cool down. You can lift the hood to help the heat escape, but leave the radiator cap alone. Since it is automotive suicide to add cold water to a hot engine (see No. 6 below), there is no need to get the cap off until the engine cools down. Keep your cool until your car regains its own!

2 For nonemergencies, just do what the garage attendants routinely do when they check the liquid level in your radiator. First, lift the lever on the safety cap, to allow the pressure to escape. Then turn the cap counterclockwise to remove it. It's a good idea to place a cloth over the cap after you've raised the lever, to keep the cap from burning your hand if it is hot.

3 If you don't have a safety cap, place a cloth over the cap and turn it counterclockwise to its first stop. This will allow the pressure to escape. If you see liquid, or a great deal of steam, escaping, retighten the cap and wait for things to cool down. If not, continue to turn the cap counterclockwise to remove it.

4 When you remove the cap, *tilt* it as you remove it, so that the opening is away from you (and anyone else around). In this way, if there is still enough heat and pressure to spray hot stuff around, it will land on the engine, or inside the hood, where it can do no harm. Be particularly sure to do this if you haven't bought a safety cap.

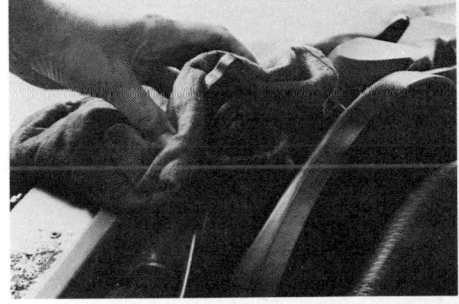

How to Remove a Radiator Cap Safely
Richard Freshman

5 Of course, if the car is completely cold, there is no risk at all, so try to do routine peeking into your radiator in the morning, before you warm up the car. If you get in the habit of checking the liquid level in your radiator every week, you won't have to bother the gas station attendants with it, and they will be free to devote themselves to cleaning your car windows instead.

6 *Never* add cold water to a hot engine! Adding cold water to an engine that is hot can crack the engine block, since the hot metal contracts sharply when the cold water hits it. If you must add water to an engine that is still *warm*, always do it with the engine running. This allows the cold water to join the stream of hot water that is circulating through the system, rather than falling all at once into the system when the engine is started again.

7 If you keep the radiator filled to within a couple of inches below the cap—or to the fill line if you have one—there will never be any need to have the gas station add water to your warm engine. Plain old tap water will do—you can use the garden hose if

you like, but try to maintain a good coolant level, too. If you are unsure about what the liquid level should be, just be sure that it covers the radiator tubes that are visible when you look down the hole. If you overfill, the extra liquid will get hot, expand, and flow out of the **overflow pipe**, coolant and all.

8 When you are finished, replace the cap by screwing it on, clockwise, and then push the lever down again.

Radiator safety caps cost less than $3. Almost every gas station stocks them, but they are cheaper in auto supply stores. Check your manual for the amount of pressure in your system and look for the proper number of psi on the new cap.

These safety caps are well worth the money. I know of one person (myself) whose mysterious car problems were eliminated by a new safety cap (see Chapter 1 for *that* adventure!). In my case, I got off with only about $40 in unnecessary repairs, but I recently met someone who had been through $200 worth of new water pumps, radiator rebuilding, and assorted other unnecessary heartaches and expense before he discovered that all he needed was a new radiator cap.

You know, that really sums up the major difference between doing the work yourself and taking it to a professional. If you don't know exactly what is causing your trouble, there are usually several possibilities to consider. Professional mechanics may go for the most potentially lucrative solution first. If that doesn't do it, they try the next thing, and continue to try things until they hit the right one. This method can cost you a bundle.

On the other hand, when *you* are the one who is doing the diagnosing, you tend to try the cheaper solutions first. So, if your car has been overheating consistently, you would first replace the radiator cap, pressure-test the system, check the coolant level and the thermostat, *before* you go for a new pump. If the pump wasn't leaking, you'd check the radiator thoroughly too. And, if it finally came down to changing the pump, you would try to find a rebuilt one and you might consider installing it yourself (this is not usually difficult). The money you would save would be well worth the effort of doing it yourself.

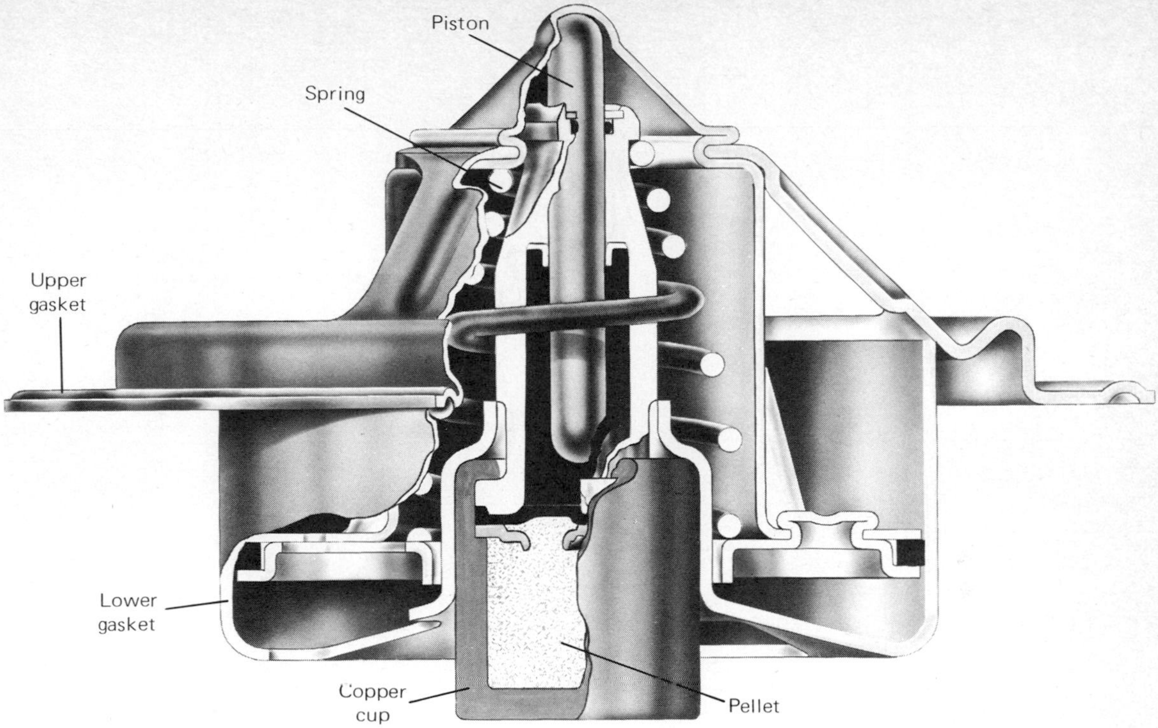

Piston

Spring

Upper gasket

Lower gasket

Copper cup

Pellet

Anatomy of a Thermostat
Fulton Sylphon Division, Robertshaw Controls Co.

The Thermostat

The last link in the cooling system does *not* help to keep the car cool. In fact, it helps it to warm up on cold mornings so your engine can operate efficiently.

The **thermostat** is usually located where the upper radiator hose meets the top of the engine. On a few foreign cars it is found where the bottom hose joins the engine. Your owner's manual should tell you where yours is.

Here's how the thermostat helps your car to heat up:

1 In the morning, when you start the car, the engine turns the fan, which is attached by a fan belt to the water pump.
2 The pump draws water and coolant from the radiator, through the bottom hose, into the engine.
3 The liquid leaves the cold engine via the upper radiator hose, on its way to the radiator, as usual. But on the way it passes through the thermostat.

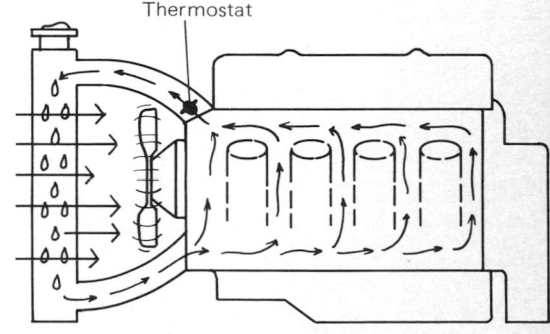

Thermostat

The Thermostat Keeps the Hot Water from Leaving the Engine Until the Car Warms Up.
Jack Herlihy

SCLAR
000-159

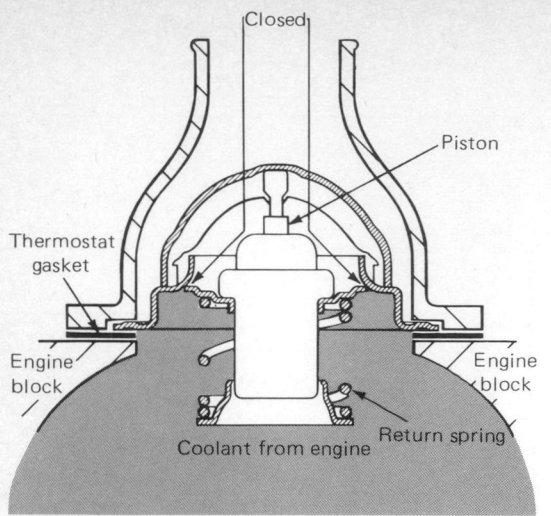

Thermostat Valve Closed
(Engine Cold)

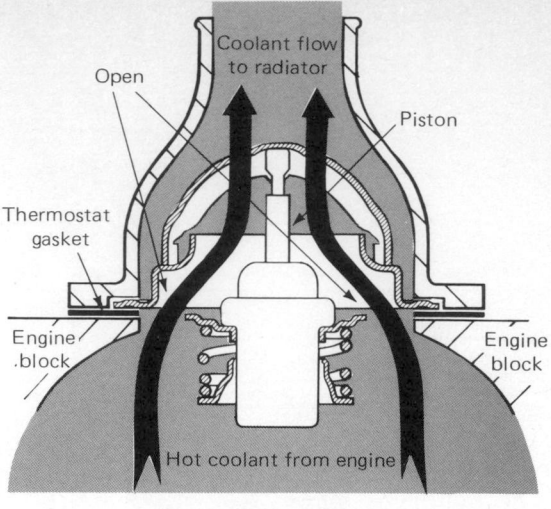

Thermostat Valve Open
(Engine Hot)

How a Thermostat Works
Standard-Thomson

4 The thermostat is just a small metal part that is sensitive to heat. When it feels hot liquid, it allows it to pass through. But when it feels that the liquid is cold, it shuts and does not allow the liquid to circulate through the radiator.

5 As a result, the liquid stays in the engine, where it gets hot as the engine warms up, and in turn, the increasing heat of the liquid helps the engine to warm up more quickly. As a result, the car runs efficiently and burns less fuel.

6 When the engine has reached the proper temperature, and the liquid reaches anywhere from 180 to 205 degrees, the thermostat begins to open and allows the liquid to circulate to the radiator and cool off.

This supply of hot liquid is also used by your car's heater when you want to heat the interior of your car. Blowers force the air that is heated by exposure to the hot liquid in the heater through vents to the passenger compartment.

And that is all you need to know about the cooling system in your car! Oh, some cars have more complicated systems, or variations on the theme. (For instance, Jaguars and VW Rabbits have two fans that are run by electric thermostats that are not connected to the water pump at all. These go on independently and draw air in to cool the engine when necessary.) But in general, if you understand the way the basic cooling system works, you should have little trouble handling the one in your car. Most cooling systems need little maintenance, and if things break down, you generally have to replace them completely or get professional help.

There are, however, a couple of things that you can do to be sure that your car's cooling system is operating efficiently. You should make it a habit to check it out fairly often—once a month for a new car, every week for an older model, right away if the car has been overheating or losing liquid regularly.

1 *Check your radiator cap.* If you don't have a safety cap, or if you haven't replaced yours in two years, buy one, whether your car is working well or not. Give the salesperson the make, model, and year of your car, but check the pressure limits on the cap against your manual to see that it is the proper cap for the amount of pressure in your car's system.

2 *Look under your car* in the morning to see if there is any liquid on the ground under it. If there is, stick your finger in it and smell it. If it's oil, see the chapter on lubrication (oil is black and greasy). If it's transmission fluid, see your mechanic (transmission fluid is pinkish and greasy). If it's coolant, then look around the parts of the car that are over the puddle and feel around for wetness.

3 *Check all the hoses* under the hood of your car whether or not you have been having trouble. If you find a hose that is:

a soft and squishy

b bulgy

c hard or brittle

d cracked or leaking

e marked with a whitish deposit where stuff has leaked and dried

you should replace it immediately. If, however, you find a hose that has collapsed when the engine is cold and that springs back when you remove the radiator

How to Check for Leaks

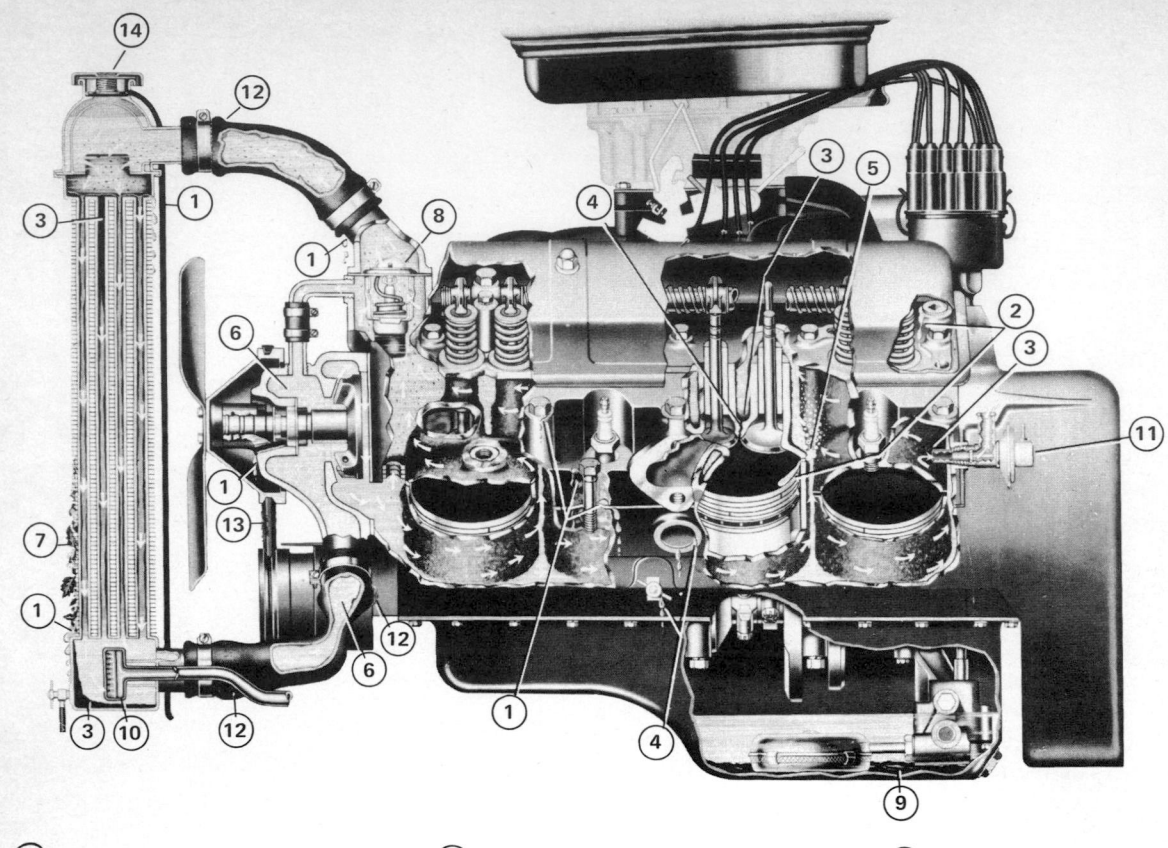

1	External leakage	**6**	Air suction	**11**	Heater control valve
2	Internal leakage	**7**	Clogged air passages	**12**	Hose deterioration
3	Rust deposits	**8**	Stuck thermostat	**13**	Fan belt deterioration
4	Heat cracks	**9**	Sludge formation in oil	**14**	Pressure cap leakage
5	Exhaust gas leakage	**10**	Transmission oil cooler	**15**	Leaky core plug

Cooling System Trouble Spots—Where to
Check for Leaks
Union Carbide Corp.

pressure cap, it is the cap and not the hose that is at
fault. For instant panic, there is nothing like having a
hose burst while you are driving. If it's a radiator
hose, the resulting shower of steam is frightening at
best and dangerous at worst. If it is a vacuum hose
that goes, the sudden loss of vacuum can stop your
car in the midst of traffic. Watching your hoses and
replacing the funky ones is the kind of preventive
medicine that can save your nerves and your pocket-
book in the long run. Later in this chapter, I'll show
you how to replace your hoses.

4 *If you can't locate the source of the leak* and your car is
   losing liqiuid from the radiator on a regular basis,
   there is a more "professional" way to find the leak
   and to check out your radiator cap.

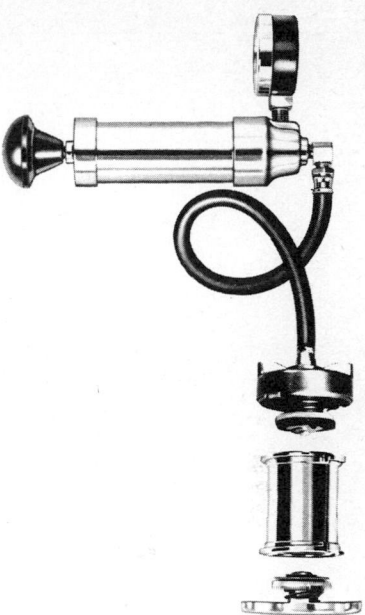

There is a "cooling system pressure tester" sold that
consists of a gauge, a hose that leads to what looks like
a radiator cap, and a little hand pump or bulb. These
gadgets cost from $25 to $40, so if you are tired of
buying tools, just drive to your gas station and ask
them if they will use theirs. They may do this for
nothing, if they are nice. All it entails is replacing your
radiator cap with the fitting on the pressure tester and
pumping air into the cooling system with the hand
pump until the dial on the gauge reaches the amount
of pressure that your cooling system is supposed to
operate under. (So if your car operates at 15 psi, they
will pump the system until the needle on the gauge
reaches the 15.) At that point, if there are any leaks in
the system, the gauge needle will drop and liquid may
start squirting out of the leaky places right before
your eyes! Simple, isn't it . . .?

A cooling system pressure tester
Stant Manufacturing Company, Inc.

5 *If no leaks appear* as a result of the pressure test,
   have them remove the radiator cap from their pressure tester and replace it with the radiator cap from
   your car. The same gauge will show whether your
   cap can withstand the 15 psi pressure. If it can't,
   you've found the culprit. If you've used the tester at
   your gas station, it might be nice to buy the new
   safety radiator cap from them, as a thank you.
   (Never let some strange gas station attendants hook
   you into buying a new radiator cap unless you make
   them test your old one with this type of tester. It
   might be smart to have them test the new one as
   well. I've been sold faulty caps to replace faulty
   caps.)

Once you've found the leak, you will have to decide
whether you can handle it yourself or if you must use
a professional. Here are a few pointers to help you
decide:

**What to Do After You've Found
the Leak**

Radiator Leaks

1 Look around your radiator for whitish deposits or rust-colored stains. These indicate old leaks that have dried. They may not be very old; water tends to evaporate quickly on a hot radiator.

2 If the radiator is leaking badly, see a reliable radiator repair shop (doctors aren't the only specialists, you know). If you are on good terms with your local garage, they may be able to steer you to one. They just take the radiator out of your car and send it to radiator specialists, so you might as well go directly to the specialist yourself and discuss the matter in person.

3 Ask the radiator specialists what they intend to do, and if they cannot be firm about the costs involved, request a written estimate *before* they do the work. If the estimate seems very high, call another radiator shop (use the Yellow Pages), tell them what needs to be done, and ask them for an estimate. Never let anyone undertake major work on your car without a *written* estimate. Some of the trusting souls among us have found that the final costs were hundreds of dollars more than they expected, and current law in some states allows the garage to *sell your car* and keep the money if you refuse to pay their bills! The same law requires them to honor a written estimate and to lose the additional money if they do extra work and do not notify you first. If you have no written estimate, the sky's the limit! Many states are working to change these laws, but it is best to be cautious. If you have a hassle about getting a written estimate, look elsewhere.

Leaks in the Engine-Block Core Plugs

On the sides of the engine block you will see little circular depressions. These are called **core plugs**, or **freeze plugs**. They plug the holes where the sand was removed when they cast the engine block. If you see rusty streaks leading away from the core plugs on your engine block and you have been losing liquid lately, you may have to have the core plugs replaced. It is best to seek professional help on this one. Always be sure they use brass plugs rather than steel ones. Brass won't rust.

Sometimes a leak right under the **cylinder head** can be the result of an ill-fitting gasket, or the fact that the bolts that hold the cylinder head on the engine block are too loose or too tight. It is possible that if you try to tighten these bolts yourself you might damage the gasket, so I think that the best thing to do would be to get professional help here too. If they just have to tighten the bolts, the cost will be minimal. If the gasket needs replacing, remember that even if you can't do the job yourself, you are still ahead if you go to a professional mechanic with a good idea of what is wrong and what it will take to correct it.

Leaks Near the Cylinder Head

Often a **water pump** that is about to break down will send out noisy warning signals and then start to leak before it goes completely. You can check your pump by either shaking the fan when the engine is shut off to make the pump rattle, or by removing the fan belt, which drives the water pump, and running the engine to see if the noise has stopped. If it has, the water pump was the noisy culprit.

Leaks in the Water Pump

If the pump is leaking in the front where it rotates with the belt, it must be replaced. If the leak is around the gasket that lies between the water pump and the engine, you may be able to stop it by tightening the bolts that hold the water pump in place. If this doesn't do the job, then you probably will need a new pump.

It is a lot easier to replace a water pump than it is to fix one. You can get a **rebuilt** pump for about half the price of a new one. Ask for at least a 30-day guarantee. A new pump, replaced and installed by a good mechanic, might run about $40 for the pump, plus about $20 for labor. You can get a rebuilt pump for $10 to $15 and install it yourself to save 75 percent of the money!

How to Replace a Water Pump

If you want to do the job yourself, be prepared to do the following:

1 Drain all the liquid out of your cooling system by opening the drain cocks in your radiator and letting

the rest of the stuff drain out when the pump is removed. (It doesn't all have to go, but most of it will.)

2 Remove the fan and the fan belts (see Chapter 5 for instructions on how to remove and replace fan belts).

3 Unscrew the bolts that hold the water pump in place. Be sure to lay everything you've removed down in the order in which you removed it, with each part in the same direction as it was on the car. This will help you to put everything back in reverse order, with no guessing about which end was up or which bolt went where.

4 Disconnect the hoses that led to and from the pump. If the **hose clamps** look funky or brittle, replace them with new ones of the gear-type.

5 Remove the pump and its gasket. Scrape the spot clean, put some water-resistant sealing compound on the area, and put down the new gasket.

6 Replace the pump, the bolts, the hoses, the fan and fan belt and test-drive the car to see if there are any leaks.

If all this seems like too much of a challenge, by all means have a professional do it for you. But call around for prices on a rebuilt pump first and bring it to the mechanic. Make sure the pump comes with a gasket that matches the old one.

A Word About Sealer If you find a leak in your radiator or engine block— and if the leak is just a small one (a couple of drops a day, with no need to add water more frequently than once a week)—you might want to try a **sealer** before you head for the repair shop.

Sealer is something you add to the liquid in your cooling system. It circulates around with the water and the coolant and when it finds a hole where a leak is occurring, it plugs it up.

There are several kinds of sealers, or "stop-leaks," as they are sometimes called. The trick is to choose one that will do the best job without gumming up the cooling system. Ask for advice on this at the auto supply store. It is especially important that the sealer be compatible with your coolant. The label should tell you.

Sealers are added through the radiator just as you add water and coolant. Some coolants have a sealer built in, but these are rarely strong enough to deal with established leaks. If you try a sealer and the leaks recur in a couple of days, you'd better get professional help.

On the other hand, if the leaks occur in any of the hoses, it is quite simple to replace them yourself.

How to Replace a Radiator Hose (and Almost Any Other Hose, for That Matter)

If you have checked the hoses in your car and found a leak in one of them, or if they are deteriorating in any of the ways listed on page 161, it is a simple and inexpensive matter to replace them. The following instructions deal with replacing radiator hoses, but they can be adapted easily to any other hose in your car. *With one exception*: Never, never attempt to replace the hoses connected to your air conditioner (if you have one), or to deal with that air conditioner itself. Air conditioners and their hoses contain a special type of refrigerant, under pressure, that can literally blind you. If you have any air-conditioning problems, or if the hoses leading to and from the air conditioner do not appear to be in good shape, let a professional deal with the problem. Nothing is worth the potential danger involved!

So much for the scary stuff. Here's how to change the rest of the hoses on your car:

1 If you have another way of getting to the auto supply store, remove the hose and take it with you. That way you can check the one they give you, right on the spot, to be sure it is the correct hose for your car.

While you are removing the hose, take a look at the clamps that are holding it in place. If they are cruddy and brittle, get new clamps when you buy the hose. Clamps are very cheap—two will usually cost less than $1.50—and most of the difficulty involved in hose changing is getting the old clamps off and putting them back on again. If you buy new clamps, you can cut the old ones off and replace them with new ones that are easy to work with. You might make it a practice to buy new clamps whenever you are buying a new piece of hose. Here are a few popular kinds:

Gear-type Clamp

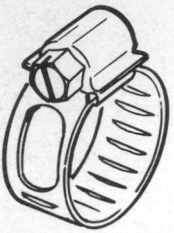

Wire Hose Clamp

Screw Type Clamp

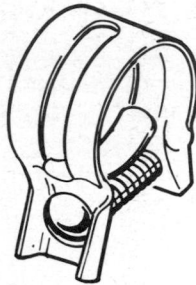

Hose Clamps
Everco Industries, Inc.

a *Wire Hose Clamps*

I hate these. You need a special kind of tool to deal with them. It is called a "wire hose clamp pliers," and it comes with a slit inside each side of its jaws for gripping the ends of these clamps. If you are going to replace a hose that has these clamps, buy a new set of gear-type clamps and throw the old wire ones away.

b *Gear-Type Clamps*

These are installed with a screwdriver. Just turn the screw to loosen the clamp, slip it over the hose, slip the end of the new hose in place, and turn the screw clockwise to tighten the clamp. Easy? These are my favorites.

c *Screw-Type Clamps*

These are hard to loosen, so they are used on radiator hoses and the like to keep them in place. Unscrew the screw completely. When you've removed the screw, slip a screwdriver under the clamp and loosen it. When you replace the hose, throw away the clamp, unless it has been *most* cooperative, and use one of the gear-type clamps to install the new hose.

2 If you must drive the car to the auto supply store, take along the spec sheet with the make, model, and year of your car. They may also want to know the size and type of engine and whether or not your car has air conditioning—depending upon which hose you are buying. But by now you have all that information at your fingertips, right?

3 Tell them which hose you want:

a If it is a *top radiator hose*, I recommend you get one that does *not* have wire inside it. Radiator hoses have to bend to fit properly between the radiator and whatever they lead to. Some hoses are straight tubes, with wire coiled inside the rubber casing. These are called "universal" hoses; they are designed to be bent to fit many cars. Often the wire will break or work its way through the top covering of the hose and cause the hose to leak.

The kind of hose to look for is called "preformed" hose. It is made with the proper bend already in it. There is no wire inside the rubber.

A Preformed Radiator Hose
The Gates Rubber Company

Another reason why you do not want a top radiator hose with wire inside it is that it should be squeezable. This way, if you have problems with your cooling system, you can squeeze the hose to see if the system is operating under pressure. The hose should be hard to the touch when you squeeze it with the car idling.

b If it is a *bottom radiator hose* that you need, it *must* have a wire coil inside it to help it keep its shape and withstand the vacuum caused by the water being drawn out of the radiator by the water pump. In this case, look for a hose with a wire coil insert inside it.

c If it is any other hose, either drag the salesperson outside to see which one it is, or indicate in the following terms which hose you need:

—its *name*, if you know it

—what it *connects* (ex., the rubber hose that runs between the carburetor and the fuel pump.)

—the *diameter* of the hose. Most hoses are sold by their *inside* diameter, and, you may have to take one end of the hose off, measure its inside diameter, then put it back on and drive to the auto supply store. (They will also need to know *how long* a hose you need in this case.)

Don't forget to buy new clamps, if you need them. They should be large enough to fit the outside diameter of the hose.

4 If possible, check the hose against your own before you remove your own hose. If the hose does not look, feel, or seem to be the same size as your old one, take it back.

5 Now you are ready to replace the old hose. If it carries water or fuel, you will need something to catch the liquid that will run out when it's removed.

a Hoses that carry fuel will lose only the fuel in the hose. This is because, when your engine isn't operating, the fuel generally remains in the gas tank. All you need is a can in which to put the first end of the hose that you remove, in order to catch whatever drains out of it.

b If you are going to change a radiator hose, especially the bottom one, you will need a bucket to catch all the liquid that drains out of the

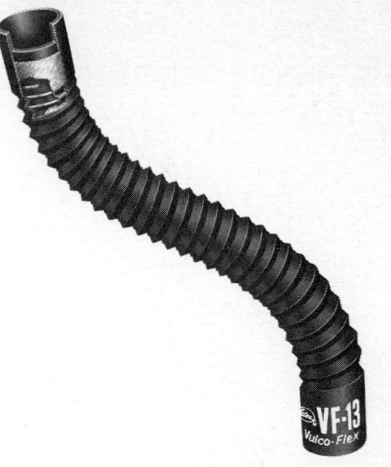

A Flexible Radiator Hose with Wire Insert
The Gates Rubber Company

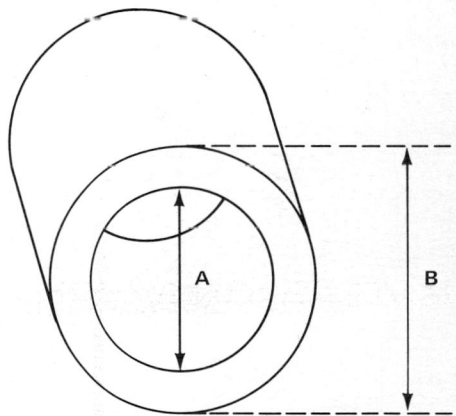

How to Measure the Inside and Outside Diameters of a Hose
Alexandra Soto

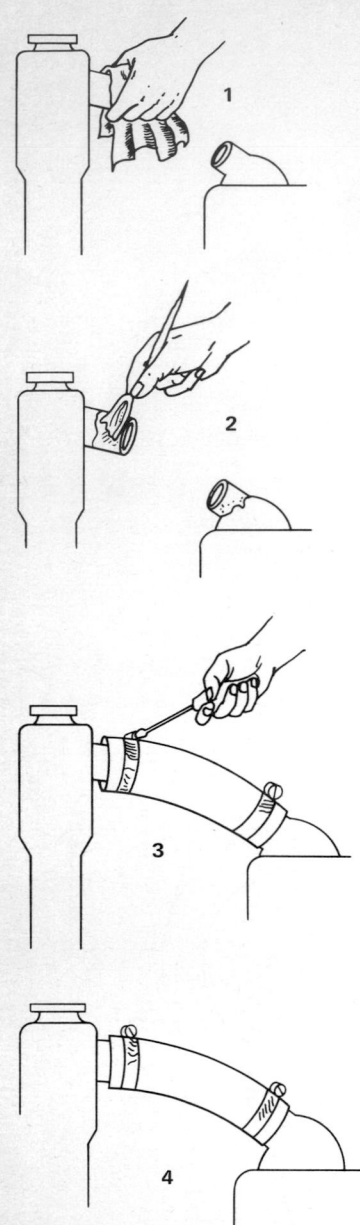

How to Install a Hose
The Gates Rubber Company

1. Wipe pipe end clean.
2. Use sealer if you want to—or try doing without it first.
3. Install clamps and tighten with screwdriver.
4. That's all there is to it!

radiator and the hose. (If you haven't had your coolant changed for almost a year, it might be a good idea just to let the stuff drain and combine replacing the hose with flushing your cooling system and adding new coolant. Instructions follow on how to do that.)

6 Remove the clamps at either end of the hose. If liquid drains out, catch it as we've described above. If you are going to replace the clamps with new ones and the old ones are hard to remove, you can saw them off if necessary. Wipe the pipe ends clean.

7 If you are replacing a hose that normally contains liquid under pressure, some manuals advise putting a water-resistant sealer on the ends of the pipes to which the hose connects. This is to prevent leaks. Because these sealers tend to make the hoses very hard to remove when it is time to replace them again or to do minor repairs, I would suggest you try it without sealer. Then if the hose leaks, you can always go back and use the sealer as recommended. In most cases, if the hose is the proper one and the clamps are on tight enough, you should be able to get by without sealer.

8 Attach the new hose, attaching and clamping one end in place before you tackle the other end.

9 If it was a radiator hose, you will have to replace the water and coolant that drained out. If the coolant is new and the water looks free of rusty junk, just remove the radiator cap and pour the liquid back through the opening after the new hose is in place. Use a funnel if necessary.

If it was a fuel hose, dispose of the fuel that leaked out when you removed the hose. If there is a lot of it and if you managed to catch it in a clean container, you can put it back into your fuel tank.

10 Check, with the engine running (make sure that the parking brake is on and that the car is in "Neutral" or "Park"), to be sure that the clamps are nice and tight so that no air, water, fuel, or whatever was in there to begin with, leaks out. You don't want your clamps so tight that they can cut the hose—but if you leave them too loose, the hose will either leak or come off.

It is impossible to tell someone, in a book, how tight or loose a clamp should be. Use your best judgment. If the clamp is so tight that it appears to be cutting into the hose, loosen it. If you can hear or see air or liquid escaping from the ends of the hose, the clamp should be tighter. In any case, the worst that can happen is that the hose will come off, and then you just have to put it back in place and tighten the clamp some more.

How to Flush Your System and Change Your Coolant

There are three things that you should do to keep your cooling system in good shape: check for leaks, replace worn hoses before they split, and flush the system and change the coolant at least once a year. We've already discussed the leak situation, and you now know how to change your hoses, so let's get on to the proper way to flush your system and change the coolant in it.

This is definitely a job that you should do yourself. It is very easy, and the difference in cost is tremendous. Remember, not only will your service station expect to make a profit on the coolant (they bought it and stocked it, didn't they?) but they will charge you for labor at around $12 an hour. Even if the "labor" consists of just waiting around for the radiator to flush, they will still charge you for that time. So be smart and do it yourself.

How to Tell If Your Coolant Needs Changing

There are two situations when you should definitely change your coolant. The first is if you haven't changed it in a year. The second is if your car has been losing water for some time and is overheating easily. The reason for this is that, after continually adding water to your cooling system, you have probably significantly lowered the level of the coolant in the system to less than half the mixture.

If neither of the above is true, you may still be in need of a change, so here are a couple of things that you can do to ascertain whether or not you should do the job:

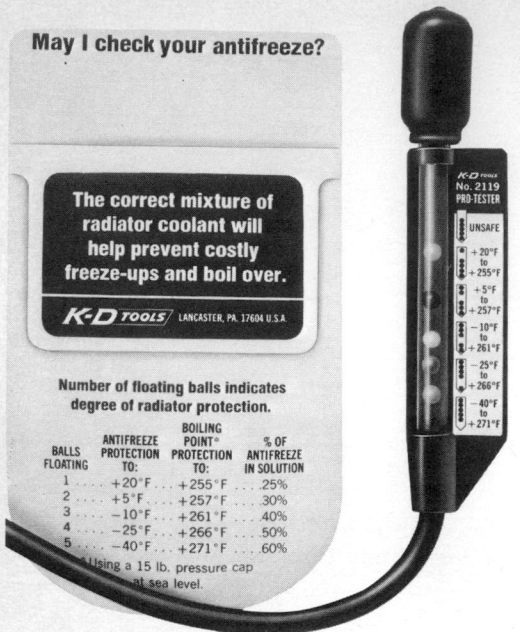

May I check your antifreeze?

The correct mixture of radiator coolant will help prevent costly freeze-ups and boil over.

K·D TOOLS LANCASTER, PA. 17604 U.S.A.

Number of floating balls indicates degree of radiator protection.

BALLS FLOATING	ANTIFREEZE PROTECTION TO:	BOILING POINT° PROTECTION TO:	% OF ANTIFREEZE IN SOLUTION
1	+20°F	+255°F	25%
2	+5°F	+257°F	30%
3	−10°F	+261°F	40%
4	−25°F	+266°F	50%
5	−40°F	+271°F	60%

*Using a 15 lb. pressure cap at sea level.

A Coolant-Protection Level Tester
K-D Manufacturing Co.

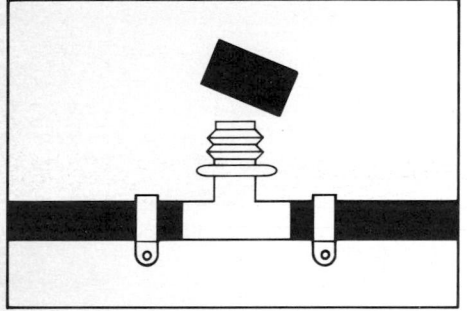

How to Use a Flush 'N Fill Kit
Union Carbide Corp.

1. Remove cap from tee. *(continued on next page)*

1 Unscrew the radiator cap and look in. Is the liquid inside clear? Or are there "things" floating around in it? Does it look rusty? Coolant can be pink in color, so don't mistake coolant for rust. Rusty water has particles floating around in it. Coolant can also be green, greenish yellow, or blue.

2 Have you been adding water every couple of days or weeks? Then your antifreeze/coolant protection level is probably low. There are little testers for sale that will tell you if you have enough coolant in your system. These are cheap and easy to use, and you might want to use one to check protection level, especially if coolant has been changed recently but you've had to add a lot of water. The instructions are on the package. They usually involve drawing a bit of liquid out of the radiator into the tester. Then little balls or a float in the tester will tell you whether you need to add coolant. While you're at it, you might check the liquid in the tester for rust.

3 If you live in a place where it gets very cold in the winter or very hot in the summer, be sure you have enough coolant in your system before extreme weather sets in. In most areas, a 50–50 solution of water and coolant is recommended for year-round use. If the weather turns *extremely* cold, you can add a higher proportion of coolant without hurting your cooling system at all. You should also be aware that, although the air conditioner in your car does a fine job of keeping the interior of the car cool, it also raises the temperature in your engine. So if you have an air conditioner, be sure to have at least a 50–50 mix during the months when you use your air conditioner most. If during your seasonal check, you find that the level of coolant is very low, it might be a good time to flush your cooling system.

Flushing Your Cooling System Can Be as Easy as Washing the Dishes

Your owner's manual will give you difficult instructions to follow when it comes to flushing your cooling system. Ignore them. There is a gadget on sale that costs less than $3 and makes flushing the system and changing the coolant a breeze. It is called the "Prestone" Flush 'N Fill Kit, and it is available in auto supply stores. Instead of having to disconnect hoses, drain the radiator, haul and measure water and coolant, all you have to do, once the Flush 'N Fill tee is installed, is unscrew your radiator cap and the little cap on the tee, screw on the end of your garden hose, and let the water run right through the cooling system and out the radiator fill hole to the ground. This flushes the entire system, not just your radiator! When the water has run for several minutes and is coming out of the system as clear as it went in, you just add the proper amount of coolant through the radiator fill hole. This displaces an equal amount of water at the other end through the tee. You screw both caps back on, and you are finished! There's no mess, no measuring, no dirty hands. The whole thing takes less than 10 minutes—5 of which are engaged in watching the water run out, or in sunbathing.

There are instructions on the package, but just in case you are worried about the difficulty involved, here's all there is to it. After you locate the proper hose on your car (they tell you how to find it easily), you loosen your radiator cap and:

1 You cut the hose.
2 You insert the tee.
3 You clamp the tee in place (the clamps are the easy kind you install with a screwdriver).

That's all! *(See illustration on page 174)*

You can consult your owner's manual, the back of the coolant jug, or the charts that the coolant manufacturers supply, for the number of quarts your cooling system will hold. Then simply divide the amount by two and buy that amount of coolant. This will give you a 50–50 water/coolant mixture, which is fine for everything but extremely cold weather. If you want to beef up the level of coolant in your system at any time, with the flushing tee installed (it stays in place permanently), just open your radiator cap and the cap on the tee and add additional coolant down the fill hole. An equal amount of liquid will come out of the tee at the other end. Then just shut both caps, run the engine until the car heats up, and add more water or coolant if the level of liquid in the radiator drops.

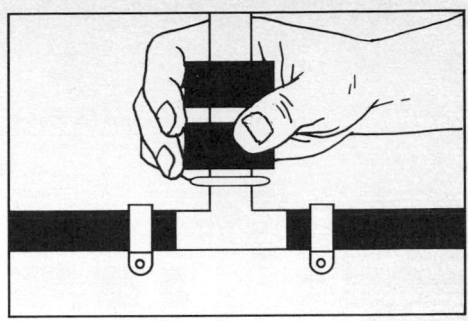

2. Connect garden hose.

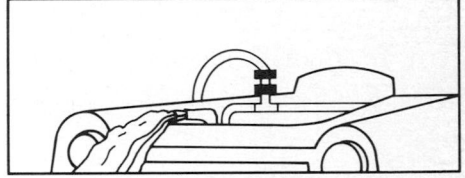

3. Remove radiator cap and insert splash tube in fill hole. Let water run through system.

How to Install the Flush 'N Fill Kit

4. When water runs clear, remove splash tube and hose and pour anti-freeze/coolant into radiator.

How to Tell How Much Coolant You Need

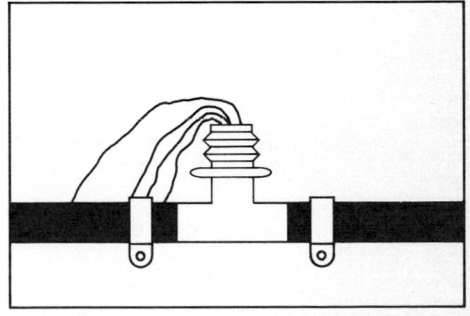

5. An equal volume of water will leave the system through the tee. *(continued on next page)*

000-173

Cooling System Cleaners

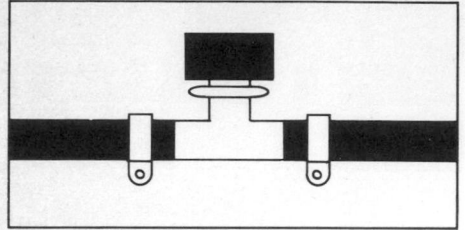

6. Replace tee cap and radiator cap.

If your car is old, or if your cooling system seems to be rusting a lot, you may want to use a cleaning chemical when you flush the system. There are several different types, but they are all easy to use. Just follow the directions on the package. They all involve adding the stuff to the system and then flushing it out again. With that flushing tee, it's no extra trouble.

Coolant Recovery Systems

If your car tends to overheat, you will often notice liquid pouring out from under the car—especially if you are using your air conditioner on a very hot day. This liquid is usually colored, and it sometimes has white foam on it. It is just the water/coolant mixture pouring out of the overflow pipe on your radiator.

When your car heats up, the pressure in your system rises, and if it exceeds the level of pressure that your radiator cap is built to withstand, the liquid in the

How to Install a Flush 'N Fill Kit
Union Carbide Corp.

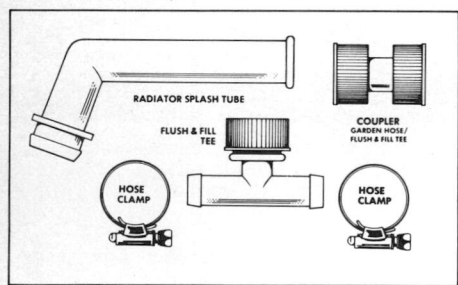

1. Cut hose.

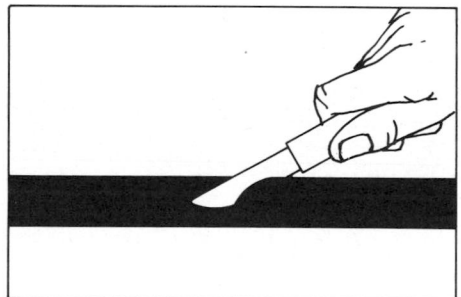

2. Insert tee.

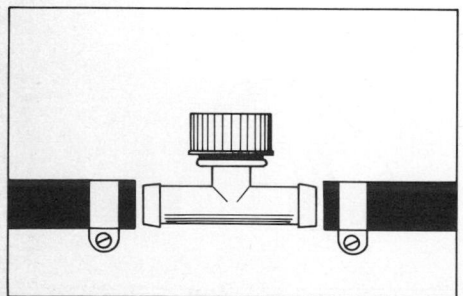

3. Tighten clamps.

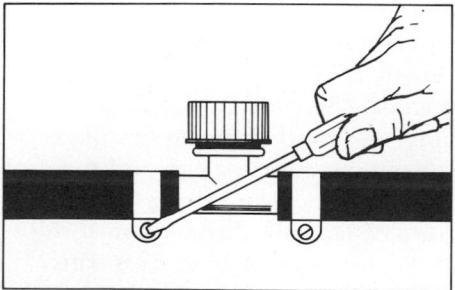

system will bypass the radiator cap and escape through an **overflow pipe** located near your fill hole. This pipe is there to provide a safe way for your car to "let off steam." Of course, if this kind of overflow occurs often, your car will lose enough water and coolant to substantially lower the level in the cooling system. You will have to keep adding water, and eventually, the level of coolant protection will be inadequate. To prevent this, there is an inexpensive gadget on the market that you might like to try.

A **coolant recovery kit** is simply a plastic bottle with two little hoses coming out of the cap. You usually attach one hose to the overflow pipe on your radiator and mount the bottle anywhere it will fit but slightly lower than the overflow pipe. A new radiator cap comes with the kit, too. When your cooling system heats up and starts to overflow, instead of constantly pouring out of the overflow pipe and onto the ground, the liquid will now pour out of the overflow pipe and into the bottle. When the system has cooled off, the pressure drops and the liquid is drawn out of the bottle and back into the radiator. The second hose serves as an overflow for the bottle, in case more liquid overflows than the bottle can hold.

These kits usually cost less than $3. Installation is simple: you just attach the bracket that holds the bottle to the frame of your car under the hood. With one of these recovery kits, when you want to add coolant or water to your system, you can just pour it into the bottle instead of into the radiator. Although a recovery system is considered "sealed," it would still be a good idea to open the radiator cap now and then and check the level in the radiator just in case you are losing liquid through a leak somewhere else in the cooling system. You can find a coolant recovery kit at your auto supply store.

If you have not been able to locate any leaks and if your car is overheating constantly, you will have to check out a different set of alternatives:

How to Install a Coolant Recovery Kit

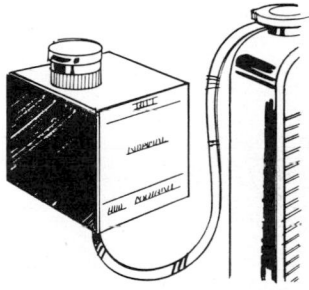

Coolant Recovery Kit

What to Look for If Your Car Is Overheating and You Can't Find Any Leaks

How to Replace Your Thermostat

If your car has been overheating or does not warm up properly, you may need to replace your **thermostat**. You will recall that this little gizmo simply stays closed and keeps the liquid in the engine block until the car heats up. Although it is a simple device, it, like everything else, can malfunction. If it sticks in the *open* position the thermostat will not keep the liquid in the engine long enough, and you will have trouble getting your car warmed up. If it sticks *shut*, the liquid will not be allowed to get to the radiator, and overheating will result.

It is quite a simple matter to replace a thermostat, and since they are quite inexpensive (definitely less than $5, and I've seen some for as little as 97 cents), you might want to try this before going on to more drastic measures:

1 Locate your thermostat, if you haven't already done so. Since most of them are found where the top radiator hose joins the engine, let's deal with this type. If your thermostat is in the bottom radiator hose, the principle is the same.

2 Get a new one. Supply the usual information (make, model, etc.) to the auto supply store. You should be an old hand at this by now, and they will probably say, "Here comes the sixty-seven Mustang" (or whatever you drive) when you come in the door.

3 Unscrew the clamp that holds the end of the radiator hose where your thermostat is located.

4 Pull off the hose. Some liquid will escape, so have a bucket handy to catch it, and return it to the radiator when you have finished the job or use this golden opportunity to change it.

5 Remove the bolts that hold the thermostat in place, and lift out the old thermostat. There is a gasket around it. Get that off too. Scrape off the pieces of gasket that may be stuck, but be sure not to let these pieces fall into the hole.

6 Lay the new gasket in place. If it doesn't match the old one, you probably have the wrong thermostat.

7 Drop in the new thermostat. Be sure to place the spring side *down.* Then replace the bolts.

8 Replace the hose, and screw down the clamp. Screw it down tight but not tight enough to cut the hose.

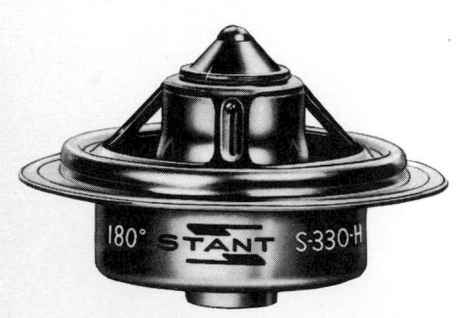

Thermostats Are Replaced Spring-Side Down.
Stant Manufacturing Company, Inc.

9 Replace whatever liquid ran out of the hose by
pouring it out of the bucket and into the radiator
fill hole (of course your bucket was clean when you
put the stuff in it, right?).

If your car continues to overheat, with the new thermostat in place, then you will have to look elsewhere
for the cause.

Other Things That Can Cause Your Car to Overheat

If you haven't tuned and timed your car recently, it
may be the fault of your timing. Late timing sometimes produces an overheated engine by having the
spark fire the fuel/air mixture after the piston has
moved back down from the top of its stroke. This
causes the spark plugs to fire too late to allow all the
gases to burn properly, and more heat will burden
your cooling system. Late timing alone will not cause a
car to overheat by more than a few degrees, but cou-
pled with other problems, it can bring the temperature to a critical point. The remedy is simple: just
check your timing and adjust it as in Chapter 5.

Timing

Some radiators get so plugged up with rust, sediment,
or small insects that even cleaning and flushing them
does not do the trick. Since plugged passages cut
down on the circulation of the liquid in the system, it
cannot cool efficiently. The remedy is to have the
radiator removed and steam-cleaned by a radiator
specialist. It should cost about $20, but it's worth it.

Plugged Radiator

Check your fan belt to be sure that there is no more
than about ½ inch of "give." If it is looser than that, it
may not be driving your water pump properly, and
that can impair circulation and overheat the cooling
system. If your fan belt seems loose or very frayed,
replace it according to the instructions in Chapter 5.

Slipping Fan Belt

Occasionally, a bottom radiator hose will begin to col-
lapse under the vacuum created by the water pump,
and the impaired circulation will cause overheating. If

Collapsing Bottom Radiator Hose

your car starts to overheat, stop and open the hood, with the car in "Park" and the parking brake on, without shutting off the engine. Then take a look at the bottom hose (be careful not to get your hair or clothing caught in the fan or the fan belt) and see if it has collapsed. If it has replace it.

Low Oil Level Check your oil dipstick if you still can't find the cause of overheating. If your car is low on oil, it will tend to overheat because the oil removes from 75 to 80 percent of the "waste heat" in your engine (besides doing its other numbers). If you are one quart low in oil and your car holds 5 quarts, there is a 20 percent reduction in the amount of heat that the oil can carry away (it cools off in the crankcase).

What to Do If Your Car Overheats from Natural Causes Even the happiest, most beautifully tuned car will overheat occasionally. If you find yourself in stop-and-go traffic, on a rotten hot day, the chances are that your car's dashboard temperature indicator will rise. There are a couple of things you can do to help your car keep its cool under these circumstances:

1 At the first sign of overheating, shut off your air conditioner and open your car windows. This will decrease the load on the engine and help it to cool off.

2 If you continue to overheat, turn on the car heater and blower. This will transfer the heat from the engine to the interior of the car. (It will do wonders for your overheated engine but very little for you!)

3 If you are stopped in traffic and the temperature gauge is rising, shift into "Neutral" and rev the engine a little to make the water pump and the fan speed up and draw more liquid and air through the radiator. The increased air and liquid circulation should help to cool things off.

4 Try not to "ride your brakes." Brake drag increases the load on the engine and makes it heat up. Lag behind a bit if traffic is crawling, and then move up when the gap between you and the car in front of you gets too wide. Try to crawl along slowly, on little more than an idle, rather than moving up quickly and braking to a stop.

5 If you think your car is about to boil over, drive to the side of the road, open the hood, and sit there until things cool off. Remember, *don't open the radiator cap* under these circumstances, and if your engine has boiled over, *don't add water* until the car is quite cool again. If you must add water when the engine is still a little warm, add the water while the engine is running in neutral gear.

Vapor Lock

I ought to say a word about a condition that often occurs under overheated circumstances. This is called **vapor lock**, and it can be quite disconcerting if you don't know what is happening.

Occasionally a car will get so hot that the gas boils in the fuel line. When it boils, it forms bubbles that keep the fuel pump from pumping the gasoline to the carburetor. This situation is easy to spot. Your car just suddenly stops going. And the condition is easy to fix once you know what has occurred.

1 If you are on the freeway, stay in your car until a member of the highway patrol comes along and helps you get to the side of the road. If you are in normal traffic and it is safe to get out and push the car to the side of the road, do it.

2 Once you are at the side of the road, lift the hood and place a wet cloth on the fuel line and the fuel pump. (You remember where to find them from Chapter 6, right?) If you have no place to wet a rag, you'll just have to sit and wait until things cool off naturally. The wet rag does it much faster.

3 Once you have cooled the line until the gasoline is no longer boiling and the bubbles have dissipated, wrap the rag around the line (some tinfoil wrapped around the line helps tremendously. If you often get vapor lock, carry some foil in the trunk of your car) to help keep the gasoline in the line from overheating again. You can also place metal clothespins along the fuel line to radiate the heat.

4 Get back on the road as though nothing had happened. This sort of thing will occur only under extreme conditions; in most cases, if you are traveling at speeds under 25 mph or idling a lot, the fan

in the car will keep the fuel cool enough to avoid vapor lock.

If Your Car Is a Chronic Hothead

If your car is a chronic overheater, you might want to consider replacing its radiator with one with a greater cooling capacity, or installing a separate cooling device where the trouble occurs. There are devices sold to cool transmission systems, for instance. Often, these coolers are sold as part of a trailer-towing package, because most cars were not designed to tow or carry very heavy loads for long periods of time. The resulting strain will cause them to overheat. Again, a professional you can trust is the proper one to consult if you think you may need these extras. (Later on in this book, I'll get into how to choose a mechanic who is honest and competent.)

Now, before we get into the mysterious secrets of the brake system, let's take a little time to go over something everybody is supposed to know (and surprisingly few of us do)—how to jack up your car without hurting it and yourself and how to change a flat tire. . . .

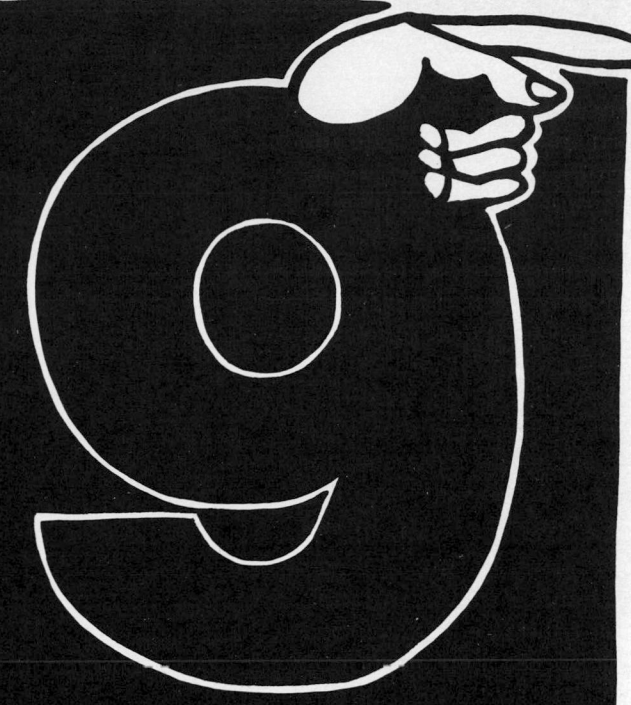

How to Jack Up
Your Car and
Change Your Tires

Up to now, most of the work we've discussed has been the "under-the-hood" kind of stuff that did not require you to get underneath your car. However, if you've reached this chapter you are probably ready to contemplate the nether regions of your automobile without flinching, so this seems as good a place as any to tell you how to jack up your car with relatively little effort or danger. And while we're at it, we'll get into the proper way to change a tire. Even if you are a member of the AAA, there is always a chance that you will find yourself stuck with a flat tire on a remote road with no telephone in sight. On these occasions, all traffic generally vanishes, leaving you helpless unless you know how to do the job yourself. We all have a general idea of what's involved, but there are a couple of places where the job gets sticky, and unless you are properly equipped, you can find yourself out of luck and in for a long wait for help to come along.

Jack Stands Hold Your Car Up Safely
Petersen Industries, Inc., Fredonia, W.I.

We've already discussed **jacks**, way back in Chapter 2, and, I hope, you've already checked to see that the jack that came with your car is working properly. If you feel that you need a new jack, you can buy either the tripod or the scissors type, or if you plan to get into under-the-car work, such as lubrication, you might want to invest in a 1.5-ton **hydraulic** jack, which is faster and safer than the other kinds and not terribly expensive.

You will also need a pair of **jack stands** if you plan to work under your car. With these, you can jack up the car, place it on the jack stands, and remove the jack. The stands will keep the car off the ground with less danger of slipping and will enable you to jack up more than one side of the car at a time.

Substituting boxes, or stones, or bricks, is very dangerous. They can slip out or break while you are under the car. A jack can do the same thing, so if you are going to work under your car (and you should plan to change your own oil and do your own lube jobs), be sure to buy a pair of jack stands. Fairly good ones cost less than $5, and the money you save by getting under there yourself will easily pay for the stands in no time.

If you are going to spend a lot of time lying around under your car, you will probably want a **creeper**. That's just a board with casters under it. You can lie on it and move around easily. You can make one yourself from some plywood and a couple of old roller-skate wheels, but if you were that mechanically inclined, you probably wouldn't be reading this book. Try lying on an old bedboard or a ratty old blanket instead if you are fed up with buying things.

If you are not yet game for a lot of under-the-car work, and you just want to change your tires, change your oil, and be done with it, forget about the creeper and just be sure you have a jack and jack stands that work properly and that you know how to use them. Your owner's manual will tell you how to use the jack that came with your car, or you can take the jack to an auto supply store and ask them to show you how it works.

What You'll Need
A Jack

Jack Stands

A Creeper

A Creeper Makes Working Under Your Car More Comfortable.
Sparkomatic Corp.

How to Jack Up Your Car

1 Check your manual for the proper place to position the jack for your model car. Remember, there is a difference in where you place the jack stands for a one-wheel job like tire changing or brake checking, and where you place them for a two-wheel whole-end job like lubrication and repairs.

2 Never place the jack so that the weight of the car rests on something that can bend, break, or "give." If your manual is incomprehensible, or lacking in this kind of information, try to place the jack so that it will touch either the car frame or the big bar that supports the front wheel suspension. Jacks can also be placed near the rear wheel **axle**. Until you become more proficient at this, I'd stick to jacking up one wheel at a time. It may mean more work, but the practice will be good for you.

3 Place the jack under the part of the car that it should contact when raised. If you have jack stands, place them near the jack.

4 *The following is important!* Before you attempt to jack up your car, observe these safety precautions:

a *Always park the car on level ground before you jack it up.* If you get a flat tire on a hill and you can't coast to the bottom of the hill without killing the tire completely, then park it close to the curb, turn the wheels toward the curb, and block the downside wheels securely to prevent the car from rolling. Even with these precautions, however, I'd be nervous.

b *Never jack up a car without blocking the wheels.* Even if the car is on level ground, use bricks, wooden wedges, or metal wheel chocks to block the wheels at the opposite end of the car from the end that is to be raised. This will keep the car from rolling after it has been jacked up. Keep the blocks in the trunk of your car so you won't have to go hunting around if you have to change a tire on the freeway. If you find yourself faced with the job of changing a tire and you have been foolish enough to disregard all these italics and have nothing with which to block the wheels, then at least park it near the curb with the wheels turned in. This may not keep you from getting hurt if the car rolls off the jack, but at least innocent motorists and pedestrians will not have to deal with a runaway driverless car!

You Can Use a Screwdriver to Pry a Hub Cap Loose.
Richard Freshman

  c *Be sure that your car is in "Park" and that the emergency brake is on, before you jack it up.* The only time you don't want the emergency brake on is if you have to be able to rotate a *rear* wheel or remove the rear brake drums to inspect the brakes.

5 If you are going to remove a wheel to change a tire or check your brakes, remove the **hub cap** and loosen the **lug nuts** *before* you jack up the car. Once the car is jacked up, the wheel will turn freely, and it will be harder to get the hub cap off and almost impossible to start the nuts.

How to Remove a Hub Cap

1 Use a screwdriver or the flat end of a **lug wrench** to pry the hub cap off. Just insert the point where the edge of the cap meets the wheel and apply a little leverage. The cap should pop off. You may have to do this in a couple of places; it's like prying a nonscrew cap off a jar of jelly.

2 Lay the cap on its back so you can put the lug nuts into it to keep them from rolling away and heading for the nearest sewer.

How to Loosen Lug Nuts

1 These are those big nuts under the hub cap that hold the wheel in place. They are usually retightened with a power tool by most garages, and unless you've done the job yourself by hand, they are going to be pretty hard to get started. If you've taken my earlier advice and bought a cross-shaft **lug wrench**, now is the time to pat yourself on the back. Before you begin, you will have to ascertain whether the lug nuts on the wheel you are working on are right-hand threaded or left-hand threaded. This is not a "left-handed hammer joke"; the threads determine which way you have to turn the wrench. The lug nuts on the right side of a car are always right-hand threaded, but the nuts on the left side *may* be left-hand threaded. Look at the lug nuts on your car. In the center of the lugs you will either see an "R" or an "L" or no letter at all. Lugs with an "R," or with no letter, are right-threaded. Lugs with an "L" are left-threaded. You turn right-threaded nuts *counterclockwise* to loosen them. You turn left-threaded nuts *clockwise*. Frankly, the whole thing

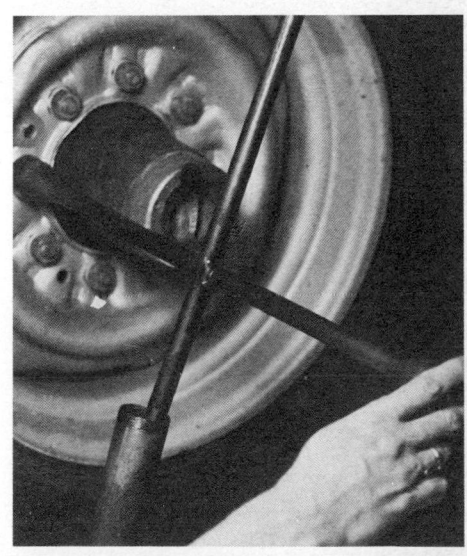

A Hollow Pipe and a Cross-Shaft Wrench Can Loosen the Tighest Lug Nuts.
Richard Freshman

seems crazy to me, but that's how it is, friends. For the purposes of sanity, let's assume that your car has right-threaded nuts. If you have a couple of lefties, just use the wrench in the opposite direction, O.K.?

2 Find the end of the wrench that fits the lug nuts on your car and fit it onto the first nut. Always work on lug nuts in rotation. That way you won't forget to tighten any later. Apply all your weight to the bar on the *left*. This should start the nut turning *counterclockwise*, which will loosen it. If the nut has been put on with a power tool and you can't get it started, a piece of hollow pipe, fitted over that left-hand arm of the cross-shaft wrench, will magically add enough leverage to start the nut easily. After you've replaced the nut yourself, this aid will no longer be necessary. But remember, the longer the arms on your lug wrench, the more leverage it will give you.

3 Do not remove the lug nuts completely, just get them loose enough so you can remove them by hand once the car has been raised.

Back to the Jack Now you can use the jack to raise the car. Apply nice even strokes, taking the jack handle from its lowest to its highest point on each stroke, to cut down on the labor involved. When the car is high enough so that the wheel is completely clear of the ground and you can easily reach and see whatever part concerns you, you can stop. Then, do the following:

1 If you have jack stands, place them under the car, near the place where the jack is touching the car. Raise the stands until they are high enough to just fit under, and lock them in place. Lower the jack until the car is resting on the jack stands. Then remove the jack.

2 Before you begin to work, wiggle the car a little to make sure it is resting securely on the jack or the jack stands. This will also tell you if you have the wheels blocked properly. It is better if the car falls while all four wheels are in place (it will just bounce a little). If you remove a wheel and begin to work without checking to be sure you've jacked it and blocked it securely, it will do itself—and you—a lot

of damage if it falls. This is not meant to frighten you away from jacking up your car and working on—or under—it. It should simply dramatize that a few simple precautions will remove any danger.

3 Everything secure? Fine! Then you can go ahead and remove the lug nuts and put them into the hub cap.

How to Change a Tire

Now that we've got the car up and the lug nuts off, here's the proper way to change a tire:

1 Remove the spare from the trunk, if you haven't already done so. Actually, it is easier if you do this before you jack up the car. If you haven't checked your spare recently, keep your fingers crossed that there is enough air in it! Roll the spare to the scene of the action.

2 Grasp the flat tire with both hands and pull it toward you. It is sitting on the exposed bolts that the lug nuts screwed onto. The flat should slide along the bolts until, suddenly, it clears the end of the bolts and you find yourself supporting its full weight. Tires are heavy, and you will be quite happy to lower it to the ground (if you haven't already dropped it).

3 Roll the flat along the ground to the trunk, to get it out of the way.

4 You are now going to have to lift the spare onto the lug bolts. Since tires are heavy, you may have a little trouble lifting it into place—especially if you are not accustomed to lifting heavy things. If this is the case, a bit of ingenuity will help.

I have a friend who is a newly liberated female of small stature. Recently, when her first flat occurred while she was on the road, she found herself in the infuriating position of being unable to lift the heavy spare onto the lug bolts—while a macho truck driver, whose offers of help she had spurned, enjoyed the scene (he'd decided to hang around and watch the "little lady" change her tire). After hearing her sad tale, I suggested that she cut an old wooden crate into a ramp that could get the tire high enough to fit onto the lug bolts, and that she should keep the ramp in the trunk of her car for future tire changes. She did it and is now gloriously independent once more. In fact, she now gets her kicks by stopping to offer bewildered males her services when they are stopped at the side of the road with a flat tire and a lack of knowledge about how to change it! The illustration shows how to make a ramp like hers.

5 After you have the spare tire in place, replace the lug nuts and tighten them by hand. Give them each a jolt with the wrench to get them firmly into place, but wait until the car is on the ground before you really try to tighten them down.

6 Replace the jack and lift the car off the jack stands, if you've used them, and lower the car to the ground. Once the car is resting on the ground, use the lug wrench to tighten the lugs as much as you can. You don't want to twist them off the bolts or ruin the threads, but you don't want the wheel to fall off, either. Use your hollow pipe, if you are worried about tightening them sufficiently, or step on the right-hand arm of the lug wrench after the nut is tight. Remember, right-hand threaded nuts tighten in a clockwise direction, lefties go the other way.

7 Now place the **hub cap** against the wheel and whack it into place with the heel of your hand. Cushion

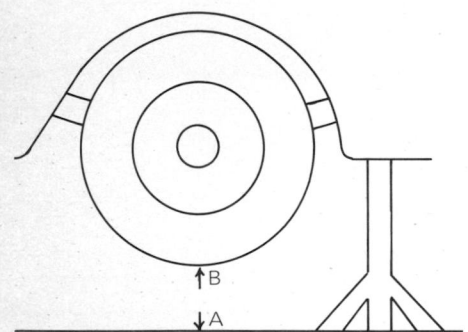

1. Measure the distance from the ground (A) to the bottom of the tire (B) while the car is jacked up.

2. Nail some boards together to form a ramp of the same height as AB above.

How to Build a Ramp
Jack Herlihy

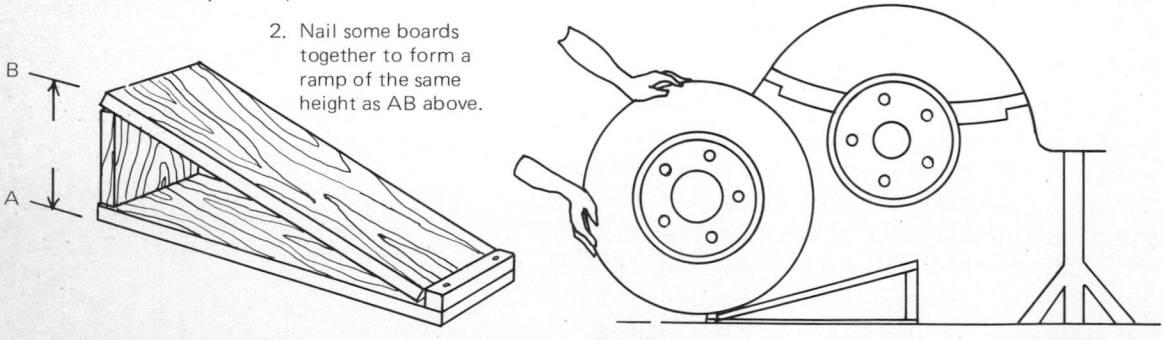

3. Now you can roll your wheel up the ramp and just push it into place without having to lift it yourself!

your hand with a soft rag first so you won't hurt it. Don't hit the hub cap with a wrench or a hammer—you'd dent it. Whack it a couple of times, in a couple of places, to be sure it's on evenly. Even second-hand hub caps can cost as much as $15 apiece to replace. If it is too much of a hassle, or if you don't have the time to replace the hub cap, you can take it home and install it later; it is mostly ornamental and you can drive for a while without it. But *do* replace it soon because it helps keep dust and dirt out of your brakes and bearings.

8 Put the flat into the trunk, where the spare was located, and put your tools away. Don't forget to remove the wheel blocks, and *don't forget to have that flat fixed*!

You may not find the prospect of fixing your own flat tires especially alluring, but isn't it nice to know that if a crisis does occur and you are not near a phone or haven't got the time to wait for the AAA, you have the ability to get yourself rolling again in less than 15 minutes? To make the job easier, should an emergency arise, you might want to go out and check the lug nuts on your car now. If they are on hideously tight, loosen them with a wrench and a pipe and retighten them to a reasonable tension so you won't have to struggle at the side of the road.

How to Be a Buddy to Your Brakes

Your car is sitting happily at the curb. It has a smug sort of look. Its ignition system is in tune, its carburetor is clean and well fed, and it hasn't overheated in a long time. You are both quite pleased with yourselves by now—and you should be. You can raise the hood with a practiced air and contemplate the gadgets in there with the eye of an old friend (well, maybe a new acquaintance). But before you relegate this book to the "guess-I'll-finish-it-later" pile and go on to learn macrame or fly-tying, we'd better talk about an aspect of auto repair and maintenance that most of us take for granted, even though it deals with practically the only system in your car that can kill you if you don't keep it in good repair. As you've already guessed—especially if you read chapter titles—I'm talking about your **brakes**.

Most cars today are equipped with an **hydraulic brake system**, which we've already discussed in Chapter 3. (If you've forgotten, you might want to go back and reread it now. I'll wait. . . .)

Since 1968, most cars are also equipped with *dual* brake systems to ensure that, if one set of brakes fails, the other set will still be able to stop your car; and with a dashboard light to warn you if your front or rear brakes fail.

Let's go over the brake system in greater detail and talk about the differences between **disc brakes** and **drum brakes**, between *manual* and **power brakes**, and so forth, so you can be perfectly familiar with what *should* be happening when you stop your car. Then, at the end of this chapter, I'll show you how to inspect your brake system to be sure it is in good shape; how to keep it in good shape; and how to keep from being ripped off when it is time to have your brakes adjusted or **rebuilt**.

Although it is possible to do most of the work yourself—there is nothing terribly complicated about it—I don't think that you should do any major brake work without supervision. If you don't get things back properly, you'll risk losing much more than you'd gain! However, if after reading this chapter you simply can't stand the idea of having a total stranger replace your worn **brake linings**, you can always get

Disc brake
(front)

Brake line

Master cylinder

Brake warning
light switch

Power brake
(optional)

Brake pedal

Drum brake
(rear)

The Brake System
The Bendix Corp.

yourself to a good auto repair class and do the work under the watchful eye of the instructor. Auto classes generally have the hydraulic hoists, **brake drum** lathes, **brake-shoe** arcing machines, and other expensive equipment that you'd need to do a really good job; so even if you are sure you need no further instruction after reading my enlightened and crystal-clear prose, it would still be worth the price of enrollment to have the equipment and the instructor's expertise available.

Whether you decide to do the work yourself or not, there is still a lot of ground we can cover, and a lot of preventive checking and maintenance you can do to spot trouble before it occurs and to enable you to deal on an informed level with your auto mechanic or brake specialist.

To recap: Getting your car to stop is a relatively simple matter. The hydraulic brake system is designed to operate on a very simple principle with a minimum of parts and maintenance.

In the system shown on p. 192 there is a **power booster**, and disc brakes on the front wheels. Your system may not have power brakes and may have disc or drum brakes all around. The principle's the same in any case. Let's start at the first point of contact between you and your brakes and then work down the line to the brakes themselves.

The Brake Pedal

The *brake pedal* in your car is attached to a shaft that leads to the **master cylinder**. When you step on the brake pedal, a small piston in the master cylinder forces **brake fluid** out of the master cylinder and into the **brake lines**. If your brakes are working properly, the pedal should stop a couple of inches from the floor. It should push down easily, stop firmly at its lowest point without feeling spongy, and stay put instead of sinking down slowly when you put normal pressure on it. Power brakes stop closer to the floor, with as little as one inch of clearance. We'll check yours later.

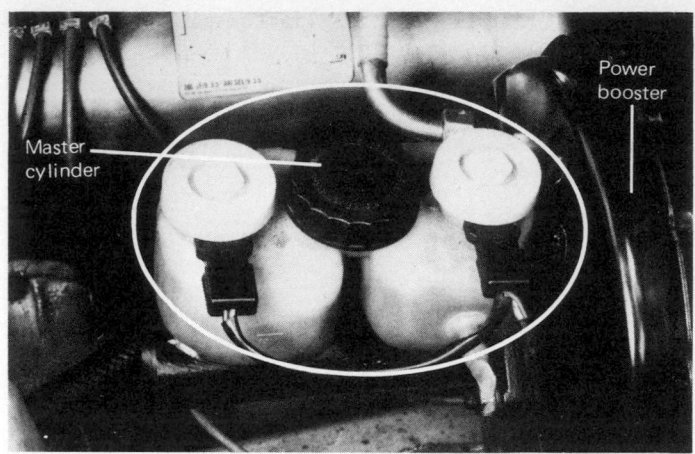

Master Cylinder with Plastic Reservoir and
Power Booster
Richard Freshman

The Master Cylinder Look under the hood of your car, up near the firewall
on the driver's side. You should see either a metal box
or a plastic bottle. Have you found it? This is your
master cylinder. It is full of brake fluid and is connected to your brake pedal, with brake lines leading
from it to the four wheels of your car. When you step
on the brake pedal, fluid will go out of the master
cylinder into the brake lines. When you release the
pedal, the fluid will flow back into the master cylinder.
Don't mess with yours now; I'll show you how to get it
open later on in this chapter, when we begin to check
the brake systems on your car.

Dual Brakes A *dual* brake system simply means that the inside of
your master cylinder is divided into *two* compartments,
each filled with brake fluid. One compartment has
brake lines that lead to the brakes on your front
wheels; the other compartment has lines leading to
your rear wheels. If you should develop a leak, or a
block, in one set of lines, the fluid in that compartment will be lost or useless. But you will still have the
other compartment and set of brakes with which to
stop your car. It may not stop smoothly, but it will
stop, and in such a case, that's all that counts! This
simple modification has saved countless lives.

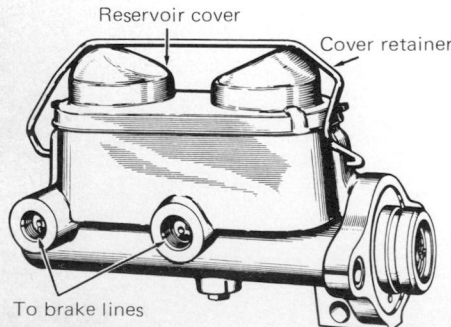

Metal Master Cylinder
The Bendix Corp.

If after checking your brake system you find you have a leak, or have to **bleed** your brakes, you will have to go to the auto supply store to buy some **brake fluid** in order to restore the fluid in your master cylinder to its proper level. Here are some things you should know:

1 Always use top-quality brake fluid, from a well-known manufacturer. Your manual will tell you which kind your car uses. Be sure to get the proper type of brake fluid for your car—drum brakes take a different type of fluid than do disc brakes.

  a **Drum brakes** use brake fluid that comes in cans that say "meets or surpasses SAE specifications 70R3 and J-1703."

  b **Disc brakes** use a fluid with a higher boiling point (around 550 degrees F.).

2 You can use disc brake fluid on a car with drum brakes providing you have the brake system thoroughly flushed first, to get rid of any traces of the former fluid. So even if you have drum brakes, check the master cylinder to see what color the fluid in it is, before going out to buy brake fluid to add to the stuff in the system. The salesperson should be able to tell what kind you have by the color.

3 If you have front disc brakes and rear drum brakes on your car, you probably have disc brake fluid in both chambers of your master cylinder.

4 *This is important!* Brake fluid becomes swiftly contaminated by exposure to air. The oxygen in the air oxidizes it and lowers its boiling point. It also has an affinity for moisture, and the water vapor in the air can combine with the brake fluid to form ice crystals that make braking difficult in cold weather. If you add water-vapor-contaminated fluid to your brake system, it can rust the system and create acids that will etch your **wheel cylinders** and master cylinder and foul your brakes, causing them to work poorly—or not at all. Therefore, if you are going to add brake fluid to your system, buy a small can, add the fluid to your master cylinder, and *throw the rest away,* or use it only in emergencies. The stuff is pretty cheap, and your car should not need more fluid after a leak has been fixed. If you keep a can with only a little fluid left in it, the air that fills up the

Brake Fluid

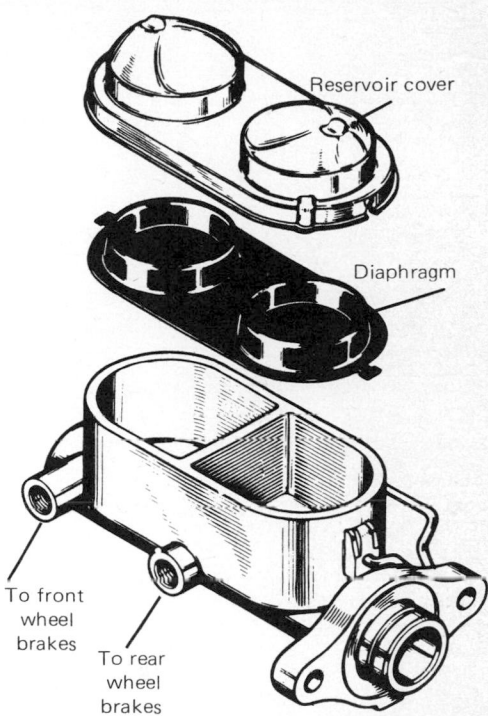

Reservoir cover

Diaphragm

To front wheel brakes

To rear wheel brakes

Dual-Chamber Master Cylinder
The Bendix Corp.

rest of the space in the can will contaminate the fluid, no matter how quickly you've recapped it. One more thing, keep brake fluid away from painted surfaces—*it eats paint*. (If this stuff seems scary, remember that many of the same statements can be made about turpentine or nail polish remover.)

Brake Lines

Leading away from the master cylinder, along the frame of your car to each wheel, are the **brake lines**. These are made of steel except for the portions that lie right near your front wheels and your rear **axle**. These portions of the brake line are made of rubber that is flexible enough to contend with the greater amount of movement that takes place in these areas when you steer your car.

Up to now, most of the brake systems on your cars have been pretty much the same. But now we get to the major differences between the various kinds of hydraulic brake systems. Most cars have **drum brakes** on all four wheels, but others have drum brakes on the rear wheels only and **disc brakes** on the front wheels. Still others have four-wheel disc brakes. Then there are cars with *power-assisted* drum or disc brakes. And to confuse you completely, since 1963 most brakes are *self-adjusting*, but there are still a couple of oldies with *manually adjusted* brakes around. Your owner's manual will tell you what kind(s) of brakes you have on your car, in case you don't already know, but it's more fun to see for yourself. I'll describe each type of brake in detail and then show you how to check each part of your car's brake system to see if it needs help.

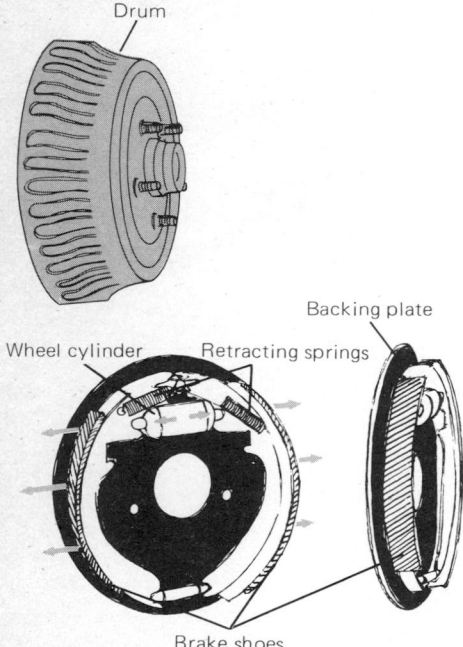

Drum

Backing plate

Wheel cylinder   Retracting springs

Brake shoes

Anatomy of a Drum Brake
Automotive Information Council (AIC)

Drum Brakes

Wheel Cylinders

1 In this type of brake system, the brake fluid that has been forced through the brake lines by the piston in the master cylinder goes into a smaller **wheel cylinder** located inside the **brake drum** on the **brake backing plate**.

2 The fluid then activates the two small pistons located inside the wheel cylinder by forcing them farther apart.

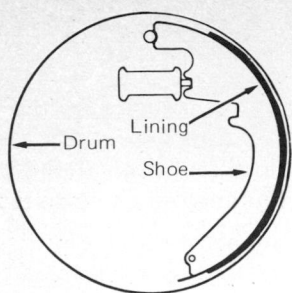

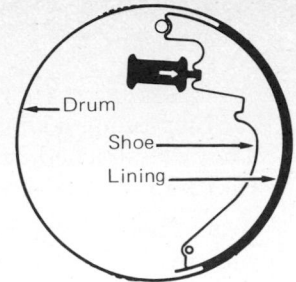

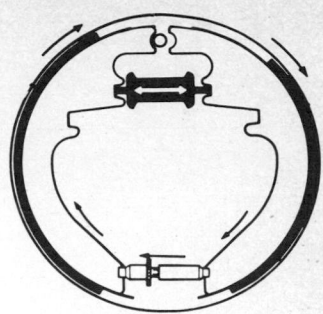

1. Before Braking.

2. Fluid in the Wheel Cylinder Pushes the Piston Outward.

3. As the Brake Shoes Are Forced Against the Drum, the Car Stops.

The Brake Fluid in the Wheel Cylinder Pushes the Brake Shoes Outward, Forcing the Linings Against the Drum.
The Bendix Corp.

3 The fluid pushes against the *pistons*, forcing them to emerge from either end of the wheel cylinder and push against the **brake shoes**, which forces the **linings** against the brake drum.

4 Seals inside the wheel cylinder, called *cups*, keep the brake fluid from leaking out of the wheel cylinder.

5 *Dust boots* on each end of the wheel cylinder prevent dirt and dust from entering and fouling the cylinder.

Whenever brakes are relined, the cylinders should be taken apart and honed with a special tool. This is because the new linings will be thicker and will push the pistons farther into the center of the cylinder when they return to their original position after the brake pedal is released. If there is dirt in the cylinder, the cylinder cups will get jammed against it and become malformed, causing leaks.

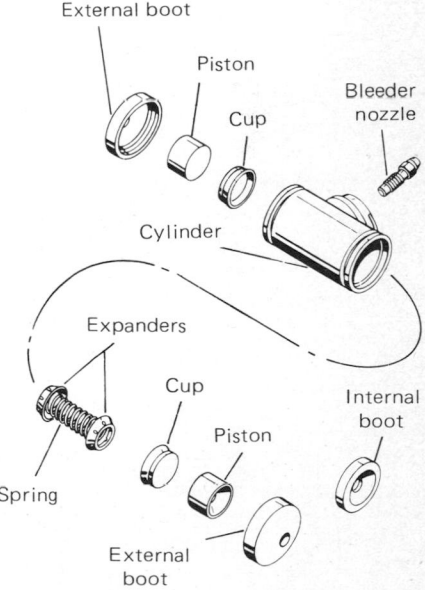

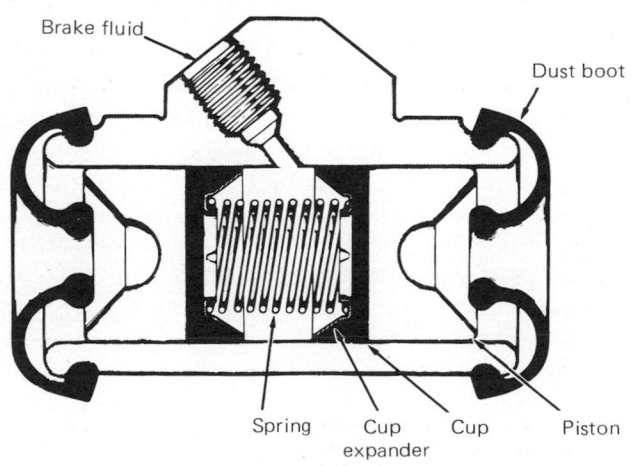

(*above*) Exploded View of a Wheel Cylinder
Delco Moraine Division, General Motors Corp.

(*left*) Anatomy of a Wheel Cylinder
The Bendix Corp.

Brake Shoes

Brake shoes are curved pieces of metal which stop the car by pushing against the inside of the brake drum. They are attached to a set of springs that draw them back into place when you take your foot off the brake.

Brake shoes can be fitted to the shape of the drum with an arcing machine. If you are told by a mechanic that your brake shoes need to be replaced, remember that almost all "new" brake shoes are really **rebuilt** ones! When the mechanic replaces your old brake shoes, he sends them to a company that removes the old linings and attaches new ones. Then the "new" brake shoes are resold. The mechanic gets a partial refund for every set of old shoes he sends in. Ask for that refund (called a "**core charge**," which really stands for "*Cash On Return*") if you need new brake shoes.

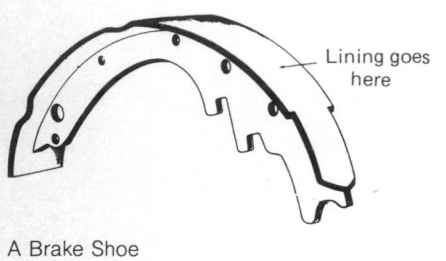

A Brake Shoe
The Bendix Corp.

Brake Linings

Either bonded or riveted to the brake shoes are curved **brake linings** of a tough asbestos material, which is very resistant to heat. When the brake shoes are forced against the insides of the brake drum, the linings create friction, which causes the brake drum to stop turning around. This in turn forces the wheels of the car to stop turning, and the car comes to a stop. Brake linings can last from 10,000 to 40,000 miles, but they should be checked for wear every 10,000 to 20,000 miles. Riveted linings are better than the bonded kind because they can more efficiently conduct the heat caused by braking. They also tend to squeak less and don't come off as easily.

Adjusting Devices

Located at the bottom of the brake backing plate is either a *manual adjusting wheel* or a *self-adjusting device*. These are used to adjust the distance between the surface of the brake lining and the inside of the brake drum when you step on the brake pedal. As your brake linings become worn, the distance increases, and this adjustment compensates for it. If you didn't have this gadget and your linings became very worn, eventually the brake shoes would not reach the inside of the drum and your car would not stop.

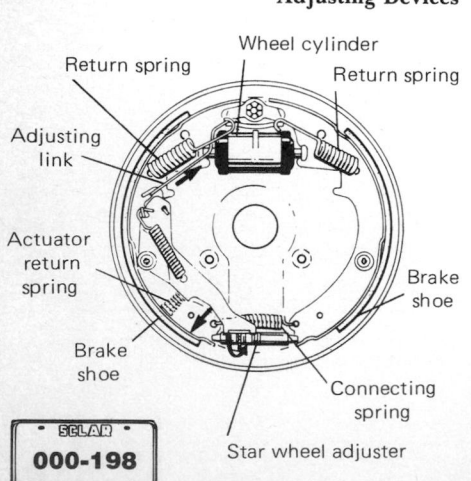

Return spring
Wheel cylinder
Return spring
Adjusting link
Actuator return spring
Brake shoe
Brake shoe
Connecting spring
Star wheel adjuster

SCLAR
000-198

Self-adjusting Delco Moraine Brake: When you back up, the adjusting links and springs adjust the brakes automatically.

Adjusting Devices on Three Popular Brakes
Delco Moraine Division, General Motors Corp.

Manually Adjusted Brakes are almost never found on cars built since 1962. If your car is old and has manually adjusted brakes, they must be adjusted periodically. Only a professional mechanic should do this.

Self-Adjusting Brakes should not require any work. When you drive and stop your car in reverse, the mechanism is automatically adjusted. So if you think your brake pedal is too low, something may be wrong with the self-adjusting device, since under normal conditions we all tend to back up enough to keep our brakes in adjustment.

Brake drums are hollow steel cylinders located in back of each wheel. Because those same lug bolts go through them that go through the wheel, they turn when the wheel turns. If you keep your brakes in good condition and change your brake linings before they become too worn, your drums should last for the life of your car. If they become worn, they can be "reground" or "turned" to a smooth surface—unless they are worn below .060 of an inch. Then, you'll need new ones.

If you are told that your brake drums cannot be turned and must be *replaced*, ask your mechanic to let you watch while he checks them with a special instrument called a brake drum *micrometer*. The instrument will show you whether the drums are worn below the legal level.

If it looks as though you must have a new drum, ask your service station to get you a used reground one. These are much cheaper than new ones and should be just as good if they are not too worn. (The difference on drums for my husband's macho-mobile was $10 to $15 for a used drum vs. $40 for a new one!) If your garage says they can't find any, try calling a couple of auto wreckers yourself (see the Yellow Pages) and ask for used drums for your car's make, model, and year. Be sure the drums look *exactly the same* as your old ones, and don't forget to specify drums for *front* or *rear* wheels. Have a professional mechanic install them for you, as the brake shoes must be adjusted to fit. It is best to use drums of the same size (front or rear) for even braking performance.

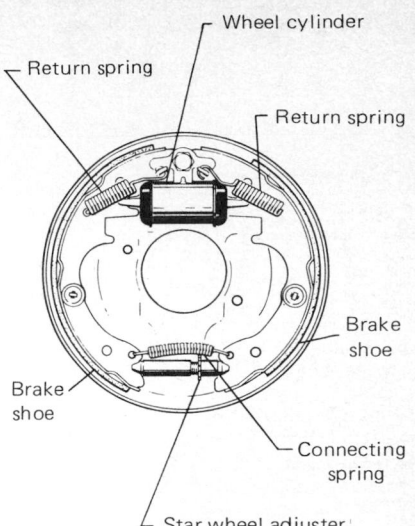

Manually Adjusted Brake: You turn the star wheel adjuster by hand to adjust the brakes.

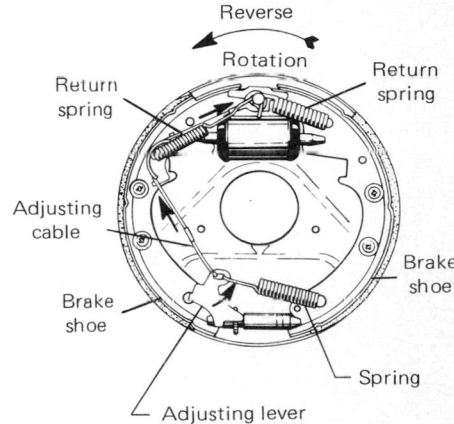

Self-adjusting Bendix Brake: When you back up, the adjusting cable is automatically tightened and the brakes adjust themselves.

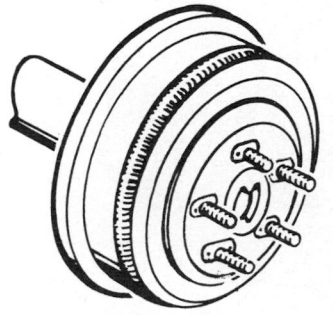

The Brake Drum in Place
Delco Moraine Division, General Motors Corp.

Advantages of Drum Brakes

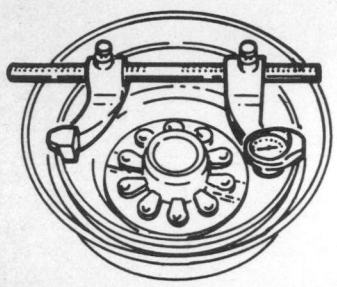

Checking Drum Wear with a Micrometer
Delco Moraine Division, General Motors Corp.

The main advantage of drum brakes is that they require less hydraulic pressure to stop your car, because the brake shoes tend to screw themselves into the brake drums once they have been pushed there by the pistons in the wheel cylinders. To help absorb this pressure, the brake linings on the front wheel brakes have a larger surface than those on the rear wheels. This is because the front wheels bear most of the pressure of stopping because the weight shifts from the rear to the front when you brake. However, on each set of brake linings, on any given wheel, the lining toward the rear of the car is larger and often is darker in color.

Disc Brakes

Disc brakes are often touted as a "special feature," and some car manufacturers provide them as an "optional extra." They are composed of a flat steel *disc* (surprise!) sandwiched between a pair of **calipers**. These calipers contain one or more pistons that are forced into the disc by the brake fluid in the brake lines. Between the disc and the pistons are *brake pads*, which operate in the same way as brake shoes do: they grab the disc with their rough asbestos linings and force the disc to stop turning, which in turn forces the wheel to stop turning and the car to stop moving. The effect is the same as on a bicycle when the brakes grab the wheel directly to stop it from turning.

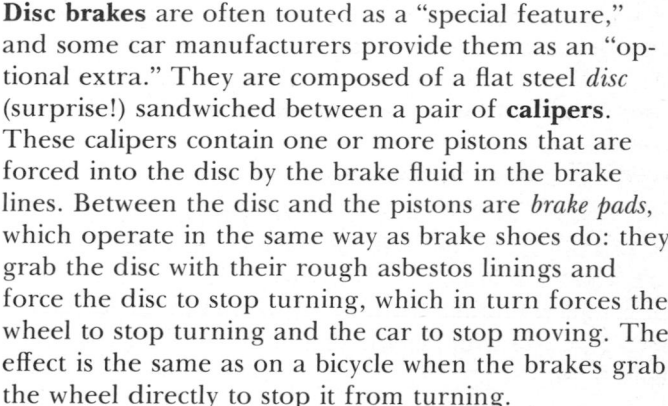

As you can see, the **hydraulic** principle (which means liquid under pressure, in this case) is the same for drum brakes as for disc brakes. But disc brakes do have advantages. Because they operate in the open air (instead of inside brake drums) they are less prone to overheating. They are also affected less by water, because the leading edge of the brake pads scrapes the water away before it can get between the pads and the disc. When drum brakes get wet, the brake linings don't grab the brake drum satisfactorily, and often the car won't stop.

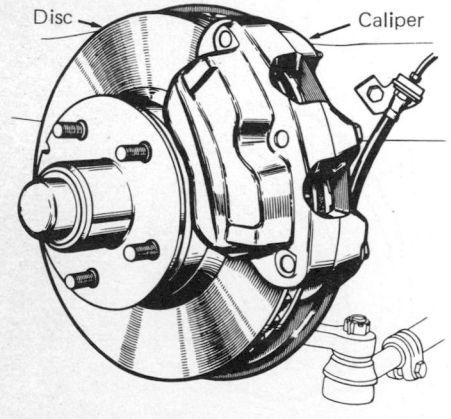

A Typical Disc Brake
The Bendix Corp.

Disadvantages include the difficulty of attaching an **emergency brake** to the rear disc brakes, and the fact that disc brakes usually need to be power-assisted.

Many car manufacturers compromise by producing cars with disc brakes on the front wheels and drum brakes on the rear wheels. This is fine, since the front wheels do most of the job of stopping the car.

Disc brakes need very little service and require no adjusting. A set of them will usually perform better than either conventional drum brakes or power drum brakes—particularly under high-speed, wet, or over-heated conditions.

If your car is braking properly, everything is probably fine. If the disc brakes are squealing, groaning, or rattling, have a professional take a look at them.

Power brakes are available with either drum or disc brakes. Power brakes, or "power-assisted brakes," are simply conventional brakes that are hooked to a device called a **power booster** that uses engine vacuum to help you push the brake pedal down. Power brakes are an "optional extra" on most cars but are considered most necessary on cars with disc brakes and cars that are big and heavy. I didn't realize how necessary the power brakes on my husband's macho-mobile were until they failed one night and we had to drive home with only the basic brake system. Herb had to *stand* on the brake pedal to stop the car even though we were traveling very slowly. I just can't see the logic of buying a car with a big frame that weighs so much that you need power brakes to stop it, power steering to steer it, a big engine to move it around, and a lot more fuel to keep the whole mess running. That's a big price to pay for "status," and why should obvious waste be a status symbol anyway? If you want a car with status, try a beautifully made, highly efficient, well-designed small car. They can be expensive too.

If you have power brakes on your car, and it gets really hard to push the brake pedal down, your power booster is probably the culprit and your brakes may be O.K.

Without getting too technical, here is how power brakes work: There is a power booster between the brake pedal and the master cylinder which contains a diaphragm. A metal arm runs from the brake pedal,

Power Brakes

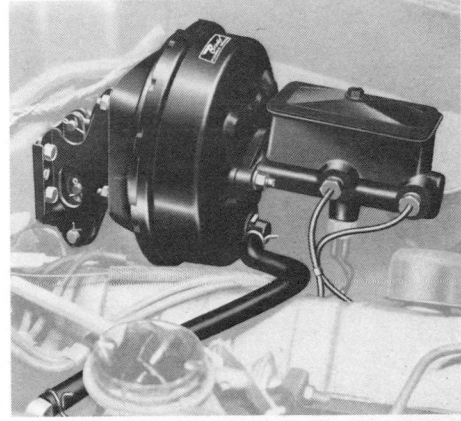

The Power Booster Is Located Right Behind the Master Cylinder
Brake and Front End magazine

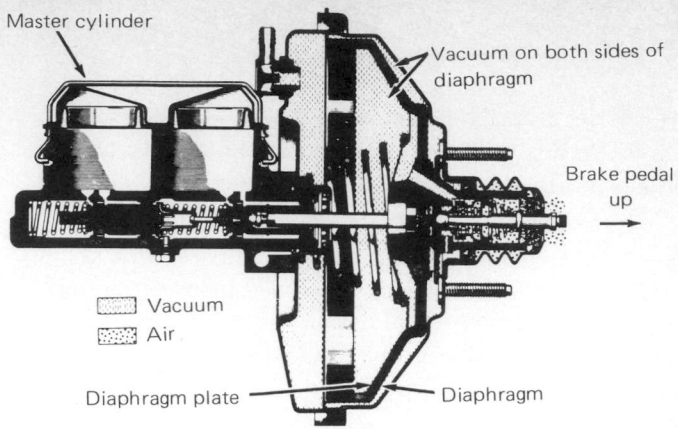

Master cylinder

Vacuum on both sides of diaphragm

Brake pedal up

Vacuum

Air

Diaphragm plate — Diaphragm

Brakes Released

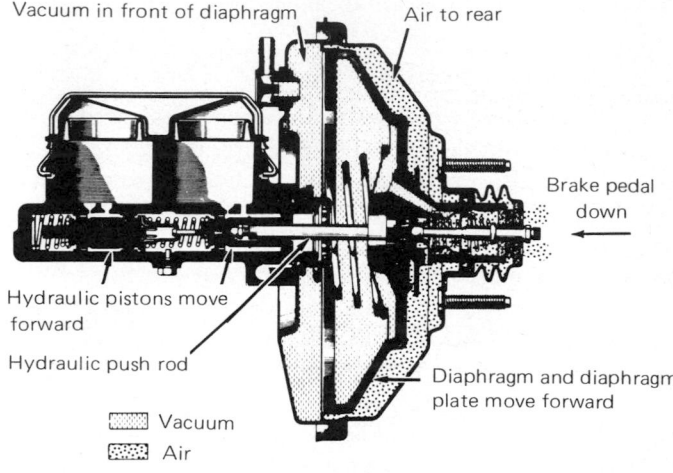

Vacuum in front of diaphragm

Air to rear

Brake pedal down

Hydraulic pistons move forward

Hydraulic push rod

Diaphragm and diaphragm plate move forward

Vacuum

Air

How a Power Booster Works
The Bendix Corp.

Brakes Applied

through the diaphragm, to the piston on the master cylinder. When you step on the brake, a valve opens in a pipe connecting the booster to the engine vacuum. That vacuum sucks the diaphragm forward, which moves the arm attached to it. Since the arm is really an extension of the brake pedal, it pushes the piston in the master cylinder, which forces the brake fluid out into the brake lines. So, all that is really happening is that you are using engine vacuum to help you push on that piston instead of just doing it yourself via the brake pedal alone.

Here are a few final notes about the anatomy of brakes: Because most of the weight is in the front of the car (on front-engine cars), the front brakes bear most of the brunt of stopping the car. Consequently, the front brake shoes are usually longer and wider than the rear ones. A friend of mine had his brakes relined recently and complained that they worked miserably. We took them apart and found that the brake "specialists" had installed the larger brake shoes on the *rear* wheels and the shorter shoes on the front! Isn't that a good reason for finding an auto repair class and—under supervision—doing the job yourself?

The **parking brake**, or emergency brake, is usually attached to the rear wheels of your car. On cars with drum brakes, the parking brake is attached with cables to the rear brakes. The cables run underneath the car and can be easily adjusted by turning a screw that controls the tension on the cable. These are called *integral* parking brakes.

On some cars, other devices do the same job. Some parking brakes are linked to the transmission, and rather than activating the rear brakes, they stop the driveshaft from turning the rear wheels. With these *transmission-type* parking brakes, the band and lining are attached to a drum on the transmission. When you pull the lever, the band squeezes the lining against the drum, and the driveshaft stops turning. If you can't find a typical parking brake linkage under your car, you may have this type of brake. If it doesn't seem to be performing properly, have it checked by a professional.

You will know when your parking brake needs adjusting because it will fail to keep your car from moving when you try to drive with the brake on. Also, as the mechanism loosens up, the brake will have to be pulled up farther (if it is a hand brake), or it will end up nearer the floor (if it is a foot pedal), before you can set the brakes properly. To be set properly a good parking brake has to be moved only about one third of the total distance along its shaft to set the brake.

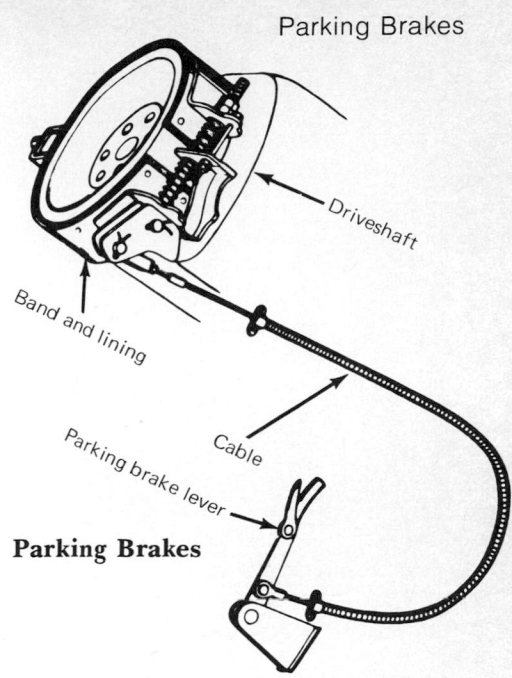

Parking Brakes

A Transmission-Type Parking Brake System
The Bendix Corp.

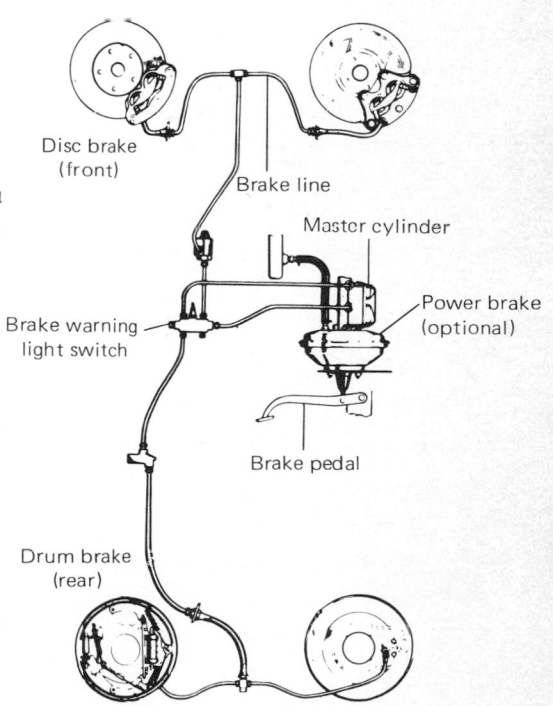

An Integral Parking Brake System
The Bendix Corp.

How to Check Your Brake System

Now that you understand how the brakes on your car work, you are in a good position to check them and be sure they are working properly. Check your brakes every 10,000 to 20,000 miles, depending on the age of your car, the history of its brakes, and how much stop-and-go driving you do. If you tend to "ride your brakes" when you drive, they are going to get that much more wear and should be checked more frequently. Riding your brake will cause your brakes to overheat more often, and you will pay the price in worn linings, worn drums, or brake shoes that have warped out of shape. Although it is always a good policy to be cautious, try to anticipate stopping situations well enough in advance to be able to slow down by releasing the pressure on your gas pedal, whenever possible, and then using your brake pedal for that final stop. If you have a **manual transmission**, **downshift** to take the pressure of stopping off your brakes. In situations that call for slowing down, rather than stopping, it is better to pump your brake pedal a couple of times to reduce speed than to jam on your brakes and screech to a halt. Good driving is guaranteed to make your brakes last longer than the most expensive maintenance.

Let's go back over the brake system in your car and check each part for wear and proper performance. Whenever it is safe for you to do the necessary maintenance, I'll tell you how to do it. If it is relatively complicated, I'll recommend professional help and tell you what that professional *should* be doing. Figure labor at $12 to $18 per hour, add on the cost of parts, and you will know whether or not you are being ripped off. And don't forget to look at the worn drums yourself to be sure they're worn below the legal tolerances of .060 of an inch.

How to Check Your Brake Pedal

1 With the car at rest, apply pressure to the brake pedal. Does it feel spongy? If it does, you probably have air in your brake lines. This is not difficult to correct; you can probably do the job yourself with the help of a friend. For instructions, see the end of this chapter under "How to Bleed Your Brakes."

2 Apply a slight amount of pressure to your brake pedal when it is once again at rest. Does it stay

where it was when you stopped depressing it? Or does it seem to sink slowly to the floor, away from your foot. If it sinks, your master cylinder may be defective.

3 Drive the car around the block, stopping every now and then, without driving the people behind you crazy. The pedal should stop around 3 inches from the floor if you have ordinary self-adjusting brakes. If you have power brakes, the pedal should stop in an inch to an inch and a half. (Always test power brakes with the motor on.)

4 If you feel that your brakes are "low" (that the pedal goes down too far before the car stops properly), try pumping the brake a couple of times while you are driving around. Does it come up higher? If so, a brake adjustment is probably in order. After we check the brake fluid situation, if you find that you are *not* low in fluid, drive to your friendly service station and ask them to adjust your brakes. After that, the pedal should not travel as far down before your car stops.

5 While you are driving around, take time to notice how your total brake system is performing. Ask yourself these questions:

a Does the car travel too far before coming to a stop in city traffic? If it does, your brakes need adjusting or you need new linings.

b Does the car pull to one side when you brake it? You may have a leak in one of your wheel cylinders, which will cause the brakes on that wheel to "grab." Or your brake drum may be warped. We'll get to checking wheel cylinders and drums in a minute.

c Do your brakes "squeal" when you stop fairly short? This condition can impair your car's braking efficiency if that squeal means that your linings are worn down to the metal. If when you check your brake linings, you find that they are not terribly worn, just slick or glazed-looking (glazed linings reflect light like a mirror), you can roughen them up a bit with sandpaper. Just be sure that you get every last bit of sand and dust off them before you reassemble the wheel. Use nothing but sand or flint paper—carbide, emory, or aluminum oxide paper will leave a residue, and the teeniest bit of grit will cause your drums to wear out more quickly. Glazed linings are not the worst thing you can have, so if your linings seem to be wearing well and your car is braking efficiently—and if you can stand the noise—you may be better off just leaving them alone.

d Does your car bounce up and down when you stop short? Your **shock absorbers** may need to be replaced. We'll get to them in another chapter.

If any of these checks shows that you have a problem, finish this chapter and then *take care of the situation immediately.* Never put off brake work. If your brakes fail, you (and a lot of other people) may be in serious trouble. Other kinds of automotive trouble may keep your car from going—brake trouble keeps your car from stopping. . . . The rest, and you, may be history.

How to Check Your Master Cylinder

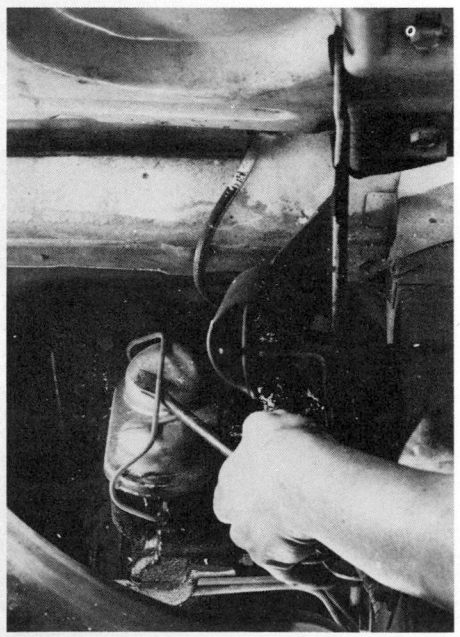

Releasing the Lid of a Metal Master Cylinder with a Screwdriver
Richard Freshman

1 Open the top of your **master cylinder**. If you have the kind with a little plastic bottle on top, just unscrew the cap. If you have a metal one, use a screwdriver to pry the retaining clamp off the top. Be sure not to let any dirt fall into the chambers when you open the lid. If your hood area is full of funky grime and dust, wipe the lid before you remove it.

2 Take a look at the lid. Attached to the inside surface is a rubber diaphragm with two rubber cups. As the brake fluid in your master cylinder recedes (when it is forced into the brake lines), the diaphragm cups are pushed down by air that comes in through vents in the lid. The rubber cups descend and touch the surface of the remaining brake fluid, to prevent evaporation and to keep the dust and dirt out. When the fluid flows back in, the rubber cups are pushed back up. If your fluid level is low, or if the rubber cups are in their descended position when you remove the lid, you will have to push them back up with your finger before you replace the lid.

3 Look inside the master cylinder. The brake fluid should be up to the fill line or within half an inch of the top of the chamber. If it isn't, you will have to buy brake fluid and add it.

A low brake-fluid level may not mean anything if it has been a long time since any fluid was added, and if your car has been braking properly. If you have reason to believe that your brake fluid level has dropped because of a leak, then check the rest of your system very carefully as we go from part to part, looking for leaks.

If you are going to buy brake fluid, reread the brake fluid section in this chapter to be sure you are buying the proper kind. Be sure that your fluid does not become contaminated by oxygen or water vapor in the air.

4 If both chambers of your master cylinder are filled with brake fluid to the proper level, close it up carefully, without letting any dirt fall into it. If dirt gets into your master cylinder, it will travel down the brake lines. If it doesn't block them, the dirt will end up in your wheel cylinders and damage your brakes.

5 Remember, brake fluid evaporates easily, so don't stand around admiring the inside of your master cylinder. Close it quickly, and be sure that the cover is securely in place. Since most master cylinders are pretty airtight, you should not lose brake fluid in any quantity unless it is leaking out somewhere else. If your fluid level was low, we'll find the cause as we continue to check the system.

6 Take a flashlight, or a work light, and look for stain marks, wetness, or gunk under the master cylinder and on the firewall near it. If your master cylinder is—or has been—leaking, there will be evidence.

7 It's a good idea to check your master cylinder every couple of months; more often if it was low in fluid when you last checked it. This should be part of your regular under-the-hood check.

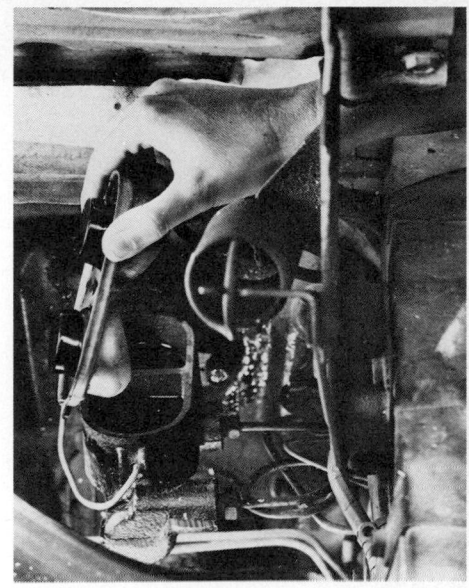

You Can See the Rubber Cups Inside the Lid of This Master Cylinder.
Richard Freshman

How to Check Your Brake Lines

1 If the fluid level in your master cylinder remains full, chances are that there is no need to check for leaks in the **brake lines**. If, however, you find that you are losing brake fluid, or if the insides of your tires are wet and look as though something has been leaking and streaking them, it could be a

brake fluid leak in the wheel cylinders or the lines—or a visit from a neighbor's dog!

2 The easiest way to check brake lines is to put the car up on a hydraulic hoist, raise it over your head, walk under it, and examine the lines as they lead from the hood area to each wheel. There may be leaks coming from holes in the lines—or where the steel lines become rubber ones—or where the brake lines connect with the wheel cylinders. Check carefully along the lines for wetness and for streaks of dried fluid. If you see rust spots on your lines, gently sand them off and look for thin places under them that may turn into holes before too long. Feel the rubber parts of the brake lines for signs that the rubber is becoming sticky, soft, spongy, or worn. Your brake lines should last the life of your car. If they look very bad, have a professional take a look at them and give you an idea of whether or not they should be replaced. If the car is fairly new and the brake lines look very bad, I'd go back to the dealer with the problem and ask him to replace the lines free of charge.

3 If you do not have access to a hoist at the auto repair shop at your local school, or at a friendly garage, then you will have to jack up your car, one end at a time, and get down there with a flashlight or work light to look at your lines. Before you do this, be sure to check for instructions and safety tips in the chapter on how to jack up your car! Remember to look at the insides of your tires for drippy clues about leaking wheel cylinders.

Getting at Your Brakes

The next thing to do is to check your brakes in order to see whether they are in good condition. This is not as scary as it sounds; in fact, it's quite a simple job—with two qualifications. The first is that you do not attempt to fiddle with anything unless I tell you to. The second is that when you go about disassembling the stuff that covers your brakes, you do so in the proper manner. This will keep you from getting into a situation where you cannot put the pieces back together again. It is this fear that keeps most of us from poking around in our cars, which in turn prevents us from discovering the cause of most trouble ourselves.

We turn to others for the diagnosis and then get angry when they come up with the wrong answers.

Once you learn to take a mechanical gadget apart properly, you will be able to put it back together again without trouble. Over the years, Don, my instructor, has given a lot of thought to this and has come up with as foolproof a set of instructions as possible. With them he has enabled hundreds of students to take apart brakes, carburetors, and other automotive gizmos, with no fatalities! I pass them along to you:

1 Before you start, get a *clean rag* and lay it down on a flat surface, near enough to reach without having to get up or walk to it. As you remove each part, you are going to lay it on this rag. Consequently, the rag should not be in an area where oil or dust or anything else will fall on it and foul the parts. If you are going to use something that blasts air for cleaning purposes, you can leave enough of the rag uncluttered to lap it over the parts resting on it while you blast.

2 Before you begin to remove each part, stop and ask yourself the following questions:

a What is this thing?

b What does it do?

c How does it do it?

d Why is it made the way it is?

e How tightly is it screwed on (or fastened down)? Most amateurs tend to put things back very tightly, in the hope that the part won't fly off. But there are things like the bolts that hold **rocker-arm cover** gaskets in place that should not be tightened too securely, because the **gasket** would be squeezed out of shape and whatever it is holding in would get out, or the bolt threads could be stripped. So try to remember how hard each thing was to remove. If you are worried about forgetting, make notes.

3 As you remove each part, lay it down on the rag *in clockwise order, with each part pointing in the direction it lay when it was in place.* This is the key to the whole thing. It will tell you when to put each thing back,

How to Disassemble Anything (and Get It Back Together Again)

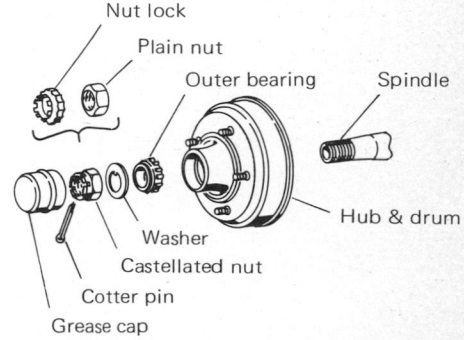

The Things You Have to Remove to Get at Your Brakes
Delco Moraine Division, General Motors Corp.

and how it went, when it is time to reassemble things. If you are making notes about tightness, etc., just call each part by the number in which you removed it—part #1, #2, etc. If you work systematically and understand the function of each thing, you won't be left with those little "extra" nuts and bolts at the end of the job. You can even put numbers on them with masking tape if you are afraid the rag might be moved accidentally.

4 Remember, if you take something off that looks too difficult to trust your memory about, write yourself a note. It needn't be a long one, just something like: "Part #6—the hook at the end of the arm on the left hooks on to the little knob to the right of part #7." With a picture, if it will help.

5 Never, never, do a job in a hurry. Allow yourself plenty of time. If things get rough, have a soft drink or a cup of coffee. You may get a whole new perspective when you go back to work. Keep the kids and the dog away and relax. If you hit a snag, sit quietly and think about it—don't panic. If the thing fitted together before, it will fit together again.

This kind of procedure works for anything—brakes, toasters, bicycles, etc. I've never been able to follow the instructions to put my kids' toys together, but I can take a carburetor apart and get it back together again—slowly but accurately. Actually, your brakes are a good place to test this procedure on yourself. They aren't hard to disassemble, and we're not going to touch anything that will keep your car from braking properly if you goof, so get up your nerve and let's go!

How to Check Drum Brakes

It is always wise to check one of your front brakes first, because the linings wear faster on the front brakes than on the rear ones. If your front brake linings are not too worn, chances are that the rest are in good shape, too.

1 Remove a *front* wheel according to the instructions in the previous chapter. Observe safety precautions with that jack!

2 Use a pair of combination slip-joint pliers to pry the grease cap off the end of the hub.

3 Take a pair of needle-nosed pliers and straighten out the **cotter pin** that is sticking out of the side of the *castellated nut.* (Look at the pin first. In which direction is it lying? How are the legs bent? How does it fit through the nut? How tight is it?)

4 Pull the cotter pin out and put in on your rag (where the grease cap is already residing, right?), and be sure to lay it down in the same direction as it pointed when it was in place.

5 Slide the *washer* off the **spindle**. Wipe it off, if it is greasy, with a lint-free rag. Lay it on the rag next to the cotter pin.

Note that some cars just have a nut with a cotter pin sticking through it; others have a nut with a nut lock over it, to hold the cotter pin in place. Which kind does your car have?

6 Grab the **brake drum** and put it toward you. *Do not slide the drum off the spindle yet.* Now push the drum back into place. The things that are left on the spindle are the *outer wheel bearings.*

7 Carefully slide the outer **bearings**, with the washer in front of them, off the spindle. Take a look at the bearings. Can you see little specks of silver in the **grease** that coats them? If you can, your bearings are wearing and you'll need to replace them. If not, are the bearings covered with a nice layer of grease? Or are they kind of dry?

   If they look dry, they need to be "repacked." Chapter 12 will tell you how to do this (all it involves is squishing wheel bearing grease back into them), so you might want to look ahead and get the necessary stuff.

8 If you don't want to get into packing your bearings right away, *do not* attempt to wipe any grease off the bearings, no matter how icky they look. Just put them in a little plastic bag and lay them on your rag, pointing in the right direction. The bag will keep dust from getting into them. A speck of dust can quickly wear a bearing out.

9 Look at the drum again. In the center hole you can see another set of bearings. These are your *inner wheel bearings.* If you are *not* planning to

repack them, *do not* attempt to take them out of their seat in the drum. This would break the **grease seal**, and you would have to get a new seal to replace it.

10 Slide the drum off the spindle, with the inner bearings still inside it, if you aren't repacking them now. If you have an air gun, take the drum well away from the parts rag and blast it inside and out to remove the clouds of dust that cover it. Don't inhale while you are doing this; a lungful of dust is no fun. You can also get asbestos emphysema (just thought you'd like to know).

If you have no air gun (you're probably glad you haven't after that last one, right?), then wipe the drum, first the inside and then the outside, with a clean, *grease-free* rag. A clean whisk broom is also excellent for dusting brake parts and brake drums.

11 Take a look inside the drum. There are probably grooves on the inner walls from wear. If these grooves look unusually deep, or if there are hard spots or burned places, you should have your mechanic check the drums out with that special micrometer that we mentioned before. If the drums are not worn below legal tolerances, they can be reground (or turned) rather than replaced. There is a special machine, called a "brake-drum lathe" that does this job in a relatively short time. It should not be a major job in terms of expense. You could do it yourself at a school auto shop, as most classes have the machine.

12 Now, look at the rest of your brakes, which are still attached to the **brake backing plate**.

a Your **wheel cylinder** should show no signs of leaking brake fluid.

b Your **brake linings** should be evenly worn, with no bald spots or thin places. They should be at least $1/16$ inch thicker than any rivet. They should be firmly bonded or riveted to the brake shoes. Most brake linings will give from 10,000 to 20,000 miles of wear. Some will last even longer. If yours have been on your car for some time, they will have grooves in them and may be somewhat glazed. If your brake drums have been wearing evenly and your car has been braking properly, disregard the grooves and the glazing unless your linings look badly worn.

c If your linings are worn, have them replaced at once. This will involve replacing the brake shoes with "new" ones that have new linings on them. Don't forget to ask about a **core charge** refund.

d Do not attempt to replace shoes, linings, or wheel cylinders yourself unless you do it under the eye of an auto shop instructor. If you choose to do this, the money you save will more than pay for your tuition! The job is neither difficult nor complicated. It just needs supervision.

e To have the work done for you, find a reliable brake shop. Try the Yellow Pages, or have the mechanic at your local service station steer you to one. Call a couple of places and ask for estimates on rebuilding your brakes. Avoid the cheapest place as well as the most expensive!

f Always replace **brake shoes** in sets (four shoes for two front or rear wheels is a set) for even performance. Replacing them all at once is even better.

g Take a look at the self-adjusting devices on your brakes. Trace the cable from the anchor pin above the wheel cylinder, around the side of the backing plate, to the adjuster at the bottom of the plate. To help you, there are illustrations of the most common self-adjusters in the earlier part of this chapter. Is the cable hooked up? Does it feel tight? If your brake pedal manages to apply your brakes before it gets halfway down to the floor, the adjustment is probably just fine. If not, and if the cylinders, linings, shoes, etc., are O.K., then the adjusting devices may be out of whack. Just making a couple of forward and reverse stops should fix them. If this doesn't work, you may need an adjustment at a service station. Don't attempt to fiddle with these yourself.

When you have finished inspecting your brakes, it is time to replace everything. Here's how to do it:

How to Reassemble Drum Brakes

1 Blow the dirt off the brake backing plate if you have an air gun. Otherwise, use a whisk broom or leave it alone.

2 Replace the wheel hub and the brake drum on the spindle. Make sure it is clean inside. (You can wipe the inside with a lint-free cloth and some alcohol if you aren't sure. Don't use water!)

3 If you've followed the instructions in the next chapter and have repacked your wheel bearings, check those instructions again and replace the grease seal and the inner bearings.

4 Replace the outer wheel bearings and the washer. Don't let any dirt get on these! Take a look at how you've laid the bearings down on your rag, checking with the illustration on "things you have to remove to get at your brakes," to be sure you will put them back properly. Don't wipe off the grease!

5 Replace the adjusting nut by screwing it on firmly and then backing it off half a turn and retightening it "finger tight." Another way to do this is to back the adjusting nut off one full notch (60°) and, if the notch doesn't line up with the hole in the spindle, back it off just enough until it does. Then, spin the wheel by hand to be sure that it is turning freely. If it isn't, loosen the nut a bit more.

6 Insert the cotter pin into the hole in the castellated nut. It should clear the outer grooves and go all the way through.

7 Bend the legs of the cotter pin back across the surface of the nut to hold it in place.

8 Replace the grease cap.

9 Follow the instructions in the last chapter for replacing your wheel, lug nuts, and hub cap.

10 Go clean yourself up with some nice hand cleaner.

Here are a couple of "nevers" to remember when working on your brakes:

—Never step on your brake pedal when you have the drum off your brakes. You can literally blow the brakes apart! The pistons can fly out of the ends of the wheel cylinders because the brake shoes will not be stopped from moving outward by the drum.

—Never use anything but brake fluid in your brakes.

—Never get oil anywhere near your brake system. It blows up rubber and will destroy the cylinder cups and dust boots on your wheel cylinders. If it gets on your brake linings, they will not grab the brake drum.

—Never get brake fluid on a painted surface—it will destroy it.

—Never remove wheel cylinders, brake shoes, or tamper with the self-adjusting device on your brakes without supervision.

How to Check Disc Brakes

1 Follow the instructions for jacking up your car and removing a front wheel in the previous chapter.

2 Look at the disc. Do not attempt to remove it from the car. Check it for heavy rust and for uneven wear. Rust generally does no damage unless the car has been standing idle for a long time and the rust has really built up.

3 If your brakes have not been working properly—if they've been grabbing or causing the car to swerve to one side—remove the two screws from the **splash shield**.

4 Look at the brake pads inside. If the linings look very worn or unevenly worn, they will probably have to be replaced. If the linings have worn to the metal pads, the disc will probably have to be reground as well.

Disc linings should be checked every 10,000 miles. Relining, caliper maintenance, and disc grinding should be left to a professional unless you do the job at school. Go to a brake shop (use the Yellow Pages or ask a friendly mechanic to steer you to one) for this kind of work rather than to the corner garage. Call a couple of shops and ask for an estimate. Choose neither the cheapest nor the most expensive. And read all the "nevers" mentioned above.

How to Reassemble Disc Brakes

1 Screw the splash shield back on (if you've removed it).

2 Lift the wheel back onto the shaft, making sure the bolts for the lug nuts go through the holes. Finish replacing the wheel, lug nuts, and hub cap according to the instructions on tire changing.

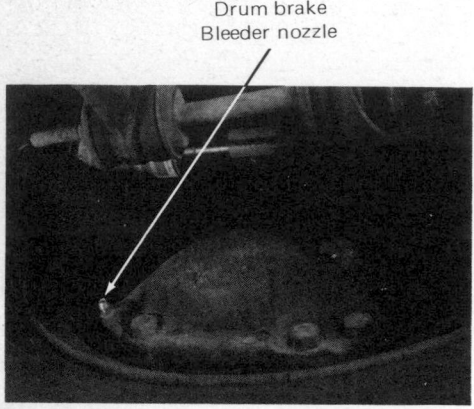

Drum brake
Bleeder nozzle

If the first set of brakes you look at seems to be in good condition, and if your car has been braking properly, there is probably no need to check on the other three. Just remember to check a different set the next time. However, if your car has not been behaving properly, then go on checking each set until you've found the culprit. Don't be surprised to find that the brakes on your rear wheels seem a bit different. There are no wheel bearings on rear wheels, and the shoes and linings are shorter and narrower. Also, your parking brake is usually hooked up to your rear brakes if you have drum brakes on your car.

How to Bleed Your Brakes

For those of us with squishy-feeling brakes, there is an easy way to get the air out of your lines. This is called **bleeding brakes**. To do the job, you will need an *ignition wrench*, a can of the proper brake fluid, a clean glass jar, and a friend.

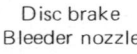

Disc brake
Bleeder nozzle

1 Behind each of your brakes is a little nozzle called a *brake bleeder nozzle*. It may be easier to reach this if you jack up the car. If you are going to crawl underneath, lay an old blanket, or a thick layer of newspapers, down first to keep from getting chilly on the cold cold ground.

2 Find the ignition wrench that fits the nozzle and loosen the bleeder nozzle. Now tighten it again (not too tight).

3 If you have a small piece of flexible hose that will fit over the end of the bleeder nozzle, attach it and place the end of the hose in the jar. Then fill the jar with brake fluid to cover the end of the hose. If you haven't anything that will fit, just keep the jar near the nozzle so that any fluid that squirts out will land in the jar.

Bleeder Nozzles on Drum and Disc Brakes
Richard Freshman

4 Have your friend pump your brake pedal a few times. If the car is jacked up, be sure that the wheels are blocked in the direction in which the

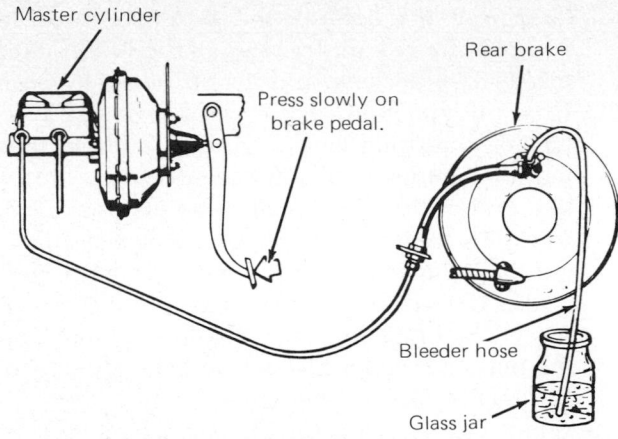

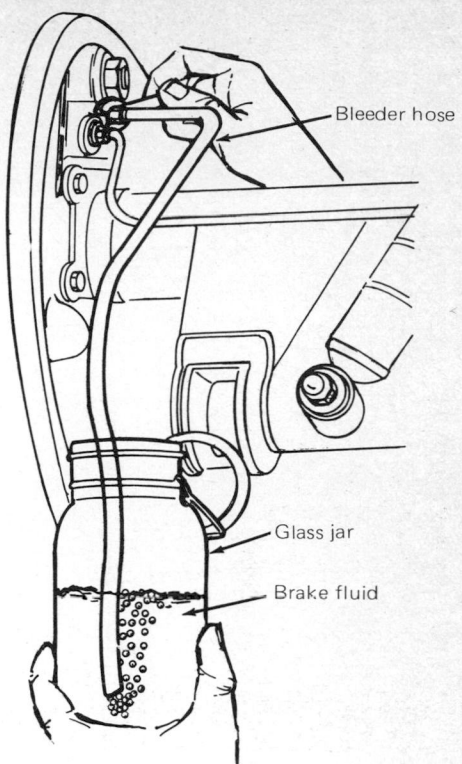

Using a Bleeder Hose to Bleed Your Brakes
The Bendix Corp.

How to Bleed Your Brakes
The Bendix Corp.

car would roll, and that the car is not parked on a hill, before you let your friend get into the car with you underneath it. Leave your tires in place so the car will bounce and leave you some clearance if it should fall.

5 Have your friend say "down" when pressing the brake pedal down, and "up" when releasing it. This will sound like an exercise class, but what the heck!

6 When your friend has pumped the pedal a few times and is holding the pedal *down*, open the bleeder nozzle. Brake fluid will squirt out (duck!). If there is air in your brake lines, there will be air bubbles in the fluid. It is easiest to see these bubbles if you are using the hose-in-the-jar method, but you can also see them without it.

7 *Before* your friend releases the brake pedal, *tighten the nozzle.* If you don't do this, air will be sucked back into the brake lines when the pedal is released.

8 Tell your friend "release" and listen for "up." Then repeat the whole loosening and tightening sequence again and again until there are no more air bubbles coming out with the fluid. Do this to one brake after another until the air is out of each brake line.

9 *This is important:* After you have finished bleeding *each* brake, open your master cylinder and add some more brake fluid to the fill line. If you ne-

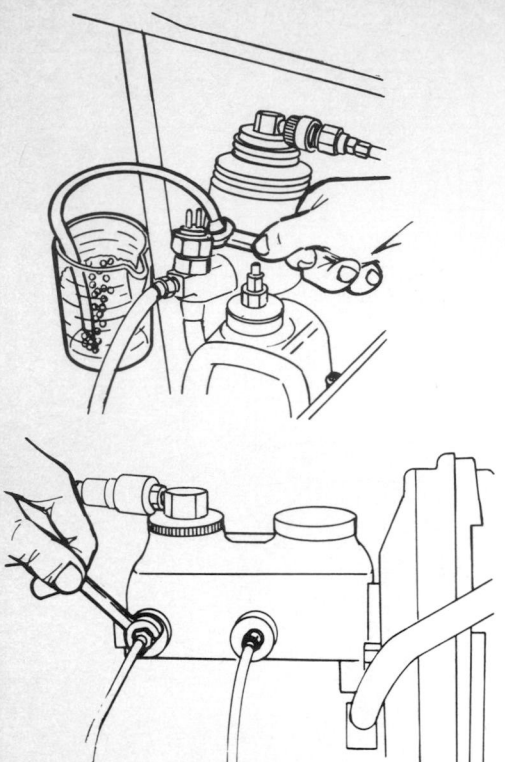

Bleeding a Master Cylinder
Delco Moraine Division, General Motors Corp.

If you have a bleeder nozzle, use the hose-and-jar method. Or bleed the cylinder at the brake line connections.

glect to do this before going on to the next brake, you run the risk of draining all the fluid out of the master cylinder and drawing air into the lines from the top. Now, that isn't fatal—it simply means you would have to go back and bleed your master cylinder until you had sucked the air out of that end of the system—but who needs the extra work? In case you goof and have to bleed the master cylinder, it's the same deal as bleeding your brakes (friend and all). Just bleed it at the point where the brake lines attach to the cylinder, and at the master cylinder bleeder nozzle if there is one. Meanwhile, back to the brake lines . . .

10 When you have finished the job, and brought the brake fluid level in the master cylinder back to full for the last time, drive the car around the block. The brake pedal should no longer feel spongy when you depress it. If it does, check the master cylinder again to be sure it's full and try bleeding the brakes one more time (this is not unusual, and it doesn't take as long as it sounds). If there is no air left in the lines and the brakes still don't feel right, you may need a new master cylinder. You should definitely consider installing it yourself—at an auto shop. All it involves is disconnecting the old one (a bolt or two and the hoses leading to the brake lines have to be released), removing it without spilling brake fluid on anything painted, installing the new one, filling it with brake fluid, and bleeding it. If it seems like too much of a hassle, then have a professional do the job. There shouldn't be much labor to pay for, and if you choose a brake shop wisely, the whole deal shouldn't cost too much. But I had Tweety's master cylinder replaced before I got smarter, and it cost me about $60. Later, I helped a friend to replace a master cylinder with a rebuilt one. The rebuilt master cylinder cost $28, instead of the $40 I'd paid for a new one, and there were no labor charges (naturally). Whatever you do, just be sure that, when the job is finished, they (or you) bleed the brakes and the master cylinder to get all the air out of the lines.

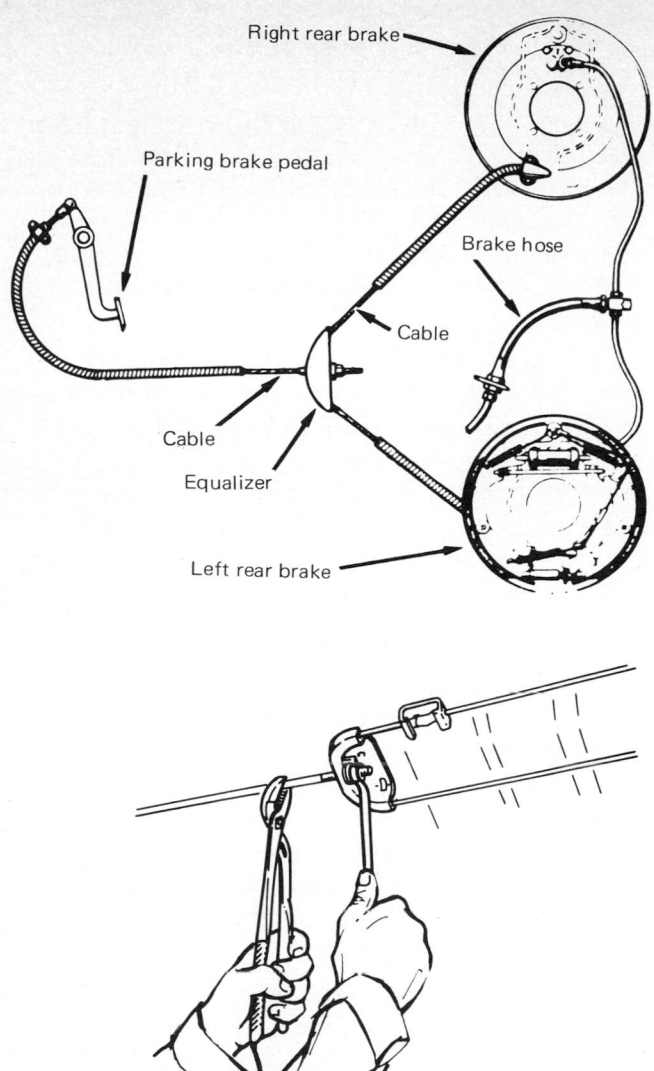

Right rear brake

Parking brake pedal

Brake hose

Cable

Cable

Equalizer

Left rear brake

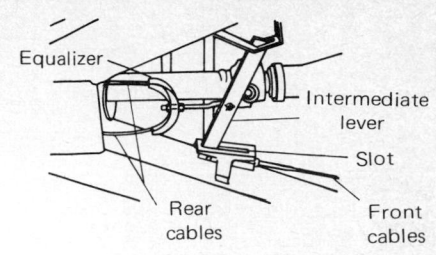

Equalizer

Intermediate lever

Slot

Rear cables

Front cables

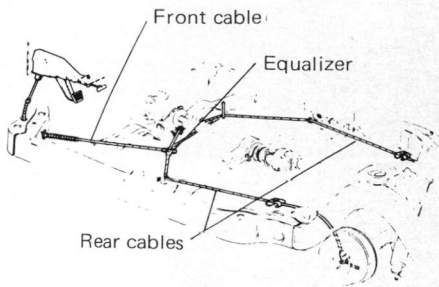

Front cable

Equalizer

Rear cables

Integral Parking Brakes and How to Adjust Them
Bendix Corp. and Delco Moraine Division, General Motors Corp.

They may look different, but they all adjust in the same way.

Here's how to adjust your parking brake:
These instructions will work only if you have **drum brakes** on your *rear* wheels. If you have a **manual transmission** you may have a transmission-type parking brake, and this should be adjusted professionally. Your service manual may tell you which kind you have, or you can crawl under the car and see for yourself. Since most of us have the traditional kind (sometimes called *integral* parking brakes), let's deal with them:

How to Adjust Your Parking Brake

Under-the-Car Views of Two Popular Parking Brake Adjusters
Richard Freshman

1 Jack up the car (a hoist would be lovely) and make sure it is secure. You can also slide underneath with a work light if you don't want to jack it up. Leave your parking brake off.

2 Trace the thin steel cables that run from each of your rear wheels until they meet somewhere under the back seat of the car.

3 Where they meet, there should be a device (usually a bar and a screw) that controls the tension.

4 Turn the screw (or whatever else you've got) until the cables tighten up. Then tighten the screw nuts to hold it in place. You may have to hold the cable to keep it taut.

5 Get out from under there and test-drive the car to see if the parking brake is working. It shouldn't have to be pulled or pushed to the most extreme level to make it work. As the cables loosen up again, you will have to pull the handle up higher, or push the pedal down lower, to engage the brake. You should not be able to drive with the brake on.

6 While you're at it, is the parking brake warning light on your dashboard working? If not, check or replace the bulb or fuse. If that doesn't work, get someone to check the connection between the light and the brake; there may be a short in it.

Well, that's it. If you get in the habit of checking your brakes every 10,000 miles (and more frequently as they get worn), you will be able to stop worrying that they might fail you at a crucial moment. If you are a good buddy to your brakes (and this involves driving properly as well as those periodic visits), they will prove to be your very best friends. After one of those breathtaking emergency stops on the freeway, I always say "Thanks, pals" and promise myself that I'll peek in soon to check on my brakes and lines to be sure they are in good shape.

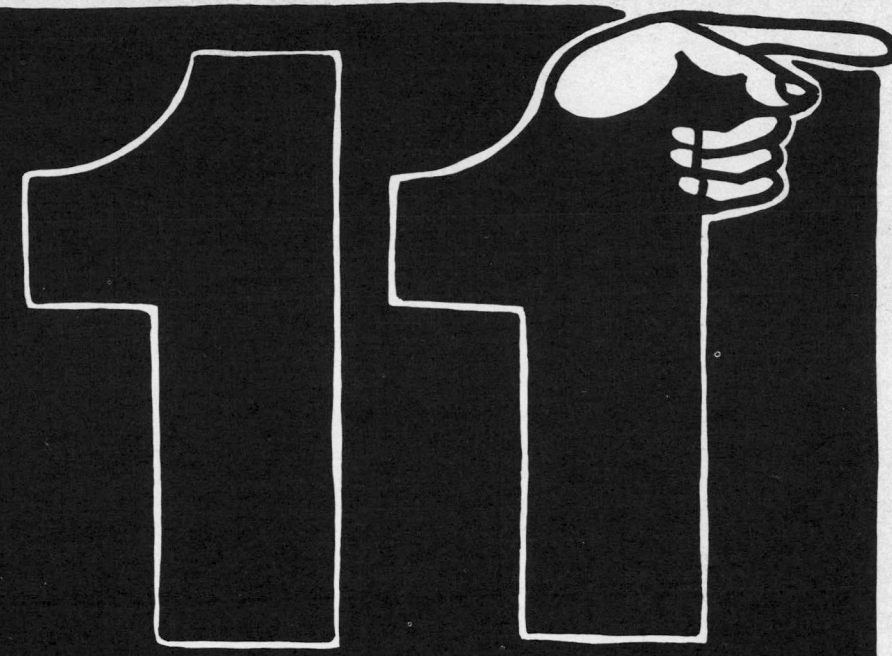

11

Wheels and Tires: How to Keep Your Car from Getting Sore Feet

Now that we've covered your brakes, let's talk about your **tires**. There is a two-way relationship between your brakes and your tires. Just as poor braking action will result in increased tire wear, if your wheels are properly balanced and aligned, and if your tires are properly inflated and in good condition, they can help to stop your car up to 25 percent faster!

There is also a strong correlation between tire inflation and tire wear. If your tires are underinflated, the outer treads will wear out faster. If they are overinflated, the center of the tread area will go. So to get more mileage from your tires, plus better braking action and a smoother and quieter ride, you ought to know a bit about buying, checking, and maintaining the tires on your car.

In this chapter, I'll tell you something about the different kinds of tires available. There are many different types, made of several different materials, and just as you wouldn't choose sneakers for a formal evening (or wear your finest shoes to the beach), you don't want to be silly about putting the most expensive, long-lasting, high-speed radials on an old car that is just going back and forth to the shopping center.

We'll go into how to check the tires on your car and how to "read your treads" for clues about how well your car is performing. If these clues show that you need to have your wheels balanced or aligned or your tires replaced, I'll provide enough information for you to be sure the work is done, done properly, and for the right price. Your treads can also tell you if you've been driving properly, and we'll go into that too.

There is practically nothing you'll have to do (in terms of physical labor) with this chapter, so just find a comfortable place to read this, relax, and enjoy it.

Tire Construction   Every tire has three major parts:

The Tread   The *tread* is the rubber part of the tire that gets most of the wear and tear. The tread patterns help the tire to grip the road (as the ad used to say) and to resist

Anatomy of a Tire
The Goodyear Tire & Rubber Company

puncturing. These patterns are also excellent indicators of tire wear, and we will get into reading these
clues later in the chapter.

The Bead

The *bead* is a strip of steel wire that is wrapped
around and around to help hold the tire on the rim of
the wheel.

The Casing

It is here that the specific character of the tire is
determined. The *casing* helps the tire to keep its shape
when inflated, instead of blowing up like a balloon. It
is basically made up of various materials, called *cords*,

The Three Basic Types of Tires
The Goodyear Tire & Rubber Company

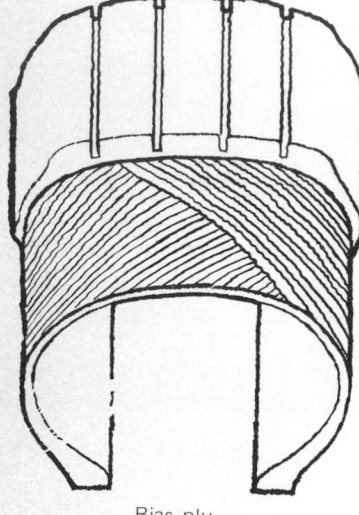

Bias–ply

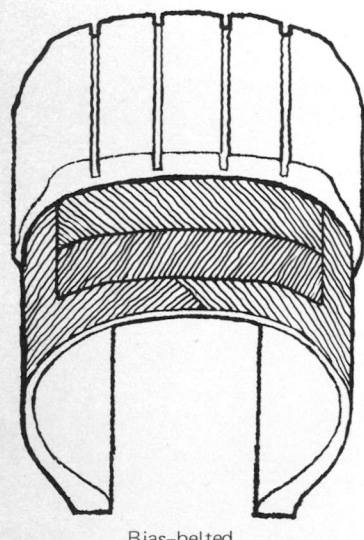

Bias–belted

that are wrapped around the *bead* in different ways. The cords can be made of different materials, and it is the type of material and the way it is wrapped that determine the kind of tire and its price. Originally, cotton was used for the cords in the casing, but this soon gave way to other materials with greater advantages. Here they are in order of durability and cost:

1 *Bias-ply tires.* This means that the cords are wrapped around the bead at angles that form overlaps. They come in a variety of materials:

   a *Nylon.* Very strong and relatively low-cost. The basic disadvantage of nylon cord tires is that they tend to lump a bit when the car is not being used. Consequently, drivers experience a slightly bumpy ride for the first few minutes. After a short time, the cords smooth out and the ride is smooth for the rest of the trip. This condition is called *flat-spotting.* If you don't mind a little roughness at first, nylon cord tires are still a good buy, especially if you tend to drive locally in street traffic and don't do a great deal of long-distance, high-speed driving.

   b *Rayon.* These are also quite strong. They cost a little more than nylon but do not develop flat-spotting.

   c *Polyester.* Even stronger, with no flat spots and a smooth ride. They last longer but are more expensive. If you don't expect to get more than another 20,000 miles out of your car, or don't want to keep it for more than two more years, forget these.

2 *Bias-belted tires.* These are constructed in the same manner as bias-ply tires but feature belts of another material which wrap around the circumference of the tire to give you longer wear, to resist punctures, and to provide more directional stability. This last feature cuts down on "tire squirm," a term used by manufacturers to indicate a tendency of unbelted tires to move from side to side as they track down the road.

   a *Glass-belted tires* are usually made of polyester, in the same manner as the bias-ply polyester tires, but have fiberglass belts for better high-speed performance.

b *Steel-belted tires* are the same, but with steel belts for greater strength and longer wear.

3 *Radial-ply tires.* These are quite different in structure from bias-ply and bias-belted tires. A recent development, they provide better handling, especially at high speeds. They tend to grip the road more, especially when cornering, and will deliver up to twice the mileage of traditional tires. Most of the radial-ply tires available are steel-belted, but there are glass-belted radials around as well.

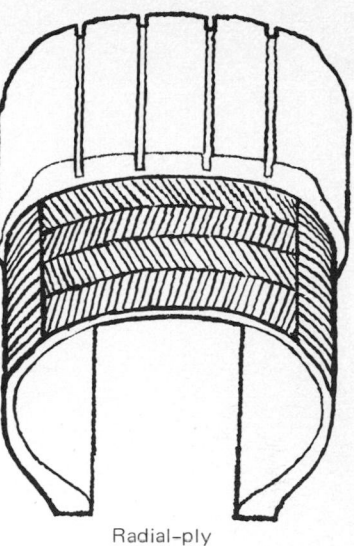

Radial-ply

Now, before you rush out and buy a set of steel-belted radial tires, there are a couple of other things to think about. Tire wear is a direct result of a few major factors: driving at high speeds, which causes tires to heat up and to take a bit of rough wear on cornering and stopping; driving on rough roads; and driving for long distances. Obviously, the longer you drive, the more mileage and wear your tires will experience.

With this in mind, let's examine the various types of tires in terms of cost and average mileage:

Bias-ply tires:
   Cost: Around $20 per tire.
   Mileage: Roughly 20,000 miles, at speeds averaging 65 mph.

Bias-belted Tires:
   Cost: Around $30 per tire.
   Mileage: Roughly 30,000 miles, at about 65 mph.

Belted-Radial Tires:
   Cost: Around $70 per tire.
   Mileage: Roughly 40,000 miles, at about 65 mph.

Of course the above figures are rough estimates, and you can add or subtract dollars and miles for nylon, rayon, polyester, and steel-belted tires, in that order.

Now comes the kicker. Most of us *do not* average 65 mph. In fact, with the energy crisis speed laws, we aren't supposed to do more than 55 mph, even on the freeways. This lower speed substantially enhances the mileage for all of these tires. This means that if you tend to average around 40 mph in city traffic, those rayon bias-ply tires will deliver around 30,000 miles before they wear out.

The logical response to this is, "Then if I buy a set of steel-belted radials and drive at an average of 40 mph on city streets I should get 50,000 or 60,000 miles out of them, right?" Wrong. You would get the additional mileage out of the treads, but unfortunately you would not have the rest of the tire to depend on. This is because rubber tends to rot after 40,000 miles, largely because of the ozone in the air. This causes cracks and hard spots, especially in the sidewalls. The condition is called **ozone checking**. If you have used your tires for more than 40,000 miles, you should investigate new ones because basically your tires are unsafe and will be prone to blowouts and leaks as the rubber continues to deteriorate.

To sum up then: If you plan to do a lot of high-speed, long-distance driving, or if you drive in rough areas on primitive roads, you are probably better off with steel-belted radials. On the other hand, if most of your driving is spent on city streets, or at low speeds, you will find that the cheaper bias-ply or bias-belted tires will save you money even if you replace them more frequently. Judge your own driving habits, and pick your tires in terms of your personal pattern of use. Also, don't buy tires that are expected to last well beyond the remaining life of your car. It is possible to put well over 100,000 miles on a car—especially if you are checking it, maintaining it, and fixing it yourself—but if you have more than 60,000 miles on your car and you drive it pretty hard, I wouldn't buy a pair of 40,000-mile tires for it. It may surprise you and outlive its tires, but chances are it won't. I'd gamble the other way. If your car turns out to be a Motorized Methuselah, the worst that can happen is that you'll have to buy it another pair of cheapos, for those last, few, sweet miles together. Then you can send them both to that Great Used Car Lot In The Sky . . .

Tire Sizes   After a good deal of thought, I've decided not to tell you everything there is to know about tire sizes and profiles. This is a very complicated area, and the whole system has been reorganized recently to include additional information. The results are extremely confusing and totally unnecessary for those of us who just want to replace the tires on our cars. I sincerely doubt that any reputable tire dealer would want to sell you tires that did not fit your car. If you were injured as a result, the dealer would be in a bad position. Therefore, just remember that you should never buy tires that are smaller than those specified in your owner's manual. You may be able to move up to a size or two larger for better handling or load-carrying ability (providing that your car's wheel clearance will allow it), but this should be done only after discussing it thoroughly with a good mechanic or a reputable dealer.

Other things to remember when buying tires:

—Never use two different-size tires, especially on the same **axle**.

—If you are replacing just one or two tires, put the new ones on the rear wheels for better traction.

—Never buy fewer than two bias-*belted* tires at a time if your others are bias *ply*. Put the new pair in the rear.

—Never buy less than a full set of radial-ply tires. The ride is so different that these tires would throw your car out of **alignment** if you tried them in combination with traditional tires.

—Remember that new tires must be "broken in," so don't drive faster than 60 mph for the first 50 miles on a new tire or spare.

—Never buy retreads; the cheapest new tire is safer and will last longer.

—To store tires that are not being used, keep them in the dark, away from extreme heat and electric motors that create ozone.

Tire Rotation

There are two points of view on tire rotation. Certain manufacturers say that you can get up to 20 percent more wear if you rotate your tires. Others caution against rotating tires, because this will tend to hide the distinctive tread-wear patterns that provide clues to poor **alignment**, worn **shock absorbers**, and defective **brakes**. If your tires seem to be wearing evenly and

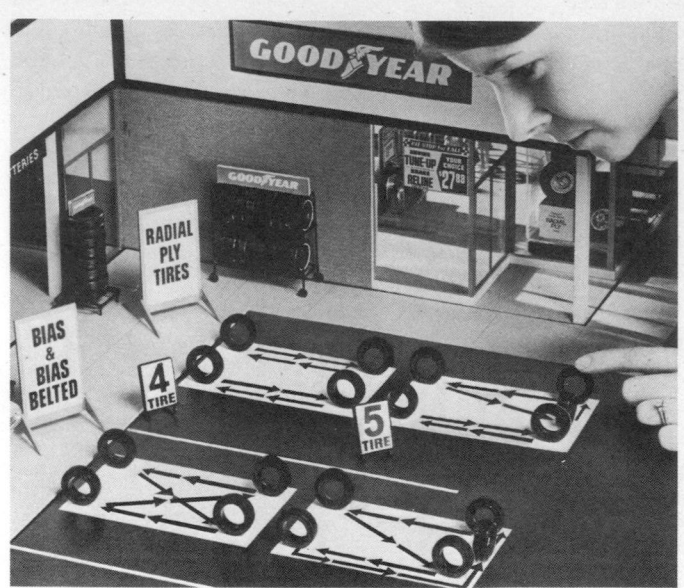

How To Rotate Your Tires
The Goodyear Tire & Rubber Company

you haven't had any of these problems, then rotate them if you like—but look at them first. One more thing: It is a good idea to balance the wheels each time you rotate your tires.

Wheel Balancing

Wheel balancing does a lot to eliminate some of the principal causes of tire wear. Since balancing is a job that should be done with the proper equipment, and since that equipment is costly and tire balancing is generally cheap, go to a professional and have them do the job for you. Just remember that there are two kinds of wheel balancing: *static* and *dynamic*.

Static balancing deals with the even distribution of weight around the axle. You can tell if you need to have your wheels statically balanced if the wheel tends to rotate by itself when the car is jacked up so that the wheel no longer touches the ground. It rotates because one part of the wheel is heavier than the rest. The mechanic will find the heavy spot and apply tire weights to balance it out.

Dynamic balancing deals with the even distribution of weight as the tire hangs vertically down. Wheels that are not balanced dynamically tend to wobble and to wear more quickly. Correcting dynamic balance is a fairly complex procedure and calls for special equipment. Most service stations have this equipment and will do the job for very little money. It should not cost more than a few dollars to have your tires balanced both statically and dynamically at a good garage.

If you plan to have your wheels balanced professionally, it is a waste of time to rotate your tires yourself beforehand. The garage will have to take your wheels off anyway to balance them, and they can put them back in any order you specify.

If you still want to rotate your tires yourself, or if you want to make sure the garage does the job properly, the illustration on page 228 shows the proper sequence for bias and radial tires, with or without a spare tire.
Note that if you have radial-ply tires, you are not supposed to move tires from one *side* of the car to the other, only from front to rear wheels on the same side.

Wheel Alignment

A cheap and easy way to substantially improve your car's handling and extend the life of your tires is to be alert to signs of misalignment and have your wheels aligned immediately if the signs appear. This job is usually called **front-end alignment**, because it is the front wheels that generally get out of line. They get that way because of hard driving with dramatic getaway starts and screeching stops, hitting curbs hard when parking, accidents, heavy loads, and frequent driving over unpaved roads or into potholes. Occasionally the rear wheels will need realignment as well, but usually only on cars with independent rear suspension like VWs, Corvettes, etc.; or on heavy-duty equipment, cars that pull trailers or boats, or cars that have had an accident that threw the frame out of line.

I used to think that front-end alignment involved taking a car that had been bashed out of shape and literally pulling it back into line. Untrue. All they do is adjust your wheels to make sure they track in a nice straight line when you drive. To do this, they use special equipment to check six points:

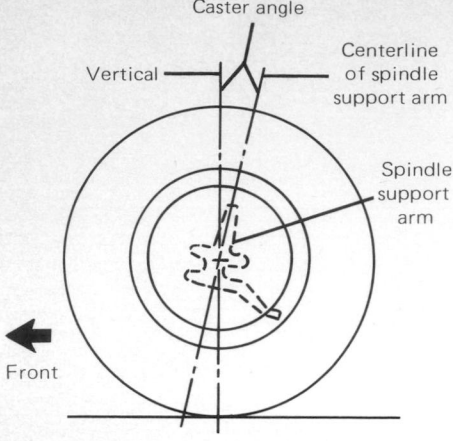

Caster angle

Vertical

Centerline of spindle support arm

Spindle support arm

Front

1 **Caster** has to do with the position of your wheels in relation to the spindle support arm. If properly adjusted, it will make your wheels track in a straight line instead of weaving or shimmying at high speeds.

2 **Camber** is the inward or outward tilt of the top of the wheels when viewed from the front of the car—how "bow-legged or knock-kneed" they are. If they don't hang properly, your tires will wear out more quickly and your car will be harder to handle.

3 **Toe-in** involves placing your tires so that they are ever so slightly "pigeon-toed" when the car is standing still. This keeps them from being forced too far out when the car is running at high speeds. The result should be a nice straight track when the car is moving quickly.

4 **Toe-out** is the opposite of toe-in (how about that!). It affects the way your car tracks on turns. No wheels should toe out. If yours do, you're in for some very freaky steering!

5 **Steering axis inclination** is adjusted so that your car will return the steering wheel to its straight-ahead position when you come out of a turn. This is done by adjusting the tilt of the steering axis so that it is directly under the center of the tread on your tires.

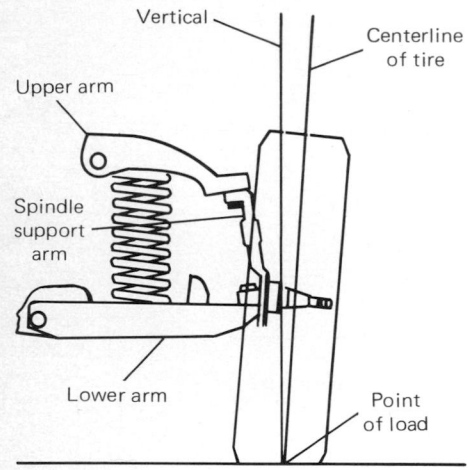

Vertical

Centerline of tire

Upper arm

Spindle support arm

Lower arm

Point of load

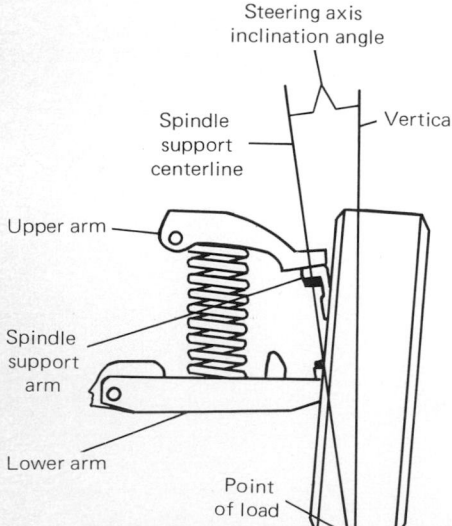

Steering axis inclination angle

Spindle support centerline

Vertical

Upper arm

Spindle support arm

Lower arm

Point of load

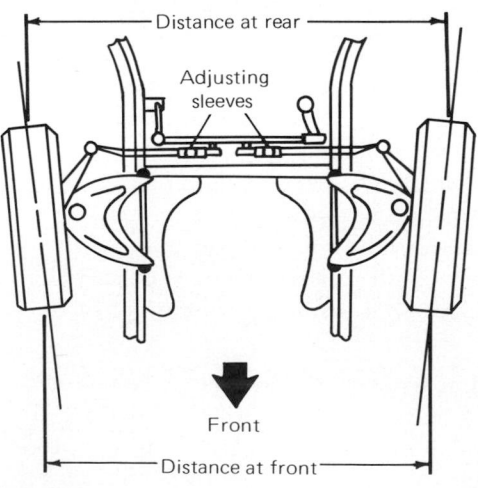

Distance at rear

Adjusting sleeves

Front

Distance at front

(*top*) Caster (*middle*) Camber (*bottom left*) Steering Axis Inclination (*bottom right*) Toe-in
Moog Automotive, Inc., St. Louis, Missouri

6 **Turning radius** is the relation of one front wheel to the other on turns. If you turn to the right, the right front tire is going to make a smaller circle than the left front tire does. To the left, the reverse holds true. Bent steering arms can cause this kind of misalignment. If your tires are "squealing" sharply on turns, this may be your problem.

How do you know if your wheels need aligning? There are two things to check: your steering equipment and your tire wear. Do this at least once a year, more often if you have been involved in any of the situations mentioned previously.

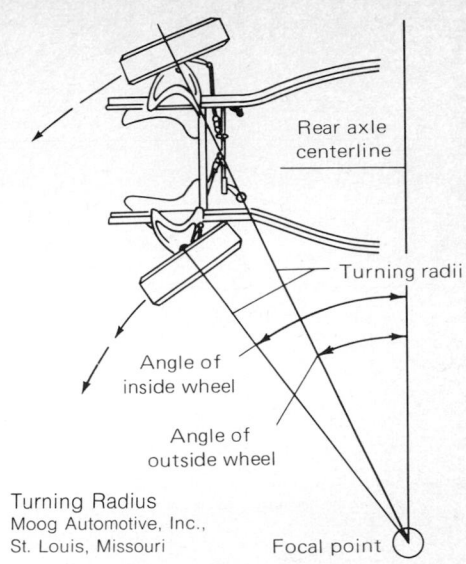

Rear axle centerline

Turning radii

Angle of inside wheel

Angle of outside wheel

Turning Radius
Moog Automotive, Inc.,
St. Louis, Missouri

Focal point

How to Check Your Steering

This is easy. Just stand outside your car, near the door on the driver's side. Stick your hand through the open window and move the steering wheel, with your eye on the left front tire. If you can move the steering wheel at all before the tire starts to move, then you need to have your steering and your alignment checked. There should be no play in the steering wheel before the signal is transmitted to the tires.

As you drive your car, be alert to signs that it is not handling as easily as before. If it seems to have a mind of its own and begins to resist you on turns (and pulling out of turns), take a good look at your tires for signs of wear caused by misalignment.

How to Check Your Tires for Wear

If you want to determine whether or not you should (a) buy new tires, (b) have your wheels balanced, (c) have your front end aligned, or (d) change your driving habits, you can tell a lot by simply "reading your tire treads." This is not like reading tread marks, as the police do when there's been an accident. It means examining your car's "feet" for clues to its health.

1 Look at each tire. Are there nails, stones, or other debris embedded in the treads? Remove them. *But*, if you are going to remove a nail, first be sure your spare tire is inflated and in usable shape. If when you pull a nail, you hear a hissing sound, push the

How to Read Your Treads

Clue	Culprit	Remedy
Both edges worn	Underinflation	Add more air Check for leaks
Center treads worn	Overinflation	Let air out to manufacturers specifications
One-sided wear	Poor alignment	Have front-end aligned
Treads worn unevenly, with bald spots, cups, or scallops	Poor alignment	Have front-end aligned
Edges of front tires only worn	You are taking curves too fast	Slow down!
Saw-toothed wear pattern	Poor braking habits	Learn to pump your brakes or slow down
Whining, thumping and other weird noises	Poor alignment or worn tires	Have front-end aligned or buy new tires
Squealing on curves	Poor alignment or underinflation	Check wear on treads and act accordingly

It's Time for New Tires When Tread-Wear Indicators Appear.
The Goodyear Tire & Rubber Company

nail back in quickly and take the tire to be fixed. If you aren't sure if air is escaping, put some water on the hole and look for the bubbles made by escaping air. If you're still not sure whether the thing may have caused a leak, check your air pressure and then check it again the next day to see if it is lower (I'll show you how to do this next). Tires with leaks should be patched by a professional. If the leak persists, get a new tire.

2 Look at the treads again. Most tires have **tread-wear indicators** built into them. These are bars of hard rubber that appear across treads that have been worn down to $1/16$ of an inch of the surface of the tire. If these indicators appear in two or three different places, less than 120 degrees apart on the circumference of the tire, the tire should be replaced. If your tires don't show these indicators and you think they are worn, place a thin ruler into the

Severe underinflation   Overinflation   Poor alignment   Poor alignment

What the Signs of Poor Tread Wear Mean
Moog Automotive, Inc., St. Louis, Missouri

tread and measure the distance from the base of the tread to the surface. It should be more than $1/16$ of an inch deep.

3 If your front tires are more worn than your rear ones and show an abnormal wear pattern, you probably need to have your front end aligned (unless, of course, you've been rotating your tires or your front tires have been on the car longer!).

4 If you keep losing air in your tires, have your local service station check them for leaks. Sometimes a leak is caused by an ill-fitting rim. The garage has a machine that can fix this easily.

5 If the garage cannot find a leak and if your rims fit properly, and you are still losing air, you probably have a faulty **tire valve** that is allowing air to escape. You can buy snap-in tire valves to replace the ones on your car. Look for the number molded into the base of the tire valves on your car; then buy new ones. At least one of the four valve caps should have a notched end for removing and replacing tire valves. If you don't have one, buy one.

Tires should be checked often to see that they are inflated properly. There is a strong correlation between inflation and wear: underinflated tires wear out faster on the outside treads, and they tend to squeal when cornering. Overinflated tires also wear out faster, this time in the center of the tread area. To make matters worse, they'll give you a bumpier ride.

Checking tires for correct inflation is a simple matter. All you need is a *tire gauge* (less than $2) and about five minutes. Here's how to do it:

How to Check Your Air Pressure

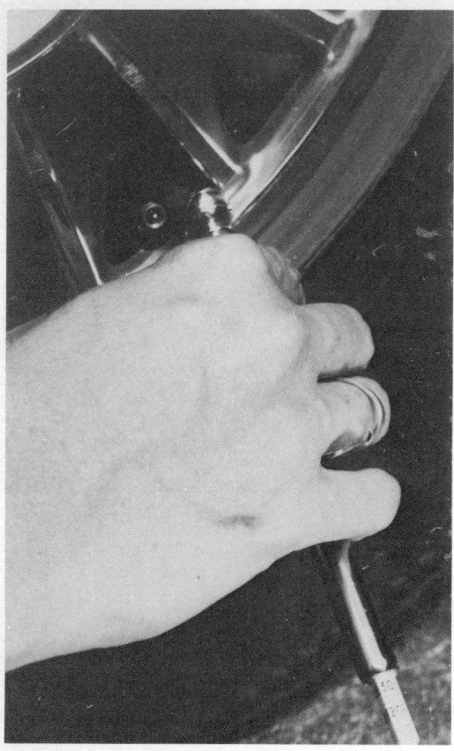

Press the round end of the gauge against the pin in the valve stem and read the numbers on the stick that emerges from the bottom of the gauge.

Use a Tire Gauge to See If Your Tires Are Properly Inflated.
Richard Freshman

1 Get a tire gauge at your local hardware or auto supply store.

2 Look at your owner's manual for, or ask your dealer, how many pounds of air pressure you should have in your tires. Most tires hold between 23 and 30 pounds of air **psi**. Sometimes a car manufacturer will specify more air in the front tires than in the rear ones, for easier handling and better traction. It is always best to check and keep the tires at the specified pressure.

3 Remember that in hot weather the pressure in your tires will rise as the air in them heats up and expands. This is also true after you have heated up your tires with a lot of driving, so check tire pressure in the morning before you use the car.

4 Conversely, in cold weather the pressure will fall as the cold air contracts. If it gets very cold and it looks as though it will stay that way for some time, you might want to add a bit of air to bring the pressure back up if you get a low reading. Generally though, tires that are correctly inflated will tend to wear properly in spite of weather ups and downs. Just check them every couple of weeks to keep things under control, and try not to check them under extreme temperature conditions or after you've been driving around.

5 *To use the tire gauge:*

a Remove the little cap from the **tire valve** that sticks out of your tire near the wheel rim. There is no need to remove your hub cap to do this.

b Place the rounded end of the tire gauge against the valve so that the little pin in the gauge contacts the pin in the valve.

c Press the gauge against the valve stem. You will hear a hissing sound as the air starts to escape from the tire.

d At this point, you will see a little stick emerge from the other end of the tire gauge. It will emerge partway almost as soon as the air starts to hiss, and it will stop emerging almost immediately. Without pushing the stick back in, remove the gauge from the tire valve.

   e Look at the stick without touching it. There are little numbers on it, and the last number showing is the amount of air pressure in your tire. Is it the right amount? If it seems too low, press the gauge against the valve stem again. If it still doesn't move, you need more air. Do this for each tire, and don't forget the spare!

6 If your tires appear to be "low," drive to your garage and use their air hose to fill the tires to the proper level. You can use the air hose in any garage for nothing. It's nice to know that some things are still free, right? But since it's free, you might like to do it yourself. Here's how:

   a Remove the cap from the tire valve.

   b Place the nozzle of the air hose against the stem as you did with the tire gauge. After a short burst of air has entered the tire, remove the hose and check with your tire gauge to see if you have reached the proper pressure. Many air hoses have a gauge built in, or are attached to a pressure meter, which is nice.

   c If the reading is now too high, let some air out by depressing the pin on the tire valve with the back of the air hose nozzle or with the little knob on the tire gauge.

   d Check again until you've got it right. No one hits it on the head the first time.

O.K., you've kept your hands clean long enough. It's time to get back to work. All this running to professionals for wheel balancing and front-end alignment and stuff has probably made you soft and lazy. So get prepared to do another job—not a big or difficult one—that can save you money and improve the life of your car and its fuel consumption if you do it more often and you do it yourself. What am I talking about? Those "lube and oil jobs" that service stations keep throwing at you . . .

Lubrication and Suspension: How to Give Your Car a Long and Happy Life

When we think about "the good life" we tend to think in terms of freedom from pressure, discomfort, and "friction." If your car could talk (mine can only sing), it would probably agree. When you consider that the temperature in your car's combustion chambers can get as high as 4,500 degrees F., with high pressures, the shock of combustion, and many metal parts rubbing and grinding against one another, you can see that a car that is *not* adequately protected against heat and **friction** will come swiftly to an untimely death. Luckily, this kind of protection is cheap and easy to ensure. It is simply a matter of providing sufficient lubrication to keep things running smoothly and then making sure your car gets this kind of regular attention.

A Tragic Tale

Before we came West, my husband's car resided, as I've mentioned before, in a garage, where it was looked after by professional mechanics. Herb was always willing to agree when he was told the car needed **oil** and **lubrication**. Yet when we took the engine apart recently, we found that a lack of proper lubrication had led to trouble, for the **camshaft** had been practically worn away! When this happens, you choose between major and expensive surgery or you get rid of the car. We got rid of the car, in favor of a new, and saner, small car with lower fuel consumption and a higher potential resale value in these economy-conscious times. As we sadly watched the macho-mobile vanish into the sunset, the major question in our minds was, "How did it happen?" The answer, unfortunately, was that we had been dependent on someone else for lubrication reminders, and we had trusted someone else to do the job properly. Not only had we been paying at least twice as much as it would have cost to do the job ourselves, but we had ended up paying to replace a car that could have gone almost twice as far if it had been lubricated properly.

If this sad story inspires you to undertake your own lubrication work, then dear old m-m will not have been towed away in vain. Besides, it is just plain silly to pay someone a lot of money to do something you can do yourself in a couple of minutes. And if you can unscrew the top of a jar and use a can opener, you can change your oil without any trouble.

The Engine

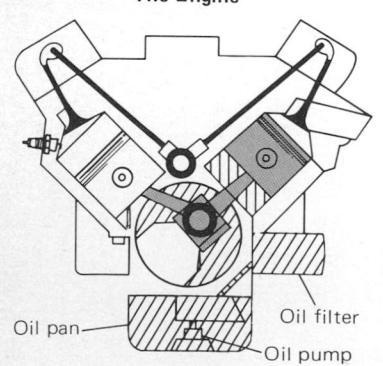

Oil pan

Oil filter

Oil pump

The Lubrication System
Automotive Information Council (AIC)

I'm very serious about changing at least your **oil** and **oil filter** yourself. There is absolutely no reason not to. If you want to chicken out of the **lube job**, go ahead. You can usually find a service station that has a "lubrication special," and it may be worth $3 or $4 to you not to have to buy a **grease gun** and crawl under your car. I'll give you all the details, and you can make your own decisions. But even if you don't do another thing to your car, if you don't try changing your oil yourself I'll confiscate your copy of this book! All it involves is unscrewing a plug and a filter, letting the old oil drain out, and pouring new oil in. You probably won't even have to jack up your car!

The figure at right shows what that costs:

The price of oil is figured at the current on sale price of 59 cents a quart. If it is not on sale, figure up to 95 cents a quart. Well? If you're convinced, let's start at the beginning.

Why You Should Change Your Oil Yourself

	At Home	At a Service Station
5 qts. oil	$2.95	$5.00
1 oil filter	1.49	5.45
Labor	——	3.00 (at least!)
Total	4.44	$13.45

To choose the proper kind of oil, you should know what the oil will be called upon to do. When your car is at rest, the oil slops around quietly in a container located at the bottom of the **crankcase**, just below your engine. This container is called the **oil pan**. When the car is operating, the oil is circulated through special channels in the engine, where it helps to cool and clean the engine and to provide a nice slippery cushion that keeps the moving engine parts from grinding one another into oblivion.

How to Choose the Proper Kind of Oil for Your Car

Since the oil pan is lower than the engine, and since it is located where the air that rushes past the moving car can cool it, the oil can pick up some of the heat as it travels around inside the engine and then cool off when it circulates through the oil pan. Although this is not enough to keep most engines sufficiently cool without water, it helps.

How Oil Cools Your Engine

Most engine oils contain some detergent, which helps to flush out the grunge and muck that accumulate inside your engine. Not only will detergent oil remove

How Oil Cleans Your Engine

and dissolve this old **sludge**; it helps to prevent new gobs of the stuff from forming. Believe me, you have no idea of the meaning of any of those yucky words until you've looked into the engine of a car that has not had its oil changed often enough. There are masses of black slimy stuff, hunks of undefinable vileness, and pebblelike particles clinging to everything. It is hard to see how these engines function at all. Even more depressing are the all-too-visible signs of wear on steel parts that have been eroded away by this ugly stuff. If your car hasn't had its oil changed in at least 6,000 miles, you can consider the growls coming out of its engine as cries of pain!

Brush the tears from your eyes—we're past the tragic part.

How Oil Cuts Down on Friction and Does Other Nice Things

By far the most important thing that the oil in your engine does is form a cushion between moving parts which helps them to slide past one another easily. This cuts down **friction**, which in turn dramatically reduces the heat and wear that friction can cause. An engine that is keeping its cool, and operating with less effort, uses less fuel. So if you change your oil on a regular basis, you can cut fuel consumption and reduce air pollution. To illustrate this, let's take another look at something we discussed earlier.

If you recall, each piston is attached to a **connecting rod**, which has a hole in it for the **crankshaft** to fit through. This makes the crankshaft and the connecting rod operate together. Take a closer look at that hole in the enlarged portion of the illustration. As you can see, there is a space around the hole that is always filled with oil. When the car is running, the oil pressure forms a cushion that keeps the connecting rod (and its bearings) from ever touching the crankshaft. Instead, each moves on its cushion of oil to prevent friction and wear, which is important since the rod exerts 4000 pounds of pressure every time it moves down. This same principle is applied to other moving parts in your car.

Oil also retards corrosion in your engine by enveloping the particles of water and acid which are present. These particles, plus the solid particles that it holds in

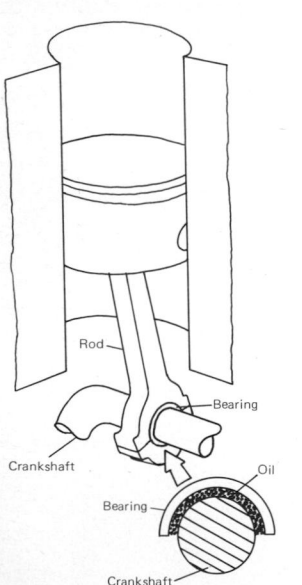

Oil Forms a Cushion to Keep Your Crankshaft and Your Connecting Rod from Wearing Each Other Away.
Jack Herlihy

suspension, are what turn oil black and thin it out. We change the oil to get rid of this stuff before it can build up to the point where the oil cannot do its job properly.

How Often Should You Change Your Oil?

Most manufacturers suggest that oil should be changed every 6,000 miles. This is an oversimplification. Oil should be changed *at least* every 6,000 miles, but you *should* do it every 3,000 to 4,000 miles or every 90 days. Cars that just do a lot of short stop-and-start driving in city traffic never get hot enough to evaporate the water that forms in the crankcase and builds up the sludge that I've so graphically dealt with above. Older cars generally are carrying around a collection of yuck that has accumulated over the years, and this stuff will foul up your nice clean oil fairly rapidly. Dirty oil just doesn't do the job as well as fresh oil does. The additives boil out; sulphuric acid forms in the crankcase and eats metal parts; and water collects over a period of time and forms sludge. Also, the oil holds more and more abrasive particles of metal suspended in it, and these particles wear away the parts of the engine which the oil was supposed to protect.

All oil looks pretty black within a couple of days after an oil change, so the only way to avoid running on oil that is so dirty it has become a liability is to keep a record of when it was last changed and to change it frequently—even as often as every 2,000 miles if necessary. By changing your oil frequently you can probably get *twice* the mileage out of an otherwise good engine!

How to Tell Which Kind of Oil to Buy

Oil is rated and identified by its **viscosity**, or its ability to flow. In cold weather, oil thickens and becomes less able to flow through your engine. In hot weather it thins out, and although it flows well enough, it might become so thin that it would not prevent friction. The questions to consider when buying oil are:

1 What kind of oil have you been using?
2 What kind of oil does your owner's manual recommend?

3 Do you live where it is very cold? Hot? Is it mountainous?

4 Are there sharp changes in temperature where you live or where you are going?

5 How old is the oil in your car? How many miles have you driven it?

6 Is your car still under **warranty**?

There are two types of oil on the market, *single-viscosity* oil and *multi-viscosity* oil. (These are also called "single-weight" and "multi-weight," or "single-vis" and "multi-vis.") Most multi-viscosity oils also have detergent added to them to help clean your engine. A few of the single-viscosity oils have detergent; others don't. The most common single-viscosity oil is 30 weight oil, which is generally considered to be the best weight oil for cars of medium age which are *not* going to face extremes of temperature. If you normally use 30 weight oil, in really hot weather you might switch to 40 weight, which is thicker. If it is really cold, 10W (the W means the oil is recommended for use during the winter) oil will be better because it is thinner and will flow more easily after the cold thickens it. Or you can use 10W–40 oil all year if you want to be covered for all weather conditions.

In the past few years multi-viscosity oils have come into their own, and most newer cars (1968 and on) are designed to use them. The most common is 10W–40. This means that it doesn't thicken when the weather is cold and it won't thin out when the temperature gets hot. This oil is fine for all year round and especially good if you are driving from a warm sea-level climate to the mountains, where it is colder.

"Aha!" you might say, "all I have to do is buy 10W–40 oil and I'm covered for everything!" Maybe, but not definitely. There are several things to consider:

1 If you have an older car that has been running on cheap 30 or 40 weight oil for most of its life, it has built up quite a bit of sludge because some of the single-weight oils don't have detergent in them. If you suddenly switch to a multi-viscosity oil, the detergent in it would free all that gook in your engine and it would start to slosh around and really foul things up. It's better to let sleeping gook lie unless

you want to invest in having your engine disassembled and cleaned. If your car is running well, don't do it. The engine would have to be taken apart and put back together again, and you might start trouble where none existed before. Just stick with the same old nondetergent stuff you've been using and forget the new-fangled stuff.

2 If your car has been logging a great many miles, and has been running on 30 or 40 weight oil, the 10W–40 stuff is not going to be consistently thick enough to lubricate the worn engine parts, which have become smaller while wearing down, leaving wider spaces between them. To keep the oil thick enough to fill these gaps, you should switch to heavier oil as your car gets older and starts to run more roughly or to burn up oil more quickly. So if you've been running on 30 weight oil, you would switch to 40 weight, at least during the summer, when oil tends to thin out. Tweety's manual called for 10W–40 oil, but I have her on straight 40 weight oil now that she has more than 80,000 miles to her credit. There is even 50 weight oil for the real oldies!

3 If you have a brand-new car, it probably has "break-in" oil in it. You must use this stuff for the first 6,000 miles; then you can switch to whatever they specify. It will probably be 10W–40, unless you live in the desert or on top of a high mountain. Then, when your car gets much older, you can switch to a heavier single-viscosity oil if you need it. Be sure to use whatever the owner's manual recommends while your warranty is in effect, or you can invalidate it.

One last note about this. No matter what you are using, if you are planning on a driving trip into the high mountains, at any time of year, use 10W–40 oil for the trip, and go back to your usual stuff when you return.

Whenever you buy oil, look for the major brands, like Pennzoil, Quaker State, Valvoline, or check *Consumer Reports*. There is a lot of reclaimed oil on the market. No matter how crazy about recycling you are, cheap reclaimed oil is junk. Stay away from it. The good stuff is often on sale in supermarkets and at auto supply stores. If you spot a sale, buy the oil and stash it away until your next oil change. Try not to switch brands, however, unless you are just stopping at a service station for a quart to "top it off." It is better to buy 40 weight oil of the same brand you've been using than to switch to 30 weight oil of another brand in order to use oil of the same weight. Most oil costs about $1.00 a can at a service station. You can usually find it on a special sale for 59 cents. If the oil crisis makes oil more expensive, the same ratio should still hold.

SAE Classification Codes

Recently the American Society for Testing and Materials and the Society of Automotive Engineers collaborated on the creation of a number of classification codes for automotive oils. You may see these codes on the oil you buy. Here's what they mean:

SA—Utility Gasoline. The lowest grade. Avoid it.

SB—Minimum Duty Gasoline. Not durable enough. Avoid it.

SC—1964 Gasoline Engine Warranty Maintenance Service. For 1964 to 1967 cars and trucks. The base minimum. Avoid it if you drive a newer car, and consider it a last resort for older cars.

SD—1968 Gasoline Engine Warranty Maintenance Service. Designed for maintenance of 1968 through 1970 models. May also be O.K. for 1971 cars. Better, but still not perfect.

SE—For 1972 Gasoline Engine Warranty Maintenance Service. This is the best around. It is designed to provide maximum protection against oil oxidation, high temperature engine deposits (gook), rust, and corrosion. If your car is an older model and the owner's manual specifies SC or SD oil, you can use this with even better results. This is the oil to buy if possible.

A Word About Additives

There are three basic types of **additives**. The first type extends viscosity. The second loosens junk and dissolves gummy deposits. The third acts as a friction lubricant to make the oil "tougher" under high extremes of temperature and usage.

Most popular additives are basically viscosity extenders. They thicken your oil when it starts to thin out. They also keep the oil from foaming at speeds of over 100 mph. And by making the heavy-weight oil even thicker, they can also keep a very very old engine that is running poorly on 40 or 50 weight oil from clanking.

Other additives have already been added to the oil you buy to help it in the following ways:

1 To pour better in cold weather.
2 To prevent corrosion of the metal parts of the engine.
3 To cut down on friction between moving parts.
4 To prevent foaming at high temperatures.
5 To clean the engine.

Remember that most oils that do not advertise the presence of additives already have most of this stuff in them. Also, no amount of additional additives will improve the performance of oil unless the oil you started with was of the best grade. So if you buy a well-known brand, you are going to get all the protection you need in these categories if your engine is in reasonably good shape. If you use high-grade oil of the proper weight and classification and change it often, you would do well to leave the rest of the additives on the store shelves. They may provide *temporary relief* if your engine is in the process of disintegrating, but they are not a *cure* for a worn-down, filthy, miserable, old engine.

If you have one of those sad, clanking workhorse engines, you must investigate the following alternatives:

1 Put it out of its misery. You might be able to get $100 from a junker, because junkers will sell its body parts.
2 Find out if it would respond to rebuilding. The price will depend on how many parts have to be replaced and how much work is involved. Prepare to pay up to $500, or even more, for this. Is the car worth it?
3 Buy a new engine or a good **rebuilt** one, and have it installed. This is still expensive, and I'd do it only for a classic car.

4 Just keep putting in heavier and heavier oil, get used to the noise, and drive it into the ground.

What About Oil Filters?

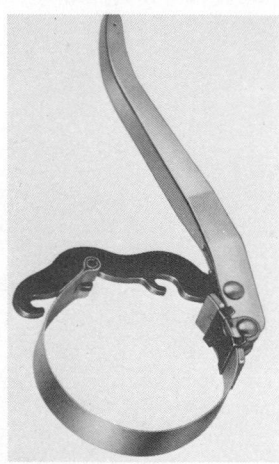

Oil Filter Wrench
K-D Manufacturing Co.

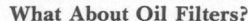

Oil Filter

Under the hood of your car, sticking out of the engine, is what looks like a tin can screwed into your engine block. This is your **oil filter**. As the oil circulates from the oil pan through your engine, it passes through this filter, which cleans it and removes some of the sludge. Although it's recommended that the oil filter be changed at every other oil change, I'd change it every time you change your oil (especially if you are going to do it less frequently than every 3,000 miles). Oil filters sell for between $1.25 and $2.00 at auto supply stores; they'll charge you as much as $5.45 if you buy it at a service station.

Most filters screw on and off. Oil filter wrenches are sold for a dollar or two. They are usually necessary for unscrewing the old filter, but plan to tighten the new one by hand.

How to Change Your Oil

1 Check your owner's manual for the type of oil recommended for your car. If you have no manual, call your friendly neighborhood service station (the ones who changed it last time), and ask them what weight oil they used in your car. If you can't do that, call a local dealer who sells your kind of car and ask him. Also find out from one of these sources how many quarts of oil your car requires.

Most cars require around 5 quarts of oil.

2 Go to the auto supply store and buy your oil. Also buy an oil filter for your make and model car. An **oil drain plug** gasket is also cheap, and it is wise to buy one in case the one on your car needs replacing. If it doesn't, just save the **gasket** for later.

3 If you do not have an old basin that you'd like to misuse, there are two products on the market that are designed for do-it-yourself oil-changing. The first is a large flat plastic can with two caps. It is designed to be laid on its side, which is shaped like a trough with a drain hole in it. You let the oil

drain onto and into the container, screw the cap on the drain hole, use the handle to carry the can to a place where you can get rid of the oil, and empty it via the cap on top. The can sells for around $4 and is endlessly reusable.

The second is a simple kit consisting of a basin, an oil can spout, and an oil filter wrench. One I saw at Sears was $1.97—a true bargain! Whatever you use, just be sure it will fit under your car without having to jack the car up, and that it will hold as many quarts of old oil as there are in your engine (the same amount as you are going to add).

4 Take all this stuff, plus a funnel or an oil can spout (if you have neither, a screwdriver or a beer-can opener will do), to your car. You should also have a lint-free rag and a dirty old thick rag as well.

5 Warm up your car so that the gook will get churned up and will flow out of the engine easily. You *don't* want it so hot that you will burn yourself. When the car is fairly warm, shut off the engine.

6 Look under your car. You should be able to see and reach a large nut located under the **oil pan** at the bottom of the engine. This is the **oil drain plug**. It unscrews with the aid of a combination wrench. Feel around to see what size wrench you will need. If the plug is too hot to touch, let the car cool off for a while longer.

7 If you cannot reach your oil drain plug easily, you will have to either crawl under your car to reach it or jack up the front end. If you choose to jack up your car, be sure to reread Chapter 9 to be sure you do it *safely*. Don't jack it up too high though, or the oil may not drain out of the oil pan completely.

8 Push the basin or container under the oil drain plug so that it can catch the oil. It would be wise to place all the stuff you are going to use within easy reach, so you won't have to jump up and run around in the middle of the job.

9 With your combination wrench, unscrew the oil drain plug until it is *almost* ready to come out.

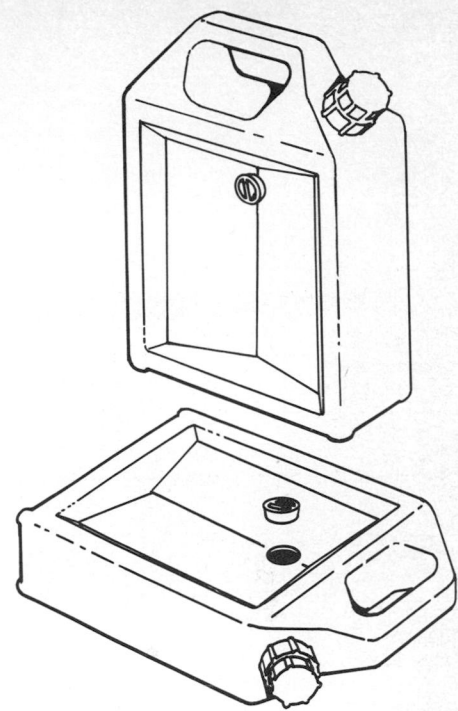

Oil Drainer-Container
Jack Herlihy

Oil Can Spout

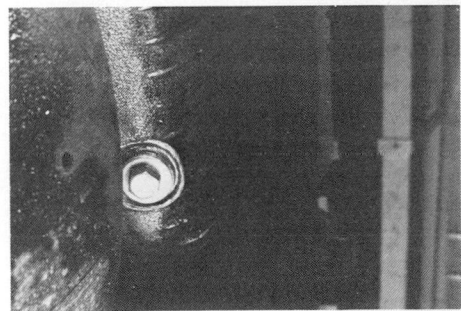

The Drain Plug Is Located at the Bottom of Your Oil Pan.
Richard Freshman

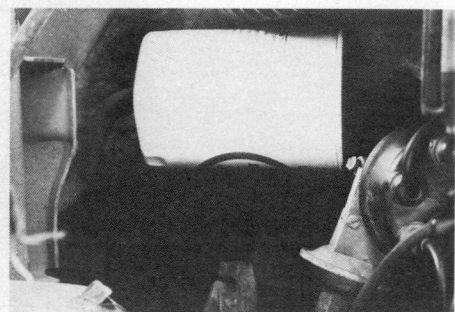

An Oil Filter Is Screwed into the Side of Your Engine.
Richard Freshman

Then take that dirty rag in your hand and give the plug a last quick turn by hand to release it. Pull your hand away quickly so you will not get oil all over it. If the plug falls into the container, you can retrieve it later. The oil will now drain out of your engine into the container. While it is doing this, get out from under the car and take a look under the hood.

10 Under the hood, and sticking out of the side of your engine, is your **oil filter**. It looks like a tin can (as I've mentioned before).

On many cars, you can easily reach the oil filter by leaning under the hood. Unfortunately, other car manufacturers have placed the filter so that it must be reached from under the car. If your car is one of these, you will have to get under your car. When you really get down to it (no pun intended), jacking the car up and getting under it isn't really too horrendous. It only takes about three extra minutes of your time, and if you lie on an old blanket or mattress pad, you won't find the task more tiresome than changing a light bulb on a ceiling fixture. Not the stuff that dreams are made of, but not a nightmare either.

Unscrew the oil filter with an oil filter wrench if you can't do it by hand. Remember that, like most other things you'll find on a car, the oil filter unscrews if you twist it counterclockwise. The filter will have oil in it, so be careful not to dump it on anything when you remove it. Throw the old oil filter away.

11 When all the oil has drained out of the engine, take your new oil filter and smear a bit of oil around the gasket on the open end. This will help it to fit better.

Here's the best way to open a can of oil:

a If you have an oil spout, just jam the end into the can. It will open the can and form a handy spout for pouring. If you have no oil spout, put the can on the ground, place one foot on the can to steady it, and jab a long screwdriver into the top of the can near the rim. That will make a hole for the oil to pour out of. (Of course, you can always use a beer can opener, but the screw-

driver has more macho in automotive circles.)
Don't make more than one hole; you don't want
the oil to pour too fast or you'll get it all over
the engine before you hit the fill hole.

12 Take a new oil filter and screw it into the engine
where the old one was. It should fit tightly, but
never use the oil filter wrench to tighten it. The oil
filter wrench might screw the filter on improperly
or tighten it so much that the built-in gasket might
warp. In either case it would leak. Instead, hand-
tighten it as tight as you can. If you lack strength,
get your mother.

13 Now get under the car again and wipe around the
place where the oil drain plug goes. If your oil
drain plug hasn't been leaking, and the old gasket
looks (or feels) all right, just wipe the area and
replace the plug.

a If you need a new gasket, scrape the old one off
the outside of the oil pan with a screwdriver or
a paint-scraper and place the new one on the
pan before you replace the plug.

If you don't use the new gasket and, later on,
you find that your car is leaking oil from around
the plug, it's not the worst thing that can happen. Just remove the plug again, catch the oil in
a nice *clean* container, and pour it back into the
oil filler hole when the new gasket is in and the
plug is back in place. Most gaskets will hold
through several oil changes. I've never replaced
mine.

14 Here is a helpful hint that I got from Don, my
advisor: Always use a *system* when you do an oil
change. This means you should do each part of
the job in order and not change that order from
job to job. This may sound unduly restrictive to
those of you who like to improvise, but if you
ignore this advice, you may find you've added the
new oil before replacing the plug or before changing the filter. In either case, you're going to wind
up with your brand-new oil all over the ground
and not enough oil in the engine to drive to the
store for more. Also, the *minute* you replace the oil
drain plug, *always* tighten it completely and put the
new oil in. That way you won't forget to put in the

Pour Fresh Oil down the Oil Fill Hole at the Top of Your Cylinder Head Cover.
Richard Freshman

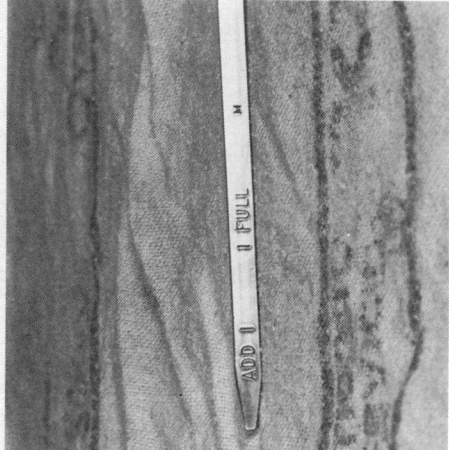

An Oil Dipstick
Richard Freshman

new oil (don't laugh; people have done that and ruined their engines in a couple of miles).

Here's how to add new oil:

15 When the oil filter is installed and the oil drain plug is back in place, remove the cap from the **oil filler hole** on the top of your engine. The cap is easy to recognize because it is a large cap that lifts or screws right off revealing a largish hole. Now, using a funnel, or the oil spout in the can, or just good aim, pour the oil into the cylinder head through the fill hole. Stop one quart short of the amount your car should hold and check your **dipstick**. Be sure to remove the dipstick, wipe it with a lint-free cloth, and replace it before pulling it out again to check it. Keep adding oil and checking the stick until you reach the "Full" line.

16 Replace the oil filler cap and start the engine. Watch the oil pressure indicator light on your dashboard. If it does not go out in 10 to 15 seconds (or if your **oil gauge**, if that is what you have on your car, does not move off "Low"), cut the ignition and check the oil level with your dipstick. If it does not indicate that the level is *near* full, look for the cause. This probably won't happen; it is just a safety check in case you forgot the plug or the filter and the oil has leaked out, or in case you did not add the required amount of oil. It's always best to be on the safe side. If you can't find a reason, yell for help; do *not* drive the car if it looks as though there is no oil pressure.

17 Assuming that everything is fine (and it will be in 99.99999 percent of the cases), drive the car around the block a couple of times—after making sure you've removed the container from under the car. Then let the car cool off a little and check the dipstick again. If the level looks lower, that's because some of the oil (about 1/2 quart) is now in the new oil filter. Add the remaining oil until you reach the "Full" line on the dipstick again. And that's it!

Oh, what do you do with that container full of cruddy old oil? Just take it to the same friendly service station that used to do your oil changes. They probably save the stuff and sell it to an oil reclaimer. They'll be glad to have your donation. If you don't want to bother with that, just dump the oil into an old can or a sturdy plastic trash bag, and throw it out.

Although this took 17 steps to explain, it should not take more than 15 minutes to accomplish once you've bought the necessary stuff. When you see how easy it is, you will tend to change your oil more frequently and your car will ride better, last longer, and burn less fuel. And you will feel pretty happy with yourself, too!

If you are really feeling good about the oil change and you've got the car jacked up anyway, you might want to consider doing the lube job now.

What a "Lube Job" Involves

Basically, a **lube job** involves applying lubricants (various kinds of **grease** and oil) to some of the moving parts under your car, and to some of the rubber parts to keep them supple. This is what you will need:

1 *A decent grease gun.* These can cost between $1.98 and $30.00. Borrow one for the first job; if you hate it you won't have made a big investment. If you can't borrow one, buy a cheap one. You can always sell it to a friend who is just getting into auto maintenance and buy yourself a super one if you plan to do the job repeatedly. Most **grease guns** come with a couple of adapters to fit the grease fittings on your car, and with an extender for hard-to-reach places. If your gun doesn't have these, you can get an adapter or an extender for a dollar or two if you need one. (You may not. Some grease guns are fitted to take grease cartridges, which saves you the time and mess of loading them.)

2 *The proper kind of grease.* Consult your owner's manual, service manual, or the salesperson at the auto supply store. They have manuals that tell all.

3 *Some rubber lube.* This is a very refined liquid for lubricating the rubber parts under your car. It will keep them from drying out and cracking.

Your **transmission fluid** and **brake fluid** are lubricants, too. See Chapter 5 about checking these, if you haven't already done so.

There are other parts of your car that need periodic lubrication. These can include **steering** parts, **transmission** shift linkage, **clutch** linkage, **parking brake** cables, **differential**, and **driveshaft universal joint** fittings. Since some of these are hard to find, hard to reach, and most require a special kind of lubricant, and since you can get into trouble if you don't deal with them properly, I'd suggest that once or twice a year you take the car to a good dealer with service facilities and have him lubricate *everything*, including your distributor. The rest of the time, just lubricate the things I point out and you will be way ahead of the game.

O.K. Just what *are* you going to lubricate? First, the **grease fittings** under your car:

Everything You've Always Wanted to Know About Grease Fittings (and Probably a Good Deal More . . .)

Grease fittings are those places on your car that hold lubricants that protect moving parts from one another. These parts must be kept packed with grease to keep them moving freely without friction. Naturally, these are usually the parts that move the most, aside from the parts inside your engine (which are lubricated with oil).

Think about your car. Where does most of the movement take place when you drive? (Not counting the kids in the back seat, if you have any.) Well, the front wheels turn on **wheel bearings**, and they can change direction when you steer because of the **steering linkage** between the steering wheel and the front wheels.

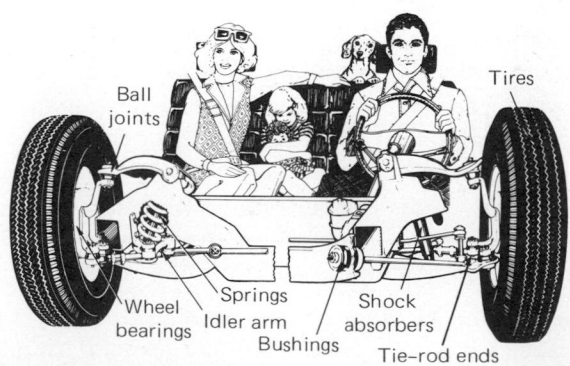

Ball joints   Tires
Wheel bearings   Springs   Idler arm   Shock absorbers   Bushings   Tie-rod ends

Where Most of the Movement Takes Place When You Drive
Moog Automotive, Inc., St. Louis, Missouri

The car moves up and down on its **suspension system** and **shock absorbers**, which keep the car level although the wheels may be bobbing up and down on a rough stretch of road. All these areas can have grease fittings called **lubrication points**, and replacing, repacking, or replenishing the grease in them is called a "lube job," a "grease job," or a "chassis lube," depending on who is doing the talking. Your car should be lubricated every 2000–3000 miles.

The steering linkage and ball joints are the areas that you are going to go after with your grease gun. The steering linkage is the system that connects your steering wheel with your front wheels. When you turn your steering wheel, the steering linkage causes your front wheels to respond by moving in the proper direction. Along the steering linkage, whenever two parts meet, there is a type of **ball joint** called a **tie rod end** that is filled with grease. As the two parts of the linkage move against each other, they are cushioned by the grease in these tie rod ends. This keeps them moving freely and prevents friction that would wear them away.

The steering linkage actually connects to the wheels,

The Steering Linkage and Ball Joints

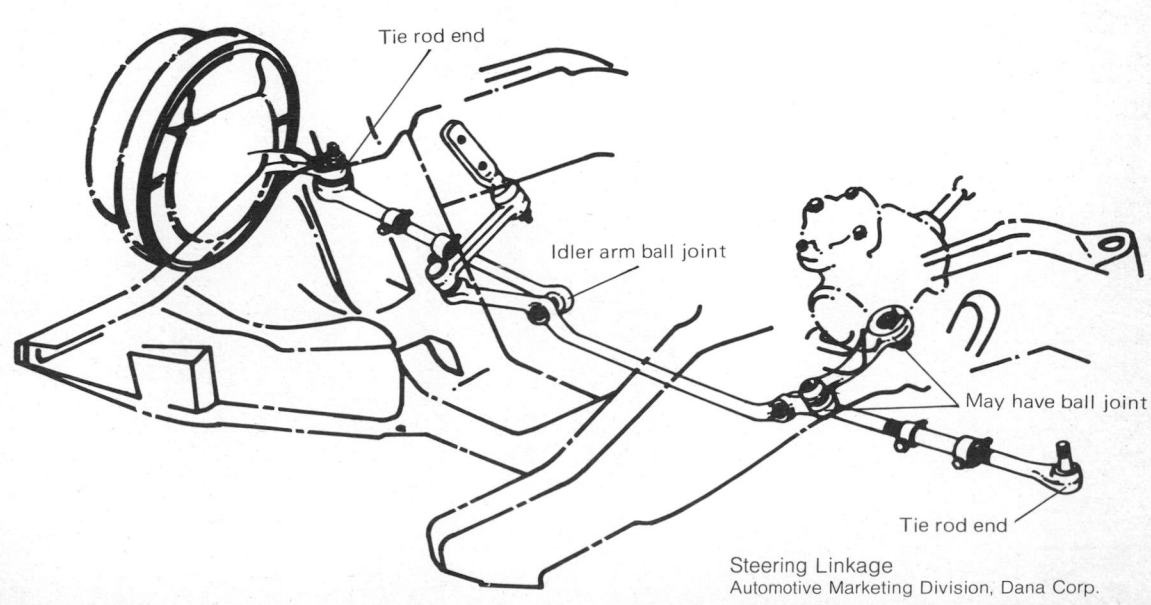

Tie rod end

Idler arm ball joint

May have ball joint

Tie rod end

Steering Linkage
Automotive Marketing Division, Dana Corp.

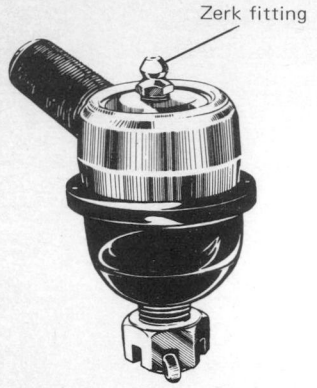

Zerk fitting

A Closer Look at a Tie Rod End Grease Fitting
Moog Automotive, Inc., St. Louis, Missouri

which are held in place by a **spindle** that goes through the wheel and is attached to upper and lower **control arms**. (That's the same spindle as the one the brake and bearing assembly fitted onto in Chapter 10.) The control arms allow the wheels to turn in any direction. To keep things moving freely, ball joints are located at the points on the control arms where the movement takes place. We keep the ball joints (and the tie rod ends) filled with grease to cut down on friction. Each ball joint and tie rod end should have a grease fitting that allows you to lubricate it.

On some cars, all or some of these ball joints are designed for *lifetime lubrication*, which means that the grease has been pumped in and sealed so it can't get out. Because this kind of sealed system also prevents dirt, air, and water from getting *in*, these lifetime lubrication systems seem to last pretty well. And you don't have to lubricate them yourself, ever. Of course if they break down, it is a bit more expensive to install a whole new part, but they don't break down very often. If your owner's manual tells you that your car

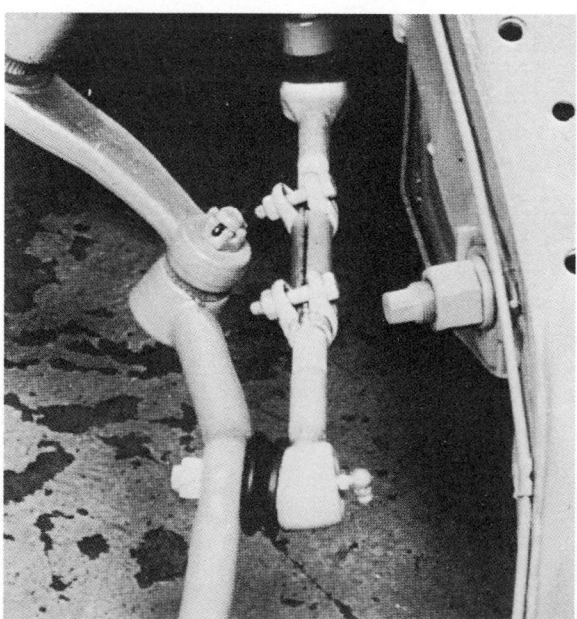

Tie Rod Ends
Moog Automotive, Inc., St. Louis, Missouri
Tie rod ends cushion the friction caused by steering your car.

has one of these, be happy, skip the rest of this portion, and go on to the **suspension system**.

For the rest of us, each ball joint has two basic parts: a rubber ball-shaped **boot** and a little metal nozzle called a **zerk fitting**. Some cars come with *plugs* on the ball joints instead of with zerk fittings. You can replace the plugs with zerk fittings by unscrewing the plugs and screwing in the fittings. The fittings then become permanent fixtures on the ball joints, and you can throw the plugs away (or save them for a rainy day).

The boot holds the grease, and the zerk fitting lets the grease into the boot and keeps it from getting out again. Most ball joints are sealed, in the sense that the only place for the grease to go in and out of the joint is through the zerk fitting. If you fill this type of joint too full, the boot will burst and have to be replaced or lubricated more frequently (as were the joints on cars before the booted ball joint was invented).

Other ball joints are designed to allow the grease to escape so that the new grease you insert pushes the old grease out the other end. Be sure to check under your car to see which type of ball joints you have. Your car dealer can also tell you if you aren't sure whether those gooey ball joints are sealed ones that have burst or the kind that are supposed to have a back door.

Another way to tell is, if only *one* of the ball joints has a mound of grease coming out of it when you put the new grease in, then it is probably a sealed joint that has burst. If they all tend to leak grease when you add more, they are probably supposed to do so. In any case, *never* add grease until the ball is tightly packed. There should be plenty of "give" when you squeeze the sides of the ball. Simply wipe the zerk fitting, fit the grease gun onto it (use an adapter if you need one), and *gently* squeeze a *little* grease into the joint.

If you squeeze too much grease in and the ball feels hard, you will have to unscrew the zerk fitting with an ignition wrench and squeeze enough grease out of the ball joint to relieve the pressure. Then you will have to screw the zerk fitting back into place. This is not a terribly pleasant thing to have to do—it is time-

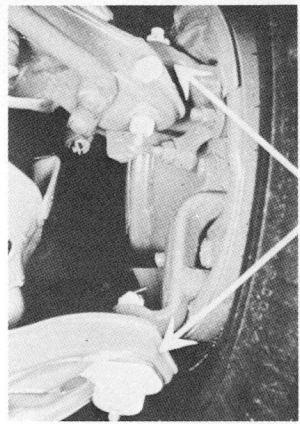

Upper control arm

Lower control arm

Ball Joints Are Located on the Upper and Lower Control Arms.
Moog Automotive, Inc., St. Louis, Missouri
Each front wheel has an upper and lower ball joint, mounted on the control arms. Ball joints permit the steering and suspension movement of the wheels.

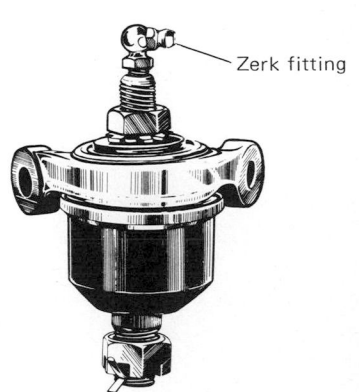

Zerk fitting

A Closer Look at the Zerk Fitting on a Ball Joint
Moog Automotive, Inc., St. Louis, Missouri

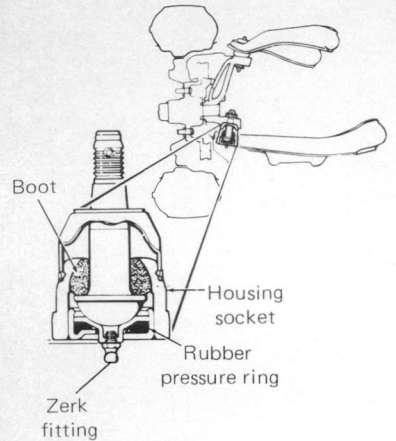

Boot

Housing
socket

Rubber
pressure ring

Zerk
fitting

Anatomy of a Ball Joint
Moog Automotive, Inc., St. Louis, Missouri

consuming and messy—so be careful to squeeze the grease in a little at a time. I know this because I've done it, and those teeny greasy zerk fittings are hard to hang onto. But if you goof, take heart. If "Thumbs" Sclar can do it, so can you!

"Fine!" you say, "but how do I find the ball joints in the first place?" O.K., here's where to look:

1 Some of the more enlightened owner's manuals will tell you, but not many of them.

2 The service manual for your car will tell you the location and nature of each lubrication point (or grease fitting or ball joint or whatever they call them in your book).

3 Every service station has a *lubrication manual* that is published by one of the major oil companies each year. These manuals show every lube point and grease fitting for every car manufactured during the year of publication. Your service station probably has the last couple of years on hand. If you don't have a service manual for your car, ask to see the lube manual if you are having trouble locating the lube points on your car.

4 Before you go down to the service station, however, why don't you try to find them yourself by looking under the front end of your car. Trace the bar that runs from one front wheel to the other. Grease fittings are usually found at the base and top of the arms that attach your wheels to the steering linkage (these are the **steering knuckles**) and at the center of the steering linkage where the tie rods meet the center. Some cars have as many as 8 or 10 of these ball joints. Others have none. Most have 4 to 6.

If you really have trouble finding yours and you are unwilling to throw yourself at the mercy of your service station for just a look at the lube manual, then give in and take the car in for a lube job someplace where they will let you hang around and ask questions. Casually ask for a look at the lube manual, or ask them to point out the lube points that they are going to work on. Say, "How many lube points does this model have?" They will usually be happy to show you and to answer your questions. People who work on cars love to talk shop (and most of them never suspect that

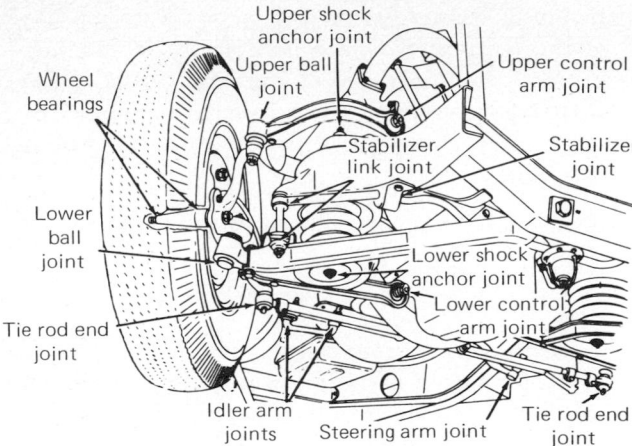

Upper shock
anchor joint

Upper ball
joint

Upper control
arm joint

Wheel
bearings

Stabilizer
link joint

Stabilizer
joint

Lower
ball
joint

Lower shock
anchor joint

Lower control
arm joint

Tie rod end
joint

Idler arm
joints

Steering arm joint

Tie rod end
joint

Some of the Places to Look for Grease Fittings on Your Car
Moog Automotive, Inc., St. Louis, Missouri

"civilians" are secretly planning to do the work themselves next time). If you get a real talkative one, you've found a gold mine, and be sure to ask about the rest of the job too.

For you lovers of recipes, let's go over the whole thing again, one step at a time:

1 Find out how many, and where, your lube points are.

2 Wipe off the first zerk fitting and try to fit your gun to it. Does it fit? If not, you may need an adapter. Can you reach it? If not, you may need an extender.

3 Load your grease gun with grease. The kind you want is called *suspension* **lube grease.**

4 Place the grease gun to the fitting and *gently* squeeze a little bit of grease into it. If the joint looks too hard and full, squeeze some out if you have the kind of fitting that has a back door. If you have a sealed joint, just add enough grease to fill it out a little. It should not be hard and full of grease. If the joint looks full before you start, don't add any grease at all; just go on to the next joint.

5 Repeat this until you have serviced all the ball joints.

6 If you've overfilled a sealed joint, take an ignition wrench of the proper tiny size and unscrew the zerk fitting (counterclockwise). Squeeze the excess grease out and replace the fitting.

Grease Gun with Adapter and Zerk Fitting
Richard Freshman

7 If one or more of your ball joints has burst, have it or them replaced *immediately.* The parts these joints protect get a lot of action, and you can be in for a very expensive job (or risk losing your ability to steer) after a very short trip on a nonfunctioning ball joint.

Now let's talk about the rest of the suspension system.

Lubricating the Suspension System

The **suspension system** technically includes the steering linkage, but in my mind, it is easier to deal with these things in terms of the function they perform. Therefore, try to see the steering linkage as concerned with the *horizontal* directions in which the car can go, and the suspension system as concerned with the *vertical* movement of the car as it travels over the road. An automotive engineer might quarrel with these distinctions, but we are basically concerned with understanding how a car works and how to fix it, and for these purposes, the two systems should be viewed separately.

What Does the Suspension System Consist Of?

Underneath your car are the main elements of the suspension system that supports your car and keeps the passenger compartment relatively stable on bumpy roads. Many of the key parts are made of hard rubber, for flexibility. To prevent these rubber parts from drying out, we apply *rubber lube* to them. This is simply a matter of getting under the car, looking for all the rubber fittings, and squirting or spreading the rubber lube oil all over them. The lube manual or service manual will point them out, but you can find them easily if you use a flashlight or a work light and take a good look around. The stuff won't hurt anything if you put it on something that turns out not to be rubber—just keep it away from your brakes.

But while you are crawling around down there, you might be curious about how the system works, so here is a general view of the basic parts of the suspension system.

There are various types of **springs** used to absorb the bumps and keep your car level on turns. These can be **coil springs**, **leaf springs**, or **torsion bars**—or a combination of more than one of these. A good many U.S. cars have leaf springs at the rear wheels, and coil springs at the front wheels. Some trucks and buses have air suspension systems, but this is rarely, if ever, used for passenger cars.

Leaf springs are usually made up of several metal plates, piled one on top of the other. These are called *leaves.* The reason for using several relatively thin metal leaves instead of one thick metal bar is that, as a bar bends, the top of the bar has to stretch a little. If the bar bent too far, it could split from the top down. The leaf springs can bend more flexibly because each leaf bends independently and they can slide on one another instead of breaking. Each end of a set of leaf springs is attached to the *frame* at the rear of the car

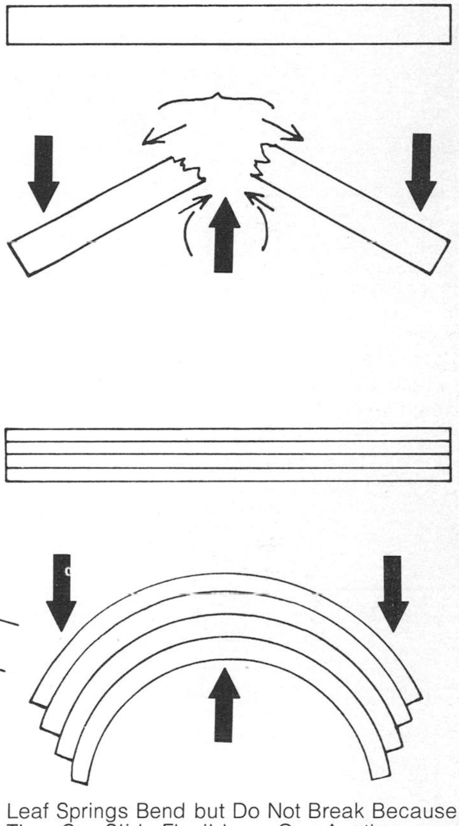

Springs

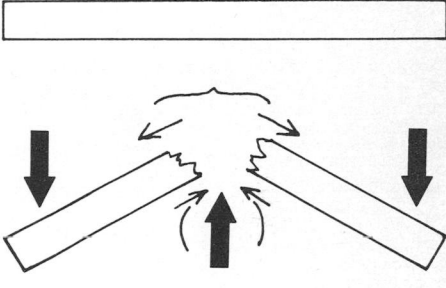

Leaf Springs Bend but Do Not Break Because They Can Slide Flexibly on One Another.
Alexandra Soto

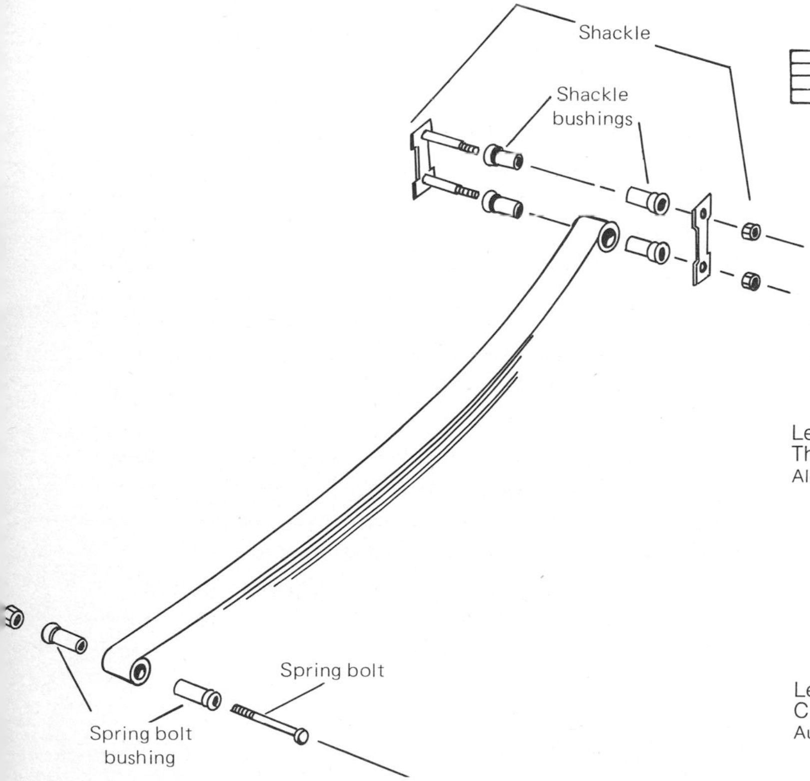

Shackle

Shackle bushings

Spring bolt

Spring bolt bushing

Leaf Springs Have Rubber Bushings to Cushion Them.
Automotive Marketing Division, Dana Corp.

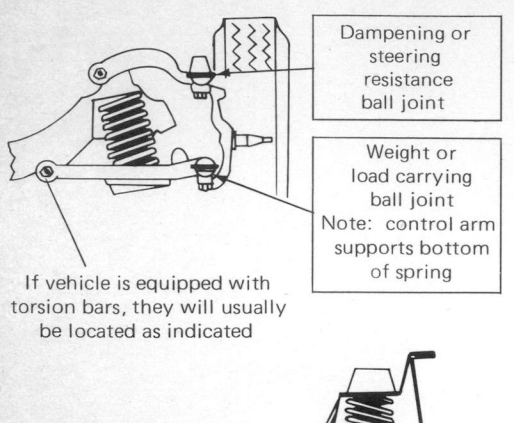

| Dampening or steering resistance ball joint |
| Weight or load carrying ball joint Note: control arm supports bottom of spring |

If vehicle is equipped with torsion bars, they will usually be located as indicated

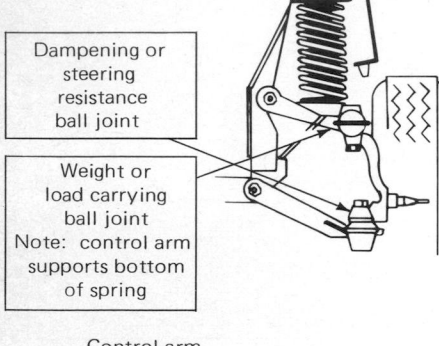

| Dampening or steering resistance ball joint |
| Weight or load carrying ball joint Note: control arm supports bottom of spring |

Control arm bushings (upper)

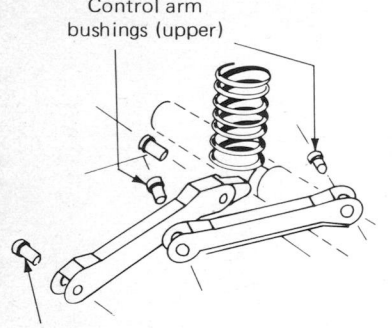

Control arm bushings (lower)

Front and Rear Coil Springs
Automotive Marketing Division, Dana Corp.
(*top & middle*) Front coil spring can sit on either the upper or the lower control arms. They are cushioned by the ball joints. (*bottom*) Rear coil springs have rubber bushings to cushion them.

Shock Absorbers

with fittings that allow the springs to bend and move freely. These fittings usually have rubber **bushings** that allow the fittings to bend and twist freely and also absorb some of the vibration and prevent it from reaching the passenger compartment. These rubber bushings should be lubricated with rubber lube.

Coil springs look like old-fashioned bed springs. They are usually found at the front of the car, although they can be at both the front and the rear. At the front end, they help to cushion the bumps, vibrations, and steering movements. At the rear, they are suspended between control arms that have rubber bushings that should be lubricated with rubber lube.

Torsion bars are used mainly in Chrysler products. These are located in the front of the car, connected to the lower control arms. They twist to accommodate differences in the load that the car may be carrying, allowing the front wheels to move up and down freely.

There are other kinds of suspension systems, but the main thing to know is that most of them involve the use of rubber bushings to cushion the shock of the bumps and to allow the metal parts to move. Look near the wheels to find most of them. There are also various kinds of **stabilizers** in use. These keep the passenger part of the car from swaying and lurching on sharp curves and turns and when the wheels are traveling over uneven ground (a better solution than the legendary mountain goat that had its legs shorter on one side than the other for traveling along slopes!). Again, all you need to know is that you can lubricate the rubber parts yourself. If the suspension system gets out of whack, get a professional to diagnose and deal with the trouble.

Shock absorbers do most of the work of protecting the passenger compartment from bumps. These are located near each wheel. The way they cut down on vertical movement is interesting. When a car wheel hits a bump, it will tend to keep bouncing up and down long after the bump has been left behind, unless this is controlled. The bouncing effect is not only due to the fact that the wheel has an inflated rubber tire. It is also due to the fact that a coil spring that is either pulled or compressed will not just snap back into its

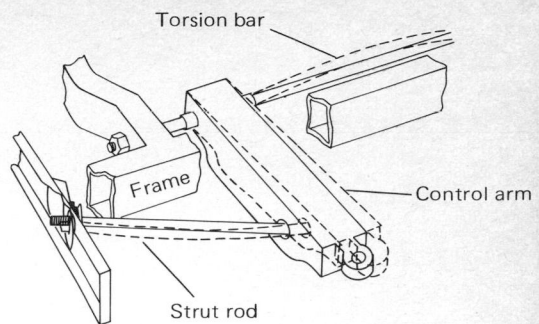

Chrysler Products Have Torsion Bars for
Load-Carrying Stability.
Moog Automotive, Inc., St. Louis, Missouri

former shape but will keep *oscillating*, or moving up
and down, for some time afterward. Since the wheels
are connected to the springs, they would move up and
down with the springs until the motion finally died
out. Shock absorbers allow the springs to compress
freely and to return or rebound slowly—like the door
check on a storm door that opens quickly and easily
but closes slowly. For this reason, you can tell if your
car needs new shock absorbers by leaning heavily on a
fender or placing your weight on a bumper, and then
releasing it suddenly, watching to see if the car returns slowly to its original position. (If it continues to
bob up and down you need new shocks.) Another
way is to stop fairly short. (If your car dips up and
down a couple of times before coming to rest, you
need new shocks.) Bad shock absorbers also increase
tire wear, and they can cause you to lose control of
the steering if you go over bumps and dips at high
speeds. If any of these things seems to be happening
to you, you should have your shocks replaced.

Replacing shocks is not difficult to do, but it is easiest
to do if you can put the car up on a hydraulic hoist. I
would suggest that you consider doing it at an auto
class shop, or buy the shocks on sale and have a
professional install them. I would hate to have to
replace shock absorbers on a car that had to be jacked
up and crawled under. It just isn't worth it.

It is a good idea to buy the shocks on sale, as I've
mentioned, because you can be sure you are getting
good ones at a fair price. Again, the store will know
which ones you need. It is important to note that
"heavy-duty" shocks can carry heavier loads but give a
slightly harder ride; other shocks may not do as well
with the entire family and two Great Danes in the car,
but they will give you a softer ride. Suit yourself.
Other special shocks provide *automatic level control* for
those cars that sometimes carry very heavy loads and
sometimes carry almost no weight at all. These are not
necessary for those of us who drive under normally
varying conditions.

So much for the suspension system. There's still one
more thing you can do yourself that involves lubrication.

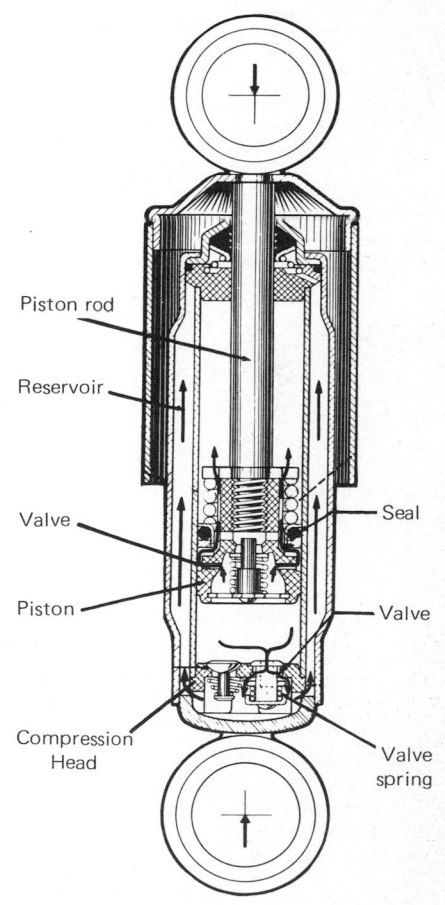

Anatomy of a Shock Absorber
Automotive Parts & Accessories Association (APAA)

How to Pack Your Front Wheel Bearings

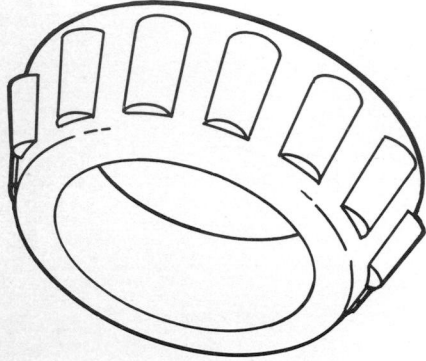

Front Wheel Bearings
Jack Herlihy

This is a job that can be done either when you are checking your brakes or as part of a lube job. I prefer to do it when I am checking my brakes, because I have the wheels off and the whole thing taken apart anyway, and that is most of the work involved. The only reason I've put the instructions in this chapter is that, technically, packing bearings is a lubrication job and is not concerned with brakes, really. At any rate, check your bearings every 10,000 miles.

Front wheel bearings come in pairs of *inner* and *outer* bearings. They allow your wheels to turn freely over thousands of miles by cushioning the contact between the wheel and the spindle it sits on with frictionless bearings and lots of nice gooey grease. This grease tends to pick up dust, dirt, and little particles of metal although the bearings are to some extent protected by the hub and the brake drum. It is important to check the bearings at least as often as you check your brakes, to be sure the grease has not become fouled with this stuff. If it has, the particles will act abrasively to wear away the very connection it is designed to protect, and the result will be a noisy, grinding ride. In extreme cases you could even lose the wheel! So be sure to check your bearings, and if they look cruddy, either repack them yourself or get a professional to do it. A good time to have your wheel bearings repacked is when they do a front-end **alignment** or a brake job, because they will have the wheels off anyway and this will eliminate paying for duplicate labor.

To check your bearings, or to repack them, here's what you do:

1 Turn back to Chapter 10 and, starting with "How to Disassemble Anything" on page 209, follow the instructions right through to the part about "How to Check Drum Brakes." Keep reading, even if you have disc brakes, because these instructions will show you how to get at your wheel bearings.

2 When you get to the part about sliding the outer bearings off the spindle, slide them off and take a good look at them. They are, usually, tapered *roller bearings*, not ball bearings (although I've heard that some cars have ball bearings).

3 Look in the spaces between these bearings. Do not wipe the grease off! Look at the grease. Does it have little sparkly silver slivers or particles in it? If it does, you must replace the bearings. If there are no particles in the grease, then you can start re-packing your bearings with nice fresh grease (see 6 through 8 below for instructions) and then go on to the inner bearing.

4 Now, you cannot remove the inner bearing from its seat in the hub unless you have a new **grease seal** for it. So if this is just a checking expedition, leave the inner bearings alone until you're sure from the condition of the outer bearings that re-packing is in order. Generally speaking, if the outer bearings look O.K., the inner ones are O.K. too. Just check each wheel, and put everything back according to the instructions for reassembling drum brakes in Chapter 10.

5 If, however, you are planning to repack your bear-ings, then slide the drum toward you, with the inner bearings still in place; but do not slide the drum completely off the spindle. Instead, screw the adjusting nut back in again and pull the drum or disc toward you and push it back. The adjusting nut should catch the inner bearing and its grease seal and free them from inside the hub. (If you have disc brakes, you will have to remove the **cali-per** to get the disc off the spindle. If you have to get a disc caliper off to get at the inner bearings, I think you should do the job under supervision. It is not a difficult job; it's just that you might not get the calipers back on right, and that could cause your brakes to misfunction—which might be an-other good reason to consider an auto repair course.)

6 Take a good gob of wheel bearing grease (this is different from most chassis-lube grease), and place it in the palm of your left hand (if you're a righty). You might want to invest in a pair of 10-cent throw-away plastic gloves for this job, but there's something kind of nice about fresh, clean grease, and if you use gloves, you'll miss one of the more sensual aspects of getting intimately involved with your car. Hand cleaner will get the grease off easi-ly, in any event.

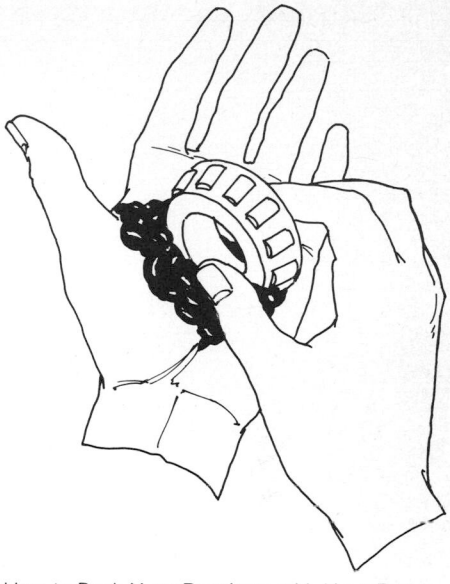

How to Pack Your Bearings with Your Bare Hands
Jack Herlihy

7 Take the bearing and press it into the gob of grease with the heel of your other hand. This should force the grease into the bearing and displace the old grease out the other end. Be sure the grease is worked into every gap in the bearing. You want it nice and yucky. Now put your bearing down in a clean place, and do the inner bearing the same way.

8 Take a rag and wipe out the hole in the hub of the drum or disc where the inner bearing went. Then take another gob of grease and smooth it into the hole. Be sure the grease fills the *races* inside the hub where the bearing fits. Wipe off excess grease around the outside of the hole, or it will fly around when the car is in motion and maybe damage your brakes.

9 Insert the inner bearing into the hub, with the small end first. Take a new grease seal, and spread a film of grease around the sealing end—the flat, smooth side.

10 To fit the new grease seal into place properly, it should go in evenly, or it will bend or break and you will lose your grease. You can use a hollow pipe or a large socket from a socket wrench set that has roughly the same diameter as the seal. With the flat, smooth side of the seal toward you, place the seal in the hub opening, and use the pipe or socket to move it into the hub gently and evenly. It should end up flush with the outside of the hub or slightly inside it.

11 Now wipe the dirt off the spindle, and slide the drum or disc back on. Do it gently so you don't unseat the grease seal.

12 Now replace the outer bearing, smaller end first.

13 Then replace the rest of the stuff according to the instructions in Chapter 10, and be sure the adjusting nut is properly adjusted. If this has involved turning back and forth between chapters, please forgive me. The alternative was to say it all twice, and that would have increased the cost of this book. The effort should be worth the savings. In partial compensation here is a repeat of the diagram, anyway, to make things easier.

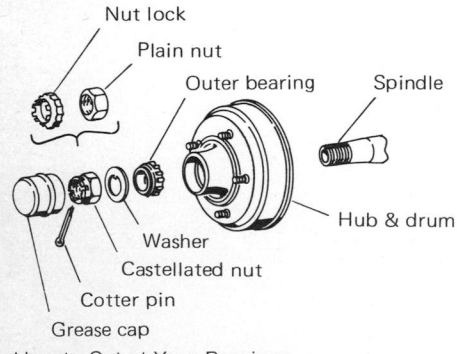

Nut lock
Plain nut
Outer bearing
Spindle
Washer
Castellated nut
Cotter pin
Grease cap
Hub & drum

How to Get at Your Bearings
Delco Moraine Division, General Motors Corp.

That's all. You will be glad to hear that there are no wheel bearings to pack on your rear wheels. There are *axle bearings*, however, but these must be replaced if they wear out; you cannot repack them. If your car is quite old and you hear a clicking or grinding noise from the vicinity of your rear wheels, you should have these bearings checked and replaced if necessary. It is easiest to hear worn axle bearings when you drive down an alley or a narrow driveway as the noise will echo loudly.

If you have found that your car needed most of the attention called for in this chapter, the chances are the other parts that are more difficult to lubricate should be attended to as well. Go to a good dealer with a service area, and ask them to lubricate your steering gear, power steering unit (if you have one), transmission shift linkage, clutch shaft, differential, distributor, and anything else that needs help. These parts don't have to be lubricated nearly as often as do bearings, but you should remember to have them professionally lubricated at least once a year (more often is better). There are instructions for checking and lubricating your differential in Chapter 13.

You will be pleased to know that this ends the dirty work that you can do on your car. The rest of the book is devoted to information that will help you to keep from getting ripped off if you need transmission work or if you want to buy a car. If you've enjoyed tuning your car and caring for its various systems and you want to continue and do more-difficult work, by all means enroll in an auto repair course at a local school. Otherwise, do not attempt to do anything else yourself, no matter how easy it looks. I have deliberately left out those repairs that can get you into trouble if you attempt to do them without supervision. You might want to move on to a more technical repair manual just to decide whether the more difficult jobs are worth doing yourself in terms of time and trouble, but don't attempt to open your engine or to rebuild your brakes or to fiddle with your air conditioning, power accessories, etc., by yourself. Of course there are things you can do to improve the looks of your car—washing, waxing, and polishing it, and you can

probably repair and reupholster the interior yourself. There are good books that can tell you how to do these jobs properly.

But before you get started (or head for the showers) you may be interested in knowing how your transmission works, in case you are ever called upon to decide whether or not it should be repaired.

Take the Drive Train: How to Understand Your Transmission System Without Losing Your Mind

The **transmission** system of your car is probably its most complex system in terms of automotive mechanics. It enables your car to move forward and backward at varying speeds, with maximum efficiency and minimum loss of power. In this sense, it is vitally connected to fuel consumption because the more power it takes to move the car, the more fuel it takes to provide that power.

Transmission systems vary from car to car. There are **manual transmissions**, for which you supply part of the power by shifting the gears and operating the clutch yourself, and there are **automatic transmissions**, which do these jobs for you.

Manual transmissions are fairly easy to explain, but I am convinced that the principles of automatic transmission were brought to Earth by some kindly extraterrestrial creature that came from a culture that operated on a very exotic system of logic. My attempts to fully penetrate the secrets of automatic transmission have been mind-boggling, and since the idea of ever fixing the thing yourself is unthinkable—except for people who have devoted their lives to it—let's be content to deal only with *what* automatic transmissions do, rather than go into detail about *how* they do it. This should give you a good idea of what should be done to keep your transmission in good condition, a good feel for diagnosing possible trouble, and at least a rudimentary knowledge of what should be done to fix your transmission if something goes wrong with it.

All cars have the capacity to move forward at varying speeds, to stop, and to move backward. Every time your car changes direction from forward to reverse, the rear wheels (or the front wheels on cars with **front-wheel drive**) have to be told which way to rotate. They must also know how fast to turn, and they must be supplied with extra power for starting, climbing hills, and pulling heavy loads.

As I've already mentioned in Chapter 3, the **drive train** on your car transmits the power from the engine to the wheels that move the car. You might want to go back to that chapter and reread the section on the drive train to get a general idea of what we're going to deal with. Start on page 36.

Still confused? O.K., let's look at it another way. Imagine that you are the captain of a ship. You have a lovely set of engines down in the engine room which are manufacturing power to move your ship. You are up on the bridge, surveying the blue ocean with your binoculars, when suddenly you see an iceberg dead ahead! You do not wish to run down to the engine room and personally reverse the propellers so that the ship will move backward. Instead, you pick up the intercom and call the engine room. You say, "This is the captain speaking. Reverse engines!" The person in the engine room hears you and does what is necessary. The ship is saved.

In a car, with a crew of one, you may be at the wheel giving orders. But you are giving them to a car that cannot hear you. How do the wheels know whether to move forward or backward? You need a piece of machinery to communicate with another machine. In this case, it is your **gearshift**. By moving the shift with your hand you can tell the transmission (the person in the engine room) what to do. Then the transmission tells the wheels via the **driveshaft**. Not only can you tell your wheels to go forward or backward, you can tell them how fast to go as well.

When you step on the **accelerator**, you are forcing the engine to produce power, but that power has to get to the wheels in the proper way for the wheels to respond most efficiently. There are ways to convey that extra power to the wheels by controlling how fast they turn in relation to the speed of the engine when you are going up a hill, pulling a heavy load, or just trying to overcome inertia and get the car started. So, your transmission has more than just forward and reverse gears; it has low and high gears too. Some transmissions have as many as five forward gears to control power and speed efficiently. The *lower* gears provide *more power* at *lower speeds.* The *higher* gears provide *less power* but allow the car to move at *higher speeds* because the wheels can turn faster in these gears at any engine speed.

Whether your car has an automatic transmission or a manual (sometimes called *standard*) transmission, you should understand how the manual transmission works. The principles involved are fairly simple, and an automatic transmission basically does the same things, but without a manual clutch and with less manual shifting.

Manual Transmissions

A manual transmission consists of a **gearshift**, located either on the floor or on the steering column, which you operate by hand to tell your transmission what to do; a **clutch**, which you operate with your left foot to disconnect the transmission from the engine so that the gears in the transmission can change without getting tangled up with one another; and the **transmission** itself, which contains the gears and responds to messages from the gearshift and the clutch.

To get the complete picture, try to see the transmission as part of the **drive train**, which conducts the flow of power from the engine to the wheels.

In the old "toe-bone-connected-to-the-foot-bone" tradition, let's trace the flow of power down the drive train, from the engine to the rear wheels. You can follow it through on the figure below.

The Drive Train
Jack Herlihy

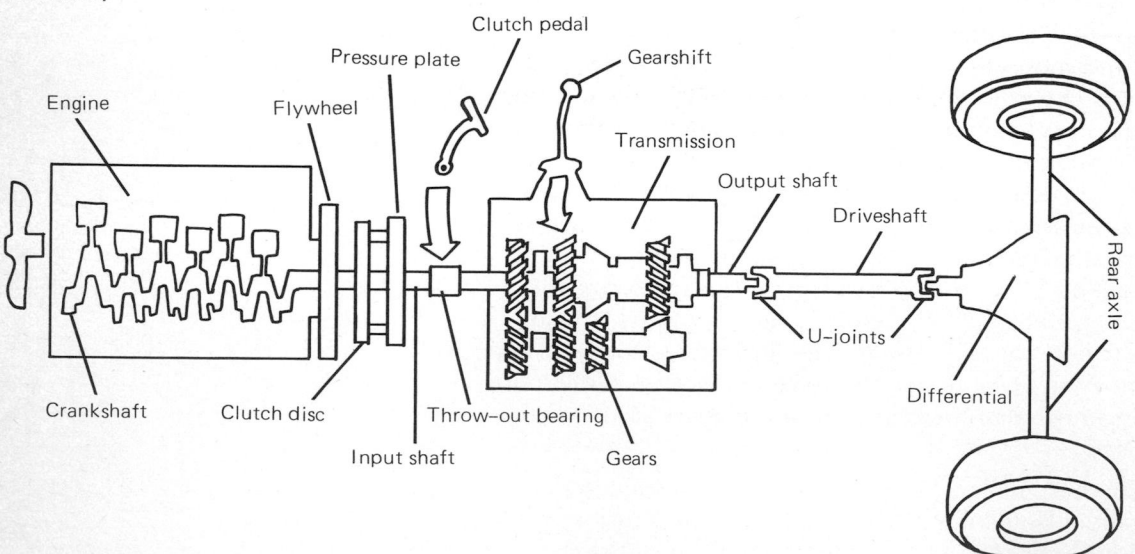

1 The running engine produces power that causes the **crankshaft** to turn at a particular rate of speed. The faster the engine runs, the more power it produces and the faster the crankshaft will turn.

2 At the end of the crankshaft is the **engine flywheel**. This is a disc-shaped plate that turns at the same rate, and in the same direction, as the crankshaft.

3 Facing the flywheel is the first part of the **clutch**. It is called a **clutch disc**, and it, too, is a disc-shaped plate. It has a tough asbestos covering. When you are *not* stepping on the *clutch pedal*, this disc is forced against the flywheel. The two plates adhere to each other, which forces them both to turn at the same speed.

4 Next to the clutch disc is the clutch **pressure plate**. This is the thing that forces the clutch disc against the flywheel or allows it to move away from the flywheel when it is time to change gears. Here's how it does that:

  a When you step on the **clutch pedal** to disengage the clutch and disconnect the engine from the transmission, a clutch *release arm* forces a **throw-out bearing** into the pressure plate's *release levers*. As a result, the pressure on the clutch disc is removed, and the disc can turn independently of the flywheel.

  b After you have moved the gearshift to the proper gear, you release the clutch pedal. This causes springs in the pressure plate to force the disc against the flywheel again, and both the disc and the flywheel resume spinning together, at a new speed.

  In this way, the clutch disc can catch up with an engine that is now turning faster—or more slowly—than before and can transmit its motion to the transmission.

5 On the clutch side of the flywheel, the drive train continues, but its name changes. It is not called the "crankshaft" anymore. It is now called the *transmission input shaft* because it carries the power, via the turning shaft, *into* the transmission. It rotates at

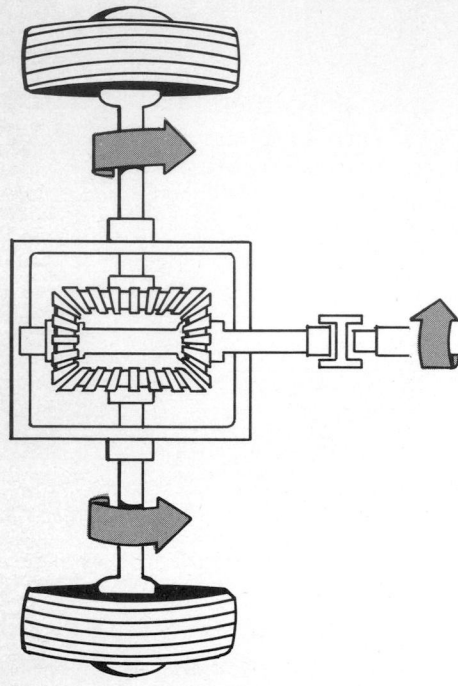

The Differential Makes the Axle and the Rear Wheels Move at Right Angles to the Spinning Driveshaft.
Jack Herlihy

the same speed and in the same direction as all the parts we've covered up to now.

6 Inside the transmission is a group of gears of varying sizes. These gears can move together and apart, in various combinations, to determine how fast and with how much power the wheels of the car will turn, and in which direction they will turn.

7 Another part of the **drive train** emerges from the other side of the transmission, with another new name. This time it is called the *transmission output shaft* because it is transmitting the power that the transmission is now putting out to the **driveshaft**.

8 The driveshaft has a **U-joint** (short for **universal joint**) at either end to allow it to move freely without affecting the more rigid transmission shaft at one end, and to absorb the vertical movement of the rear axle and wheels at its other end. These U-joints can turn and move in any direction—up, down, and from side to side. They need periodic lubrication, which should be done professionally.

9 At the end of the rear U-joint is the **differential**. This is another box of gears which takes the movement of the spinning driveshaft and transmits it to the **axle**, which is spinning at right angles to the driveshaft. It also allows each side of the axle to rotate at a different speed, because when you go around a sharp curve, the outside wheel travels farther than the inside wheel and is going to have to move more quickly than the inside wheel, just like the ice skater at the end of a snap-the-whip line.

10 The differential also provides the rear wheels with extra power by using its gears to convert every three revolutions of the driveshaft into one revolution of the rear wheels. This is called a rear-end **gear ratio** of 3 to 1.

Now, let's go back and look at each one of these components again, in greater detail:

The Gearshift Gearshifts can be located on the steering column or on the floor in front of, or between, the front seats. Generally speaking, floor shifts are more desirable because they connect more directly with the transmission (which is under the front seat of most cars). Older cars designed for the general market used to have shifts with three forward speeds located on the steering column (very old cars had a 2-foot gearshift located in front of the driver). Then the sportier models emerged, with four forward speeds. The gearshift in these cars was located on the floor, and this gave rise to the term "four on the floor." Today most cars with manual transmission have floor shifts.

There isn't much you have to know about gearshifts except that they may occasionally become hard to move. This can happen if the *gearshift linkage*, which connects the shift lever to the rods that go to the transmission, needs adjustment, lubrication, or minor repair. This is not expensive and should certainly be investigated before you let anyone talk you into major transmission work.

The Clutch

You use the clutch when you start, stop, and shift gears. In each of these cases, you step on the clutch pedal to disengage the clutch disc from the flywheel, so that the engine and the crankshaft can turn independently of the transmission. Otherwise, if you attempted to shift gears without using the clutch, the gears in the transmission would be rotating at different speeds and would clash and break their teeth.

The major parts of the clutch are:

1 The **clutch pedal**, which is located on the floor of the car to the left of the brake pedal.
2 The **clutch disc**, which moves back and forth on the *input shaft* to engage and disengage the **engine flywheel**, and to connect and disconnect the engine from the transmission.
3 The **pressure plate**, which moves back and forth on that same shaft to force the disc to engage and disengage the flywheel.
4 The **throw-out bearing**, which is linked to the clutch pedal. It activates the release levers that move the pressure plate back and forth.

Once you've got the engine going at its new speed (or going at all, for that matter), you release the clutch pedal to bring the clutch disc into contact with the flywheel again. The **friction** caused by the asbestos covering (it's the same stuff that brake linings are made of) causes them to grab each other lovingly and turn at the same rate once more. If your car responds erratically when you shift, it might be that the coverings on those plates are worn and that the clutch is "slipping." The engine will rev up loudly, but the car won't respond well—it won't change speed properly.

By keeping your clutch pedal properly adjusted, you can cut down on the wear on your clutch disc. Your clutch pedal should move down from ³/₄ to 1 inch without effort and then require a good deal more effort to travel the rest of the way down to the floor. This **free pedal play** insures that when you release the pedal, the disc will be fully engaged. Too much free pedal play is not good either, as too much pedal travel is used up doing nothing. There is not enough movement left at the bottom of its travel to compress the clutch springs and allow the flywheel and the clutch disc to separate. In this case, the gears would clash whenever you shifted into "First" or "Reverse" from a stopped position.

How to Tell If Your Bearing's Wearing

If there is no **free pedal play** on your clutch pedal, another problem can occur, even if there is enough play to allow the clutch disc to engage. In this case, the **throw-out bearing**, which responds to pressure on the clutch pedal by causing the disc to disengage, may go on spinning. If the throw-out bearing is allowed to revolve constantly in this way, it will wear out. If that happens, getting the car into or out of gear will become difficult.

Don't "ride the clutch." Riding it can cause the throw-out bearing to wear out too. You'll know that something is wrong because it will make whirring, whining sounds. If the sounds disappear when you release the clutch pedal, and resume when you step on it, you have a bad throw-out bearing. If you think you have one, or your clutch has been misbehaving in other ways, you might as well go to a reliable mechanic and have the clutch checked out.

Your clutch can be good for from 5,000 to 50,000 miles. This varies widely, depending on the type of

car, the way you drive, and how much maintenance
the car receives. It could go as far as 100,000 miles, or
it could break down after 10,000. If you are having a
clutch disc replaced, be sure to have the pressure plate
and the flywheel checked at that time to be sure they
aren't badly worn. Here are some tips about what to
expect:

1 If the flywheel is worn, have a garage mechanic
   resurface it. This means that it is ground down to a
   new flat surface and then polished to a mirrorlike
   finish. If you fail to do this, the worn flywheel can
   wear out the facing of the new clutch disc very
   quickly. And if you've had to have the disc replaced,
   the chances are that it managed to score the flywheel by the time you recognized the trouble signs
   and had the disc attended to.

2 If the **pressure plate** is excessively worn, you must
   replace it. If you replace it with a **rebuilt** unit, you
   can turn your old one in and receive a **core
   charge**, as you can with brake shoes.

3 If the springs on the pressure plate become loose,
   replace them.

Since, as I've mentioned before, excessive wear on any
part of your clutch will result in wear on the other
parts, it is generally a good idea to have the clutch
assembly, levers, clutch disc, and throw-out bearings
checked and, if necessary, replaced at the same time.
You can also have the *pilot bearing*, which is located
where the shaft meets the flywheel, checked then too.
In this way you can save money on labor charges by
eliminating the necessity of getting into your clutch
and putting it back together a second time. This is a
good practice to keep in mind when dealing with
other parts of your car as well. If your mechanics have
to open your transmission, be sure they check the
whole thing and replace gaskets, etc., that look as
though they are about to go. If they have to open
your cylinder head or get into the engine, be sure
they look for potential trouble from the rest of the
stuff in there. Of course you will want them to show
you the parts that are wearing before they proceed
with any unauthorized work—you are not giving them
carte blanche to replace anything they please—but keep
in mind that a good part of the labor costs are associ-

ated with just getting the thing apart and back together, so if they have to do it only once, you save money.

Easy so far, right? Now to the toughies. I'm sure you are dying to know what goes on in that mysterious transmission gear box. Well, here goes!

How a Manual Transmission Works

A Gear with 10 Teeth Will Rotate Completely When a 30-Tooth Gear Has Only Traveled a Third of the Way Around.
Jack Herlihy

Generally speaking, the faster your engine runs, the more power it puts out. If you need extra power to get your car up a hill, or to overcome inertia and just get that heavy monster moving in the first place, your engine must run faster than it would run simply to maintain speed once your car is on the road. Low gears supply that power, by making your wheels turn at a slower rate than your engine does.

Imagine, if you will, a large gear placed next to a small gear so that their teeth mesh. If the large gear has 30 teeth, and the small gear has 10, the large gear will turn once to every three turns of the small gear. Another way of saying this is that it would turn only a third of the way around for every complete revolution of the small gear. The gears in your transmission work on this principle. If you imagine the turning crankshaft ending in a gear that will be brought into contact with other gears of different sizes, you can see that the transmission sets up a situation where the crankshaft that runs between your engine and the transmission is turning at the same rate of speed as the engine, but the driveshaft that leaves the transmission and carries the power to the rear wheels will turn at a different rate of speed, depending on which gears in the transmission are engaged.

In low gear, the gears in the transmission make the driveshaft (and therefore the wheels) turn *more slowly* than the engine. In fact, it may turn only once for every four revolutions of the engine. All the power of the swiftly running engine is channeled into those few turns. The wheels turn more slowly, but they have more power to put into each turn, so your car can start, climb a hill, or pull a trailer. Not only does the engine run faster, but you have the mechanical advantage of having the big gear provide more leverage by turning slowly but with more force.

In second gear, the engine turns more slowly than it did in low, putting out less power but more speed, because the wheels can turn more quickly. In this gear the driveshaft may turn once for every two revolutions of the engine, or twice as fast as in low gear.

In high gear, the ratio can drop to around 1 to 1. This means that the engine and the driveshaft are turning at relatively the same rate of speed. The wheels can go very fast now; yet the engine is not putting out additional power to produce that speed. Since you have overcome inertia by the time you shift into high gear, and generally have nothing more to contend with than the wind resistance and the surface of the highway, it does not take a lot of power to keep moving at a good clip once you've gotten there. As Newton said, once something gets moving, it tends to keep moving unless it encounters something that stops it. So you don't need much power to ride the freeway. What you need is power to stop, and that is the job of your brakes.

As far as the way things look inside the transmission is concerned, I've included a simplified cutaway of a manual transmission for those of you who are curious.

Basically, all that a manual transmission consists of is a group of gears of varying sizes which are moved into and out of mesh with each other by the gearshift lever. The number of gear wheels depends on the number of forward speeds the car has. Then, there is one more gear that reverses the direction of power, so your car can move in reverse. This reverse gear works in conjunction with your lowest gear, and your car moves backward fairly slowly but with a good deal of power. Since we bring the car to a stop before we back up, and since we rarely want to hit high speeds in reverse, this low gear provides the power to get the car moving efficiently in the "wrong" direction.

There are mechanical computers and electronic computers, but did you know that an automatic transmission has a very efficient **hydraulic** computer built into

Low Gear

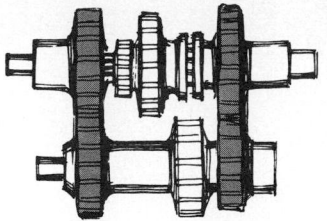

Second Gear

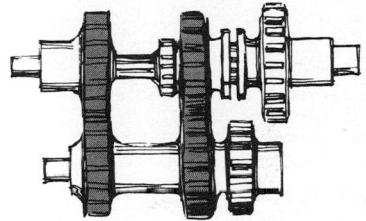

High Gear

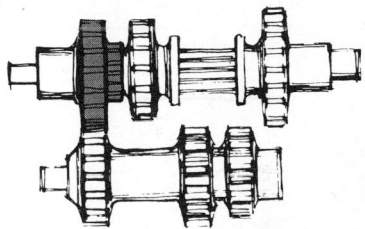

Cutaway of 3-Speed Manual Transmission Gears
Automotive Information Council (AIC)

Automatic Transmissions

it? It is a unique piece of equipment that allows the car to shift gears because little valves sense the changes in hydraulic pressure caused by changes in the speed of a pump that reacts to changes in the speed of the engine. When the engine goes faster, the pump pumps harder, and this causes the hydraulic pressure to rise. As a result of these changes in pressure, the computer helps your car to shift gears automatically.

The automatic transmission works on the same basis as a manual transmission does, with a **gear selector** on the steering column or floor to allow you to tell the car manually to park, idle, go into reverse, or into lower gears for special occasions. But instead of a manual clutch, the automatic transmission uses hydraulic pressure to change gears automatically.

This hydraulic pressure is caused by oil (**transmission fluid**), which fills the transmission system. As the speed of the engine changes, a pump, which pumps the transmission fluid to develop hydraulic pressure, also changes speed. The transmission fluid responds to the changes in pressure by flowing through the transmission at different rates. When the car is moving slowly, the pressure is low, and only the low gears respond. As the speed of the car increases, so does the pressure, and higher gears are brought into play.

There are several different types of automatic transmission systems. They are all based on principles of hydraulic pressure, which drives the transmission gears by means of friction **bands** and plates. These bands and plates do the same thing that the clutch on a manual transmission does—they pull various gears into and out of action. When mechanics tell you that your bands need adjusting, these are the bands they are talking about. This can usually be done by external adjustment, but certain jobs involve opening the transmission, draining out the oil, taking the whole thing apart, and replacing defective parts. This kind of job is expensive and must be done properly by people who really understand automatic transmission systems in general, and the kind your car has in particular. Well then, if you can't do the job yourself, how do you keep from being ripped off?

First, have your automatic transmission serviced periodically, according to the manufacturer's recommendations (usually around every 24,000 miles). Then you should know what the basic kinds of transmission work involve:

If your transmission needs "servicing" they will:

1 Change the transmission fluid, if necessary.
2 Adjust the bands if this can be done externally.
3 Replace the transmission filter.
4 Replace the gasket around the pan and change the oil it holds.

If your transmission is leaking:

1 If the *front seal* is bad the mechanic must remove your transmission to replace it, but he doesn't have to take the transmission apart. Front seals usually have the biggest leaks.
2 If it's the *rear seal* the mechanic must remove your driveshaft, but your transmission can stay in place.

If your transmission must be "overhauled" they will:

1 Remove and disassemble the transmission.
2 Replace the seals, clutches, bands, and bushings that are worn or defective.

So you can see that the ability to tell the kind of transmission work that is necessary can save you from paying for more work than you need. There are also a number of other things that can go wrong and seem to indicate that you need major transmission work to correct them; yet they really can be fixed for very little money. An unscrupulous mechanic can diagnose one of the problems as a major transmission breakdown and charge you hundreds of dollars when the real solution could be achieved for under $5. Here are two of these:

The **vacuum modulator** can be replaced for very little money ($1.50 to $10, depending on the car and where you buy the part). When a vacuum modulator goes wrong, the car tends to stay in low gear all the time, or it will shift with a bang—especially when shifting into lower gears. These little devils can suck up trans-

How to Keep from Being Ripped Off on Transmission Work

The Malfunctioning Vacuum Modulator Caper

mission fluid and burn it, causing white or gray smoke to emerge from your tail pipe as you shift gears. Replace the little modulator, and your troubles may be over. You can usually replace it yourself—just unscrew the old and on with the new. It's worth trying, especially if yours is easy to reach.

Those Low Transmission Fluid Blues

1 *If your automatic transmission seems to be acting up*—by hesitating when you change gears, or by shifting with a "clunk"—first check your transmission **dipstick**. Your transmission fluid may be low, or dirty, or it may have dried. Chapter 5 tells you how to find and check your transmission dipstick, and how to buy the proper kind of transmission fluid for your car. It's a good idea to do this fairly often anyway as part of your regular under-the-hood check. A good many "band jobs" have been bought and paid for when a quart of transmission fluid would have solved the problem for about $1.

2 *If your transmission fluid level is low*, add some down the dipstick hole (use a funnel to avoid spilling it). If the level is low again in a couple of days, look under the car for a leak around your transmission. You may need a seal replaced, or the plug may have jolted loose and just need to be tightened.

3 *If your fluid level is fine but your transmission isn't working well*—or if your fluid keeps disappearing and no leaks are evident—you probably need some transmission work. We'll get to that in a moment.

4 *If your transmission fluid looks or smells burned or dirty* but everything else is normal, you might want to consider changing the fluid. Unfortunately, changing transmission fluid can sometimes cause more problems than it remedies, so it should be done only when there are really serious reasons for doing so. The reason for this is that just changing the fluid can cause your transmission to leak even if it hasn't been leaking before. The old transmission fluid has formed a deposit around the front transmission seal. When it is replaced with fresh fluid, the new stuff tends to dissolve that deposit and the old seal may start to leak. Don, my automotive advisor, who is a transmission guru on his father's side, says that the best bet is not to change transmission fluid at all until the transmission goes. Then rebuild

it. Just keep the fluid level up to the fill mark or as close to it as you can. This should not stop you from having your transmission serviced, because it may hold as many as 11 quarts of transmission fluid and you will usually lose only 3 quarts or less in the process of ordinary servicing.

How to Keep Your Drive Train Running Smoothly

Your manual or automatic transmission system will work better and live longer if you have the **U-joints** in your drive train checked and replaced with new ones if they are loose, and have your **differential** lubricated at regular intervals. Even if you are now lubricating your steering linkage and suspension system yourself, you should still take the car to a service station to have *everything* lubricated at least once a year. Be sure to check to see if your rear end (sorry, that's the way they refer to the differential) needs lubrication. Here's how to do it:

Find the inspection plug in the differential (that's the gear box between the two rear wheels of the car). You can usually remove this plug by putting the square end of a 1/2-inch drive **ratchet** into the square hole in the plug. If, when the plug is removed, fluid drips out, you're O.K. If nothing comes out, add differential/manual transmission grease until it is full. If your car has a "limited slip" or "positraction" rear end (very few cars do), it will require a special fluid. Check the specifications in your owner's manual, or call your dealer, to find out for sure.

Checking the grease level on a manual transmission is the same as checking the differential on cars with either a manual or an automatic transmission. You just locate the inspection plug, remove it, and see what comes out. If nothing does, you use the same differential/manual transmission grease to fill it up again. (On cars with an automatic transmission, the transmission dipstick does this job for you, as we've already mentioned.)

How to Undertake Transmission Repairs Wisely

For transmission repairs, take your car to reputable transmission specialists and ask them to diagnose the trouble and give you an *estimate* of the costs. *Do not let them take the thing apart.* Once your transmission is in pieces, you are a sitting duck. Have them drive the car, listen to it, ask you questions about its history and its symptoms, and give you their ideas. They may say, "You may just need your bands tightened, or you may need a new transmission; we can't tell until we open it up." Fine. Ask them for estimates for both jobs and move on to the next place.

Get three estimates, or more if the first three vary widely. Discard the high estimates. Discard a *very* low one, too, if it seems way out of line with the others. It may be a hustle. Then return to the place with the lowest prices and/or the best vibes. Of course if someone you know who is fairly knowledgeable about cars, recommends a place enthusiastically, this is usually worth extra points when you are deciding. But I'd get estimates anyway.

Once the work is underway, ask to be notified about what they find when they open it up. Will it be a simple adjustment? Or a major rebuild? Get the estimated costs on the receipt, signed by you, *before* the actual work begins, and ask to be called if that estimate changes because they uncover other problems. Ask them to save you the parts they replace so that you can see what you paid for. There are consumer laws in many states which hold the mechanic responsible for failing to give the customer a written estimate, for failing to notify the customer if the estimate becomes way out of line because more serious problems have been uncovered in the course of the work, and for failing to turn over parts that have been replaced when the customer asks that they be saved.

Now go home, cross your fingers, and wait for the operation to be over. Of course you may still be ripped off, but you'll know that you've done everything possible to prevent it. And since you've been so canny about estimates, open about shopping around, familiar with the transmission itself (drop words like "hydraulic pressure," "modulators," and "bands," etc.) and insistent about written estimates and such, you just might scare someone who would like to cheat you into doing a good job and charging you properly for it.

If this whole thing sounds paranoid, that's just because there are bad apples that give the good, honest, hard-working, car-loving, competent transmission specialists a lot of competition. Most specialists are all of the above positive things. But the baddies are the ones you tell your friends about, and so we have all become a bit paranoid when dealing with an unknown mechanic for delicate and expensive work. Go ahead and be paranoid. It can't hurt. You haven't done anything to insult the mechanic. You've just been careful. He's probably the same way about dealing with other people when he is faced with an expensive job that must be done by strangers. And if the mechanic does his job well, for a reasonable price, you can always sing his praises to your friends and refer them to him when they have problems.

There is one thing more that you can do to keep from ripping *yourself* off, and that is to learn some driving habits that will extend the life of your transmission.

Driving your car with expertise can prevent many of the most common causes of transmission failure. This means getting into the proper gear to reduce the strain on the engine and on the transmission, and not riding your clutch. Remember, an automatic transmission works with gears, too. If you are in low gear, you are transmitting more power to your rear wheels, and your transmission will be feeling the strain. If you attempt to speed in a low gear, you will be straining the transmission even more. On the other hand, if you attempt to climb hills in high gear, you will be forcing the car to make the effort in a gear that lacks the power for the job. Result, more strain. People with a manual transmission learn to watch the **tachometer**, or just "feel" the car's need for more power or more speed, and shift into the proper gear for each occasion. But people with an automatic transmission tend to shift into drive and GO—up hills, with heavy loads, and into jackrabbit starts—happily oblivious to the fact that even automatic transmissions have gear selectors that provide one or two lower gears for these occasions.

Using a lower gear can save wear and tear on your brakes too, especially if your car has a manual trans-

How to Keep From Driving Your Transmission Crazy

mission. If you are driving along in high gear and you see that a traffic light is changing to red or that traffic is slowing ahead, instead of using your brake to take on the full job of slowing the car down, try **downshifting** (shifting into the next lower gear) after the car has slowed down a bit. The lower gear will help your car to slow down still further, and this will save your brakes. Also, if you are going down a steep hill, use a lower gear to help your car move at a slower pace without the need to ride your brakes all the way down.

On cars with an automatic transmission, **passing gear** provides the same kind of help as downshifting does. In this case, you use passing gear when you are already in high gear and need an extra burst of power to pass a car or enter a freeway. If you have been traveling at less than 50 mph, the sudden flooring of the gas pedal will make your car downshift automatically from high to second, which provides more power by speeding up the engine. When you release the pedal, the car goes back to high.

If you have a car with **overdrive**, you have an extra, higher, gear that allows your rear wheels to turn even faster while maintaining the same engine speed. Once you are really traveling along, shifting into overdrive means that your car can move at the same speed but the engine can turn more slowly and consume less fuel as you cruise along.

Once you have the car moving along swiftly, it is always a good idea to shift into the higher gears as soon as possible. There is no need to speed the engine to supply extra power when it is not needed. But if you come to a steep hill—or if you are carrying four kids, everything you'll need for a month in the country, and those two dogs—go for the lower gears instead of trying to haul the whole mess as fast as you can. This way, you avoid engine strain (this is called "lugging") and the power goes toward carrying the load rather than into maintaining speed. When the engine is lugging, always shift into a lower gear so that it can turn faster and carry you along with less strain. Once you get everything moving freely, you can return to a higher gear—until you reach the next steep hill. Then back to low again for the power to carry the load up the hill against gravity, with less strain on the car. In this way, even drivers of cars with automatic transmissions can extend the lives of their engine and their transmission.

Although this has been a "clean-hands" chapter, rather than a work chapter, it is probably the most difficult one in the book. If you understood the whole thing, fine—you probably would have made a terrific engineer or mechanic. If the principles of transmission design have failed to penetrate, don't worry— that's what we pay transmission specialists for. Just go over the parts of the chapter that deal with driving properly until it gets to be a habit, and you may never have to worry about your transmission at all. If your luck turns bad and your transmission acts up, reread the parts about diagnosing and getting help wisely. If you "fake it" you can probably get everything taken care of with a minimum of pain.

The next chapter is a kind of catchall chapter that will tell you how to save on fuel by driving "eco-logically," and what to do if your car breaks down suddenly.

14

On the Road: Driving Your Car for Fuel Economy and What to Do If It Drops Dead on the Freeway

It is one thing to understand how your car works and to be able to tend to its maintenance and minor ills. But cars are for driving, and in the long run, it is how well they perform on the road that counts. There are two aspects of this question that we've touched on briefly but haven't covered in sufficient detail: how to drive your car efficiently to save gas and cut down on air pollution, and what to do when it just won't go. I'll deal with each of these questions in this chapter.

How to Drive "Eco-logically"

In previous chapters, I have touched on the relationship between good maintenance and fuel economy. If your car is well tuned and lubricated, it will burn less fuel and contribute less pollution to the ecology. This is no longer news to anybody, and if you have become involved to the point where you are regularly changing your oil, tuning your carburetor, replacing your points and plugs, and generally keeping your car at the peak of efficiency, you are probably already happily aware that you are now getting better mileage than you ever did in the past. But there are several other ways to save fuel. The fuel crisis may go away, and we may all be rolling in money someday, but unless every driver learns to drive efficiently, we are going to go on wasting fuel and dumping the unburned residue into the ecology. So here are some ways to do your bit for the ecology when you and your car are on the road. I call it "eco-logic" because it makes sense to view your car and your driving techniques from an environmental perspective as well as from an automotive point of view. The two are intimately related, as you will see.

Starting Up Without Warming Up

When you start your car in the morning, do you warm it up before you drive off? No good! Most manuals will caution you not to indulge in lengthy warm-ups. They waste fuel, pollute the air, and increase wear on your car.

What exactly happens when you start your car? When you kick the gas pedal once or twice, the **choke** on your **carburetor** automatically closes (unless you have a manual choke). It does this to cut down on the amount of air that is going into the carburetor. This increases the vacuum in the **venturi** and draws more fuel than usual into the engine. This enriched **fuel/air** mixture helps the car to heat up more quickly. It is also necessary because part of the fuel will condense on the cold metal walls of the **intake manifold** and not get to the engine at all. The whole thing takes only a minute or two, and once the car is warm, the choke opens and things go back to normal. At this point you simply waste fuel by sitting there with the engine **idling** at zero miles to the gallon. And if you happen to be sitting in a closed garage, you can waste *yourself* with carbon monoxide fumes.

If your car keeps stalling unless you warm it up, check the choke:

How to Check Your Choke

Before you start the car in the morning, remove the **air cleaner** and look into the **carburetor barrel**. The choke is probably open. Have someone kick the gas pedal once or twice, and the choke should close. (If you can get someone to help, you'll save yourself a lot of running around. If that doesn't work, try jiggling the **throttle** linkage; it may just be stuck.) Have your helper start the car and let it idle. After a minute or two the choke should open again. If it doesn't, or if it never closed, it could be stuck. A little carburetor cleaner can be squirted in to free it, or a teeny drop of oil might help. If it still won't work properly, check the choke adjustment according to the instructions in Chapter 7.

If your choke appears to be working properly but the car continues to stall if you don't warm it up, then check the **carburetor settings** with a tach/dwell meter after the car has heated up. You may find that the idle mixture is too lean or that the idle speed is too low. Either can cause the car to stall when it should be idling. On the other hand, a too-rich mixture, or a too-fast idle speed, will waste fuel. Chapter 7 can help you here too.

If your carburetor is properly adjusted and the car still doesn't seem to warm up properly until you've driven it for several miles, it might be the **thermostat** that's at fault. As you probably remember, the thermostat simply keeps the water from circulating out of the engine until the engine warms up. This helps the

engine to warm up more quickly. If your thermostat is on the blink, the whole process will take longer. Consult Chapter 8 for instructions on locating, testing, and replacing your thermostat.

Checking Your Car Out Eco-logically

While you're at it, take another look at your air cleaner. If the **air filter** is dirty, you can lose a mile per gallon at 50 mph. Remember, if you can improve your mileage by only 10 percent, you can save an average of 77 gallons a year! And according to the Automotive Parts and Accessories Association (APAA), if every car owner saved just one gallon a week, the nation could save more than 300,000 barrels of fuel per year!

Other things to check while you are under the hood:

The PCV Valve

If your **PCV valve** is not functioning properly, you are going to be running your engine less efficiently, and you might be burning and polluting your oil, too. Check it according to the instructions in Chapter 7.

The Points and Plugs

Misfiring **spark plugs** can cost you up to 25 percent in mileage! If you haven't tuned your **ignition system** in the past 10,000 miles, do it now! A simple **tune-up** can reduce carbon monoxide and hydrocarbon exhaust emissions (that's air pollution, folks) by 30 to 50 percent! It is also a good idea to check your **dwell** and examine at least one spark plug every 5,000 miles, to be sure your car is running efficiently. If the dwell is off, the **rubbing block** could wear away and your **points** would stop opening and closing. If you check at least one of your plugs against the chart in Chapter 5, it will tell you if you are running too hot, burning oil, or losing power in some other manner.

The Fan Belt and Other Drive Belts

Since these belts connect your **fan**, **water pump**, **alternator**, and a variety of other devices, a belt that's too loose or too tight can result in a serious loss of efficiency. It should have about half an inch of "give" and should not be frayed or badly worn. A properly adjusted **fan belt** will keep your **battery** charged and help you to start faster, with less fuel consumption.

O.K. Now you are ready to get in and drive away.

Eco-logical Driving Techniques

First, you must view your driving techniques in terms of *fuel consumption*. In other words, if you are driving at 55 mph and you accelerate to 65 mph and have to step on the brake after a block or two, you have wasted the gasoline it took to accelerate the car, because you've had to return to the original speed so soon. So check before putting on extra speed to be sure you won't have to waste that effort by slowing for a blinker, crossroad, or curve ahead. This kind of thinking is the key to driving efficiently. Every time you step on the gas pedal you are using gas. Every time you step on the brake pedal you are losing the speed that you used the gas to achieve.

It takes power to move a car from a stationary position. Either you can apply that power efficiently, by starting and accelerating slowly, or you can blow the whole thing by slamming on the accelerator for a quick getaway. A fast start may cost you 8 miles per gallon for the first 4 miles. A slow start can carry you 50 percent further on the same amount of gas! Try to go slowly, at least for the first mile. Once you are underway, keep an eye on the speed limits and pace yourself accordingly, especially in city traffic. Unless you are racing the stork to the hospital, you will probably want to keep within the speed limits anyway. So if the limit on a city street is 35 mph, don't jump off at each light, speed down the street, and have to stop for the light at the end of each block. Those traffic lights are set for the speed limit. If you maintain a nice, steady 35, you will find that the lights will magically turn green as you approach them and you will not have to stop—or start—so often. Results: less work for you and 15 percent less fuel consumed. The AAA reports that your gasoline efficiency could be increased by as much as 44 percent if all your stop-and-go driving techniques were improved!

What about changing lanes and passing other cars on the freeway? Each time you do this you accelerate to pass or change lanes and then usually have to step on the brake to fit back into the traffic pattern. The result is up to 30 percent more fuel wasted. Try to stay in lane if you can. And when you get stuck behind a slowpoke, wait for the opportunity to pass without any automotive histrionics.

My mother used to tell me that the mark of a fine chauffeur was that the passengers were never aware that the car was moving. She never had a chauffeur,

to my knowledge, but she was—and is—a good driver. She taught me never to stop short if I could help it, but to anticipate the stop and to slow down gradually. Sometimes you can slow down by just taking your foot off the accelerator. Great! You can't use extra gasoline when your foot is off the gas pedal. The same goes for dramatic changes in speed. Try to set a steady pace on the road and around the curves. If you are not speeding, you may be able to account for a lot of the slowdowns by decelerating, rather than by braking. You won't wear out your brakes as quickly, and you will save fuel. If you have a **manual transmission**, you can **downshift** to slow down, as well.

Try to accelerate slowly and smoothly. It may fool your **accelerator pump** into not supplying an unneeded extra squirt of fuel to your carburetor. And, if your carburetor has secondary barrels that cut in at higher speeds (some two-barrel and all **four-barrel carburetors** have this feature) try to stay below the cut-in level, especially if you are going to have to slow down soon, anyway.

Arrange your car seat so that you are as comfortable as possible. Research has shown that a comfortable driving position will help you to tread lightly on the gas pedal. A light foot on the gas pedal saves gas. By traveling at 50 mph, a "featherfoot" can get 20 percent better gas mileage than someone can who is tromping on the pedal and doing 70. This is because wind resistance increases at higher speeds, and every mile per hour over 50 costs you more than 1 percent in mileage. An extra 5 mph will cost you 7 percent, and so on. Besides, your car's **chassis** will age twice as fast at 70 mph! It may get you there sooner, but will it be waiting for you when you're ready to go home?

When you approach a hill, try to build up speed slowly before you get there. The extra momentum will carry you at least part of the way up the hill. Don't accelerate to maintain your speed while you are climbing unless you are holding up traffic. Try to keep the gas pedal steady, and never, never crest the top of a hill at high speeds; you'll only have to brake on the way down, wasting the gas that got you up there so quickly in the first place. Try coasting down the other side, using the weight of the car and its momentum to carry you down with your foot off the accelerator.

You can use your **transmission** to save fuel, too. If you have an automatic transmission, ease up on the gas pedal at around 18 to 22 miles an hour. This will allow the transmission to shift into high gear more easily. As you may remember, the higher the gear, the less strain on the engine—and the less fuel consumed. Does the car have **overdrive**? It can save another 10 percent! Owners of cars with manual transmissions can do the same thing by shifting into higher gears as soon as possible. The APAA suggests that you shift into second gear at about 5 to 8 miles per hour and into higher gears at the lowest speed that the engine will take without laboring or lugging. If you haven't already practiced this, start now.

Here's a really way-out way to save gas. Did you know that a *left turn* uses more gas than a right turn? That's because you generally have to wait, with the car idling at 0 mph, until the road is clear for the turn. Then you have to overcome inertia and get into low gear to get moving again. If you really want to be a gas saver, try to structure your trips around the city to include as few left turns as possible. By the same thinking, it is more eco-logical to go around the block than to make a U-turn if the turn involves a lot of stopping and starting as you shift from forward to reverse, and to forward again. A nice slow cruise around the block uses less gasoline and probably won't take much more of your time.

While you are tinkering around with structuring trips to save gas, try the following:

1 Don't make a lot of little trips; keep a list and combine them into one longer one. A one-mile trip on a cold engine can cut fuel economy by as much as 70 percent.
2 Eliminate unnecessary trips by letting your fingers do the driving through the phone book, or by writing letters.
3 Arrange a car pool to work or to school if you can. These are not only eco-logical; they often result in new friendships as well.
4 Have you ridden a bike lately? How about the bus?
5 A local store may have slightly higher prices than the one at the edge of town, but in terms of time, gasoline, and wear and tear on your car, the neigh-

borhood store may be cheaper. If you are committed to the distant markets, experiment with shopping only once a week, or every ten days, instead of hopping over there whenever you run out of something. You can car-pool to those distant shopping centers too.

6 If you can, choose your routes carefully. A "short-cut" over a poorly paved road can cost 15 percent in fuel penalties—and a gravel road ups that figure to 35 percent!

Streamlining Your Car Ecologically

We've already mentioned *wind resistance* and its relation to mileage. Take a trip from racing drivers and from the designers of fast cars and planes. Look at your car to see what you can do to cut down on wind resistance and otherwise improve its fuel consumption:

Did you know that a highly *waxed* car cuts wind resistance dramatically? And it looks good too.

Those light-looking *roof racks* are deceptive. They create quite a bit of drag, especially when fully loaded, and the ensuing wind resistance substantially interferes with the air flow around the car. As a matter of fact, a small trailer loaded with the same gear is probably not as big a liability. Trailers travel in the "wake" of the car and meet with less air resistance. Of course they weigh more too, but once underway, they follow along easily if you don't try to speed. Besides, you always disconnect the trailer when you don't need it, but you tend to carry the empty roof rack around even when you have no load to put on it.

Open side windows also increase wind resistance. Try to use the interior vents and the vent windows whenever you can. An air conditioner may seem to be a good answer in terms of wind resistance, but you will still lose mileage if you have one. First, the car has to carry around the weight of the air conditioner and its coolant. Second, it has to put out extra power to make the air conditioner work. You pay your money and you take your choice—air conditioners consume an extra $2\frac{1}{2}$ miles per gallon!

Did you know that **radial tires** can save you up to 10 percent in fuel consumption? They roll more freely than conventional tires do. If your car cannot use—or does not need—radial tires, you can compromise with bias-belted tires the next time you need tires. Underinflated tires consume about 1 mile per gallon of extra gasoline. And they wear out faster too. Air costs nothing, so be sure your tires are getting all they need. On long trips, add about 4 pounds more than is recommended to your tires, but don't go above 32 psi. To get an accurate reading, always put air into your tires in the morning before you drive the car (except to get to the air pump, of course). After a car has been driven for a while, the tires heat up and the air in them expands. Get the snow tires off the car as soon as possible—they consume a lot more fuel, too.

Check your *brakes* if you haven't already done so. Sometimes a poorly adjusted brake will "drag" while the car is in motion. It takes more power to move the wheel against the dragging brake, and the result is that your brake linings—and the gas in your tank—won't last as long. To check for dragging brakes, jack up each wheel and spin it. If a brake shoe is dragging, you will feel it as you try to turn the wheel on the hub.

Worn wheel bearings will cut fuel mileage in the same way. Check them at the same time by listening for a rumbling sound as you spin each wheel. If your bearings or your brake shoes seem to be preventing your wheels from moving freely, have the situation remedied quickly or you will soon be paying for new brake linings, a new brake drum, or a worn axle.

The overall *weight* of your car is significant, too. Every 500 pounds of chrome, steel, and power accessories which you haul around will cost you from 2 to 5 miles per gallon! A car that weighs only 2,500 pounds will get you twice the mileage of a car that weighs 5,000 pounds. And it will get you there just as fast. . . .

While you are at it, clean the junk out of the *trunk compartment.* You use extra fuel to haul that weight around, too.

Possibly the most dramatic way to save fuel is to trade that faithful old gas-eater in for a good used *compact car.* Most small cars don't need power accessories either, so you win twice. And while you are considering it, did you know that a car with a big, wide front-end creates enough wind resistance to substantially increase its fuel consumption over that of a car with a smaller, narrower front-end?

How about this one for eco-logical sophistication: A car with a 10-percent-higher **rear axle ratio** can save you from 2 to 5 percent in mileage. It really doesn't matter if you don't know what rear axle ratio is; just look at the specs the next time you are trying to choose another car and pick the one with the higher ratio if everything else is equal. The higher the rear axle ratio, the slower the engine has to turn at any given speed. That's why it saves you fuel.

Filling 'er Up Eco-logically

Did you know that, like everything else, gasoline expands with heat? Ten gallons of gas will expand by $8/10$ of a quart (that's the same as $4/5$—as in a bottle of whiskey) with a temperature increase of 30 degrees? So if the day is going to be a scorcher, try to fill up in the early morning or in the evening, when the air is cooler. This way, your gas tank will hold more gasoline at no extra cost, and you won't have to make as many trips to the filling station.

If you really want to fill the tank efficiently, shake the car a bit while it is filling, to get rid of trapped air in the tank. If you think this is compulsive, consider that gas expands $1/10$ of 1 percent for every 10 degrees of heat. If you are judging your fuel consumption by dividing the number of gallons in your tank into the number of miles you drove before it needed refilling, you will get more impressive results if the tank is *really* full to begin with—and not partially full of heat-expanded gasoline and partially full of air.

This does *not* mean that you should jam those extra ounces of gasoline into the tank after the filler hose has automatically shut itself off. Many station attendants like to do this because it means extra money for that extra gas, but it also increases the danger that the overfilled tank will simply run over and spill that gasoline on the ground if you should travel up a hill soon afterward or park in the heat of the sun. The lost gasoline is not only a waste of fuel, but the fumes from it contribute substantially to air pollution. So fill your tank efficiently, but don't overfill it. And check your fuel tank cap to be sure its gasket is in good shape.

That brings us to the second half of this chapter. Since we are talking about trips, let's consider that old bugaboo. . . .

What to Do When Your Car Drops Dead on the Freeway

This is really a trouble-shooting section. Whether the car has died on the freeway or in front of the house, it is always a time of unrivaled panic and stress. But an informed, well-organized approach to diagnosing your sick monster's ills will pay off by getting you moving again with a minimum loss of time, money, and composure. The problems involved are seldom serious, and you can usually solve them by keeping a cool head and following these instructions.

First, if you are on a freeway, try to get to the right-hand shoulder of the road. Very often, if a car is going to do its swan song while in motion, it will give you a couple of hints first. Be alert to any sudden loss of power. Do you suddenly have to floor the accelerator to maintain speed or to keep moving at all? Have any of your warning lights gone on? It is worth while to stop immediately and check the cause. Is the car suddenly running roughly? Is the engine misfiring? Are there any new noises? Is the car pulling to one side? All of these are good reasons to head for the side of the road.

Safety Precautions

While the car is still going, try to coast down the shoulder until you are well away from any curves behind you. This will pay off when you are ready to get back onto the freeway, because you will be able to spot oncoming traffic before it's on your tail.

If the car has died right on the freeway and you can't get off the road, *don't do anything*! I know that it is unnerving to sit in a dead car, with traffic piling up behind you. But it is literally suicide to attempt to cross a high-speed freeway on foot. Most freeways that are heavily traveled are also heavily patrolled, and some nice highway "patrolperson" will be along before you know it. Once the officer is on the scene, it will be a simple matter to stop traffic long enough to push your car to the right shoulder.

Once you have reached the side of the road, take these additional safety precautions:

1 Don't work on your car from the left side, unless you will be standing well away from the right-hand lane. If you can't move the car farther off the road, climb into the area from the front or the right, if necessary, but keep away from traffic. That goes for changing left-hand tires, too.

2 If it is daylight, put on your emergency blinkers or your left-turn signal to alert oncoming traffic to the fact that your car is not moving.

3 If it is nighttime and you carry flares, place them about six feet behind the car to alert traffic. If you don't have any flares, you may carry a lantern, a large battery-operated light, or a couple of milk cartons filled with wax and a wick. If you have nothing, leave the right-hand car door open so the interior lights will go on and alert traffic.

Once you are safely off the road and ready to deal with the problem, try to view what happened in dietary terms. Your car lives on a mixture of air, fuel, and fire—as you probably remember. If it won't go, it is not getting one of these ingredients.

Air This is simple and probably not the problem. The car gets its air through the air cleaner. Unless the **air filter** is totally clogged, it should get enough air to keep it going. Of course your **choke** or **throttle** may be stuck in a closed position, and this could keep your car from breathing properly. Remove your air cleaner and look into the carburetor barrel. Is the choke open? Move the throttle linkage with your finger (that's the arm that makes the car rev when you push it). Does it seem to be moving freely? Then that's not your problem. Check your **PCV valve** to be sure it's clear and functioning. Look at those hoses—have any of them become disconnected or broken? Do you hear air whistling while the car idles—if it can? One strategic hose lost can slow or stop your car. Reclamp the wanderer or tape the hole, and you'll soon be on your way. Of course if you've made a habit of checking and replacing worn hoses before disaster strikes, you have avoided this trouble completely.

If the car will **turn over** but won't start running, it may not be getting any fuel. Are you out of gas? Even if your **gas gauge** says you still have some, the gauge may be on the blink. When did you fill the car last?

Did you lose power before the car died? Look down the carburetor again and push the **accelerator pump** arm. Is fuel squirting into the **venturi**? Then the **float bowl** is full. Still, it may not be getting a fresh supply when it needs it. Disconnect the hose that leads from the carburetor to the **fuel pump**. Somewhere along that line is the **fuel filter**. This could have jammed—especially if it hasn't been changed in ages. Place the end of the hose in a jar or plastic bag. If you don't have anything to put it in, let it hang down so the gas can run onto the ground. Don't let gasoline run out of the hose onto your clothes or all over the engine. If it's very hot, fan the area to disburse the fumes. Bump the starter and see if gasoline squirts out of the hose. If it does, then your fuel filter and fuel pump are probably all right. If nothing comes out of the hose, you probably either have a plugged fuel filter, a defective fuel pump, a broken fuel line, or you are out of gas.

If you can, try to eliminate the fuel filter as the villain by taking it out to see if gas comes out of the hose. If you have changed the filter recently, ignore this step and look under the rear end of the car to see if fuel is leaking from a broken fuel line. If you find nothing and you fail to find any other cause of trouble, tie a white rag to your door handle or antenna and wait for help, or try to get to a phone and contact a rescue unit or the AAA. With luck, help should arrive within half an hour.

Sometimes the problem is *too much* fuel. If you open your hood and find that everything is covered with gasoline, *don't try to start the car*! Gasoline is too inflammable to monkey around with. Just hoist that white flag and get some help.

If it's a very hot day and you've been on the road in stop-and-go traffic, you may have **vapor lock**. Chapter 8 tells you everything you need to know about it, and about all the other causes of overheating. For the time

Fuel

being, simply wrap a wet rag (assuming you are near a source of water) around the fuel line between the fuel pump and the carburetor and wait for things to cool down. If you haven't got a wet rag, try some tinfoil, and leave it in place after you get started. No tinfoil? Then just sit there and wait for the darn thing to cool down, and the vapor lock will go away.

Fire If the fuel is entering your carburetor as it is supposed to, then you are probably having ignition trouble. As you know, the "fire" is really electric current that is stored in the **battery**, replaced by the **alternator**, amplified by the **coil**, and directed by the **distributor** to each **spark plug**. If something along the way goes wrong, all the air and fuel in the world will not produce **combustion** in the car's **cylinders**, and it won't go. So follow along the route of the current to see if it has been prevented from getting to the plugs.

It is probably not the fault of the battery, **solenoid**, or **starter**, since the car has been going. Pull the middle wire out of the center of the **distributor cap** and hold it close to a piece of metal on the engine *that is not near the carburetor.* Hold yourself away from the metal sides of the car (to avoid grounding yourself), and have someone **crank** the motor. An intense bright blue spark will jump between the wire and the engine if your ignition system is working properly. (If you have no one to help you, you'll just have to wait for help.) Is that wire securely pushed down where it enters the coil? How about the two little coil wires?

If you don't get a spark, remove the distributor cap and look at the **points**. Do they open and close when you bump the starter? If not, adjust them so they do and check again for spark. If there is still no spark, your points could be oxidized, or fouled by a bit of grease or oil. Bump the engine so the points are closed, and insert the tip of a screwdriver, fingernail file, matchbook cover, or feeler gauge to rub the point surfaces to eliminate the oxidation or dirt. If you *still* don't get a spark, there's still another thing to try.

It is a good idea to keep your old **rotor**, points, and **condenser** in the trunk of your car after you replace them during a tune-up. First, try replacing the rotor

Testing for Spark
Richard Freshman

with the old one. If that doesn't work, replace the condenser. If that doesn't work, replace the points. Don't worry about gapping them; as long as they open and close, the car will run. I have been told that the most frequent cause of car failure is improper lubrication of the **cam** when the points were changed. Because of this, the little **rubbing block** gets worn down, and then, even when the block rests on the **cam lobe**, there is not enough surface to force the points apart. That's why it's important to check your **dwell** every 5,000 miles and replace points every 10,000 miles.

If you've checked everything out and the car still won't go, then you are probably going to have to wait for help. Sometimes it's your coil or part of your engine that has given out. Sometimes it's the **transmission**. If that's the case, you may be saying good-bye to Old Faithful. All the comfort I can offer is that the next chapter will tell you how to buy a good used car. Most of the time, however, you will find the cause of the trouble by checking as I've outlined above. Or you will have plenty of warning before the car gives up the ghost. If you have not checked and maintained your car properly, if you have ignored the warnings, the **knockings**, the smoke from the **tail pipe**, the hesitations and the stalls, well—you asked for it.

Symptoms of Trouble Ahead

As you work on your car, you will get to know it better. Before long you will find that you are becoming more sensitive to its signals. If something "sounds funny" or "smells funny" or just doesn't feel "right," you will soon sense it. This will help you forestall those sudden-death routines, because you will be preventing trouble or catching it before it reaches the terminal stage. Here are a couple of "funny" things to be alert to:

Sounds

1 *If your fan belt is singing*, readjust or replace it. If it breaks on the road, you will hear a loud knocking sound. Don't attempt to drive with a broken **fan belt**. If you have kept a spare, or an old belt, in the trunk of the car, you can replace the broken one at the side of the road if you want to spare

yourself the cost of having someone else do it. Some rescue units won't do this kind of thing on the road and you have to pay tow charges (with possible damage to the car) so that they can fix it at the station.

2 *If your radiator is singing,* check the cap.

3 *If your tires are squealing on curves,* check the **tires** and **alignment**.

4 *If your tires are "tramping,"* check inflation and tire wear.

5 *If something is ticking rhythmically when your car is idling,* check your oil level. The hydraulic lifters that lift your valves can make these noises if you are as little as 1 to 1½ quarts low in oil. If your dipstick indicates that you have enough oil, then have someone check your valve adjustment.

6 *If there's a knocking sound in your engine,* it may just be a loose **rocker arm**, but it could be a loose bearing or a faulty **piston**. Have this checked fast, because if it's one of the last two, you can blow the whole engine and destroy the car if you let it go unheeded.

7 *If there's a whistling noise,* check the hoses for vacuum leaks.

8 *If there's an unlocatable sound,* get an old stethoscope from a medical supply house or ask the family doctor. Take off the rubber disc and insert a piece of tubing in its place (about 1½ inches will do). Then put the plugs in your ears, run the engine, and move the tube end of the stethoscope around the hood area. It will amplify the sound as you near the part that's causing it. A metal wrench will work this way too. Place one end of the wrench on the bone behind your ear, and, leaning over, place the other end of the wrench on the parts that seem to be the source of the noise. Be careful not to get your hair tangled in the fan.

9 *If your brakes are squealing,* you may have grease loose in the brake drum, or glazed or very worn linings. **Disc brakes** tend to squeal naturally. Have the brakes checked, or follow the instructions in Chapter 10 and check them yourself. The linings may be worn, too.

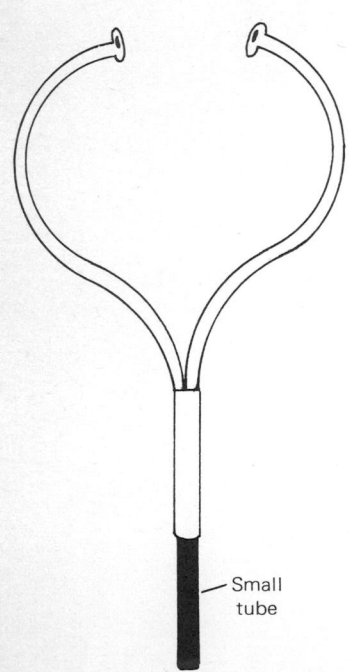

Small tube

A Piece of Tubing and an Old Stethoscope Make an Efficient Trouble-Shooting Device
Alexandra Soto

10 *If the car sounds like an old taxi,* especially when it is driven on a bumpy road, it probably just needs **lubrication**. You may get used to the squeaks and groans, but they also indicate wear, because they are caused by parts rubbing together or moving without the proper lubrication.

11 *If your car is idling peculiarly,* with an offbeat rhythm, it is not becoming creative, it is probably **misfiring**. Check the **spark plug** cables and the connectors in the **boots** at either end of them to be sure that all your plugs are firing. A quick way to do this is to pull each spark plug cable (one at a time) off its terminal on the **distributor cap** and hold it a short distance away from the terminal. Have someone **crank** the motor. If your cable is working at that end, a spark will jump across from the terminal to the cable. Don't lean on the metal parts of the car when you check cables in this way—you don't want to ground yourself.

   a If you do this for each plug and you don't find a problem, then hook up your **tach/dwell** meter and turn the knob to "**Tachometer**."

   b Pull each cable off the spark plug it connects to (one at a time). As you pull a cable, keep your eye on the tach. The reading should drop sharply when you pull the cable. If it doesn't drop but continues to read the same as when the cable was hooked to the plug, you've found the culprit.

   c Check the cable for breaks or shorts in the wiring. If that reveals nothing, pull the plug and check it to see if it is clean and properly gapped.

An easy way to see whether or not your car is **idling** evenly is to place your hand, or a stiff piece of paper, against the end of the **tail pipe** while the car is idling (with the **emergency brake** on, please). Either will amplify the sound and enable you to hear the rhythm. A misfiring **cylinder** will come through as a pumping or puffing sound. An even but rough idle is a clue that it's time to retune your **carburetor**—especially the **idle mixture** and **idle speed screws**. Go back to Chapter 7 for instructions on how to do this easy job.

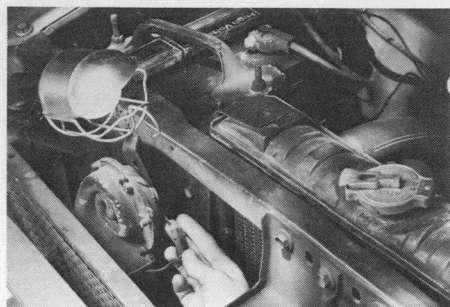

If Your Horn Gets Stuck, Pull the Wire to
Silence It.
Richard Freshman

12 *If your car sounds like a jet plane* or makes some other kind of really loud abnormal sound, a hole in the **muffler** is probably the cause. Replace it immediately: traffic cops hate noisy mufflers, and carbon monoxide hates people!

13 *If the horn is stuck*, your car is producing probably the worst noise it can make. Before this happens, have someone honk your horn until you can locate it under your hood. There are usually two horns. Each has a wire leading to it. If your horn gets stuck, pull these wires and it will stop. Sometimes you have to pull only one. Then find out, or have someone find out, why it stuck. When the horn is fixed, reconnect the wires.

14 *If the car continues to run roughly,* try a compression check.

How to Check the Compression in Your Cylinders

A Compression Gauge
Karcheck Products, Otsego, Michigan

For this job you need a **compression gauge**. This is a device that tests the amount of pressure that the **piston** exerts on the **fuel/air mixture** before the **spark plug** fires it. If there isn't enough pressure, the mixture won't explode. If there is less pressure than there should be, the mixture won't explode as efficiently. If one or more **cylinders** have a good deal less pressure than the others, the car will not run evenly, and this is what you are checking to see. Now, why shouldn't there be enough pressure? Because something is letting the pressure escape from the cylinder. Where can it go? Basically, two places. Either out through one of the **valve** openings, because the valve is improperly adjusted or so worn that it doesn't close properly, or down past the **rings** on the piston. These rings are supposed to keep the pressure at the top of the cylinder in, and the oil that lubricates the engine from entering the cylinder. When the rings get worn, oil gets in and pressure gets out. Your compression gauge can tell you whether or not your cylinder is firing efficiently and whether your rings or your valves are worn or out of adjustment. And it doesn't cost much to buy one of these gauges or take much time and effort to use it.

a Have someone sit in the driver's seat with the car in "Park" and the emergency brake on. Pull the wire from the center of the **distributor cap** (the big one that leads to the **coil**).

b Remove the #1 spark plug and insert the plug at the end of your **compression gauge** into the hole where the spark plug screwed into the cylinder. (If you've forgotten about the compression gauge, consult Chapter 2.)

c Have a friend press the starter button until the engine **cranks** over about five times (the fact that you've pulled the wire will keep the car from actually starting). Be sure to keep the gauge plug firmly inserted while the car is cranking.

d Look at the gauge and write down the reading. Then replace the spark plug and go on to the next plug. Don't forget to reset the gauge each time.

e When you have done this to each cylinder, look at the readings. The highest and the lowest readings should not vary by more than 15 percent. If one or more of the cylinders read way below the others, go back and squirt a couple of drops of motor oil into the spark plug opening and retest it with the gauge. If the cylinder reading stays the same, the valves are either worn (and letting pressure escape) or out of adjustment. If the reading rises dramatically after you've put in the oil, you probably need new rings on the piston in that cylinder. If the pressure is less than 100 psi, the cylinder probably isn't even firing! Once you've determined what is wrong, you'll have to decide whether or not it is worth correcting. If the car is on its way out anyway, get rid of it. If it is otherwise in fine shape, then new rings may be a wise, though costly, investment.

Oh, one last thing: If the low readings were on the first few cylinders you tested, it may be that your car wasn't properly warmed up and your **choke** was still closed. This would keep the air supply low, and the pressure would be lowered, too. So if you think this might have happened, take the time (before you take action) to retest the cylinders that seemed below standard.

1 *Do you smell rubber burning under the hood?* One of your hoses might have come loose and landed on a hot part of the engine. Rescue it before it melts through.

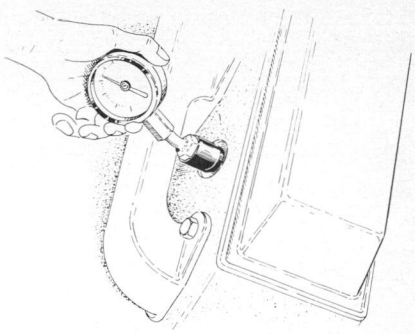

Checking Compression
Actron Manufacturing Company

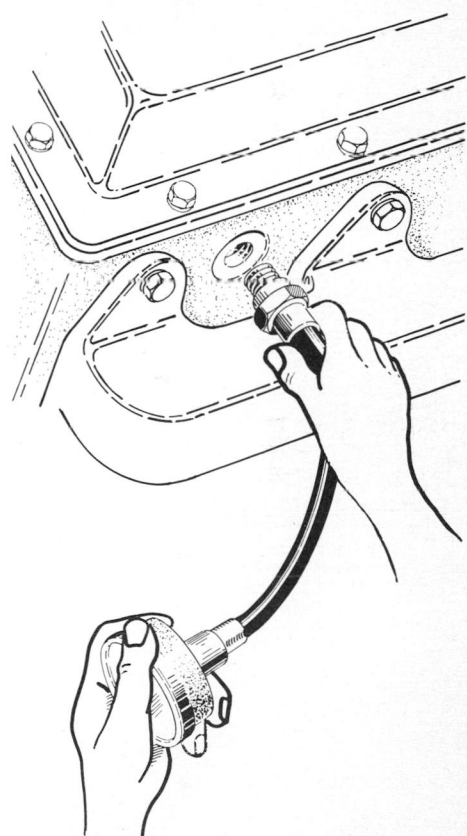

Some Gauges Have Long Hoses That Screw into the Spark Plug Opening, So You Can Do the Check Unaided
Actron Manufacturing Company

Smells

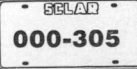

2 *Do you smell burned rubber with the hood closed?* Feel your wheels. If one is hot, a **brake shoe** may be dragging.

3 *Do you smell oil burning?* First check the **dipstick**; your **oil gauge** may be lying and you may be out of oil. Or your engine may be overheating and your temperature gauge may be broken. If neither is the case, look around the engine for an oil leak that may be frying in the heat of the running engine. If the oil situation seems to be O.K., check the **transmission fluid dipstick**. Sometimes a faulty **vacuum modulator** can siphon the fluid out of the transmission and feed it to the engine, where it is burned. Also, if the transmission fluid is very low, it can be burned in the transmission because the gears are not lubricated enough and are getting very hot.

4 *Do you smell oil or exhaust fumes in the passenger compartment?* The cause could simply be burned oil from the engine area—but it could also be a faulty **exhaust pipe** under the car which is letting **exhaust gases** get into the car through the floorboards. Exhaust fumes are full of carbon monoxide, so if you smell oil or exhaust in the car, be sure to keep your windows open at all times and have the problem checked out as quickly as you can. We've all heard stories about people who have died on the highway from carbon monoxide or from passing out at the wheel because of it. Such stories are true.

5 *If you smell gasoline*, check your **carburetor** to be sure it isn't leaking fuel. If it seems all right, check down the **fuel line** all the way to the **fuel tank** for leaks. A look under the car, after it has been parked overnight, may help, but remember that fuel evaporates quickly, so the clues may be stains rather than wet spots. Check your **fuel pump** for fuel leaks. The gasoline will wash a clean streak across it, which can be seen with the naked eye.

Strange Sensations   This is a catchall category for those things that "feel funny" but are not obviously related to a specific part or situation. Try to locate the source of the sensation by the process of elimination and then check to see what's wrong. Check **hoses**, **tires**, **brakes**, **oil** levels, spark plug connections, the **carburetor**, the **cooling system**—in short, anything that may cause your car to operate roughly. If it seems to be associated with the **clutch**, **gearshift**, or **steering linkage**, have those checked out. If your steering is difficult and you have **power steering**, be sure to check the **dipstick** in the cap on the little reservoir that is attached to the unit to see if there is sufficient **automatic transmission fluid** in it. If it is low, and if it gets low again very soon after you've refilled it, check for leaks in the hoses leading from the unit to the front wheels. Consult the Under-the-Hood Check in Chapter 5 if you can't find your power-steering unit.

If Your Car Won't Start

Before we end this section, let's consider those wonderful days when your car simply refuses to start. We've covered most of this before, but there are a few more things that you should know.

If you have left your lights, heater, radio, or some other electrical gizmo on after you parked the car, then you know what the trouble is. Your **battery** is dead. You can get going again if you know how to jump a start from some Good Samaritan's car to your own.

How to Jump a Start

1 If you have found a Good Samaritan, be sure his or her battery has at least as much voltage as your own. It doesn't matter if your car has negative **ground** and the GS's car has positive ground, or if your car has an **alternator** and the GS's car has a **generator**, as long as you hook up the cables properly (and the proper way is the same in every case).

2 Take out those nice **jumper cables** you bought as soon as you read about them in Chapter 2. If you didn't, you'll have to find a Good Samaritan who has cables too.

3 Remove the caps from the top of your battery and the GS's battery. Remember, batteries produce hydrogen gas, which is explosive, and we are dealing here with jumping a spark that just could set it off. If the batteries are open, the gas disperses and so does a potential explosion. If the batteries remain closed (especially the kind with screw-on caps), then

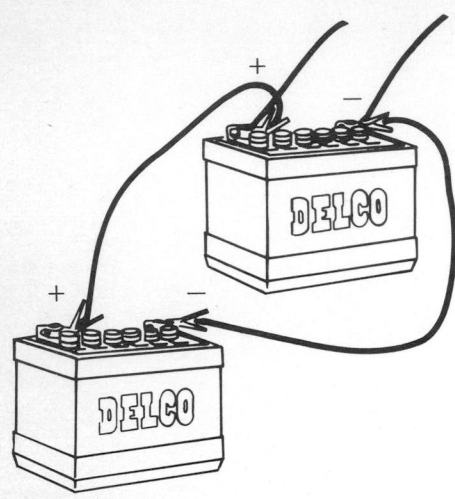

Connect the Positive Cable to Each Battery
and Then the Negative Cable
Delco-Remy Division, General Motors Corp.

the pressure that could explode is much greater. So this step is a safety measure.

4 The positive cable has red clips at either end, and the negative cable has black clips. First, attach one of the red clips to the **positive terminal** of your battery (it will have "pos" or "+" on it, or it will be bigger than the negative terminal). Then attach a red clip to the positive terminal of the GS's car.

5 Now attach one of the black clips to the **negative terminal** on your battery, and the other black clip to the negative terminal of the other car.

6 Up to now, both cars have been in "Park," with the **ignition switch** off and the **emergency brake** on. Now get into your car and turn on the ignition. The car should start.

7 Disconnect the cables, thank the Good Samaritan, and resume your life.

If your alternator light stays on, or your gauge continues to point to "Discharge" after your car's been running, check your fan belt to see that it is tight enough to run your alternator properly. If your battery keeps going dead, have it and your alternator checked professionally. In any case, do not drive around with a light or gauge that reads "Trouble"; have it checked out immediately—that's why they put those gauges in there.

Now let's run through the rest of those Won't Start symptoms for one last time:

Car is silent when key is turned in ignition. Check **battery** terminal cable connections. If they look very corroded, force the point of a screwdriver (with an insulated or wooden handle) between the connector and the post and twist it to lodge it firmly. Then have someone try to start the car. If it starts, you need to clean or replace your cables.

Car makes a clicking noise but won't start. Usually a dead **battery**. If not, check the **starter** wiring for a loose connection.

Car cranks over but won't start. Check the fuel supply to your **carburetor**. If that's O.K., check your **distributor cap** to see if the spark is getting through.

Car starts but dies. Check your **carburetor** adjustment and your **choke** to see if the choke is first closing, then opening.

Car won't start on rainy days. Check inside the **distributor cap** for dampness. If you find moisture, carry some mechanic's solvent in the car (get some from your friendly service station—they use it to clean car parts—and it's also sold in aerosol cans). When you find dampness inside the distributor cap, turn the cap upside down and pour some solvent into it. Swish it around and pour it out. Then dry the cap as best you can and replace it. The solvent will evaporate the water; just be sure to only use *clean* solvent. Gasoline won't do; the spark can ignite the fumes.

Car won't start on cold mornings. Check the **choke**. Is it closed? Does it open?

Here are some more trouble symptoms:

Engine misses while idling. Check the **points**, the **idle speed** and **mixture screws** on the **carburetor**, and look for leaky air hoses.

Engine misses at high speeds. Check the **points, spark plugs, fuel pump, fuel filter**, and **carburetor**.

Engine misses or hesitates during acceleration. Check the **accelerator pump** in the **carburetor**, the **spark plugs**, the **distributor**, and the **timing**.

Engine knocks or pings. Check your **timing**; check the octane of the fuel you are using. The owner's manual will tell you the proper octane and whether the fuel should be leaded, low-lead, or unleaded. Check the **cooling system**. Do a **compression check** on the engine cylinders.

Preventive Medicine

Two things should have emerged as a result of all the above. The first is that most of the things that go wrong with your car can be avoided by simply maintaining it properly—lubricating it frequently and replacing fan belts, wiring, hoses, points, plugs, brake linings, and other parts *before they fail.* It is much

simpler to diagnose car failure if you know that you've checked certain parts and systems recently and that they are in good shape. This is preventive medicine, and it is well worth the effort!

The second is that by understanding the way your car works, by exploring a failure logically in terms of what is happening (or not happening) and which part or parts are involved in that function, and by checking them to see if they are working properly, you will be able to quickly diagnose—and sometimes remedy—the situation. You won't feel helpless or bewildered, perhaps just frustrated by the time it sometimes takes to fix the trouble. And once you become familiar with the way things *should be*, and know why, you will be much more alert to the signs of disaster *before* disaster strikes.

I suggest you keep this book in your trunk compartment, with your jumper cables, some rags, a jack, the wrenches and screwdrivers you use most frequently, a couple of old spark plugs, your old points, rotor and condenser, and a spare fan belt for emergencies. It would be frustrating to get stuck and know that you could soon be on your way if you hadn't left your instructions and tools at home.

If your car exhibits many of the symptoms in this chapter—and shows signs of needing new rings, a valve job, or major transmission work—the most encouraging thing I can say is that you can get right on to the next chapter, which is about evaluating and buying a good used car.

Auto Recycling Without Tears: How to Buy a Good Used Car and Evaluate Your Own

We've come a long way, friends. You are no longer "dummies" when it comes to cars. You know how they work, and by this time, you have probably formed a pretty good idea of how well *your* car is working. If you've tuned it and fed it properly, and if you have been driving it efficiently and it still isn't performing well—or if you've found that it needs a lot of professional work, most of it expensive—then you may be thinking about getting rid of it and buying another car. On the other hand, if your car is pretty old but is now in surprisingly good shape, you may want to hang onto it instead of risking the chance of getting involved with a shiny new lemon.

My own feeling is that hanging onto an older car in good condition is a better risk today than buying a new one. True, the newer cars have lovely things like electronic ignition systems that don't need tuning, spark plugs that last longer, and all sorts of "extras"—radial tires, power accessories, and so forth. But recent economic problems mean that many new cars are just not being built as well as they used to be. Materials have changed, and more and more metal parts are being replaced by plastic. These cost the manufacturer less, although the savings are not reflected in a lower price for the car. The plastic parts wear out faster, and *you* have to go back to the manufacturer and pay again for new ones. The manufacturer wins twice—and you lose.

Again, cars are being made with less hand labor. Machines are building machines, and they aren't programmed to care about people. I recently pulled a lady from a new car that had overturned because its steering had locked on a mild curve. She was more angry than injured, because the same thing had happened before! The manufacturer had repaired the car, and now it had happened again. When I told the story to a few people, I found that the same model (which is *very* popular) had locked and overturned all over the country! If you think this is unfair, just look at the number of recalls in recent years and the dangerous situations that prompted them.

On the economic side, the mileage from many new models is often just not as good as you might have gotten from the same model a few years ago. And the new emission control devices have become the subject of controversy because many of them are still unproven. They waste fuel, they reduce engine performance, and some have been accused of producing new and dangerous pollutants of their own. In short, we are in a period where the technology is producing cars that are more expensive, and less efficient, than they used to be. There are exceptions, of course, and if you really want to buy a new car, you can check *Consumer Reports* and the major independent automotive surveys to locate the best buy. For my money, I'd hang onto my old car if it is running well, or I'd look for a pre-1970 used car in good condition. A car that has been built well and properly maintained can go for as much as 150,000 miles. Most of us think our cars are played out at half that mileage!

Another way to look at it is this: If you buy a new car your car payments can run to $150 a month. And if you buy a car for $5,000, it can lose as much as $3,000 in value in the first year or two. But if you buy or hang onto a well-made older car, you can keep it running well for a lot less than $150 a month. Even if you put a whole new engine into the car every year (which is totally unnecessary), it would cost you only $50 a month to pay it off. So if you have or can find a good used car, you can probably end up way ahead of the game.

If you are going to look for a car, please be professional about it. Ever since I've become automotively involved I've been horrified at car ads because they almost never deal with the most important thing you're buying. (I'm not counting the new advertising thrust toward fuel-economy sales pitches, because in most cases the data are misleading and do not reflect any major effort on the part of the manufacturer to improve mileage.) Most ads reflect the ignorant concerns of the majority of potential auto buyers. They talk about externals like vinyl seat covers, moon roofs, whitewalls, and "luxury packages." But there is little or no mention of what has been put under the hood.

What kind of engine does the car have? What is the engine made of? How efficient is it? Can you reach the sparkplugs and distributor easily? At a recent auto show I was amazed to see that they'd put a large V-8 engine into a small car that didn't need it. There was so little room under the hood (because the car had been designed for a 4-cylinder engine) that you had to hoist the engine out of the car in order to change the spark plugs! Not only couldn't the owner do it alone, but the labor costs for dismounting the engine, hoisting it, and replacing the engine mounts when the tune-up was over had to be astronomical. Not only that, any engine that has to be loosened and hauled out a couple of times a year is just not going to be as silent and stable as one that stays put. The smaller engine would have supplied more than enough power to well exceed the current 55-mph speed limit, but the potential customer who wanted this "super sports model" is going to pay more for the car, more for the fuel it will consume, and much more for tune-ups. If, because of the high cost, the owner doesn't spring for tune-ups as often, the car will run less efficiently, burn even more fuel, and contribute still more to air pollution.

Many of us cannot help viewing cars as status symbols, and car freaks such as myself dream about owning a really superb piece of automotive engineering. But even if you are in the market for a status symbol, it might be wiser (and perhaps even more impressive) to forget the new expensive macho-mobiles and look for a classic car from the 1950s or 60s instead. I recently read that a very prestigious American biggie costs $10,000 new today and will depreciate in worth to a few hundred dollars in the next ten years. But a classic car that cost $3,500 ten years ago will be worth close to $10,000 in a year or two if in mint condition. This is a good investment as well as a beautiful status symbol. The reason these "oldies" have suddenly become more valuable is simply that they were beautifully made of the best materials—by hand, in many cases. In most instances, their owners loved them and took very good care of them, and as a result, they have a longer potential life span today than many of the new cars do, in spite of the mileage that has been added over the years.

Of course the classic "oldies" are sometimes more difficult to maintain because parts can be hard to find and expensive to buy. But many of them were popular enough to assure a fairly large selection of parts in major urban areas.

If you are just looking for a family car, an oldie can still be worth while. I bought Tweety for a little over $500 two years ago. I have put about $200 into her (including a classy red paint job), and I've been offered $1,000 for her several times. I recently passed a used-car lot that wanted $1650 for her twin sister! Consequently, when the macho-mobile died, we went looking for another Tweety. We found one for $750 and spent about $100 to get it into good shape. And Sylvester has power steering, an automatic transmission, and air conditioning, too!

Now, before the car manufacturers come to get me, let me tell you how to shop for a new old car, how to get rid of your own, how to evaluate a used car to determine if it is in good condition, and how to strike a good deal with Smiling Sam, the used-car dealer.

Where to Shop for a Used Car
Auctions

There are three major sources for used cars—auctions, dealers, and private parties. Rule 1 is: Stay Away from Auctions! Although cars go very cheaply at auction, there is little or no chance for you to inspect the car, determine its past history, or get your money back if you find you've bought a terminal basket case with a lovely paint job. Car dealers go to auctions prepared to take risks. You can't. So forget them.

Sometimes you will hear of an auction or sale of police cars, fleet cars, or taxis, at very good prices. Forget these too. Although such cars have usually been pretty well maintained, they have been driven for long hours over thousands of miles by people who neither owned them nor cared for them. As a result they are often worn out and ready for pasture. The same often goes for used station wagons. These are sometimes owned by traveling salespeople who put 50,000 miles a year on them. So unless you know the former owners, a used station wagon should be checked out very thoroughly before you consider buying it.

Private Parties

It is usually cheaper to buy a car directly from the owner rather than from a used-car lot. But there are drawbacks here too. The owner usually wants to sell the car quickly because the money is needed to buy a new car. Consequently, private owners are not too happy if you want to take the car and check it out thoroughly. Some will let you, but if they have had fifty answers to their ad, they are more inclined to keep the car close to home and wait for another, more impetuous, buyer to come along. Also, if you buy the car and get ripped off, it is harder to get the old owners to give you your money back. They have no reputation to protect as a car dealer, and most private deals carry no warranty, guarantee, or money-back promises. You pay your money and you take your lumps—unless you arrange, *in writing*, that you can return the car for a full refund in a day or two—after you've had it checked. If the car is as good as the owners say it is, they may be willing to do this.

There is also the chance of buying a stolen car from a private party. If they take off and you are left holding the car, it is your loss if the police come to repossess it.

Of course if you buy a used car from a friend, relative, or business acquaintance, you may have better luck returning a lemon. But the relationship is going to go a little sour, too. I wouldn't recommend it, unless you need the car more than you need the former owner.

Car Dealers

Car dealers come in two flavors. There are the new-car dealers who have facilities for selling the used cars they take in as trade-ins, and there are independent used-car dealers who buy cars from the public and from the new-car dealers for resale.

New-car dealers are generally the safest sources for used cars. They are not really in business to move the trade-ins, so they generally keep only the nicest trade-ins on the lot and sell the lemons to independent used-car dealers or to wreckers. Also, they have spent years building their reputation in the community, and if trouble develops, they will often go out of their way to see that you are satisfied. Many dealers have service facilities to handle new-car warranty work, and so if you find that your new used car has defects, they may fix the car at less cost to you and to themselves. There are two drawbacks, however. First, if new car sales are really down, a new-car dealer may become as hard-nosed as an independent about moving the used merchandise. Second, new-car dealers generally charge top prices for used cars, higher than independents and much higher than private parties. If you can argue them down a bit, it may be worth a slightly higher price up front to have safe recourse if trouble develops.

000-315

It is a good idea to go to the classiest neighborhood around when shopping the new-car dealers for a used car. In high-income areas there is usually little demand for used cars and a high turnover in new ones, so the dealers are eager to move the trade-ins off their lots. Also, well-heeled people tend to have maintenance work done regularly, with the best mechanics and the finest parts, because they can afford it. So the used car they trade in is often in pretty fine condition. It may not have as much mileage on it either, because wealthy families often have several cars to choose from, instead of running just one car into the ground. This may be the only time you will find the best bargain in the high-rent part of town!

Used-car dealers can be good sources for bargains if they have been around long enough to have established a stake in being a reliable part of the community. An established used-car dealer is probably totally trustworthy, considerate, and worth checking as a source for a used car. But it is wise to avoid the hit-and-run independent who springs up in an unused lot like a weed, unloads a group of lemons on the local public, and vanishes before the cars fall apart. It is these fellows that have made us ask, "Would you buy a used car from this man?"

When we were shopping for Sylvester, I got a good view of the used-car hierarchy in my home town. For some reason, Santa Monica has a very large number of auto dealers. It is probably one of the main sources of cars for the Los Angeles area. The dealers vary from new-car dealers who have been in the same location since the manufacturer invented the car and gave them the franchise, through a good many established used-car dealers, to the weed-grown independents on the edges of town. Oddly enough, we got the most accurate view of the hierarchy when we were trying to unload the macho-mobile. We went first to the new-car dealer who sold m-m's. He looked at our car and said, "I don't handle anything more than a year or two old. If I take a car that's a little older in trade, I generally sell it to Dealer X, down the block. You might look there if you want a model from the early seventies. But this car is a '68. We sell those to Dealer Y, who is about a mile away. And if you can't sell it to him, then check out Dealer Z, on the edge of town. He's the one who gets the cheapest and the oldest cars." Dealer Y bought our car. I hope it didn't end up with Dealer Z.

**How to Determine
the Price of
a Car**

Of course, when you are looking for a used car, check the newspaper ads to see what they are going for. Also check to see what cars like the one you currently own are selling for, so you will know how much

money you can expect to get from selling yours. You will see that cars that are sold by private parties are generally lower in price than those from dealers. That's because the private party will still do better selling at the lower price to another private party than he or she would have done if the car were sold to a dealer. A car that is sold by a dealer for $1,000 was generally bought or taken in trade for around $500. The owner could probably have sold that car easily for $800 through a newspaper ad to a private party. Remember that newspaper ads are usually a bit inflated because the owner wants a chance to deal for the best offer.

Another good place to check prices is the NADA (National Automobile Dealers Association) **"blue book"**. This is the official used-car guide to the current wholesale and retail price for each car. It will tell you how much you can expect to get for your car and how much you can expect to pay for the car you want. It generally breaks down the price in terms of accessories, power extras, body condition, engine size, transmission, etc., so you can pretty well zero in on the price range for a car of the same age, quality, and general condition as your own. You can find the "blue book" at your local bank, at insurance companies, and sometimes in the public library. Be sure you have the most recent copy. Car values change drastically according to competition, economic conditions, and current fads. The best time to buy a used car is in the fall, when there are lots of trade-ins because people are buying the new models that have just come out.

How to Sell Your Old Car

You can get more for your car if you sell it yourself, especially if it is in good condition. If it is terminally ill, be reasonable and don't try to unload it on an unsuspecting stranger. I'm firmly convinced that deeds like that eventually come home to roost. If, however, it is not terminally ill but does need some fairly major work, you might be better off trading it to a car dealer for a newer used car. The dealer will not give you much, but it may be worth his while to make the sale. And *he* can worry about unloading your monster, or fixing it up in his own shop for less money than a private buyer would have to pay. Still, in general, selling the car privately is more lucrative—if you have the time and patience to sit through dozens of phone calls, answer silly questions, and wait while several prospective buyers kick your tires.

Incidentally, if you want to sell a sports car or a convertible, try to wait until spring. Convertibles are notoriously hard to sell during the winter or the rainy season.

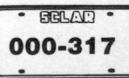

Free Advertising

The first thing to do is advertise. How can you sell something if nobody knows it's for sale? The cheapest form of advertising is *free.* Just place a "For Sale" sign in one of the car's rear side windows, with your telephone number on it in large black numbers that can be read from across the street. Then drive the car around town, or leave it parked in a large shopping area where it will get lots of exposure. If you want to avoid a lot of silly inquiries, put a price on the sign. If you'd rather wait for the best deal, just the phone number will do.

There are also a number of consumer-oriented newspapers that accept free ads from people who want to get rid of second-hand stuff. Many of these exist only on the price they get for the paper. Others will take the ad free but expect as much as 5 percent of the selling price in return if you make a sale. Check out the possibilities, and go for the most popular paper, which will reach the largest audience.

A third way to advertise free is to use the bulletin board at your local school, church, shopping center, community center, or at the office where you work. You can get a couple of index cards, write your sales pitch on them, and stick them up all over town. Use colored cards, add a colored border, or use colored lettering to make your card stand out from the crowd.

Cheap Advertising

Most local newspapers now have a Bargain Box, or a column for the sale of second-hand merchandise by private parties. Most of these cost about $1 per line and most are one-liners. Just the make, year, price (if you like), and phone number will fit. It's worth a dollar.

Newspapers also have classified sections for second-hand car advertising. These may run from $3 to $5 per ad for a three-line ad. Rates vary, and you can get a cheaper rate if you agree to run the ad for a week. Get an idea of the circulation of the paper and estimate how many prospective buyers you will hit per dollar of advertising cost. Also, choose a paper that will be read by people who live fairly near you—or by very large numbers of people all over town. Take ads on weekends in the winter and on weekdays in summer (when people tend to get out of town on Friday).

How to Write Your Ad

What can you say about Faithful Flash? It's been carrying you around for years, and you have a personal love for it, but to the eye of a stranger, old Faithful is just a heap. Well, the best ads convey the fact that the owner cared about the car. So if space permits, try to establish the fact with copy like, "Good home needed for Faithful Mustang. High-spirited, fuel-saving 6-cyl. engine, lovingly maintained, housebroken," etc. Convey whatever enthusiasm you can muster, but don't misrepresent what you are selling. If the car is only in fair shape, don't say that it is in mint condition. That isn't honest and you can be sued. "Needs minor body work," and other bad-news items are better left unsaid. But tell the customer the truth when asked. Sometimes you will find someone who is looking for a bargain and is quite willing to undertake some work themselves, if they know that the car will be worth the effort when they are through. In fact, if you get proficient enough at car repair, you might want to go looking for a classic oldie, such as we've discussed before, that is for sale cheaply because it needs some work that is within your range of expertise.

Be sure your ad contains the following information: year, model, condition (if good), mileage (if low), major equipment (air conditioning, automatic transmission, AM/FM radio, power stuff, etc.), price (if low), your phone number, and when you can be reached. If you have the time to wheel and deal, you can include the words "best offer," or "highest bid" and then sit around and wait for the best deal. You will have to put up with an awful lot of silly phone calls and tire kickers, however, because a lot of people are going to try for a bargain at a price that is much lower than the one you have in mind. Still, a golden goose may fly in and make it all worth while.

When the prospective buyers come around, you will want to show your car to its best advantage. Also, by knowing what to do to make your old car look its best, you will also be wise to similar tactics on the part of those who want to sell you their cars. Here's what should be done to bring out the best in your car:

How to Get the Best Price for Your Car

1 Clean your car inside and out. Wash the car, the upholstery, and vacuum the rug. Empty the ash trays. Make it look loved!

2 This is important. Wash the car's windows inside and out. This may sound silly, but most people drive around with a layer of dirt on their car windows. The only ones that get washed are the windshield and rear window—if they have a conscientious gas station. When a prospective buyer gets into a car with clean windows, the effect is scintillating. The car seems spacious and roomy, the world looks brighter as they drive around. No kidding, this really works!

3 Have the car waxed. A nice shiny finish can add $50 to the price.

4 *Don't* have the car painted. Most prospective buyers will assume that the new paint job is there to cover up recent body work after a smashup.

5 Repair torn upholstery, worn pedal covers, and floor mats. But don't wait till the last minute to make the replacements. If you replace a brake pedal or an accelerator pedal, do it a couple of weeks in

advance so the new pedal will be a bit scuffed. This is because a badly worn pedal cover or floor mat is a sure sign of high mileage, and a sparkling new pedal or mat will convince the alert buyer that the old one must have been worn through.

6 If your engine looks really cruddy, you can clean it with an aerosol can of engine degreaser. Be sure to cover the distributor before you wash the stuff off, however. But before you turn the under-the-hood area into a Mr. Clean fantasy, you should be aware that many buyers consider a totally clean engine to be a cover-up for the fact that some mechanic opened the engine and found a terminal illness inside, then closed it up and eliminated the signs of his exploratory surgery by cleaning everything. But do clean the worst parts up, because a well-kept engine is generally a good selling aid.

7 To give your car a well-maintained look, clean off battery deposits with 1 tablespoon of baking soda in a cup of water. Then take a look at the underside of the hood. A sure giveaway of a poorly functioning PCV valve, or bad rings, is a huge greasy spot on the undersurface of the hood, right over the air cleaner. This is called **blow-by.** It is usually worse-looking than the condition that causes it. Wipe this off before you show the car.

8 If you can, have the receipts from past maintenance handy to prove mileage and show the car's history of maintenance and repair. Also try to have an up-to-date service sticker on the door. It is a good idea to tune your car and get it into good working order so that the test drive will be a positive experience for the prospective buyer. Avoid major repairs, however; they very rarely raise the price enough to compensate for what they cost. The same goes for new tires.

How to Shop for a Used Car

You should have a good idea of what you want, and how much you are prepared to pay, before you go shopping. Read the ads, look at the "blue book," car-watch a bit on the street, and talk to people who own the cars you like for a firsthand view of the pleasures and problems associated with that particular model.

Be wary of the following kinds of cars:

1 Car models that have gone completely out of production unless the one you want was so widely sold that there are still lots of parts available. Of course you may want to buy an Edsel as a collector's item. . . .

2 Cars with engines that have been modified. If a major change has been made by the owner, find out what went wrong with the original equipment and ask a professional what damage the defective part might have done to other parts of the car.

3 Sports cars with racing modifications. Most of these souped-up darlings are miserable in stop-and-go traffic and at lower speeds. Many have been worn out by leading fast lives and aren't good for anyone anymore.

4 Very new cars that are up for sale. These may be lemons or might have been wrecked.

5 Any car that has been in a wreck. Although the car may have been completely restored, it's possible that the frame is bent and less stable, that the spot welds may not hold, or that the steering may be damaged. And remember, even though you may be convinced that the car has been restored and is as good as new, when the time comes for *you* to sell it, you may have trouble finding a buyer who feels the same way.

6 Station wagons owned by traveling salespeople, fleet cars, police cars, ex-taxis, etc. As I've mentioned before, these are usually driven hard and may be worn out.

Now that you know what you *don't* want, figure out a general range of makes and models that appeal to you. Go for a pre-1970 car if possible. Although there are many good cars made since then, generally speaking the '60s were way ahead in terms of construction and materials. Don't limit your choice to just one car. But if you have a favorite brand, go to a dealer who sells new cars of that make, because they will tend to have more used cars of the same kind that they have taken as trade-ins. Follow these guidelines:

1 Do your shopping during daylight hours. Floodlights tend to make cars look more exotic, and they can hide a lot of damage, especially to the underbody of the car.

2 If you are looking for a trade-in on your old car, park it about half a block away and *walk* to the dealer's lot. This is a good procedure to follow even if you are shopping for a new car. Most dealers will appraise your old car to decide how much they are going to have to give you in trade for it (whether you say you want to trade it in or not). They'll tack that onto the price they'd like to get for the car you are looking at. It is better to get a nice low price on the car you want and *then* talk trade-ins, so keep your car an unknown quantity until you are ready to deal.

3 Shop several places. Buying a car is like hiring a mechanic for an expensive repair job. Establish that you are shopping around. They will be more eager to offer you a good deal to keep you out of the hands of the competition.

4 Make it clear that you are looking for a car in *fine condition* and that you value condition over price. This will prevent the dealer from trying out the lemons on you. They will know that you are going to be very upset if they sell you a car that is not in good shape.

5 Check each car that you really like, and road-test it according to the instructions in the next part of this chapter. It will help you to identify the cars that you want to consider and will impress the dealer a lot, especially if you are female. If you can, bring a friend to help you test the car.

6 Visit several dealers this way. Then go back to the car you liked best and tell the dealer that you are there to buy if the deal is good. (In all of this, it is wise to remember that you want to *buy*, not *be sold*, a car.) Now is the time to trot out your trade-in and deal for the best price. It is your turn to be the car dealer here, so talk up your old car. Say that you've had better offers (even if you haven't) if you feel your car is being undervalued. And it will be undervalued at first. That's car trading. Tell the dealer that you know that the "blue book" value is above what was offered and that you know what other dealers are selling your model for. Eventurally you will reach a price that is less than you'd like to get but more than the original offer. If the new price seems in line, take it.

7 Before you drive the deal home, tell the dealer that you want to take his car to a mechanic to have it checked. Dealers will usually let you do this, although some may have reservations about letting the car off the lot overnight.

8 Do have the car checked by a mechanic. It shouldn't cost more than $20 to $30, and a mechanic has the ability to *hear* things you'd miss, a sixth sense to diagnose them, and the hoists and equipment to check the car fully. Unless the mechanic is a personal buddy, don't tell where you got the car.

Financing Your New Used Car

When you are satisfied that the car is the one you want, go back and buy the car. If you have to finance the cost, be sure you can pay down at least 30 percent of the total price of the car, including sales tax, license, and registration fees. Check the various finance deals offered by the dealer, your bank, and local finance companies. Car financing is very complex, with a great deal of opportunity for you to lose your shirt, so check carefully. There have been books written on the subject, and I'd rather you got professional advice than the superficial coverage I could offer you here.

Getting a Guarantee or Warranty

Most dealers have some sort of **guarantee** arrangement, although almost no used cars carry warranties. If the car is a very late model, its original **warranty** may still be in effect, but I'd question why such a new car has been traded in so soon.

The basic guarantee is a 50–50 split between you and the dealer to cover any repairs that have to be made within the first 30 days. I don't care for it, because if the car turns out to need major work, you are going to get hung for half the retail cost of the parts and labor involved in the job, while a dealer with service facilities or good friends is only going to pay cost for parts and about half the retail cost of the labor. So it isn't really a 50–50 split. However, if that's the best you can do, and if a good mechanic has checked the car and it seems to be in good shape, then take the deal and cross your fingers. But try for a full money-back guarantee over the first few weeks to cover surprises. One major used-car dealer offers "a full refund toward the purchase of any of our other cars if you are not satisfied with the one you've bought." Of course a dealer may not have another car you want, so this is not the best deal.

If a dealer refuses to let you take the car to a mechanic for a checkup or refuses to consider any kind of a guarantee, RUN! If he has no faith in your chances of happiness with that car, he probably knows what he is *not* talking about.

This is not meant to replace having a professional mechanic check a car you are ready to buy. But it is the best way to decide whether the car is worth considering, and it may be your only chance if you are buying from a private party who has a lot of other interested people waiting to view the car. Besides, as I've already pointed out, it will impress the dealers no end, and possibly prevent them from trying to sell you a car that is not in good shape.

How to Check Out a Used Car Yourself

When Herb and I went looking for Sylvester, I had the most marvelous time checking out the prospects. Most used-car dealers we encountered tended to be "old-boy" types, who were convinced that the only thing the "little lady" would be interested in was the color of the car. When I asked one of them to open the hood, he said, "Will you know what you're looking at if I do?" That fellow's eyes popped as I wrenched open the master cylinder and poked around. "What is she doing?" he asked my husband in astonishment. "Oh, she's a mechanic," Herb replied. "I'm just along for the ride." The salesman wiped his brow, "Now I've seen everything," he murmured. After I got through telling him what was wrong with the car and what it would probably cost to fix it we left.

1 First, walk around the car and just form a general opinion of it. Does it have "good vibes," or do you get a general impression of seediness? If that's how it looks to you, that's how it will look to others when you drive it.

Checking the Outside of the Car

2 If the car has severe dents or very chipped paint, then prepare to add the cost of body work and maybe a paint job to the price of the car.

3 Sight along the sides of the car to catch ripples in the light reflections from the surface of the body. If the reflection is distorted, it can reveal body work, spot welds, and paint cover-up after an accident.

4 Look at the chrome trim. You can have a bumper rechromed for about half the cost of a new one($20 to $30 for rechroming), or you can find a good bumper at a wrecker's if the car is a popular model. Trim is usually cheap to replace, ditto hub caps; but a grill is hard to find and expensive, even at a wrecker's.

5 Check for rust around the headlights and trim and on the underside of the car. This will need immediate removal and a paint touch-up because rust is a "disease" and tends to spread if not checked immediately. If the car is old and has recently had an undercoating, this may have been done to hide the fact that the bottom has rusted out. If you live in an area that gets snow in the winter, check the underside for corrosion due to the salt put on the streets. You may have trouble finding a pre-1970 car in such an area that has not rusted through because of these conditions.

6 Look at the windshield and at the rear window. The glass is expensive to replace, and cracks tend to enlarge with time. If the glass is cracked or severely scratched by the wiper blades, you will have to replace it. Side windows and side vents are generally much cheaper to replace.

7 Look for sagging doors, loose door handles, and trunk and hood lids that don't fit properly. These could mean that the car has been thrown out of line in an accident. If it's been driven a lot since then, parts of that car are now dangerously worn.

8 Check under the hood, in the trunk, and around the door jambs for signs of repainting. If the car is new and has recently been repainted, it has probably been wrecked and restored. If it is quite old and is otherwise in good condition, consider the new paint a plus.

9 Look under the car for signs of a bent **frame**, spot welding, etc. These are clues to accidents. If you see them, don't buy.

10 Check the **tires**; they will tell you how the car was driven.

a If the outside treads of the tires are worn, the car has probably been driven hard and is worn out. (See the tire chapter for pictures of tire wear.) If only the front tires show this kind of wear, the car probably just needs wheel realignment.

b If the tires are unevenly worn, either the car is out of **alignment** or, simply, the wheels are poorly **balanced**. Having the wheels realigned or balanced is not expensive, but you may have to get new tires if the present ones are in bad shape.

c If the tires simply show signs of overinflation or underinflation, correction is no problem.

d If the tires are worn *very* unevenly, or cupped, steering, suspension, shock absorbers, or brakes may be defective. Draw this to the attention of your mechanic if the car is otherwise O.K. and you are having it checked.

e If the tires are worn evenly but are very worn, the car has at least 20,000 miles on it no matter what they tell you.

f Is there a spare tire? Is it in good shape? If not, you will have to pay for a new one. Does a **jack** go with the car? Do you need one?

g Grab the top edge of each of the front tires and try to pull it toward you and push it away from you. If you hear a clunking sound or if there is a lot of movement, the **wheel bearings** may be worn or out of adjustment.

h If you can, get a rear wheel off the ground, jiggle it up and down. If there is any up-and-down movement of the wheel while the axle remains stationary, the rear axle bearing may be worn. The **axle** and the wheel should move as a unit.

11 To check for sagging **springs**, look at the profile of the car as it sits in the lot. The front and rear ends should be on the same level—also the left and right sides of the car. Lean on the front and rear fenders on each side and let go. Do you hear squeaks? Sometimes these mean that lubrication is needed; sometimes they mean that the suspension has had it.

12 Check the **shock absorbers** by stepping on the front and rear bumpers and placing your weight on them. Then take your weight off the car abruptly. If the car continues to bounce up and down for a while, the shocks are worn. The car should return to its former level and stay there when you take your weight off it. New shocks can cost as much as $20 each. You can get them for under $5, but installation is expensive unless you install them yourself at an auto class.

13 Back the car up a car length and take a look at the surface of the lot where it was parked. Are there fresh spots or puddles on the paving? Dip your finger into each one:

a If it's water, check the **radiator** and hoses for leaks.

b If it's black oil, figure out which part of the car was over the puddle and check for leaks around the **oil drain plug**, the **crankcase**, the engine, etc.

c If it looks like a light fluid, check around the **master cylinder**, **brake lines**, and in back of the wheels for **brake fluid** leaks (depending on which part of the car had been parked over the puddle or spot).

    d If the leak seems to be pink oil and is coming from under the center part of the car, check the **transmission** for leaks. In all cases, just run your hands around the area, if you can reach it, and *feel* for wetness.

    e If it smells like gasoline, check around the **fuel pump** and the **carburetor** if the leak is near the hood area. If it came from the center of the car, check the **fuel lines**. Check the **fuel tank** if it came from the rear.

14 Ask how long the car has been standing in that spot; it's possible that the leaks have come from another car. Later, if you take the car off the lot for a test drive or to have a mechanic check it, park it and let it stand for about 15 minutes; then back up and again check the pavement for leaks.

Checking the Inside of the Car

Now open the door and get in. Look around you.

1 Is the rug in good shape? Is the upholstery torn? It will cost money to buy a new rug or to repair or recover the seats.

2 Is the lining of the roof torn? More expense.

3 Are the springs in the seats sagging? Forget the car—new seats are expensive.

4 Worn floor mats and pedal covers are cheap to replace, but they may mean that the car has been driven many miles.

5 Try to move the steering wheel without starting the car. If there is more than 2 inches of play in the steering wheel before the wheels begin to move, the steering is unsafe.

6 Put the **emergency brake** on, and turn the key in the ignition. With the car in "Park," look at the gauges. A broken gauge can be replaced cheaply, but if the gauges are operating and indicate low oil pressure, a discharging **alternator**, brake trouble, etc., then be wary of buying the car.

    a While you have the motor running, try out the windshield wipers and washers, the clock, and the radio. Are they working properly? How about the heater, the defroster, and the air conditioner (if there is one)?

    b Turn on the headlights. Check to see if the directional signal flashers on the dashboard are working. If they aren't, check the directional lights in the front and rear. Have a friend look to see if the headlights are on and if they go to high beam when you press the button. Have your friend look at the brake lights to see if they go on when you step on the brake, and at the back-up lights to see if they are functioning.

7 Now race the engine, still in "Park" or "Neutral," with the emergency brake on. Have someone look to see if there is smoke coming out of the **tail pipe**.

  a If it is a cold morning, you may see some white water vapor. Disregard it if it stops when the car warms up.

  b If white vapor continues to come out of the tail pipe after the car is warm, a cracked **engine block** or **cylinder head** may be letting water leak into the engine.

  c If black smoke comes out of the tail pipe, you may need only to adjust the carburetor because the **fuel/air mixture** is too rich. You can check this by running your finger around the inside edge of the tail pipe (make sure first that it is not hot). If carbon comes off on your finger, the mixture is probably too rich. Ask your mechanic to adjust it if you take it in for a checkup.

  d If there is light or dark-blue smoke coming out of the tail pipe, the car is burning oil. This can indicate that the car needs its **piston rings** replaced because oil is leaking into the **combustion chambers**. Forget the car. Rebuilding the engine can cost as much as $300 to $1,000 (and that's why the previous owner probably wanted to get rid of the car). Even if the smoke means only that the oil was not changed and has been allowed to get so low and cruddy that it is smoking, this would indicate that the moving parts of the engine are worn owing to improper **lubrication**.

  e If the smoke is light gray, the car is burning **transmission fluid**. Check the transmission **dipstick**. Is the fluid dark and burned-looking, or does it smell? Have the transmission checked carefully by your mechanic if you are still interested in the car. If there are signs of transmission trouble, forget the car completely. Sometimes a faulty **vacuum modulator** can suck transmission fluid into the engine, where it is burned in the **cylinders**, causing the same type of smoke to come out of the tail pipe. If this is the case, you can replace the vacuum modulator for between $5 and $10. In most cases all you do is unscrew the old one and screw in the new one. The mechanic will be able to tell you if this is the case with the car in question.

8 Shut off the engine and step on the brake (leave the engine running if it is a **power brake**). Check for sinkage of the brake pedal. It should stay put after you have depressed it. If it continues to sink slowly toward the floor, the master cylinder is probably defective. Get out and check the brake lines around the master cylinder, and behind each wheel for leaks.

9 Run the **gearshift** through each gear if the car has a **manual transmission**. Does it move smoothly, or does it stick?

Checking Under the Hood of the Car

Now lift the hood and peek in. How do things look in there? Most used-car dealers have the engine area cleaned so that it will look as though it is in mint condition. But remember that this can hide signs of repair work, or that the dealer may have opened the engine, taken a look at a worn **crankshaft**, and closed it up again. Be wary and look for signs of leaks (these don't have to be wet; sometimes stains can clue you in).

1 Look at the **radiator** and the principal hoses. Run your hands around them. Are there signs of wetness, or are there stains that show that coolant leaked the last time the car was driven (because of the pressure) and then dried up? Make a note to have the cooling system checked with the pressure tester we talked about in Chapter 8. Leaky radiator hoses can be replaced for a couple of dollars; leaky radiators can cost a lot of money to fix or replace.

  a Open the radiator cap and look in. Is there much rust floating around inside? The radiator may need flushing (which is easy to do), or it may need replacing, if it is rusted through. Ask if they've replaced the **coolant** recently.

  b Look carefully around the **water pump** to see if there are rusty areas that can indicate leaks. (In case you've forgotten, the fan is usually mounted on the water pump.)

2 Look at the **battery**. If it is very corroded (they'll have cleaned up the acid deposits, but the cables will tell the story), you will need a new one. Maybe the dealer would like to throw one in as part of the deal. Look inside the battery. Is it filled with water?

3 Look at the engine.

  a Run your finger around the edge of the **cylinder head** where it meets the **rocker arm cover**. Is oil leaking out? You may need a new **gasket**. That's not too expensive if you replace it yourself. You'll have to unscrew the bolts, pull off the head, remove the old gasket, put in the new one, and screw everything back. Just make sure to tighten all the bolts a little at first, then go back and tighten them all down, skipping from front to back and from side to side to get the pressure even. Don't tighten them so hard that you crush the gasket, however, or it will leak again.

  b Look at the **core plugs** in the sides of the engine. Are there signs that these have been leaking? They can cost as much as $75 to $80 if they must all be replaced. If only one plug looks rusty, the others probably have as much rust and will soon begin to leak, too.

  c Check the engine block, cylinder heads, and **manifolds** for cracks or rust (which can indicate leaks). If you find cracks, RUN!

  d Check around the **crankcase** and the **oil pan**. Are there leaks there?

e Check the oil dipstick. Is the oil clean? Does it have particles in it? Is the level low? This can indicate a leak or just poor maintenance. Does the dipstick have drops of water on it? They could be there because the car has been driven too long without an oil change, or they could be clues to a blown head gasket or a cracked block that has allowed water to leak into the oil. Ask when the **oil**, **oil filter**, **air filter**, and **fuel filter** were last replaced. Most dealers will replace these as a matter of routine when getting a car ready for resale. If they haven't, they should do it as part of the deal. If you're buying from a private party, you'll have to do it yourself, but the whole mess will cost you only about $10.

f Feel the hoses that run into and out of the engine. Are they cracked or leaky? Sticky? Soft and mushy? Stiff or brittle? If they have any of these symptoms they will have to be replaced or they could blow at any time. Again, not a big expense if you do it yourself. Actually, the dealer should do it for you.

4 Now ask the dealer to take off the air cleaner (or do it yourself). Notice if the filter has been changed recently. If it is really filthy, the car may not have been properly maintained.

5 Look at the carburetor. Are there signs of leaking fuel from the bottom or from the gasket area where the top of the carburetor meets the **float bowl**? If you haven't run the engine yet, is the choke closed? It should be.

a Look at the inside of the hood itself, above the carburetor. Can you see a **blow-by** stain? Have the **PCV valve** and the compression checked.

b Start the car again, with the **air cleaner** off. Did the choke open after a while? Remember to be careful about looking down a strange **carburetor barrel** while the engine is running, it could possibly backfire in your face.

c Move the **throttle** linkage with your finger. Does it move easily? Does the car rev up promptly? Shut off the engine and move the throttle linkage again while you peer carefully into the carburetor barrel. Does fuel squirt into the **venturi** when you move the throttle? It should. A carburetor may simply need adjusting to make it run well—or it may need to be taken apart and cleaned (that's called "rebuilding"). If you think the carburetor needs to be rebuilt or replaced, think twice about the car. At any rate, checking the carburetor is a good way to shake a dealer into a better deal. Replace the air cleaner.

6 Take off the **oil filler cap** and listen to the engine. How do the **valves** sound? Are there ticking, rattling, or clunking noises coming from inside the engine? Valve jobs are expensive, and even worse things could be happening in there.

7 Is the engine shaking around a lot while the car is running? One or more cylinders could be **misfiring** because of a loose connection, bad wiring, or a carburetor that needs adjusting. If the shaking occurs only when you are stepping on the gas and accelerating, the cause could be the engine mounts. These can be replaced—for more money.

8 With the emergency brake on, put the car in "Park" or "Neutral" and check the **transmission dipstick** if you haven't already done so.

9 Take a screwdriver and open the top of the **master cylinder**. If you've forgotten how, see Chapter 10. Look inside. Is the **brake fluid** clean? Is it up to the fill line of both compartments?If it is low, there may be a leak in the lines or in a wheel cylinder. Do the rubber cups on the lid look to be in good shape? Replace the cover and run your hands around the sides and base of the master cylinder. Are there any signs of leaks? Look at the **firewall** behind and next to the cylinder. Are there any signs of wet or dried leaks?

10 Wiggle the **distributor** to see if it is loose. If there is a lot of play, the timing will be off. Check the **distributor cap** for frayed wires and cracks.

11 Remove the wire from the center of the distributor cap and lay it on a metal part of the car to ground it. Have someone crank the engine. Listen for uneven cranking. This can clue you into uncovering a poor **starter**, or broken teeth on the flywheel.

How to Road-Test the Car

Now you are ready to take the car on the road.

1 Find a quiet nearby street where you can check the **brakes**. With your seat belt on, check to be sure that there is no one behind you and then hit the brakes. Does the car pull to one side? This can indicate a leak or worn linings. Do the brakes squeal? They may need to be replaced. How long does it take to stop the car comfortably at the end of the block?

2 Drive slowly down the block with your hands off the wheel. Does the car pull to one side? The **steering linkage** may be damaged, or the front end may need **alignment**. The first is a no-no. The second is not costly.

3 Vary your speed; shift from forward to reverse. The engine should not race, and there should be no slams, jerks, or howls from the **transmission** during these shifts.

4 If the car has a **manual transmission**, check the **clutch** for slippage. Run through the gears. Does the **gearshift** work smoothly? Does the car hesitate or make grinding noises when you shift? What about the **clutch free pedal play**? Is there a $1/2$ to 1 inch of movement before it starts to disengage? Does the clutch chatter?

5 Drive a car with a manual transmission at a low speed and shift it into high gear. Then accelerate. The engine should stall and die if the clutch is in good shape. If the clutch is slipping, the engine will speed up but not the car. This is a bad sign. It is one of those few circumstances when stalling out is good news.

6 Have a friend watch while you drive the car slowly. Do the wheels wobble? The cause may be a bent wheel. If you really want the car, try the spare.

7 Are you comfortable in the car? Adjust the seats. Can you see well? How about the rear and side mirrors? Do you feel at home?

8 Head for the freeway if there is one nearby. Does the car handle well? If the front wheels shimmy, you may need an **alignment**, or the front end may be badly worn.

9 What is the car's pickup like when you accelerate, pass, or start? Is there enough power? If it has an **automatic transmission**, does it move smoothly from low to higher gears? Is there **overdrive**?

10 Drive up a hill if you can. How does the low gear feel? Does the car "just make it" up the hill? Or does it sail up smoothly, with power to spare?

11 Drive down an alley or driveway. Open the car windows and shut off the radio if it's been on. Can you hear clanking or grinding noises coming from the rear wheels? This can indicate worn rear-**axle bearings**. Check them when you get back according to the instructions in the early part of this chapter, or have a mechanic take a look.

12 When you get back home, look at the engine again for signs of leaks that may have opened up under the pressure of driving. If the car seemed to lack power, or felt "funny," you might want to run a **compression check** on the engine. This will tell you how well the **cylinders**, **pistons**, **rings**, and **valves** have worn. Look for instructions at the end of Chapter 14, or have a mechanic do it.

Before you get back to the dealer, stop and evaluate what you've discovered about the car (of course, you've been taking notes, right?). On the next page is a chart that will give you a general idea of what your findings mean in terms of expense and the future performance of the car. Actually, all these items should be taken care of by the dealer as part of the deal. A used car, bought from a dealer, is supposed to be in good condition unless it is advertised as needing work. Some states require a recent state inspection sticker before a car can be sold or

**How to Evaluate
What
You've Found**

Repair Evaluation Chart

Baddies	Think Twice About These	Cheapies
I Wreck Indicators	Needs new shock absorbers	Minor dents
Extensive dents, rust, and chips	Needs new springs	Needs front-end alignment
Misalignment of hood, trunk lid, or doors	Needs new carburetor	Needs new throttle linkage
Welded or bent frame under car	Needs new master cylinder	Needs carburetor adjustment
New paint job on a new car	Needs complete brake job	Needs new gauges, knobs, switches, wiper blades, lighter, etc.
II High Expense Items	Self-adjusting brakes out of adjustment (possibly expensive)	
Transmission leaks or poor performance	Needs new alternator, radiator, starter, muffler, flywheel, or distributor	Radio needs to be repaired
Blue smoke coming from tailpipe (unless due to faulty vacuum modulator)		Clock doesn't work
Cracked block, head, or manifold	Needs seats recovered	Needs horn, lights, or signals repaired
Valves need to be reground or replaced	Needs new side windows or vents	Needs hoses replaced
Grille missing or damaged	Needs a new rug	Needs a tune-up
Needs four new tires	Needs new chrome, or new bumper	Needs manual brakes adjusted
Needs new windshield or rear window	Needs pollution device required by law	Needs a spare tire, or just two tires
Clutch worn or defective		Needs new fan belts
Rear axle worn or damaged		(The dealer should definitely supply all of the above. In some states the law requires that the brake system, muffler, pollution devices, steering, suspension, horn, and lights be in safe condition before the car is sold.)
Steering linkage and front-end suspension worn or damaged		
Needs extensive body work or complete paint job		
Needs new seats because seat springs are shot		
Needs new convertible top, or interior		
Needs new crankshaft, driveshaft, etc.		

reregistered. If your dealer is *required* to furnish this, then he will have to fix anything found below standard if you have the car reinspected after you buy it. If you are buying from a private party or must undertake the work yourself for some reason, a good rule of thumb is, if any of the conditions listed in the "Baddies" column exists, forget the car. These problems are either unsolvable, and will lead to the quick demise of the vehicle, or they are much too costly to handle. The only time you might want to fool with any of these problems is if you are dealing with a truly classic car that will go up in value by *thousands* of dollars once it is restored. Add up the probable cost of the work required plus the cost of the car, and see if it compares favorably with the going price for that car in recent newspaper ads.

The middle column lists repairs that would cost more than $50. It may be worth while to invest if only one of these repairs is needed; but more than one of these repairs will mean $100 or more, unless you do the job yourself. And you can probably find another car that does not require expensive work.

The last column lists repairs and replacements that most used cars require. None of these is very costly—maybe $30 tops—especially since you can do most of these yourself with little or no expertise. Of course if most of the repairs and replacements are necessary, the car is probably more trouble than it's worth, unless you have a lot of time on your hands.

Evaluating Your Own Car

One final thing. Even if you are not in the market for a used car and have just read this chapter on your first sweep through the book, it might be useful to go out to your own car and run it through these checks. This will give you a good idea of the car's general condition and tell you whether or not it is worth investing your time and effort. These checks will also pinpoint the areas to concentrate on when you are ready to put down the book and go to work. Remember, whether you want to keep a good car in good condition without paying dearly to have someone else do the maintenance, or you simply want to keep your old heap running just a little longer without spending a lot of money on it, and whether you want the satisfaction of "doing it yourself," or are convinced that a well-tuned, well-maintained car will consume less fuel and contribute less to the air pollution, you won't be able to realize any of these goals unless you stop procrastinating and start *working*. Don't finish these pages and say, "Yes, I must try some of these things someday." You'll never find the time or the opportunity that way. This book will just join all the others on the shelf. So *make a commitment* right now! Whether it's running your car through these checks, or going out and buying a set of socket wrenches, or just changing your air filter, DO IT NOW. Once you've made any kind of an effort to get intimately involved with your car, you will find you'll want to carry the relationship further.

If your car hasn't had a tune-up lately, pick a day when you know you'll have a couple of free hours, and plan to change your spark plugs and install new points and a condenser in your distributor. Before the day comes, buy the spark plugs and the distributor kit and round up the tools you'll need—even if you have to borrow them. Or plan to change your oil (anybody can do that!) and buy the oil and the oil filter *now*.

Once you've spent a couple of dollars, you will make the time to get the job done. Don't put things off by planning to do *everything* in this book when your next vacation rolls around. Most of these things can be done in from fifteen minutes to three hours. Then, you can spend your vacation driving your happy, peppy car to all those lovely places you've been meaning to visit.

And the best part of it all will be that both you and your car will have the satisfaction of knowing that, when it comes to auto repair, you're not a dummy anymore!

[*On the following pages you will find a Specifications Record and a Maintenance Record. If you make photocopies of them before you fill them in, you'll have them for several cars and be able to take them to the store with you when you go to buy parts.*]

Specifications Record Checklist

Specifications Record

Item	Car #1	Car #2	Car #3
Manufacturer			
Make			
Model			
Year			
Number of Cylinders			
Auto. or Standard Transmission			
Engine Displacement			
Type of Carburetor			
Air Conditioned?			
Smog Devices?			
Horsepower			
Dwell			
Contact Point Cap			
Distributor Kit Number			
Spark Plug Gap			
Spark Plug Number			
Cylinder Firing Order			
Ignition Timing			
Oil Weight			
Oil Capacity			
Oil Filter Number			
Coolant Capacity ($\frac{1}{2}$ total cooling system capacity)			
Air Filter Number			
Fuel Filter Number			
Tire Size			
Min. & Max. Tire Pressure			

Maintenance Record

CAR:_____   FROM:_____ TO:_____

	J	F	M	A	M	J	J	A	S	O	N	D
I. Under-the-Hood Checklist (once a month or every 1,000 miles)												
Checked Coolant Level	☐	☐	☐	☐	☐	☐	☐	☐	☐	☐	☐	☐
Flushed System and Changed Coolant (once a year)	☐	☐	☐	☐	☐	☐	☐	☐	☐	☐	☐	☐
Checked Fan Belt	☐	☐	☐	☐	☐	☐	☐	☐	☐	☐	☐	☐
Changed Fan Belt (if frayed)	☐	☐	☐	☐	☐	☐	☐	☐	☐	☐	☐	☐
Checked Battery	☐	☐	☐	☐	☐	☐	☐	☐	☐	☐	☐	☐
Replaced Battery (as needed)	☐	☐	☐	☐	☐	☐	☐	☐	☐	☐	☐	☐
Checked Oil Level	☐	☐	☐	☐	☐	☐	☐	☐	☐	☐	☐	☐
Changed Oil (every 2–3000 miles or 90 days)	☐	☐	☐	☐	☐	☐	☐	☐	☐	☐	☐	☐
Replaced Oil Filter (every other oil change)	☐	☐	☐	☐	☐	☐	☐	☐	☐	☐	☐	☐
Checked Automatic Transmission Fluid Level	☐	☐	☐	☐	☐	☐	☐	☐	☐	☐	☐	☐
Last Added Automatic Transmission Fluid	☐	☐	☐	☐	☐	☐	☐	☐	☐	☐	☐	☐
Checked Brake Fluid Level	☐	☐	☐	☐	☐	☐	☐	☐	☐	☐	☐	☐
Last Added Brake Fluid	☐	☐	☐	☐	☐	☐	☐	☐	☐	☐	☐	☐
Checked Power Stearing Fluid Level	☐	☐	☐	☐	☐	☐	☐	☐	☐	☐	☐	☐
Last Added Fluid	☐	☐	☐	☐	☐	☐	☐	☐	☐	☐	☐	☐
Checked Windshield Washer Fluid Level	☐	☐	☐	☐	☐	☐	☐	☐	☐	☐	☐	☐
Checked Windshield Wiper Blades	☐	☐	☐	☐	☐	☐	☐	☐	☐	☐	☐	☐
Replaced Windshield Wiper Blades	☐	☐	☐	☐	☐	☐	☐	☐	☐	☐	☐	☐
Checked Tire Pressure (don't forget the spare!)	☐	☐	☐	☐	☐	☐	☐	☐	☐	☐	☐	☐
Replaced Tires (record details below) (miles)	☐	☐	☐	☐	☐	☐	☐	☐	☐	☐	☐	☐
Checked Wiring	☐	☐	☐	☐	☐	☐	☐	☐	☐	☐	☐	☐
Replaced Wires (record details below)	☐	☐	☐	☐	☐	☐	☐	☐	☐	☐	☐	☐

(continued)

000-337

Maintenance Record Checklist

	J	F	M	A	M	J	J	A	S	O	N	D
Checked Hoses	☐	☐	☐	☐	☐	☐	☐	☐	☐	☐	☐	☐
Replaced Hoses (record details below)	☐	☐	☐	☐	☐	☐	☐	☐	☐	☐	☐	☐

II. Tune-Up Time Checklist
(every 10,000 miles or 6 months—more often if necessary)

	J	F	M	A	M	J	J	A	S	O	N	D
Checked Air Filter	☐	☐	☐	☐	☐	☐	☐	☐	☐	☐	☐	☐
Replaced Air Filter (once a year or every 20,000 miles)	☐	☐	☐	☐	☐	☐	☐	☐	☐	☐	☐	☐
Checked Fuel Filter	☐	☐	☐	☐	☐	☐	☐	☐	☐	☐	☐	☐
Replaced Fuel Filter (once a year or every 20,000 miles)	☐	☐	☐	☐	☐	☐	☐	☐	☐	☐	☐	☐
Checked PCV Valve	☐	☐	☐	☐	☐	☐	☐	☐	☐	☐	☐	☐
Cleaned or Replaced PCV Valve (every 12,000 miles)	☐	☐	☐	☐	☐	☐	☐	☐	☐	☐	☐	☐
Checked Spark Plugs (cleaned and regapped them)	☐	☐	☐	☐	☐	☐	☐	☐	☐	☐	☐	☐
Changed Spark Plugs (every 10,000 miles or 6 months—more often if burnt or worn—less often with electronic ignition system)	☐	☐	☐	☐	☐	☐	☐	☐	☐	☐	☐	☐
Checked Points, Dwell, & Point Gap	☐	☐	☐	☐	☐	☐	☐	☐	☐	☐	☐	☐
Changed Points, Condenser, & Rotor (every 10,000 miles or 6 months—more often if burnt or worn—not necessary with electronic ignition system)	☐	☐	☐	☐	☐	☐	☐	☐	☐	☐	☐	☐
Checked Timing	☐	☐	☐	☐	☐	☐	☐	☐	☐	☐	☐	☐
Adjusted Carburetor	☐	☐	☐	☐	☐	☐	☐	☐	☐	☐	☐	☐
Cleaned or Rebuilt Carburetor (when needed)	☐	☐	☐	☐	☐	☐	☐	☐	☐	☐	☐	☐

III. Lubrication & Brake Checklist

	J	F	M	A	M	J	J	A	S	O	N	D
Checked Grease Fittings (every 2–3000 miles)	☐	☐	☐	☐	☐	☐	☐	☐	☐	☐	☐	☐
Lubricated Steering & Suspension (every 2–3000 miles or as needed)	☐	☐	☐	☐	☐	☐	☐	☐	☐	☐	☐	☐
Had Complete Professional Lube Job (once or twice a year)	☐	☐	☐	☐	☐	☐	☐	☐	☐	☐	☐	☐
Checked Brakes (every 10,000 miles)	☐	☐	☐	☐	☐	☐	☐	☐	☐	☐	☐	☐
Had Brakes Rebuilt (record details below)	☐	☐	☐	☐	☐	☐	☐	☐	☐	☐	☐	☐

	J	F	M	A	M	J	J	A	S	O	N	D
Checked Wheel Bearings (every 10,000 miles)	☐	☐	☐	☐	☐	☐	☐	☐	☐	☐	☐	☐
Repacked Front Wheel Bearings (every 10,000 miles or as needed)	☐	☐	☐	☐	☐	☐	☐	☐	☐	☐	☐	☐
Checked Shock Absorbers	☐	☐	☐	☐	☐	☐	☐	☐	☐	☐	☐	☐
Replaced Shock Absorbers (as needed)	☐	☐	☐	☐	☐	☐	☐	☐	☐	☐	☐	☐
Had Front-End Alignment (as needed)	☐	☐	☐	☐	☐	☐	☐	☐	☐	☐	☐	☐

IV. Parts Replacement Record

Part   Date and Details

Wiring
(coil wire, ignition wires, spark plug boots, etc.

_____

_____

_____

Hoses
(top or bottom radiator hose, vacuum hoses,
fuel lines, etc.)

_____

_____

_____

Brakes
(shoes, relined, drums turned, etc.)

_____

_____

_____

Tires
(which one? where did new tire go?)

_____

_____

_____

Other Parts

_____

_____

_____

SCLAP
000-339

A Practical Glossary of Automotive Terms

[Words appearing in italics are defined elsewhere in the Glossary.]

accelerator   the gas pedal.

accelerator pump   the part of the *carburetor* which provides an extra squirt of fuel to enrich the *fuel/air mixture* and thus enables the car to respond swiftly to increased acceleration when you depress the gas pedal suddenly.

additives   substances that are added to such products as *coolant* and engine *oil* to enable them to perform better, last longer, and provide secondary benefits. Popular additives are rust preventers (in coolant and oil), *viscosity* extenders (in oil), lubricants (in coolant), and preservatives (in foods).

air cleaner   a metal can located atop the *carburetor* which contains an *air filter*, which removes dust and dirt from the air before it enters the carburetor. Also acts as a flame arrester in case of backfire.

air filter   the element in the *air cleaner* that removes impurities from the air. Some air filters are disposable; others can be cleaned and reused.

air horn   the tubular passage through which air travels to the *air cleaner* and the *carburetor*. See *venturi*.

air-cooled engine   an engine that uses air instead of water in its *cooling system*. Most Volkswagens have air-cooled engines.

alignment   the procedure for adjusting the position of the front wheels to improve handling and performance and to reduce *tire* wear. See *camber, caster, toe-in, toe-out, steering-axis inclination* and *turning radius*.

allen wrench   a wrench with a solid hexagonal head that fits into the hexagonal hole in some set screws or bolts.

alternator   generates electric current that is stored in the *battery* and is used to start the car and run the electrical equipment. Alternators generate alternating current (AC). Alternators have replaced *generators* that produced direct current (DC) but otherwise performed the same functions on older cars.

antifreeze   see *coolant*.

automatic choke   a *choke* that automatically adjusts the amount of air entering the *carburetor* by sensing changes in engine temperature. See *thermostatic coil choke, thermostatic spring choke*.

automatic transmission   a *transmission* that selects gears automatically by means of a *hydraulically* driven system of *bands* and plates.

axle   a solid metal shaft to which the rear wheels of a vehicle are attached. On most cars, the rear *axle* spins at right angles to the *drive train* and transmits the power to the rear wheels. See *spindle*.

backflushing   See *flushing the cooling system*.

ball joint   a movable joint found on the *steering linkage* and *suspension system* of a car that allows the front wheels to move like a door hinge. See *boot, grease fitting, zerk fitting*.

bands   *automatic transmissions* rely on *hydraulic* pressure to change gears by means of a system of friction *bands* and plates. These bands can be adjusted externally without taking the *transmission* apart. Adjusting the bands is part of normal transmission service.

battery   a box filled with a solution of water and acid called *electrolyte* which contains metal plates that store current generated by the *alternator* and deliver it to the parts of the car that operate electrically. See *ground, negative terminal, positive terminal,* and *electrical system*.

bearings   antifriction devices that are usually found between two moving parts. For instance, in your car the babbit bearings found between the *connecting rod* and the *crankshaft* are lubricated and cushioned with *oil*, and the front wheel *bearings* must be repacked with *grease* at regular intervals. Bearings can be ball- or roller-type.

bleeding brakes   a method for removing air bubbles from the *brake lines* in order to allow the brakes to operate more efficiently.

blow-by   a *fuel/air mixture* under compression which is lost past the *piston rings* and causes fumes that form acid and *sludge* in the *crankcase* and smoking from the *oil filler hole*.

blue book   a listing of the current prices for used cars published by the National Automobile Dealers Association (NADA). Available at banks, loan offices, libraries, and insurance companies.

boots   the rubber or plastic covers located at either end of the spark-plug cables to insulate the connections between the cable ends and the *spark plug* and *distributor* terminals. Always grasp the cable by the boot when removing it. Also, the protective cover of the *ball joint* that holds the *grease*. See *grease fitting*.

bore   the width or diameter of the *cylinder* hole. See *stroke*.

brake backing plate   a metal plate, located inside the *brake drum*, on which the *wheel cylinder, brake shoes*, and other brake parts are mounted.

brake drums   metal drums mounted on each wheel. The *brake shoes* press against the inner surfaces of the drums to slow or stop the car. See *brake system*.

brake fluid   the liquid used in the *hydraulic brake system* to stop or slow the car.

brake lines   a system of hoses and metal tubes through which the *brake fluid* flows from the *master cylinder* to the brakes at each wheel. See *brake system*.

brake lining a heat-resistant asbestos material that is attached to the *brake shoe*. When the shoe is pressed against the *brake drum*, the lining grabs the inside of the drum, which stops the car and also prevents the drum and the shoe from wearing each other away.

brake shoes curved pieces of metal with heat-resistant surfaces that are forced against the *brake drums* to slow or stop the car.

brake system a system that uses *hydraulic* pressure to enable your car to slow and stop safely. Consists of the *master cylinder*, *brake lines*, and *disc* or *drum brakes* at each wheel. See *brake drums*, *brake fluid*, *brake lines*, *brake lining*, *brake shoes*, *parking brake*, *power brakes*, *wheel cylinder*.

breaker plate the movable plate inside the *distributor* to which the *points* and the *condenser* are affixed.

breaker points see *points*.

bushing a protective liner that cushions noise, friction, or movement. Rubber bushings on the *suspension system* should be lubricated regularly.

butterfly valve a small metal disc that controls the flow of air into the *carburetor*. See *choke*, *throttle*.

calipers devices on *disc brakes* which hold the disc pads and press them against the disc to stop or slow the car.

cam a metal disc with irregularly shaped *lobes* used in the *camshaft* to activate the opening and closing of the *valves* and, in the *distributor*, to force the *points* to open.

cam lobes the bumps on a *cam* that contact and activate such devices as the lifters, which operate the *valves*, and the *rubbing block*, which causes the *points* to open and close, as the cam spins with the *distributor shaft*.

camber a wheel *alignment* adjustment of the inward or outward tilt of the top of the wheel when viewed from the front of the car. Improves handling and cuts *tire wear*.

camshaft a shaft with *cam lobes* which causes the *valves* to open and close. See *overhead cam*, *push rods*, *rocker arms*.

carburetor a device that *vaporizes* fuel and mixes it with air in proper quantities to suit the varying needs of the engine.

carburetor barrel the tubelike part of the *carburetor* through which air flows and is mixed with *vaporized* fuel. The *choke butterfly valve* is located at the top of the carburetor barrel, and the *throttle* valve is located at the bottom. Midway through, the barrel narrows, and this part is called the *venturi*. Carburetors can have one, two, or four barrels. See *dual carbs*, *four-barrel carburetor*.

caster a wheel *alignment* adjustment that positions the wheels correctly, like the casters on a chair or shopping cart, so the tires follow naturally in a forward straight line. On a turn, the wheels will tend to straighten out when the steering wheel is released.

catalytic converter a pollution-control device found on many newer cars which acts like an afterburner to reburn unburned gas in the *tail pipe*.

centrifugal advance a device found on GM cars which advances or retards the ignition spark to correspond with changes in engine speed and load. See *spark advance*, *spark retard*.

charging system a system that, using a *fan belt* driven by the engine, enables the *alternator* (or *generator*) to generate electrical current, which is stored in the *battery* and delivered to the electrically operated parts of the car.

chassis the parts of the car which are left when the body and fenders are removed.

choke the device that limits the amount of air allowed to enter the *carburetor*, thus enriching the *fuel/air mixture* and enabling the car to start and run more easily when cold. *Automatic chokes* have a *thermostatic coil* or *thermostatic spring* that activates a *butterfly valve* at the top of the *carburetor barrel*. Older cars have manually operated chokes.

circuit the path of electrical current through an *electrical system*.

clutch a device that disconnects the engine from the *transmission*, to allow the car to change gears, and then allows the engine and transmission to resume contact and turn together at a new speed. See *clutch disc*, *clutch pedal*, *engine flywheel*, *free pedal play*, *pressure plate*, *throw-out bearing*.

clutch disc a spinning plate located at the end of the *driveshaft* facing the *engine flywheel* and covered with an asbestos surface. When the *clutch* is engaged, the clutch disc is forced against the flywheel, causing the engine and the *transmission* to turn at the same speed.

clutch pedal a pedal located on the floor of the car to the left of the brake pedal on cars with *manual transmission*. When the clutch pedal is depressed, it disengages the *clutch* so the engine and the *crankshaft* can turn independently of the transmission and the driver can change gears.

coil the part of the *ignition system* which receives a small amount of electrical voltage from the *battery*, amplifies it into a big jolt of voltage, and sends it to the *spark plugs* via the *distributor*.

coil springs large metal coils, like bed *springs*, that cushion and absorb the shocks and bumps as the car is driven. They are usually found near the front wheels, but many cars have them in the rear as well. Often the *shock absorbers* run up the center of the coil springs. See *suspension system*.

combustion the intense burning of the *fuel/air mixture* in the *combustion chamber*.

combustion chamber the part of the *cylinder* where the *fuel/air mixture* is compressed by the *piston* and ignited by a spark from the *spark plug*.

compression gauge a device used to check the amount of pressure created in a *cylinder* when the *piston* is at its highest point (*TDC*) and is squeezing the *fuel/air mixture* into the smallest possible space. A poor compression-gauge reading can indicate the need for a *valve* grind, new *piston rings*, etc.

compression ratio the amount of pressure applied to the *fuel/air mixture* in the *combustion chamber*. It is determined by comparing the size of the combustion chamber, with the *piston* at its highest point (*TDC*), to the size of the *cylinder* when the piston is at its lowest point.

condenser   a small metal cylinder, usually located inside the *distributor*, that prevents electricity from arcing across the *gap* when the *points* are open by acting as a "sponge" for the excess current.

connecting rod   the metal rod that connects the *piston* to the *crankshaft* and converts the up-and-down motion of the piston into the circular motion of the spinning crankshaft. The term *throwing a rod* refers to a broken connecting rod.

contact gap   see *point gap*.

contact points   see *points*.

control arms   metal struts located at the top and bottom of the wheel *spindle*. The upper and lower control arms allow the front wheels to change direction. See *suspension system*.

coolant   an ethylene glycol solution that raises the boiling point and lowers the freezing point of the water in the *cooling system*, prevents rust and corrosion, and lubricates the *water pump*. Also called "antifreeze." Most cars require a 50–50 mixture of coolant and water.

coolant recovery kit   a small bottle that acts as a reservoir for liquid expelled from the *cooling system* through the *overflow pipe* and returns the liquid to the system when it cools down. A special radiator *pressure cap* is also part of the kit. Also called a "closed cooling system" when it is part of the original equipment.

cooling system   a system that stores, circulates, and cools a mixture of water and *coolant*, which flows through *water jackets* in the *engine block* and keeps the engine from overheating as you drive. See *fan, pressure cap, radiator, thermostat, water pump*.

core charge   "core" is an acronym for "cash on return." A sum of money is refunded for a rebuildable part that is being exchanged for a *rebuilt* part of the same type. A common core charge is for *brake shoes* that need relining.

core plugs   metal plugs in the sides of the *engine block* which can pop out because of excessive pressure and prevent the engine block from cracking. These plugs sometimes develop leaks and should then be replaced. Also called "freeze plugs."

cotter pin   a fastener shaped like a pin but split up the center. After it is inserted, the legs are bent up or around to keep it in place.

crankcase   the lower portion of the engine where the *crankshaft* is located. At the bottom of the crankcase is the *oil pan*.

cranking   the act of engaging the *starter* by turning the key in the *ignition switch* which makes the engine *turn over*. In the old days, a hand crank was used to do this, hence the term "cranking."

cranking circuit   see *starting system*.

crankshaft   the main rotating shaft in the engine. The *connecting rods* transmit power from the *pistons* to the *crankshaft*, which, in turn, transmits power to the *driveshaft* and, eventually, to the rear wheels.

crankshaft pulley   a wheel attached to the front end of the *crankshaft* which is connected by *fan belts* to the *fan*, the *alternator*, and other devices so that the rotating crankshaft can drive these other parts as well. The crankshaft pulley usually has *timing marks* located on it, and these are necessary for checking and adjusting *timing* with a *timing light*. Also called a "harmonic balance wheel."

creeper   a platform on wheels that allows you to move around easily while lying on your back when you work under your car.

cross-shaft lug wrench   see *lug wrench*.

cylinder   a hollow tube-shaped pipe in the *engine block*. The *piston* rides up and down in the cylinder to compress the *fuel/air mixture* that drives the engine.

cylinder block   see *engine block*.

cylinder head   the part of the engine above the *engine block* which contains the *combustion chambers* and, usually, the *valves*. The *spark plugs* screw into the side of the cylinder head. On most cars a *valve cover* or a *rocker-arm cover* is located on top of the cylinder head.

cylinder sequence   the order in which the *cylinders* are located on a particular car. It is necessary to locate the #1 cylinder in order to check and adjust *timing* with a *timing light*, and the #1 cylinder may be at the front of the engine on a U.S.-made straight 4- or 6-cylinder engine and at the rear of the engine on a foreign-made car. See *firing order*.

diesel engine   a *fuel system* without a *carburetor* which burns diesel oil instead of gasoline. The diesel oil is injected directly into the *combustion chamber*, where it is ignited by the heat caused by intense compression, rather than by a spark from a *spark plug*.

differential   a box of gear wheels, situated between the rear wheels, that turns the power of the rotating *driveshaft* at right angles to drive the rear *axle* and rear wheels. The differential also allows each of the rear wheels to turn at a different speed, when cornering.

dipstick   a metal stick that is inserted into a reservoir to check the level of the fluid in the reservoir by means of markings on the stick. The most common dipsticks check the levels of *oil, transmission fluid*, and *power-steering fluid*.

disc brakes   brakes that have *calipers* with heat-resistant pads, which grab a disc attached to the wheel and force it to stop turning, thus stopping the car. Many cars have disc brakes on the front wheels and *drum brakes* on the rear wheels. Most disc brakes have a *power booster*.

displacement   the volume of the inside of the *cylinders*—that is, the amount of fuel and air they can hold before compression takes place.

distributor   the part of the *ignition system* that distributes the proper amount of electrical voltage to each *spark plug*, in the correct sequence, at the precise moment for efficient combustion. See *condenser, points, rotor, spark advance, spark retard*.

distributor cap a cap that covers the *distributor*. It has a tower for each *spark plug* cable, plus a center tower where the wire from the *coil* enters the cap to conduct electrical current to the *rotor*. The cap keeps dirt and moisture from getting into the distributor.

distributor hold-down clamp a metal bracket at the base of the *distributor* that has a nut or bolt which can be loosened to allow the distributor to be moved on its shaft to readjust ignition *timing* or to open the *points* for gapping.

distributor shaft the metal shaft inside the *distributor* that has a *cam* wheel which revolves with the shaft and forces the *points* to open. (A spring causes the points to close.)

double clutching depressing the *clutch* for a second time, when the *gearshift* is in "neutral," while shifting from one gear to another. This allows the clutch to bring the *engine flywheel* and the *clutch disc* together more smoothly and reduces wear on these parts. Especially useful for cars with *manual transmission* without *syncromesh*.

downshifting shifting the car manually to a lower gear in order to use the engine to aid the brakes in reducing speed. Also called "downgearing."

drive train the path of power from the engine to the rear wheels. Consists of the *clutch, transmission, driveshaft, differential*, and rear *axle*.

driveshaft the spinning metal shaft that transmits power from the *transmission* to the *differential*, the rear *axle* and the wheels.

drum brakes brakes that use *hydraulic* pressure to force curved *brake shoes* against the inner walls of a hollow metal drum attached to each wheel. See *brake system*.

dual carbs two *carburetors* on the same engine.

dwell the distance the *distributor shaft* rotates while the *points* are closed. Also called *cam* angle. The dwell is given in degrees.

dwell meter a device for determining whether your *points* are correctly gapped to allow the *distributor* to deliver a spark of proper intensity and duration to the *spark plugs*. See *tachometer*.

electrical system a system that generates, stores, and distributes the electrical current required to start and run your car and such electrically operated equipment as the radio and headlights. See *charging system, ignition system, starting system*.

electrodes metal rods attached to the center and side of the *spark plug* to conduct current and create a *gap* across which the spark must jump.

electrolyte the mixture of sulphuric acid and water that is found in the *battery*.

electronic ignition system an *ignition system* with a *distributor* that transmits electrical current to the *spark plugs* by electronic means, eliminating the need for replacing *points* or *condensers*, and for checking *dwell*.

electronic sensing device an electronic device found on cars with *fuel injection* which senses changes in engine speed and driving conditions and determines the amount of fuel to be injected into the *combustion chambers*, thus eliminating the need for *carburetors* on these cars.

emergency brake see *parking brake*.

engine block the metal block in which the *cylinders* are bored which runs from below the *cylinder head* to the top of the *crankcase*. Also called the "cylinder block."

engine flywheel a spinning plate located at the end of the *crankshaft*, on cars with *manual transmissions*, which engages the *clutch disc*, causing the engine and the transmission to turn at the same rate of speed. Also helps to dampen engine vibration. See *clutch*.

exhaust gases the burned residue of the *fuel/air mixture* that must be refined and expelled from the car via the *exhaust system*.

exhaust manifold a set of pipes, one for each *cylinder*, through which burned *exhaust gases* can flow from the cylinders through the *exhaust system* and out of the car through the *tail pipe*.

exhaust system a system that conducts the *exhaust gases* from the *exhaust manifold* to the rear of the car and into the air. On the way, pollution-control devices are sometimes used to burn off harmful substances, and a *muffler* (and *resonators* in some cases) controls the noise of the escaping gases. See *catalytic converter*.

exhaust valve the *valve* that opens to allow the *exhaust gases* to pass from the *combustion chamber* to the *exhaust manifold*.

fan situated between the *radiator* and the engine, the fan draws air through the radiator to cool the liquid in the *cooling system* when the car is standing still or operating at low speeds.

fan belt a flexible rubber belt that connects the *fan* and the *alternator*. The operation of the engine turns the fan, and this turns the belt, which drives the alternator, enabling it to generate electric current. Other fan belts can drive air conditioners, *power steering* pumps, etc. Fan belts should be checked and replaced if they seem frayed, glazed, oily, etc.

feeler gauge a device for measuring the distance, or *gap*, between two surfaces. Use a wire feeler gauge to gap *spark plugs* and a flat feeler gauge to gap *points* and adjust *valves*.

firewall the insulated partition that runs from the windshield down between the interior of the car and the engine area. Protects the driver and passengers from engine fires, noise, fumes, and during accidents.

firing order the sequence in which the *cylinders* fire on a particular car to distribute the shock of *combustion* evenly and reduce engine vibrations. This should not be confused with *cylinder sequence*, which refers to the location of the #1 cylinder on a specific car, and where the other cylinders are located with relation to #1.

float bowl a small chamber in the *carburetor* that holds a small ready supply of fuel to be *vaporized* and mixed with air by the carburetor. The level of the fuel in the float bowl is controlled by a small float and fuel valve in the chamber.

flushing the cooling system circulating water through the *cooling system* to remove old liquid and clean the system of rust and dirt. "Backflushing" means circulating the water from the engine to the *radiator* (reversing the normal direction of flow) in order to clean the system more efficiently.

four-barrel carburetor a *carburetor* with four barrels that works like *dual carburetors*, with the second carburetor (third and fourth barrels) cutting in only at high speeds. Usually found on large *V-8 engines*.

four-stroke power cycle refers to the four movements of the *piston*—down, up, down, and up—that draw the *fuel/air mixture* into the *combustion chamber* (intake stroke), compress the mixture (compression stroke), transmit the power created by the *combustion* to the *crankshaft* (power stroke), and expel the *exhaust gases* from the *cylinder* (exhaust stroke).

free pedal play the distance the clutch pedal can be depressed before it begins to disengage the *clutch*. About ³/₄ to 1 inch of free pedal play is normally required to assure that the clutch will be fully disengaged when not in use. Without free pedal play, the *throw-out bearing*, and/or the clutch, would wear out.

freeze plugs see *core plugs*.

friction the rubbing of two moving parts against each other. Friction creates heat and wears down moving parts. The *lubrication system* uses *oil* and *grease* to reduce friction and to increase the life of your car.

front-end alignment see *alignment*.

front wheel drive a car that is "pulled" by its front wheels, rather than being "pushed" by its rear wheels, has front wheel drive. This eliminates the long *driveshaft* and the center floor hump found on cars with rear wheel drive.

fuel/air mixture a mistlike combination of *vaporized* fuel and air which is compressed in the *cylinders* and ignited to produce the power that drives the engine and the car.

fuel filter a small device that removes impurities from the fuel before it gets to the *carburetor*. Usually found near the carburetor in the *fuel line* that leads from the *fuel pump* (in-line fuel filter), or inside the carburetor or the fuel pump (integral fuel filter). Must be cleaned or replaced once a year, or every 20,000 miles, or if it becomes clogged and interferes with the carburetor's fuel supply.

fuel injection a fuel system without a *carburetor* that employs an *electronic sensing device* to deliver a specific amount of fuel to each *combustion chamber* in response to changes in engine speed and driving conditions. See *fuel injector valves*.

fuel injector valves devices that work like hypodermic needles·to inject the proper amount of fuel into the

combustion chambers in response to signals from an *electronic sensing device* on cars with *fuel injection* systems.

fuel lines the hoses or pipes through which the fuel passes from the *fuel tank* to the *carburetor*.

fuel pump a pump that draws the fuel from the *fuel tank* and sends it through the *fuel lines* to the *carburetor*.

fuel system a system that stores, cleans, and delivers the fuel to the engine in proper quantities to meet the varying needs that arise as you drive. Consists of the *fuel tank*, *fuel lines*, *fuel pump*, *fuel filter*, and *carburetor*.

fuel tank the storage compartment, under the trunk in most cars, that holds the fuel for the car. Also called the "gas tank."

gap the space between the spark plug *electrodes*, or between the *points* when they are as far apart as they can get. Adjusting this space is called "gapping." See *point gap*, *spark plug gap*.

gapper see *feeler gauge*.

gas gauge a dashboard device that indicates the amount of fuel in the *fuel tank*.

gasket a rubber, cork, paper, or metal plate that is inserted between two parts to cushion against wear and prevent leakage.

gear grease a heavy liquid grease that fills the *differential* and *manual transmission* to lubricate the gears. Also called "differential grease."

gear ratio the speed of the engine compared with the output speed of the *transmission*, and/or the *differential*, in a given gear.

gear selector a *gearshift* located on the side of the steering column on cars with *automatic transmissions*.

gearshift the stick attached to the *transmission* which selects new gears in response to the driver's commands. See *gear selector*, *stick shift*.

generator see *alternator*.

grease see *gear grease*, *lube grease*.

grease fitting a device that seals in and allows the addition of more *grease*, or some other type of lubricant, to cushion two moving parts, allow them to move freely, and prevent them from wearing each other away. See *ball joint*, *steering knuckles*, *tie-rod ends*, *zerk fitting*.

grease gun a device that can be loaded with *grease* and used for lubricating your car. Grease guns come with extenders for hard-to-reach places and with adapters for lubricating various types of *ball joints* and *zerk fittings*.

grease seal a circular, metal-backed, rubber device, that keeps *grease* from leaking out and protects wheel *bearings* and similar parts from dust and water.

ground one terminal of the *battery* is wired to the metal frame of the car to utilize the frame as a path for returning electric current to the battery and thus completing the electrical *circuit*. Most U.S. cars are negative ground—the *negative terminal* is wired to the frame of the car. In some other countries, this is called "negative earth."

guarantee a promise by the manufacturer to fix or replace a specific part if it does not last for a specific time period or distance.

head gasket the seal between the *cylinder head* and the *engine block.* This *gasket* keeps the *coolant* out of the *cylinders* and free from contamination by *exhaust gases.* A "blown" head gasket will cause a serious loss of compression.

horsepower the energy required to lift 550 pounds one foot in one second—or, 33,000 foot-pounds per minute.

hose clamps adjustable metal rings placed around a hose, where it connects to another part, to prevent leaks and to keep the hose in place.

hub cap the cap that fits over the end of the wheel *spindle* to keep dust and water away from the wheel *bearings* and brakes. Considered a decorative accessory on many cars, it is also a safety device that causes quite a racket if a *lug nut* falls off and tumbles around inside it.

hydraulic operated by the resistance offered, or pressure transmitted, when a quantity of water, *oil,* or other liquid is forced through a comparatively small opening or tube. Hydraulic devices on a car may include *automatic transmission, power steering,* and most *brake systems.*

hydrometer a device to determine the weight of a liquid. They are used to test *battery electrolyte* and the percentage of coolant in the *cooling system.*

idle the engine speed when the car is not moving.

idle air bleed screw a screw found instead of the *idle speed screw* on some *carburetors.* It allows air to enter the carburetor when the *throttle* is closed, so that the car can *idle.* It also prevents the formation of deposits in the throttle area. The adjustment of this screw is part of a basic *tune-up.*

idle mixture screw a screw located on the outside of the *carburetor* which controls the proportion of the *fuel/ air mixture.* The adjustment of this screw is part of a basic *tune-up.*

idle speed screw a screw located at the bottom of the *carburetor* on the outside which keeps the *throttle* from closing completely when the car is idling and thus controls the *idle* speed. This is adjusted as part of a basic *tune-up.* See *idle air bleed screw.*

idle stop solenoid a small cylinder located on the outside of the *carburetor* on some cars. It prevents the car from continuing to *idle* after the *ignition switch* has been shut off (this is called *dieseling*). This can be adjusted as part of a *tune-up.*

ignition switch the slot in which you turn the car key to close the electrical *circuit* that starts the car. When the key is removed, the switch is shut off.

ignition system a system that provides the electric current used to ignite the *fuel/air mixture* in the *combustion chambers* of the *cylinders.* Its parts include the *coil,* which amplifies the current it gets from the *battery* and

sends it to the *distributor,* which directs the current to each *spark plug* at the proper time.

ignition timing see *timing.*

in-line engine an engine in which the *cylinders* occur in a single row with the *crankshaft* running along the bottom. Also called a "straight engine." See *V-type engine.*

intake manifold a set of iron pipes, one for each *cylinder,* that conduct the *fuel/air mixture* from the *carburetor* to the cylinders. See *exhaust manifold.*

intake valve a *valve* that opens to allow the *fuel/air mixture* to enter the *combustion chamber.* Also called the "inlet valve."

internal combustion engine an engine that works on power released by *vaporized* fuel and air burning swiftly and violently inside the engine itself, rather than on an outside source of *combustion* as, for example, a steam engine does.

jack a device for lifting the car, or part of the car, off the ground to facilitate repairs. The most popular jacks are the tripod, scissors, and *hydraulic* jacks. Some cars come with bumper jacks for *tire* changing.

jack stand a safety device that keeps the car from falling to the ground if the *jack* is removed or faulty. Most jobs require two jack stands for safety.

journal the area on the *crankshaft* that fits into the lower portion of the *connecting rod.* A layer of *oil* and metal *bearings* cushions the impact during the power *stroke* to prevent the crankshaft from being crushed by the swiftly descending *piston* and connecting rod.

jumper cables cables used to "jump a start" by conducting current from one car *battery* to another. This allows a car whose battery has run down to start and begin to generate its own power. See *positive terminal.*

knocking a sound that occurs in the *cylinders* when the *fuel/air mixture* is being ignited too soon and the subsequent explosion is hitting the *piston* as it travels up the cylinder on the compression *stroke.* Usually it is due to faulty *timing,* low-octane gas, or fragments of burning carbon in the cylinders. Also called "pinging" or "pre-ignition." It sounds like marbles rattling in a can and can best be heard when accelerating up hills. See *four-stroke power cycle.*

leaf springs a series of steel plates, placed one atop the other, which bend flexibly to absorb the bumps and shocks of driving. Most often found near the rear wheels. See *suspension system.*

lube grease super-thick lubricating oil that has a paste-like consistency. Used to lubricate the *steering linkage,* the *suspension system,* and other moving parts outside the engine. See *gear grease.*

lube job the greasing and lubrication of the *suspension system,* the *drive train,* and other parts of the car which need it. Should be done professionally once or twice a year.

lubrication system a system that stores, cleans, cools, and recirculates *oil* through the engine to lubricate its moving parts and cool them. Includes the *oil pan*, *oil pump*, *oil filter*, and a dashboard *oil gauge*. You can check the level of oil in the system with the oil *dipstick*.

lug nuts the nuts that hold the wheel onto the car. You remove them with a *lug wrench* in order to change your *tires*.

lug wrench a wrench used during *tire* changes to remove the *lug nuts* that hold the wheel onto the car. The cross-shaft type provides the best leverage. Carry one in your trunk compartment.

manifold see *exhaust manifold, intake manifold.*

manual transmission a *transmission* system in which gears are selected by the driver by means of a hand-operated *gearshift* and a foot-operated *clutch*. Also called a "standard transmission."

master brake cylinder a device that stores *brake fluid* and *hydraulically* forces it through the *brake lines* to the brakes when you step on the brake pedal.

misfiring the failure of the *fuel/air mixture* in one or more *cylinders* to undergo *combustion* while the car is running. Misfiring can be due to poor compression caused by worn or improperly adjusted *valves*, worn *piston rings*, or a faulty *head gasket*. Or it can be caused by poor ignition due to worn or dirty spark plug *electrodes*, worn or improperly gapped *points* or *spark plugs*, poor fuel delivery, faulty ignition wiring, or faulty *distributor* components. It can be detected by placing a stiff piece of paper of the end of the *tail pipe* and listening for an irregular puffing sound.

motor mounts the rubber-covered brackets that hold the engine and *transmission* to the frame of the car and cushion vibrations.

mph an abbreviation for "miles per hour."

muffler a device for controlling the noise of the *exhaust gases* before they are released into the air through the *tail pipe*.

negative ground see *ground.*

negative terminal the *battery* terminal that conducts electric current back to the battery on cars with negative *ground*. The negative terminal is usually smaller than the *positive terminal* and has either "neg" or "−" on it.

odometer a dashboard device for measuring and indicating the number of miles a car has traveled. A trip odometer that can be set to zero in order to register the mileage on a particular trip can be found on some cars, as well.

oil a substance that lubricates and cools the moving parts of the engine and reduces the formation of rust and corrosion. Oil comes in varying weights suitable for efficient operation in cold and hot weather and for engines in varying states of wear. See *viscosity.*

oil drain plug the plug that secures the drain hole in the *oil pan*. An oil plug *gasket* lies between the plug and the hole and this gasket should be replaced if leakage occurs.

oil filler hole a hole at the top of the engine through which new oil can be added after the filler hole cover is removed.

oil filter a canlike device that screws onto the outside of the *crankcase* and cleans the *oil* as it circulates through the *lubrication system*. Oil filters should be replaced at least every other oil change.

oil gauge a dashboard device that indicates the oil pressure as the *oil* is pumped through the engine. If this gauge shows a sharp drop, reads "Low," or lights up, stop the car immediately and find the cause before driving any further. Without oil you can burn out your engine in less than a mile.

oil pan the chamber at the bottom of the *crankcase* which stores *oil*. The *oil drain plug* at the bottom of the oil pan can be removed to allow old oil to flow out of the car during an oil change.

oil pump a small pump located in the *crankcase* which circulates the *oil* from the *oil pan* to the moving parts of the engine.

oscilloscope an ignition-system and engine tester that displays variations in electrical current as a visible wave on the fluorescent screen of a cathode-ray tube.

overdrive an optional special gear that allows the rear wheels to turn faster than the engine. This lowers fuel consumption during sustained high-speed driving on freeways.

overflow pipe a tube located in the *radiator fill hole* that allows excess liquid to escape from the *cooling system* under conditions of extreme heat, pressure, or overfilling. See *coolant recovery kit.*

overhaul see *rebuild.*

overhead cam (OHC) a *camshaft* located above the *cylinder head* rather than below the *cylinders* in the *engine block*. Overhead camshafts eliminate the need for *push rods* to activate the *valves*. DOHC engines have double (two) overhead camshafts.

owner's manual a handbook provided by the car manufacturer to give the owner basic instructions for operating the various devices on the car. Many owner's manuals contain *specifications* for items associated with maintenance, but very few offer instructions for doing-it-yourself. See *service manual.*

ozone checking cracks or hard spots usually found on the sidewalls of *tires*. Caused by the action of the ozone in the air on the rubber, this condition is normal but could be dangerous on tires that either are more than 40,000 miles old or have been exposed to the ozone created by electrical machinery.

parking brake an auxiliary brake attached to a rear wheel or to the *transmission* which keeps the car from moving accidentally. Also called an "emergency brake."

passing gear an *automatic transmission* gear that shifts a car into a lower gear for a short burst of extra power to pass other cars on the highway. This gear is engaged by sharply depressing the gas pedal. When the pedal is released, the car returns to normal driving gear.

PCV valve part of the positive crankcase ventilation system, which reroutes *crankcase blow-by* to the *intake manifold* and back to the engine, where it is reburned in the *cylinders* as part of the *fuel/air mixture*. This cuts emission pollution and increases fuel economy because unburned fuel in the blow-by is consumed the second time around. It also keeps the blow-by and water vapor from fouling the *oil* in the crankcase, thus reducing the formation of engine *sludge*.

Phillips screwdriver a screwdriver with a pointed tip that is shaped to fit the crossed slots in the heads of Phillips screws.

pinging see *knocking*.

piston a cylindrical part, closed at the top, that moves up and down inside the *cylinder* to compress the *fuel/air mixture* and drive the engine by means of a *connecting rod*, which is attached to the piston at one end and to the *crankshaft* at the other. See *journal, piston rings*.

piston rings metal rings located in grooves on the outside of the *piston* which keep the *fuel/air mixture* from leaking past the piston into the *crankcase* during compression and that keep *oil* from going up into the *combustion chamber*. Faulty rings can cause poor compression, severe *blow-by* and excessive smoking from the *tail pipe*.

point gap the space between the *points* when they are fully open. Adjusting this *gap* is a primary part of the basic *tune-up* because the spark that jumps this gap is affected, both in intensity and in duration, by the width of the gap. See *feeler gauge*.

points two or more metal terminals, located inside the *distributor*, which are brought into contact and then separated by the movement of the *cam* wheel on the rotating *distributor shaft*. The points regulate the intensity and duration of the current that is conducted to each *spark plug* by interrupting the flow of current from the coil as they open and close. Also called "contact points," "breaker points," or "ignition points." See *gap*.

positive terminal the *battery* terminal that leads to the *electrical system* on cars with negative *ground*. The positive terminal is usually larger and has "pos" or "+" on it. *Jumper cables* and other devices that connect to the battery usually have red clips for the positive terminal and black clips for the *negative terminal*.

power booster a device that uses engine vacuum to assist you in braking the car. Helps the brake pedal to activate the *hydraulic* pistons in the *master cylinder*.

power brakes a *brake system* that uses a *power booster* to make braking easier.

power steering a device that uses *hydraulic* power to help the driver to steer the car more easily. Cars with power steering usually have a reservoir in the power steering pump, which requires the occasional addition of power-steering fluid (usually automatic *transmission fluid*).

pre-ignition see *knocking*.

pressure cap a radiator cap that allows the *cooling system* to operate under pressure at higher temperatures for greater efficiency. Safety pressure caps can be used to help to release the pressure before the cap is removed to prevent injuries due to escaping steam or hot water.

pressure plate a disc that is forced by springs against the *clutch disc*, which forces the disc and the *engine flywheel* against each other, causing the engine and the *transmission* to turn at the same rate of speed. See *clutch*.

primary terminal the clip found inside the *distributor* which allows electric current to pass from the *points* to the *condenser* and provides the insulation to keep the current from contacting other metal parts. See *ignition system*.

psi an abbreviation for "pounds per square inch." The term is used to measure the amount of air pressure in *tires* and the amount of compression of the *fuel/air mixture* in the *combustion chamber*.

push rods the rods that run between the *camshaft* lifters and the *rocker arms*. The lifters and the push rods are pushed up by the *cam lobes*, causing the rocker arms to make the *valves* open and close. Engines with *overhead cams* do not need push rods, because the camshaft contacts the valves directly.

radial tires see *tires*.

radiator a device that cools the liquid in the *cooling system* by allowing it to circulate through a series of water channels, which are exposed to air ducts.

radiator cap see *pressure cap*.

radiator fill hole an opening at the top of the *radiator* through which new water and *coolant* can be added. The *pressure cap* seals the fill hole.

radiator pressure cap see *pressure cap*.

ratchet a device that allows you to turn a screw or bolt in one direction, then move the handle of the wrench or screwdriver back in the opposite direction to prepare for the next stroke, without removing the tool from the screw or bolt. See *socket wrench*.

rear axle ratio the number of times the rear wheels turn compared to a particular *transmission* speed. The higher the rear *axle* ratio, the slower the engine can run and still allow the car to achieve a given speed.

rebuild to disassemble a particular device, clean it thoroughly, replace worn parts, and reassemble it. *Clutches, carburetors,* and *brakes* are sometimes rebuilt as part of the maintenance or restoration of older vehicles. You can rebuild a part yourself with a kit containing instructions and part replacements, or you can buy a rebuilt part and turn in your old part for a *core charge*. Rebuilding is sometimes called "overhauling."

resonator a small auxiliary *muffler* found on some cars which further reduces the noise of the escaping *exhaust gases*.

rings see *piston rings*.

rocker arm cover a metal lid located on top of the *cylinder head* on cars that have *valves* that are activated by an *overhead cam* or by *rocker arms*. See *valve cover*.

rocker arms curved levers each of which has one end attached to a *push rod* and the other end attached to a valve stem in order to make the *valves* open and close in response to the pressure of the *cam lobes* on the spinning *camshaft*. Cars with *overhead cams* do not always require rocker arms, because the valve stems may contact the cam lobes directly.

rotor a device that sits atop the *distributor shaft* and conducts the electric current to each *spark plug* terminal in turn. See *ignition system*.

rpm an abbreviation for "revolutions per minute." A *tachometer* measures engine revolutions in terms of rpm.

rubbing block a little block located on the movable point that contacts the *distributor cam* wheel and causes the *points* to open. (A spring causes the points to close.)

safety pressure cap see *pressure cap*.

sealed beam unit a headlight that usually contains both high and low bulbs, reflectors, and lenses and is sealed to keep out dirt and moisture. When the headlight fails, you replace the entire unit.

sealer a substance you can add to the liquid in the *cooling system* to seal leaks. Also called "stop-leak." Other kinds of sealing compounds are used to coat surfaces before installing hoses or *gaskets*. These are effective in preventing leakage but usually make the hose or gasket hard to remove.

service manual a handbook published by a car manufacturer or a specialized publishing company that contains instructions and *specifications* for the maintenance and repair of specific cars. Most service manuals deal with only one make, model, or year, and nearly all are intended for professionals or the very experienced amateur. They are useful for locating various parts on your car and for parts specifications. See *owner's manual*.

shock absorbers devices located near each wheel to cut down the vertical bouncing of the passenger compartment on the *springs* after the wheels go over a bump or the car stops short. Shock absorbers also improve handling on rough road surfaces. See *suspension system*.

sludge a combination of oxidized *oil*, gasoline, water, and *blow-by* that can foul an engine. Some engine oils have detergents to break down sludge.

socket wrench a wrench that completely covers the head of a bolt rather than fitting around its circumference. A socket set usually consists of a variety of sockets plus at least one handle (usually a *ratchet* handle), a couple of extenders, and sometimes a *spark plug socket* as well.

solenoid a device connected to electrical current which induces mechanical movement in another device. See *idle stop solenoid, starter solenoid*.

spark advance to adjust the *ignition timing* so that the *spark plugs* will fire sooner than they have been firing. See *spark retard*.

spark plug a device that delivers the electrical spark to the *combustion chamber*. This ignites the *fuel/air mixture*

and produces the power that drives the engine. See *ignition system, spark plug gap*.

spark plug gap the space between the center and side spark plug *electrodes* across which the spark must jump to ignite the *fuel/air* mixture in the *combustion chamber*. Adjusting this *gap* is a major part of the basic *tune-up*, since the width of the gap affects the intensity of the spark. See *feeler gauge*.

spark plug socket a metal cylinder with a rubber lining that fits over the exposed end of the *spark plug* to make it easy to remove the plug without damaging its porcelain surface. Can be purchased as part of a *socket wrench* set, or separately.

spark retard to adjust *ignition timing* so that the *spark plugs* will fire later than they have been firing. See *knocking, spark advance*.

specifications the size, description, or parts numbers for various items needed to maintain or repair a car. See *owner's manual, service manual*.

speedometer a dashboard device that measures and indicates how fast the car is going. The speedometer cable should be lubricated when the needle starts to move erratically, or if the cable begins to make noise.

spindle the small shaft located at each front wheel on which the front wheels revolve.

splash shield a removable device found on *disc brakes* that helps to keep water and dirt from fouling the brakes.

springs devices to cushion and absorb shocks and bumps and to keep the car level on turns. A car can have *leaf springs, coil springs, torsion bars*, or a combination of these. See *suspension system*.

stabilizers a variety of devices used to keep the passenger compartment of a car from swaying and lurching on sharp curves and turns. See *suspension system*.

standard transmission see *manual transmission*.

starter a small motor that causes the engine *crankshaft* to begin to turn, which starts the engine running and so starts the car. Also called the *cranking* motor. See *starting system*.

starter solenoid a device that uses electrical current to start and engage the *starter*. See *solenoid*.

starting system the portion of the *electrical system* that starts the car. Consists of (1) the *ignition switch*, which closes the circuit and allows current to flow from (2) the *battery* to (3) the *starter*, via (4) the *starter solenoid*. Also called the "cranking circuit."

static shield a device found on some *distributors* that reduces radio interference caused by the working of the car's *ignition system*.

steering-axis inclination an *alignment* adjustment that allows the steering wheel to return to the straight-ahead position when the car comes out of a turn.

steering knuckles a type of *ball joint* located at the ends of the tie rods on the *steering linkage*. See *grease fittings*.

steering linkage the system that connects the steering wheel to the front wheels and allows the wheels to change direction in response to commands from the driver.

Contains *grease fittings* to cushion against wear and friction. See *alignment*.

stick shift   a *gearshift* located on the floor between, or slightly in front of, the front seats. A car with a four-speed *manual transmission* and a stick shift is said to have "four on the floor."

stop-leak   see *sealer*.

stroke   the vertical distance that the *piston* moves as it travels from the top to the bottom or from the bottom to the top of the *cylinder*. See *bore, four-stroke power cycle*.

suspension system   a system that cushions the passenger compartment of the car from the bumps and shocks caused by the wheels moving over irregular road surfaces. Includes *springs, shock absorbers, steering linkage*, upper and lower *control arms, torsion bars, stabilizers*, etc. The *grease fittings* and rubber *bushings* along this system should be lubricated at regular intervals. See *zerk fitting*.

syncromesh   a *manual transmission* device that allows two gears to mesh more smoothly by causing them to spin at the same rate of speed before coming together.

tachometer   a device for measuring engine *rpm*. Many cars with *manual transmissions* have a dashboard tachometer to aid in changing gears. A portable tachometer is used to adjust *idle* speed as part of a basic *tune-up*. Often a tachometer is combined with a *dwell meter* in a single unit. Try to find one with both "Hi" and "Lo" rpm range.

tail pipe   the last link in the *exhaust system*. Conducts *exhaust gases* from the *muffler* to the rear of the car and into the atmosphere.

TDC   an abbreviation for "top dead center." This is the point at which the *piston* has reached the top of its *stroke* and has compressed the *fuel/air mixture* to the greatest extent. BTDC and ATCD mean "before" and "after" top dead center. These terms are used to refer to *timing marks*. See *combustion chamber*.

thermostat   a device that keeps the hot *coolant* and water in the engine to help the engine to warm up more quickly. Then, the thermostat allows the liquid to flow to the *radiator*, where it is cooled and recirculated through the engine to prevent overheating. See *cooling system*.

thermostatic coil choke   a sensing device mounted on the *carburetor* that automatically controls the choke *butterfly valve* by sensing the heat of the *exhaust manifold*. See *choke*.

thermostatic spring choke   a sensing device that automatically controls the choke *butterfly valve* by sensing the heat of the *intake manifold*. See *choke*.

throttle   a device that controls the vacuum created in the *venturi*. The greater the vacuum, the richer the *fuel/air mixture*. The throttle enables the engine to run on a richer mixture and produce more power for high-speed driving. It consists of a throttle arm, located on the outside of the *carburetor* and connected to the gas pedal, which activates a throttle *butterfly valve* at the base of the *carburetor barrel*, where it joins the *intake manifold*.

throw-out bearing   a part of the *clutch*, activated by the clutch pedal, that allows the clutch to disengage. If you

allow the car to *idle* in gear with the clutch pedal depressed, instead of shifting to neutral gear, you can wear out the throw-out bearing. Also called the "clutch release bearing." See *free pedal play*.

tie rod ends   *grease fittings* or *ball joints* located on the ends of the *steering linkage*.

timing   the ability of the *valves, ignition system*, and other engine-driven parts of the car to work together for maximum efficiency. Timing is checked as part of the basic *tune-up* because, if the timing is off, the car cannot perform well, just as all the pieces in an orchestra must not only be in tune but must play together to achieve a good performance. Timing is regulated by checking with a *timing light* and then adjusting the *distributor* or the *timing chain*. See *distributor hold-down clamp, spark advance, spark-retard, timing marks*.

timing chain   a chain that drives the *camshaft* by linking it to the *crankshaft* and assures that the *valves* will open and close at the proper moments for efficient ignition. See *timing*.

timing light   a device used to check ignition *timing*. The light is hooked to the first *cylinder spark plug* and blinks on and off as the plug fires. When aimed at the *timing marks*, this stroboscopic effect causes the marks to appear to stand still opposite a pointer. Xenon timing lights are usually more useful than the cheaper neon ones because they are more visible in daylight.

timing marks   a series of marks or notches usually located on the *crankshaft pully* (also called the "harmonic balance wheel"). When a *timing light* is aimed at these marks, they appear to stand still, enabling you to see if the proper mark is lined up with a stationary pointer located nearby. The proper timing marks are part of the car's *specifications*.

tire valve   a small valve, mounted on the wheel rim of a tubeless *tire*, that allows air to be added to the tire with an air hose and allows air to be withdrawn from an overinflated tire by pressing on the little stem at the end of the valve. Some tire valves have little caps to protect against leaks and keep dirt from fouling the valve. On tires with inner tubes, the tire valve is mounted on the inner tube. (Today, most tires are tubeless.)

tires   can be bias-ply, bias-belted, or radial, depending on their construction. The most popular materials used are rayon, nylon, and polyester plies. Belting can be fiberglass, or steel for extra strength. The rest of the tire (treads and sidewalls) is hard rubber. See *alignment, ozone checking, tire valve*.

toe-in   an adjustment of front-wheel *alignment* so that the *tires* are slightly pigeon-toed when the car is standing still. This improves handling at high speeds.

toe-out   a wheel *alignment* adjustment to control the way the car tracks on turns. Tires should never toe out.

torque   turning or twisting power. See *torque wrench*.

torque wrench   a special wrench that can measure the exact amount of *torque* being applied to tighten a bolt.

torsion bars   on Chrysler products, these are often connected to the *control arms* to compensate for uneven loads and to allow the front wheels to move up and down freely on uneven road surfaces. See *suspension system*.

transmission   a box of gear wheels that allow your car to move forward and backward with varying amounts of power to meet a variety of driving situations. *Manual transmissions* are operated by means of a *clutch* and *gearshift*. *Automatic transmissions* are driven by *hydraulic* pressure.

transmission fluid   a superthin *oil* that fills the *automatic transmission* system so that it can run on *hydraulic* pressure. Also found in many *power-steering* pumps.

tread-wear indicators   bars of hard rubber that appear across the treads of *tires* that have been worn below ¹/₁₆ inch of surface.

tune-up   the process of adjusting and/or replacing the various parts of the *ignition system* to ensure that it delivers a spark of the proper intensity and duration to the *combustion chamber* at the precise moment when the *fuel/air mixture* is compressed to burn at peak efficiency. Adjusting the carburetor *idle speed* and *fuel/air mixture* is a key part of the tune-up, as well. A basic tune-up includes replacing and gapping *spark plugs* and *points*; replacing the *rotor* and *condenser*; checking and adjusting *timing* and *dwell*; and adjusting the *idle mixture screw*, *idle speed screw*, and sometimes other controlling devices, such as the *idle air bleed screw* and the *idle stop solenoid* on the *carburetor*. Your car should be tuned every 10,000 miles or every six months, whichever comes first.

tune-up kit   a kit containing a new set of *points*, a *rotor*, a *condenser*, a little vial of *cam* lube, and a *feeler gauge* of the proper thickness for a specific car make, model, and year. A necessary part of a basic *tune-up* is replacing these parts and lubricating the *distributor*.

turn over   an engine is said to "turn over" when the *starter* has caused the *crankshaft* to begin to turn, which starts the *pistons* moving so that *combustion* can begin to take place in the *cylinders*, providing power to move the car.

turning radius   the relation of one front wheel to the other on turns. If your tires are "squealing" on turns, have your front-end *alignment* checked to be sure that bent steering arms have not affected the turning radius of the car.

two-plus-two   a two-door car with relatively limited seating in the rear for two people. More seating than in a two-seater but less than in a car with a full rear seat.

U-joints   an abbreviation for "*universal joints*."

universal joints   couplings located at either end of the *driveshaft* which allow the shaft to move freely, without affecting the more rigid *transmission* shaft at one end, and to absorb the vertical movement of the rear *axle* and wheels at the other end. Also called *u-joints*.

vacuum advance   a device located to the side of the *distributor* which advances the ignition spark in response to the vacuum produced by the operation of the engine.

You disconnect the vacuum advance before you check the *point gap* with a *dwell meter*.

vacuum modulator   a small, easily replaceable, and inexpensive part that can give the impression of *transmission* failure if it malfunctions. If the car tends to stay in low gear, shifts with difficulty or produces whitish smoke, has an *automatic transmission*, and is constantly low in *transmission fluid*, try replacing the vacuum modulator before undertaking major repairs. Most vacuum modulators simply screw into place.

valve cover   a metal lid located on top of the *cylinder head* on cars with *overhead cams*. The valve cover is removed when the *valves* need adjusting.

valves   metal devices that open and close to allow fuel and air to enter the *combustion chamber* and *exhaust gases* to leave it. Operated from the *camshaft*, by means of valve lifters, *push rods*, and *rocker arms* (except for cars with *overhead cams*, which don't require them), the valves can be adjusted with *feeler gauges* so that they open and close at the proper times. See *exhaust valve*, *intake valve*, *timing chain*.

vapor lock   bubbles formed in the *fuel line* when the fuel boils because of extreme heat. These bubbles prevent the fuel from reaching the *carburetor* and cause the car to stop running. A wet rag will cool the line and get rid of the problem, and a piece of tinfoil wrapped around the line will prevent its recurrence in extremely hot weather.

vaporize   to convert a liquid into a mist by breaking it into small particles and mixing it with air. The *carburetor* vaporizes gasoline to produce a combustible *fuel/air mixture*. If it is not vaporized, liquid gasoline will burn poorly.

venturi   the part of the *carburetor barrel* which is narrowed to increase the ability of the air to mix with *vaporized* fuel by creating a vacuum that draws more fuel out of the *float bowl*.

viscosity   the thickness or pourability of a liquid. *Oil* comes in a variety of thicknesses, or weights. It also comes in single viscosity (single-weight oil) and in a blend of viscosities (multi-weight oil), which enable it to flow easily in cold weather and prevent it from thinning out in hot weather. The higher the weight, the greater the viscosity of the oil. You can find the weight of the oil embossed on the top lid of the oil can.

voltage regulator   an electrical device that controls or regulates the amount of electricity generated by the *alternator*.

V-type engine   an engine in which the *cylinders* occur in two rows set at an angle to each other, with the *crankshaft* running through the point of the V. The most popular engine of this type is the 8-cylinder V-8 engine. V-6 and V-4 engines are also available, and Jaguar makes a V-12! See *in-line engine*.

warranty   a promise by a car manufacturer and a car dealer to fix or replace parts on a new car if they malfunction before a specific time or distance has elapsed.

water jackets   channels in the engine through which water and *coolant* circulate to cool the engine. See *cooling system*.

water pump   a device that circulates the liquid through the *cooling system* by pumping it from the engine *water jackets* to the *radiator*.

wheel alignment   see *alignment*.

wheel balancing   a procedure that ensures that the weight of the wheel is distributed evenly to improve performance and cut *tire* wear. Static balancing distributes the weight of the wheel evenly around the *axle* or *spindle* and is done with the wheels off the car. Dynamic balancing distributes the weight evenly as the wheel and tire hang vertically down, also balances the brake drum, and can be done with the wheels on the car.

wheel bearings   see *bearings*.

wheel cylinder   a small cylinder located at each wheel brake that uses *brake fluid* to exert *hydraulic* pressure, which forces the *brake shoes* against the *brake drums* and stops the car.

zerk fitting   a small valve that allows *grease* to be added to a *ball joint* with a *grease gun* and prevents the grease from leaking out when pressure is placed on the area.

Index

[Page numbers in italics refer to location of illustrations]